PATRICIA MEYER SPACKS has been Professor of English at Wellesley College since 1959. She holds degrees from Yale and the University of California, Berkeley. She is the author of various critical studies, including *An Argument of Images*, a study of Alexander Pope; *The Poetry of Vision*, a critical study of five Eighteenth Century poets; and *The Insistence of Horror: Aspects of the Supernatural in Eighteenth Century Poetry*. Dr. Spacks' unique and perceptive affirmation of the female voice in literature began in part with a seminar she taught at Wellesley. Incorporating the responses of her students into her own arguments, she examines the development and creative implications of "The Female Imagination," demonstrating that "women dominate their own experience by imagining it, giving it form, writing about it." THE FEMALE IMAGINATION has been nominated for The National Book Award.

THE
FEMALE
IMAGINATION

PATRICIA MEYER SPACKS

 A DISCUS BOOK/PUBLISHED BY AVON BOOKS

Cover illustration:
Mother and Child by Mary Cassatt
Courtesy of National Gallery of Art, Washington
Chester Dale Collection

AVON BOOKS
A division of
The Hearst Corporation
959 Eighth Avenue
New York, New York 10019

Copyright © 1972, 1975 by Patricia Meyer Spacks
Published by arrangement with Alfred A. Knopf, Inc.
Library of Congress Card Catalog Number: 74-21320

ISBN: 0-380-00599-9

First Discus Printing, May, 1976

DISCUS TRADEMARK REG. U.S. PAT. OFF. AND
FOREIGN COUNTRIES, REGISTRADA TRADEMARK—
MARCA REGISTRADA, HECHO EN CHICAGO, U.S.A.

Printed in the U.S.A.

For JoAnn B. Fineman

*We arrive at the truth,
not by the reason only,
but also by the heart.*
—PASCAL

Contents

Acknowledgments

Parts of this book have been published earlier, in different form: portions of Chapter Three as "Taking Care: Some Women Novelists," in *Novel*, 6 (1972), 36–51; portions of Chapter Eight as "Free Women," in *The Hudson Review*, 24 (Winter 1971–72), 157–70; a few sentences of the Afterword in "Reflecting Women," *Yale Review*, 63 (1973), 26–42.

Several women brought to my attention texts that I might otherwise have encountered. I feel indebted to them: Jane Cohen, Joyce Cole, Helen Corsa, Jane Davison, JoAnn Fineman; and to my students, for challenge, stimulation, and insight. I am also grateful to Margery Sabin, who read and usefully commented on earlier versions of two chapters; to my editor, Carol Janeway, for reactions that consistently clarified my perceptions; to my daughter Judith, who keeps before me a vivid and inspiriting image of young womanhood; and to my husband, Barry Spacks, who endured my exhilarations and despairs in writing, who dared to criticize rigorously, whose criticism has once more enriched my work.

THE
FEMALE
IMAGINATION

Prologue

What are the ways of female feeling, the modes of responding, that persist despite social change?

Do any characteristic patterns of self-perception shape the creative expression of women?

Changing social conditions increase or diminish the opportunities for women's action and expression, but a special female self-awareness emerges through literature in every period. This book examines its continuities. Women write more now, or write more publicly, than they used to. They make heroines of divorcées rather than governesses; they depict themselves in print as struggling for independence rather than for virtue. "The fear of doing wrong has been always the leading principle of my internal guidance," Fanny Burney wrote in 1819, at the age of sixty-six. In a memoir published in 1969, Lillian Hellman reports one of the significant lessons of her life: "If you are willing to take the punishment, you are halfway through the battle." Different as her orientation clearly is, she shares with Miss Burney more than one would readily suspect: shares a problem, though not a solution. To look for evidence of sharing, seek persistent ways of feeling, discover patterns of self-depiction that survive the vagaries of change: such are my purposes. And to investigate how women use their creativity to reveal and to combat their characteristic difficulties.

But also to see how a writer's patterns and problems affect her readers.

"If we study how women express themselves and how

they really feel, then that would be women's liberation."

"We need something to identify with."

Two young women made those comments, responding to a question about why they wanted to study books by members of their sex. Wellesley College undergraduates, they were among the thirty (in two groups) who elected a freshman-sophomore literature colloquium called "Woman Writers and Woman's Problems." It was clear to them from the outset that the changes of history would concern them less than its continuities. They were looking for help, for models, ways of being, of coping with perplexing perceptions and feelings. For "liberation." And they were struggling with the problem of "specialness." All adolescents feel special: that's part of their burden. For young women, the burden is particularly heavy, since they have often been bred to believe that they are not supposed to be unique, that there's something wrong with wishing to stand out, except possibly on the basis of physical beauty. If they can discover their kinship with women who have boldly asserted themselves as writers, they may be helped toward self-realization. So, at any rate, my students seemed to hope. They felt (although they suspected that they weren't supposed to feel anything of the sort, it wasn't "intellectual") that to read books by women would have direct personal meaning for them. ("I am an aspiring woman," one of them wrote, to explain why she wanted to take the course.) They thought that the investigation of other women's feelings and acceptable modes of expressing them might provide a way to justify individual intensities of emotion and to find individual forms of expression. Their ways of articulating such ideas were naïve, and so, often, were the ideas themselves. But they suggested an approach that proved illuminating and that I have tried to elaborate and extend.

Of course it is by no means true that books by women necessarily differ vividly from books by men. Male writers are often "sensitive," women frequently knowledgeable: the stereotypes don't apply. Writing novels, women deal

2

with the problems that have always concerned novelists: relationship, personal identity, the interchange between individual and society. The autobiography of a woman who has struggled to become an artist or a labor leader or a scientist may bear striking analogies to that of her male counterpart; housewives and average men seldom write their autobiographies. Still, there appears to be something that we might call a woman's point of view—except that that sounds like a column in the *Ladies' Home Journal*—a vague enough phenomenon, doubtless the result mainly of social conditioning, but an outlook sufficiently distinct to be recognizable through the centuries. Some anthropologists posit a dim matriarchal past in which women dominated society. If such a period ever existed, no written records of it survive. Women have written books only during the eras of their social subordination, books that necessarily refract the effects of that subordination in ways hardly possible for a man to duplicate. Men write often about the fact that women look in mirrors; but the eighteenth-century letter writer Lady Mary Wortley Montagu and twentieth-century novelist Doris Lessing have more in common in their allusions to this phenomenon than either is likely to have with a male writer even for her own time and place in history.

Not, again, that the male-female contrast need be extreme. Yet it is illuminating to seek the special point of view, delicately divergent though it may sometimes be, and to find how often the stories women tell shape themselves into patterns dictated by the same few clearly defined issues—patterns, if not universal, at least very widespread in female experience. My students, for example, identified with many incidents and actions and reactions from earlier centuries on the basis of their own lives. (I use their words—taken from tape recordings of the class meetings—intermittently in the ensuing pages to emphasize such continuities of theme.) To a certain extent, therefore, the existence of a female point of view challenges the myths of the writer's and the adolescent's "specialness."

Women writing directly about their own lives in letters, journals, autobiographies, or indirectly in that concealed form of autobiography we call fiction, demonstrate that the experience of women has long been the same, that female likenesses are more fundamental than female differences. It seems an obvious enough truth, but its implications, psychological and literary, are far-reaching. If the "special" woman in her expressiveness is *not* separated from her kind, therefore from herself, it is perhaps not necessary for women to fear distinction as much as often they do. The "fear of success" that Matina Horner has richly documented is among other things a form of that fear of alienation which accompanies a sense of difference. And if even some of the patterns of women's writing are distinct enough to be identified, literary critics must acknowledge the possibility that useful ways of talking about such writing will take account of such distinctions. Men and women in many respects represent separate cultures, as Kate Millett points out, although not separate species; only the avowedly political criticism of staunch feminists has thus far made important use of this important fact. But criticism need not be political in order to be aware.

This book is an investigation of some possibilities—not a history of women's writing; indeed, explicitly antihistorical in orientation, but an examination of the ways the life of the imagination emerges in the work of women writing prose directly as women. "Imagination" is a slippery term, designating a power that penetrates the inner meaning of reality but also a power that creates substitutes for reality; I am interested in both meanings. In one way or another, imagination has been for many women the seed of grace, and often the subject as well as the impetus of their writing. Directly and indirectly, women discuss the function of their creativity—expressed through their domestic and maternal life, through their artistic achievement, sometimes through their evolution and presentation of a "self." The autobiographies and novels where discussed, as well as

4

the theoretical works, illumine the nature and uses of women's creativity from many different angles.

Why these particular books, rather than others? All belong to the Anglo-American literary tradition: because analysis must depend on nuances of language, I have not wished to deal with works in translation. (The single conspicuous exception to this principle is *The Second Sex*, a work of such importance to the development of contemporary female self-awareness that it could hardly be ignored.) Almost all delineate the lives of white middle-class women. Phyllis Chesler has remarked, "I have no theory to offer of Third World female psychology in America. . . . As a white woman, I'm reluctant and unable to construct theories about experiences I haven't had." So am I: the books I talk about describe familiar experience, belong to a familiar cultural setting; their particular immediacy depends partly on these facts. My bibliography balances works everyone knows (*Jane Eyre, Middlemarch*) with works that should be better known (*The Story of Mary MacLane*). Still, the question remains: Why only these?

To some extent the choice, like all such choices, is arbitrary. I've included most, though not all, of the books my students and I read together in the colloquium, and added others, many others, because they revealed additional dimensions of fundamental female experience. The subsequent chapters are organized around certain large recurrent problems that emerge from the texts. Perception of the problems in every case derived from my reading of the books; the books were not selected to depict preconceived problems. Their selection, of course, reflects the operations of my own imagination; the meaning of the book as a whole must depend partly on the implications of the special conjunctions achieved through a particular sensibility.

The female imagination, if one may conceive of such a thing, is my subject and guiding principle; this study depends upon psychological and literary awarenesses more than political ones. I am trying to find the themes that have absorbed female minds during the past three centuries as recorded in literature written in English. Surely the mind has a sex, minds *learn* their sex—and it is no derogation of the female variety to say so. At any rate, for readily discernible historical reasons women have characteristically concerned themselves with matters more or less peripheral to male concerns, or at least slightly skewed from them. The differences between traditional female preoccupations and roles and male ones make a difference in female writing. Even if a woman wishes to demonstrate her essential identity with male interests and ideas, the necessity of making the demonstration, contradicting the stereotype, allies her initially with her sisters. And the complex nature of the sisterhood emerges in the books it has produced.

One

THEORISTS

> We may safely assert that the knowledge that men can acquire of women, even as they have been and are, without reference to what they might be, is wretchedly imperfect and superficial and will always be so until women themselves have told all that they have to tell.
>
> —JOHN STUART MILL

Theories by women about women have only recently begun to appear in print. Theories by men about women are abundant.

Among female theorists, relatively few have concerned themselves with women's literary manifestations, the subject of my particular concern. Virginia Woolf was perhaps the first, writing (in 1928) *A Room of One's Own* on the announced subject "women and fiction." Her essay strayed frequently from that focus, and this was its point: women's writing could not be considered in isolation from the social, economic, and political facts that dictate much of women's condition. Subsequent critics have agreed.

Yet such agreement itself reflects the deep resentment women may feel about the peculiarities of their lot. Simone de Beauvoir observes that "a man would never get the notion of writing a book on the peculiar situation of the human male. ... A man never begins by presenting himself as an individual of a certain sex; it goes without saying that he is a man." Masculinity is the norm, "humanity is male"; a critic may choose to contemplate the relation of a man's social situation to his literary production but the facts do not force him toward such contemplation. But there is a sense—my students were right—in which women always begin apologizing for women's writing. We have no female Shakespeare to point to—a fact that apparently obsessed Virginia Woolf. Why not? Well, women's social, economic, political conditions . . .

But most of all, certainly, their psychological condition.

9

In autobiography, poetry, fiction, women reveal themselves, their psychology; but they may make equivalent revelations in their literary and social theory. Certainly the presence of Virginia Woolf, as woman and as unique personality, is vivid in *A Room of One's Own*.

She begins the essay with an elaborate statement of insecurities. What does her topic really mean, she asks, and how is she equipped to deal with it? She is giving a lecture, and she wants only to please her audience: such, at any rate, is her claim.

The title women and fiction might mean, and you may have meant it to mean, women and what they are like; or it might mean women and the fiction that they write; or it might mean women and the fiction that is written about them; or it might mean that somehow all three are inextricably mixed together and you want me to consider them in that light. But when I began to consider the subject in this last way, which seemed the most interesting, I soon saw that it had one fatal drawback. I should never be able to come to a conclusion.

The critical questions implied by her alternatives are important and useful, but she disguises them as expressions of inadequacy. Such disguises, of course, are only figures of rhetoric, attempts to engage the audience on the speaker's side—by a mode of engagement more readily available to women than to men. In this instance the tension between the author's claim that she doesn't know quite what she's doing and the sense she conveys that she in fact knows precisely what she's doing points to a conflict running through the entire essay.

It is a clash between the necessity to assert and the need to apologize, implicit in the writer's tone and technique from beginning to end. Her stylistic elegance, her withdrawings and qualifications, her delicacies of feeling: all apologize for her presumption in undertaking such a subject. She quotes with indignation Sir Egerton Brydges,

10

who writes, "Female novelists should only aspire to excellence by courageously acknowledging the limitations of their sex," but her own acknowledgment of limitation is everywhere. Providing an account of a sequence of thought, she interpolates a description of a river ("To the right and left bushes of some sort, golden and crimson, glowed with the colour, even it seemed burnt with the heat, of fire. On the further bank the willows wept in perpetual lamentation, their hair about their shoulders. The river reflected whatever it chose . . ."). Its mannered virtuosity conceals self-justification: Don't judge me by the quality of my thought, note the fineness of my sensibility. Such descriptions appear throughout, seductive endeavors to involve the reader on a level where the writer dares feel confident. She apologizes directly (partly ironically, but only partly) when she begins to praise her own sex; and she apologizes constantly for the inadequacies of the woman writers she considers.

In particular, she apologizes for feminine anger, which she believes an emblem of feminine limitation. Charlotte Brontë's outbursts against the injustices of woman's lot Mrs. Woolf feels as weaknesses in her novels. The Countess of Winchilsea is no Shakespeare because her mind "is harassed and distracted with hates and grievances." The writing of the Duchess of Newcastle is "disfigured and deformed" by her rage at her situation. Shakespeare displayed no such rage; he rose above personal emotion into an incandescence of spirit which is the sign of his greatness. But his hypothetical sister Judith, whose imagined career fascinates Mrs. Woolf, would have been driven to anger by the injustices of her lot.

There is no question that anger exists where the critic locates it, but her conclusions about it are debatable. She quotes the Duchess of Newcastle: "Women live like Bats or Owls, labour like Beasts, and die like Worms;" she does not appear to realize that the Duchess never wrote better, never elsewhere wrote as well as in sentences of this sort. She quotes one of the Countess of Winchilsea's best po-

ems, a diatribe against the impediments placed in the way
of a woman writing. And she quotes a passionate outcry
from *Jane Eyre*, the sort of outpouring duplicated in Charlotte Brontë's other novels, which provides some of the
special flavor of these books. All these instances of anger
are to Mrs. Woolf examples of female weakness. But how
can she deplore such writing? On what basis can she assume that these women would have written better under
better conditions? Anger must have been a source of
creative energy for these and other women writers; anger
provided the impetus, the subject, and the inventiveness of
their work. Yes, there have been no woman Shakespeares.
But there has been only one *male* Shakespeare: his existence establishes no rules. Perhaps Shakespeare wasn't angry, or at least not angry about his own lot. The fact
remains that many women have written marvelously out
of anger; and one cannot assume that they would necessarily have written better out of other emotions, or out of
emotion transcended.

The fact is, moreover, that Virginia Woolf herself writes
marvelously out of personal anger. She calls the imaginary
women in her essay Mary Beaton, Mary Seton, and Mary
Carmichael, the names of figures in the Child ballad about
Mary Hamilton, who has borne a child to the king and is
in consequence hanged.

Last night there were four Marys,
Tonight there'll be but three,
There was Mary Beaton, and Mary Seton,
And Mary Carmichael, and me.

Mrs. Woolf's essay, in all its urbanity, alludes constantly
by implication to this ballad about the miserable injustice
of women's condition. Nor are its suggestions of anger all
quite so indirect. If the essay proceeds partly by displays
of sensibility, it also depends on displays of irony; and the
nature of that irony is suggestive.

It is Mrs. Woolf's belief, apparently, that the difference

between man and woman is absolute. "Lamb, Browne, Thackeray, Newman, Sterne, Dickens, De Quincey—whoever it may be—never helped a woman yet, though she may have learnt a few tricks of them and adapted them to her use. The weight, the pace, the stride of a man's mind are too unlike her own for her to lift anything substantial from him successfully." The list of proper names suggests her dilemma. These are the writers she admires; she can find few women to admire as much. Great literature is male literature. She will not go so far as to conclude that women must turn into men before they can achieve as significantly, but she *does* conclude that the greatest writing is "androgynous," that women must cultivate their masculine side and men their feminine, that people must surpass their sexual limitations in order to produce great writing.

Yet the insistent ironies point to her conviction that the quintessential feminine nature is after all a source of power. Certainly it is an important source of *her* power. Her ironies call attention not only to the inequalities of the feminine lot, but to a hidden value judgment of feminine superiority, lying beneath the surface of the frequent admissions of male social superiority. "Indeed, it was delightful to read a man's writing again. It was so direct, so straightforward after the writing of women. It indicated such freedom of mind, such liberty of person, such confidence in himself. . . . But after reading a chapter or two a shadow seemed to lie across the page. It was a straight dark bar, a shadow shaped something like the letter 'I.' " All Mrs. Woolf's praise of masculinity seems double-edged. "Direct," "straightforward," "freedom:" these are terms of approval. But they conceal a kind of contempt. By comparison to women, the language hints, men are unsubtle, crude, naïve. And insanely egotistic: this is more than a hint.

The vanity of men, a constant insult to women, is also the ground for the implicit feminine claim of superior sensitivity and morality. Life for both sexes, Virginia Woolf points out, is difficult and demanding. Self-confidence is necessary for success. Men achieve it, she suggests, by insisting on their innate superiority to women. "Women have served all these centuries as looking-glasses possessing the magic and delicious power of reflecting the figure of man at twice its natural size." The adjectives convey both the masculine evaluation of this feminine power and feminine irony at the expense of the evaluation. But the metaphor itself, which Mrs. Woolf develops at some length, is significant. In satire and moral commentary since classical times, the looking glass has been associated with women, used by male writers as an emblem of the narcissism that, long before Freud, men felt to be a dominant trait of women. Now a woman critic not only associates the mirror with male rather than female narcissism, but points out the degree to which men convert women into instruments of masculine self-love. But if it is the role of women to provide "delicious" enlargement of the male ego, it is also their nature to realize the ironies of such a role. Awareness of the ironies—more even than the injustices—of the feminine condition is a subterranean theme of *A Room of One's Own*, and a source of much of its energy.

But the problem of whether it is or is not a good thing for a woman to write out of consciousness of being a woman is one that Virginia Woolf finally cannot resolve. She tackles it, she makes a statement, but the statement is inadequate to the facts. Her explicit conclusion is unambiguous and forceful: "It is fatal for anyone who writes to think of their sex." But the pronouncement, contemplated, generates many perplexities. What does it mean, exactly, to think of one's sex? How can one avoid it? Is it really true, or only a semantic convenience, to say that Shakespeare wrote not as a man but as a man-woman? Surely the critic is imposing terminology to solve a problem that will not yield to so easy a solution.

For she concludes also, "It is much more important to be oneself than anything else." And she concludes, "I am asking you to live in the presence of reality." And to separate the idea of being oneself, the idea of commitment to reality, from awareness of one's sexual identity seems an arbitrary and dangerous disjunction. Moreover the evidence that Mrs. Woolf herself cites, for different purposes, may remind the reader of the degree to which many of the best women writers have written precisely out of thinking about their sex. *A Room of One's Own* leaves more questions unanswered than resolved. This is not to denigrate its achievement: to express, even to half-express, some of the perplexities of the feminine situation, and to connect them with the issues raised by the fiction of women—these are significant accomplishments. And the essay's inadequacies are themselves revealing. Its author's evasions of her own anger, her effort to dismiss feminine anger as a limitation on women's writing, her aspiration to escape in writing the problems implicit in her own sexuality: these aspects of the book, its logical failures, tell us as much as do its logical triumphs.

"I just don't understand what's going on here," exclaimed the one "grown-up" freshman in my class: twenty-four years old, married, a trained nurse with direct experience of what students are fond of calling "the real world." We had been discussing an autobiographical piece by Ellen Willis, an argument for Women's Liberation based on detailed rendition of the facts of a young woman's experience. The members of the colloquium brought their analytic faculties brilliantly to bear on the essay. They located and described its shifts of tone, its complexities of attitude, its principles of structure; they treated it as they might have treated an ode by Keats. It was this fact that the nurse was reacting to. "You act as though she's talking about someone else, but she's talking about our lives too. Doesn't this have anything to do with you? It has a lot to do with *me*."

Everyone was startled, then shamefaced. Yes, they admitted, they recognized the immediate applications of Ellen Willis to their own lives, but they weren't sure they wanted to talk about that. Neither were they sure they wanted to discuss theoretical differences of opinion about the nature of women's lot. Theory, too, had its discomforts; it was safer to stick to textual analysis.

But over and over the same point emerged: These books are talking about *us*. And the "us" they describe makes one uneasy. We would just as soon find someone else to identify with—but where?

By the time Simone de Beauvoir tackled the problem of the female nature, a good deal more prose had been written on the subject. Mlle de Beauvoir's defenses, and needs for defense, are much less obvious than Virginia Woolf's. Her ambition is much greater, and her range of knowledge and reference. The slowness of development in *A Room of One's Own* seems part of the stylistic apology; the ponderousness with which *The Second Sex* develops its argument is part of its authority. The questions Virginia Woolf evades, or fails to recognize, or only pretends to answer, Simone de Beauvoir confronts in detail. The literary analysis through which Virginia Woolf displays her sensibility becomes for the Frenchwoman a way of insisting on her rational powers. Yet she, too, writes finally as a woman—as a woman must, despite all arguments for the "androgynous" or the "transcendent"—and in her mode of dealing with the problem of femininity, as well as in her direct statement about it, she adds to our knowledge of what it is like to be a woman writing.

The Second Sex is six times the length of *A Room of One's Own*: the two works are hardly comparable. But both use reference to literary texts as a way of talking about the feminine situation; and both purport to add to our understanding of the woman's state.

But how unfeminine to write such a *big* book as *The Second Sex*!

A book so assertive, so argumentative, so overwhelming!

What do you mean, Mlle de Beauvoir would rejoin, by this term, *unfeminine*? What would it be to be *feminine*?

It is her contention—she takes more than seven hundred pages to support it—that such ideas have little supportable content. "It is as absurd ... to speak of 'woman' in general as of the 'eternal' man." There is no feminine nature, only a feminine situation which has in many respects remained constant through the centuries and which largely determines the characters of its victims. The notion of "femininity" is a fiction created by men, assented to by women untrained in the rigors of logical thought or conscious of the advantages to be gained by compliance with masculine fantasies. Their assent traps them in the prison of "repetition and immanence" which limits woman's possibilities. Man reserves for himself the terrors and triumphs of transcendence; he offers woman safety, the temptations of passivity and acceptance; he tells her that passivity and acceptance are her nature. Mlle de Beauvoir tells her that this is a lie, that her nature is complicated and various, that she must escape, liberate herself, shape her own future, deny the myths that confine her.

All authors talk to themselves, as well as to the readers they imagine and foresee. For a woman to write such a book as *The Second Sex* is a particularly significant kind of "talking to herself." The act of writing defines her as a being seeking transcendence. She demonstrates her logic, her grasp of reality, her capacity to deal with the abstract as well as the concrete; demonstrates thus her intellectual identity with those beings who have attempted to separate her into a special category. "Woman is still astonished and flattered at being admitted to the world of thought, of art—a masculine world." Mlle de Beauvoir does not directly betray her astonishment, but one feels at times the strain of her insistence that she really belongs to this world. For she is explicitly conscious that the facts of feminine experience necessarily limit the possibilities of greatness for a woman:

Art, literature, philosophy, are attempts to found the world anew on a human liberty: that of the individual

creator; to entertain such a pretension, one must first un-
equivocally assume the status of a being who has liberty.
The restrictions that education and custom impose on
woman now limit her grasp on the universe; when the
struggle to find one's place in this world is too arduous,
there can be no question of getting away from it.

In these sentences, Mlle de Beauvoir suggests both her
aim and her sense of its frustration. What she has finally
to say to herself (and to other women) is that she can
never hope to be as much as she can imagine herself
being. Many thinkers would say that this gap between
imagination and fact is essential to the human condition, a
partial definition of mortality. Only a woman would say
that her experience as a member of her sex makes it definitely impossible for her to "found the world anew"
through the power of her mind.

True, she carefully explains that "it is not a special destiny that limits" women—only a historical accident lasting
for many centuries. The future is unknown; she dreams of
a future in which women, finding new liberation, will also
discover new capacities. Their genius then may express itself as freely as men's. Anything is possible. But the
weight of those seven hundred pages, standing behind
that optimistic assertion of faith in the possibilities of the
"free woman," contradicts it. It is the weight of all human
history; by comparison, the insistence that things are
changing now, that women are claiming their rights, that
everything is going to be different, seems whistling in the
dark. Here is the final sentence of the book's penultimate
chapter, on "The Independent Woman": "What is certain
is that hitherto woman's possibilities have been suppressed
and lost to humanity, and that it is high time she be permitted to take her chances in her own interest and in the
interest of all." It is a surprisingly weak conclusion. Compared to the finality of "suppressed and lost," the insistence that "it is high time" matters should change has a
petulant shrillness; the dubiousness implicit in the use of

the passive voice in the final clause betrays the author's belief that woman is finally dependent on men, who must grant her "permission" to "take her chances." One is hardly convinced—and one hardly believes the author is convinced—that the future will be appreciably different from the past. Like the rest of us, Mlle de Beauvoir seems riddled with internal conflicts. More important to her book even than the disparity between what she wishes to be possible and what her knowledge and observation tell her, is the clash between masculine and feminine values expressed in her prose.

Which brings us full circle: She doesn't *believe* in feminine values as something apart from masculine ones; how can there be such a clash? Well, as in Virginia Woolf, what she demonstrates is not quite compatible with what she asserts; and in the incompatibility lies much of the interest of her book. Her long and penetrating analysis of how women live, how their physical being affects them, how they feel, adds up, after all, to a convincing evocation of " 'woman' in general"—that being of whom Mlle de Beauvoir considers it "absurd" to speak.

All women share the same physical nature. Here is Mlle de Beauvoir on the subject:

Blood pressure rises before the beginning of the [menstrual] flow and falls afterward; the pulse rate and often the temperature are increased, so that fever is frequent; pains in the abdomen are felt; ... many subjects have sore throat and difficulties with hearing and sight; perspiration is increased and accompanied at the beginning of the menses by an odor sui generis, which may be very strong and may persist throughout the period. ... Glandular instability brings on a pronounced nervous instability. The central nervous system is affected, with frequent headache, and the sympathetic system is overactive; unconscious control through the central system is reduced, freeing convulsive reflexes and complexes and leading to a marked capriciousness of disposition. The woman is more emo-

*tional, more nervous, more irritable than usual, and may
manifest serious psychic disturbance. It is during her
periods that she feels her body most painfully as an obscure, alien thing; it is, indeed, the prey of a stubborn and
foreign life that each month constructs and then tears
down a cradle within it. . . . Woman experiences a more
profound alienation when fertilization has occurred. . . .
Gestation is a fatiguing task of no individual benefit to
the woman but on the contrary demanding heavy sacrifices. . . . All that a healthy and well-nourished woman
can hope for is to recoup these losses without too much
difficulty after childbirth. . . . The conflict between species
and individual, which sometimes assumes dramatic force
at childbirth, endows the feminine body with a disturbing frailty. . . . In the end woman escapes the iron
grasp of the species by way of still another serious
crisis. . . .*

A woman can hardly read this without an answering pang
in the vitals. And this is only a truncated version of the
elaborate, detailed account *The Second Sex* provides of
the physical experience shared by half of humanity.
Equally compelling, and only a trifle less detailed, is its
narration of the social and psychological experience of
women: what it is to be a young girl, a wife, a mother, an
old woman. Female readers on a different continent from
the author, separated in time from the writing of the book
by almost a quarter of a century, must give assent to essential aspects of this account. Details differ in different
social contexts, but the irritability of menstruation, the difficulties of reconciling the claims of family and career, the
problem of preserving love in marriage: these seem ineluctable.

It is true of course that social revolution, or even drastic
evolution, might produce conditions so different as to alter
many facts of feminine experience. Many, but surely not
all—not the experienced alienation from the body or the
sense of being at the disposal of forces beyond the individ-

ual. And such facts must be crucial in the psychic life, consequently in the character and personality, of the human being who experiences them. How can women fail to be in some vital respects—psychic as well as physical—different from men? Surely there must be something we may call "woman in general": Mlle de Beauvoir makes us believe in her even while denying her existence.

The point is an important one, for it bears on the problem of evaluating feminine accomplishment, actual and potential. Despite Mlle de Beauvoir's penetrating criticism of male writers' "myths" of women, her standards of accomplishment are masculine; her acceptance of those standards total. *Middlemarch* is not the equal of *War and Peace* because George Eliot lacked the "richness of experience of a Dostoyevsky, a Tolstoy"; no woman "has that madness in her method that we call genius"; "woman exhausts her courage dissipating mirages and she stops in terror at the threshold of reality." Without challenging these descriptions of literary reality—although they are controversial—we may question the value judgments they imply. Is it necessarily true that only the combination of madness and method is to be called genius, that richness of experience (richness meaning, apparently, breadth, variety) is a prerequisite for the highest literary accomplishment, that the dissipation of mirages is not an adequate literary goal? "They [women] rarely create masculine heroes as convincing as Heathcliff: in man they comprehend hardly more than the male. But they have often aptly described their own inner life, their experience, their own universe; attentive to the hidden substance of things, fascinated by the peculiarities of their own sensations, they present their experience, still warm, through savory adjectives and carnal figures of speech. Their vocabulary is often more notable than their syntax because they are interested in things rather than the relations of things ..." All this somehow adds up to the second-rate. Mlle de Beauvoir explains that most men are also limited in their literary accomplishments, that it is by comparison with male geniuses—"the few rare male artists who deserve to be called 'great men'"—that woman seems "mediocre" in her artistic achievement. Male artists alone set the standard of greatness.

It is not only in explicit judgments that the critic betrays her rather startling bias. Her treatment of woman writers always suggests an *a priori* tendency to take them less seriously than their masculine counterparts. In discussing "the myth of woman," she treats in detail five male authors: Montherlant, Lawrence, Claudel, Breton, Stendhal. Although these writers represent divergent attitudes toward women, all are finally inadequate in their treatment of the opposite sex. Mlle de Beauvoir demonstrates this fact through careful and on the whole sympathetic analysis of individual texts. She offers no equivalent investigation of any woman writer. Do the various "myths of woman" survive unchanged in female renditions? She doesn't tell us. Instead, she frequently cites passages from woman writers—notably Collette, Katherine Mansfield, and Isadora Duncan—as direct testimony about the nature of woman's lot. Oddly enough, she cites the imaginative writing of men—Zola, Tolstoy, Ibsen—in exactly the same way for the same reason, to provide examples of female experience. Men make "myths" about women, yet they can also be trusted, apparently, to render the facts of her condition. Women may or may not make or reproduce myths (Mlle de Beauvoir expresses no view about this question), but their literary significance depends mainly on their direct rendition of actuality—a source of their literary limitation, as Mlle de Beauvoir elsewhere points out. Not even an intelligent woman, dedicated in the most serious way to the cause of feminism, takes them seriously in the way she takes men. And her judgment that they are not to be taken as seriously apparently lies too deep for her to question it.

Like Virginia Woolf, then, Mlle de Beauvoir believes that women must transcend the condition of being women in order to be great artists. But the conclusion is more surprising in her because of the nature of the demonstration by which she reaches it. We believe what Mlle de Beauvoir tells us because she tells it so well: with endless convincing detail and with profound, meticulous empathy. I am a female, she seems to say, and nothing female is alien to me. The situation of the prostitute, the narcissist, the mystic, the woman in menopause—she presents all with the same exactness and conviction. Perhaps the most remarkable aspect of this remarkable book is the way in which it transforms history and sociology into psychology. The virgins, brides, mothers, and grandmothers who inhabit it are most often imagined figures. Case histories provide supporting evidence, but the author generalizes from them to "type" characters of extraordinary vibrancy. What they feel, how their lives seem to them, their psychic as well as physical experience: these internal facts, understood as crucial, shape their presentation. The turmoil of the adolescent girl emerges not as set a set of data but as a compelling congeries of emotion. That girl evokes what every woman remembers, as a figure in imaginative literature might. In some ultimate sense, this scholarly book *is* imaginative literature.

Like Virginia Woolf (although it is not for her as important an image as it is for her predecessor), Simone de Beauvoir is interested in the mirror, metaphor and reality, as a key to the feminine condition. Women concern themselves with their own images; men require the enlarged self-image provided by their reflection in a woman. The difference is that between an active and a passive orientation. "In woman particularly, the image is identified with the ego. . . . Woman, knowing and making herself object, believes she really sees *herself* in the glass. A passive and given fact, the reflection is, like herself, a thing." For a man, the situation is more complicated. "Woman has often been compared to water because, among other things, she is the mirror in which the male, Narcissus-like, contemplates himself: he bends over her in good or bad faith. But in any case what he really asks of her is to be, outside of him, all that which he cannot grasp inside himself, because the inwardness of the existent is only nothingness and because he must project himself into an object in order to reach himself."

Virginia Woolf's emotional ambivalence about the value judgments to be made of men and woman recurs here in subtler form. Contempt controls the description of woman's willingness to accept herself as a thing; but a shadow of contempt also hangs over the account of men unable to grasp their own inwardness, dependent on those willing to make themselves objects. And what is the relation between the special "inwardness" of women, the ability to perceive, to accept, and to project the reality of inner states, and their accepted status as objects? Mlle de Beauvoir declares transcendence to be the proper goal of human endeavor. But in the course of her demonstration of the horrors immanence, the female state, she also suggests its special value—not only for man, who makes of woman "the Other," but for woman herself, whose self-acceptance may give her, if not unique possibilities of knowledge, at least special ways of knowing.

Writing a historical, philosophical, and psychological account of the state of women, Mlle de Beauvoir quite properly concentrates on the injustices of the female lot and on the consequences of injustice in female experience. She too is angry, as thinking women can hardly fail to be; her anger expresses itself in her essentially masculine posture of defense. Trying to write as she believes only men have written—lucidly, logically, with a firm grasp of wide experience—she indeed demonstrates her power as a thinker, but also her power as a woman. Strangely, she never seems to realize this fact.

Everyone faces choices about what aspects of his experience he will allow himself to realize, what he will ignore. Even the fundamental choice, for a woman, of whether to recognize the unfairnesses of a woman's lot can be a difficult one. The frequent resistance of theoretical discussion of the female situation in my class partly reflected a reluctance to deal with the possibility that one was a victim of social injustice. Although one young woman firmly asserted, "The greatest problem for women is self-hatred," most of her contemporaries merely demonstrated this fact. In some ways they appeared afraid to think—afraid of what thought might reveal to them. "To me," one girl observed, "—and this really worries me—the opposite of feminine is intellectual." A sense of this opposition is buried deep in many women. What does it mean to be feminine? they ask themselves, and find the answer difficult, resenting the stereotypes such definitions involve them in. But they feel unavoidably clear about what is *not* feminine: serious thought is not. This is not to say they will necessarily refuse to engage in it, but it suggests the strain they are likely to feel in serious confrontation of intellectual issues. The first question is whether they are really capable of such confrontation; the second is whether they *should* test themselves in this particular way. If to do so is *a priori* unwomanly, it may be self-defeating. Few women wish to deny their womanhood; and many feel that to investigate its meaning is itself an act of denial.

On the other hand, they are not necessarily willing to commit themselves openly to their feelings. Feeling may be "feminine," but exposure is dangerous. And feeling with no support of reason is embarrassing partly because it suggests exactly the kind of inadequacy many women are all too ready to suspect in themselves. "I've had some really emotional things going on inside me but I always feel like I have no business saying anything unless I can really back it up." "I come here to listen to other people's ideas, I don't want to tell you what I feel."

The last of these remarks is perhaps the most revealing: it suggests the speaker's eagerness to take advantage of the passive role socially assigned her, to be a recipient, not to face the dangers of self-exposure inherent in verbal giving. (When young men came to the class, they avoided the same danger in the opposite way: by insistent, though largely meaningless, talk.) The disinclination to talk about personal feelings is very deep. It characteristically seems to reflect a sense of an absolute split between the emotional and the intellectual. Emotional responses are private and vaguely shameful, indices of vulnerability, even of feminine inferiority; intellectual equipment functions in the classroom, is more respectable, but provides no convincing grasp on or response to actuality. My students had no notion of the unified sensibility even as a possibility. They accepted disjunction as the natural condition of women, accepted it too deeply even to regret it.

These three responses—self-contempt, reluctance to risk emotional exposure, belief in the eternal separation of the intellectual and the emotional—all create problems for students talking about writing by women, making it difficult for them to know what their reactions really are and difficult to express a reaction even when it is recognized. But these are responses not only of adolescents, and the difficulties they create appear not only in the classroom. To a striking degree the problems of young woman critics are duplicated in the writing of the women they aspire to criticize.

In *Thinking About Women*, Mary Ellmann describes Rebecca West's classification of women as idiots, men as lunatics. She points out that in making such a classification, Miss West avoids the danger of being included in it: "The person capable of describing idiocy and lunacy cannot herself be confined by either of them." Mrs. Ellmann herself escapes the potential fate of condemnation to some dismissive category of the feminine by locating the chief categories in terms so penetrating that the classifications themselves become ridiculous. It would be a bold critic who would presume to comment on Mrs. Ellmann's striking lack of shrillness in her account of women's lot, having read her observations on the widespread tendency to damn women as shrill or praise them as not shrill. Woman as balloon, as shrew or witch, the formlessness, passivity, instability, piety, irrationality, compliancy, materiality of women—all these stereotypes, and more, Mrs. Ellmann economically describes and dismisses. None can contain her.

Yet as clearly as Virginia Woolf, although less apologetically, Mrs. Ellmann writes in the distinctive voice of a woman. What that means, in her case, is a display not of sensibility but of a peculiarly feminine sort and function of wit. A new category suggests itself for her: not the passivity of formlessness or the purposelessness of instability, but the feminine resource of evasiveness. The opponent who would presume to attack her finds her not where she was when he took aim. She embodies woman as quicksilver, always in brilliant, erratic motion. The traditional metaphoric association between mercury and wit is to the point here; and so, perhaps, is the fact that mercury makes a backing for mirrors. But Mrs. Ellmann's mirror provides a fun-house view of the men it reflects. In it, Norman Mailer is all paunch, and the Shakespearean critic E. E. Stoll looks rather like the straw man in *The Wizard of Oz*: overstuffed head of undistinguished content.

Evasiveness is the triumph and the limitation of *Thinking About Women*, and at the heart of the literary program the book seems—evasively—to advocate; it is central to Mrs. Ellmann's technique, and she reveals it, indirectly, as a primary resource of women in their social victimization.

Not that she ever speaks of the social victimization of women. In many important respects, *Thinking About Women* is diametrically opposed to *The Second Sex*, despite that fact that both can be loosely characterized as feminist documents. Simone de Beauvoir tries to overwhelm her audience with facts; Mary Ellmann charms them with allusions. She has facts at her disposal too: white mice sometimes rape other white mice, and Dryden knew it; Evelyn Waugh's first wife was named Evelyn, sufficient cause for a disastrous marriage. But the function of such facts is implicit in their nature. They are incidental

27

illustrations rather than pieces of evidence. The primary evidence for Mrs. Ellmann's case is the texture of her mind. This is enough to suggest the injustice of masculine dismissiveness, the power of feminine intellection—understood as distinctively different from its masculine counterpart.

That women suffer social injustice is a crucial fact in the background of the argument, but only in the background. Mrs. Ellmann's declared interest is in the uses of language, particularly the ways in which the language men use about women suggests their assumptions. Mrs. Ellmann speaks of the words used in referring to the processes of parturition, pointing out how the stress on *attendance* and *delivery* emphasizes the passivity of women in this crucial role, although the admission that *labor* takes place at least acknowledges some female activity. (She does not discuss, as she might, the ambiguities inherent in the word *delivery:* traditionally the mother, unlike the postman, does not deliver the infant, it is delivered to the recumbent mother; also the woman is delivered from her nine-month burden. Vocabularly thus grants, after all, that giving birth is not simply the "creative" activity that, as Mrs. Ellmann points out, men are fond of declaring it.) If these words reveal significant social attitudes, so do such accompanying facts as the proud role of the doctor in blood-specked smock, and Mrs. Ellmann evokes the image of that doctor in precisely the same spirit that she looks into the words used in describing him. Recognizing how artificial is the separation between words and facts, she nonetheless persists in declaring blandly her primary concern only with the verbal.

As she points out how strikingly patterns of metaphor and allusion may change from one century to the next, however, she suggests how her concerns penetrate beneath the linguistic level. Her first chapter deals, in witty and illuminating fashion, with the uses of sexual language to describe literary activity. Analogies between sexual and literary creativity have always presented themselves to writers; but their usage in our own time is different from the patterns of the seventeenth and eighteenth centuries.

At the crudest level of this metaphoric struggle, the writer finds his professional and sexual activities incompatible, on the grounds of the distribution of resources. This anxiety seems distinctly modern. The association of the two faculties, intellectual and sexual, is ancient, but the expressed inability to reconcile them is recent. Blake, for example, celebrated "the lineaments of gratified desire," and seemed to sense no contradiction between them and artistic gratification. In fact, he considered sexual intercourse, rather like having breakfast or a walk in the garden, an essential prelude to composition. Hemingway, instead, found a young writer to warn against making love during periods of composition: the best ideas would be lost in bed.

Why has this change taken place? Mrs. Ellmann does not offer to tell us. She is not a spinner of theories, not a writer of history, only an observer and commentator. She exposes a problem to our attention and proceeds to the next, with the air of someone merely passing the time. And the problems she reveals or suggests do not always, or even mainly, involve the persecution of women by men. If the book keeps reminding us of ways in which women are forced into uncomfortable roles for the convenience of men, it never directly asserts anything of the sort. Its direct assertions, by and large, confine themselves to literary facts.

This mode of indirection is of course itself a particularly effective kind of evasiveness. Claiming so little, Mrs. Ellmann is difficult to attack; implying so much, she is difficult to refute. When she wishes to make Norman Mailer look ridiculous, she indulges in no diatribes: she simply quotes him. "The real interplay of the novel exists between the characters and the objects which surround them until the faces are swimming in a cold lava of anality, which becomes the truest part of her group, her glob, her impacted mass." This is Mailer on *The Group*; Mrs. Ellmann comments, "A fine polemical bit, though it is not at once clear why, since the world is full of a number of things, they should all be seen as shit." Apparently praising her subject for his rhetorical skill, she mildly criticizes his limitation of perspective. Such is the entire content of her commentary sentence. Its effect, however, is far more devastating: the woman critic demonstrates how feminine charm can combat masculine forcefulness. Her simplicity of language exposes Mailer's pretentiousness; her question suggests the perversity of his metaphor; her air of common sense reveals how far Mailer is from the sensible, and how completely she refuses to be infuriated by him. And the victim would be hard pressed to find a way out. He might sputter that he is as capable as the next man (or woman) of saying *shit*; he would only seem ridiculous. The fact would remain that in this instance he chose to obscure what might be summarized in an Anglo-Saxon word by meaningless elaboration of metaphor. He might proclaim that he does not choose to be merely "sensible"; Mrs. Ellmann would silently wait for him to explain what it is that he chooses to be instead. Victory belongs to the devious: finally there is only that for Mailer to complain of.

What *Thinking About Women* does not say, but irresistibly implies, is as interesting as what it says. Its long discussion of feminine stereotypes has a consistent hidden dimension, its nature suggested by one of Mrs. Ellmann's comparisons between women and Negroes. "Feminine passivity is closely related to Negro apathy. In both cases, having restricted the participation of the group, the observer finds that inactivity is an innate group characteristic. . . . Women and Negroes are also linked in the stereotypes of frivolity and fecklessness, respectively." The writer does not go on to point out that the psychological strategy of individual blacks has often been to exploit these stereotypes to his own advantage, nor does she indicate the further implications of the comparison she has drawn. But the abundant literature analyzing the psychological and

30

social experience of the blacks indicates how much further the comparison might be taken. Stereotypes, the imposition of one group's ways of thinking and speaking on another, affect the group imposed upon as well as the group imposing. Blacks declared to be shiftless may enjoy and exploit the advantages of shiftlessness. Women labeled frivolous or passive have corresponding resources open to them: resources of indirection, deviousness, evasiveness. Both oppressed classes, of course, may also take the opposite way, of openly resenting and defying imposed stereotypes. But if they are acting only as individuals, they are unlikely to be as successful with openness as with evasiveness. Feminine anger often expresses itself in indirect ways. Mrs. Ellmann's book constantly reminds one of this fact, both through what it says and implies and through its indirect way of saying it.

It is no surprise to find, in the second half of this study, that the author sees the greatest literary possibilities for women as lying in the abandonment of authority as a rhetorical pose. Before the twentieth century, she believes, one can make a general distinction between masculine writing, marked by its note of authority, and feminine, characterized by commitment to sensibility. In our own time, however, "the authoritative mode is no longer the mode of original, which is more than competent, expression. At the same time, the exertion of sensibility is not marked in the most interesting writing by women now." The temper of the age is such that claims of authority are now likely to seem ludicrous. This fact provides a significant opportunity for women writers. "Quite simply, having not had physical or intellectual authority before, they have no reason to resist a literature at odds with authority." The rejection of authority in many instances implies a retreat from the public pose of the novelist, making announcements to the world at large, to a more private position. The novelist now suspects that he may be talking to himself; and often he (more often, she) talks only *about* himself, herself. Mrs. Ellmann finds introspection, on the whole, boring. She recognizes the fact that women have always been alienated from the main stream of society, and that it is natural for them to write about this alienation. Yet what impresses her most in Doris Lessing's *Children of Violence* sequence is its tedium of depressed self-analysis and self-discovery. Her ritual gestures of respect toward Mrs. Lessing do not conceal her preference for writers of quite another sort.

For the kind of fiction Mrs. Ellmann admires is in some ways analogous to the kind of criticism she writes. The woman writers who seem to rouse her enthusiasm are Ivy Compton-Burnett, Jane Bowles, Dorothy Richardson (with resservations). Their escape from authority depends on irony, the preservation of psychic distance; most of all, on indirection. "The interest in phenomena is unlimited, the customary urge to categorize them is retrained. The novelist may, in this way, escape the necessity to be a representative, of her sect or sex or era. If anything is accented, it can be eccentricity—as natural and ubiquitous as type. So a freedom can come about at least from pomposity . . ."

Escape. Freedom. It is striking that Mrs. Ellmann should choose to characterize feminine literary success in these terms. The implication is that triumphant women writers in their writing solve the problems that face all women as women. They *escape*, find freedom from the restrictions that limit their experience. They do so by avoidance: of categories, of pose, of authority, of representativeness. In devious feminine fashion, they find a way through the perplexities of the novel, the perplexities of life. For a woman, often, the devious and the triumphant are identical.

Mary Ellmann's avoidance of any claim to authority, her darting, glancing attacks, her technique and advocacy of evasiveness suggest the same thing as Simone de Beauvoir's straining for masculine authority: a hidden level of female self-doubt. It is not that Ellmann thinks it preferable to be a man: she delights in the special possibilities of womanhood. On the other hand, her way of

32

proceeding is a mode of concealment, covering anger, although it also indirectly expresses it, evading full commitment to emotional involvement with subject by witty (i.e., intellectual) logic and rhetoric. The writer *escapes* masculine categories by defining them; escapes the trap of emotion by analysis; escapes imitating a man by demonstrating the resources of femininity. In other words, she solves the problems my students recognized in themselves. Solving them, she demonstrates, like other women writers, that they exist for her too.

"You can't expect anyone to maintain their toughness forever."

The issue of "toughness" kept coming up in class. If women's problems, as expressed directly and indirectly through their writing, have a dreadful monotony, so do many of their solutions. And the solutions raise further problems, all returning to the fundamental question of whether there is or should be a feminine nature distinct from the masculine.

The association between masculinity and aggression is profound. Aggression is okay for men, maybe; at any rate, most adolescents seem relatively content to think it's inevitable. But for women? *The New York Times Magazine* reported that someone had experimented with injecting small quantities of testosterone into females. (Females of what species? someone immediately asked. No one seemed to know.) The result was an immediate increase in aggression. Members of the class were fascinated, but scared. A frightening idea: aggression really *was*, in a provable, chemical sense, innately male; and it might conceivably be inflicted on females.

But the problem of anger remains, and how it is to be expressed.

If you give up your anger and aggression, you necessarily buy into the game you hate and fear.

If you preserve it, you're imitating men.

Is there a "feminine" way? Should there be?

Kate Millett has successfully maintained her toughness. One distinction of *Sexual Politics* is that it made so many people angry. Mary Ellmann didn't infuriate anyone, even Simone de Beauvoir invited scholarly consideration rather than political polemic as response. But Miss Millett had it both ways: she constructed an elaborate exercise in political rhetoric, and for it she got a Ph.D. in English. So Irving Howe got upset, and Norman Mailer, and many others. And it was necessary to read the book, or at least to pretend to have read it, if only for the sake of cocktail party conversation. However clumsily stated, unoriginal, muddled, Miss Millett's was an idea whose time had come, the idea that relations between men and women have always been more fundamentally a matter of politics—meaning manipulations of power—than of sentiment.

The evidence for this truth is historical—the record of centuries of male domination; literary—the writings of such "male chauvinists" as D. H. Lawrence, Norman Mailer, and Henry Miller, and more deviously, of the homosexual Jean Genet; and psychological—the nature, recorded or intuited, of actual feminine experience. And the voice in which this account is offered—well, the voice is the problem. In some ways it seems impersonal, the sexless voice of twentieth-century politics. On the other hand, it has also an odd quality of intense, imperfectly concealed personal emotion. The emotion is anger: one encounters it everywhere in women writing about their own condition. Virginia Woolf considers anger a defect in feminine writing. Simone de Beauvoir conceals it behind her accumulation of data and logic, Mary Ellmann uses it as an impelling force for her wit, evasively presenting wit rather than anger as her justification. Kate Millett, feeling justified in her anger, uses it as a rhetorical weapon. Anger breeds anger: it is not surprising that hers should be a book that enrages male commentators, and some female ones as well. But in accepting anger about the limitations imposed on women as sufficient self-justification, Kate Millett embraces one kind of limitation for the sake of avoiding others. She seems representative in this respect of a considerable group of female commentators.

Mary Ellmann claims that the tone of authority is not comfortable for a woman; Kate Millett fairly wallows in it. The difference between her sureness and Simone de Beauvoir's is instructive. Although it is true that *Sexual Politics* owes a large, and largely unacknowledged, intellectual debt to *The Second Sex*, its emotional assumptions are different. Simone de Beauvoir seeks authority by imitating a masculine approach; she gains it largely by her capacity for detailed and convincing empathy. Although she sees men as the oppressors of women, she admires masculine capacity. Kate Millett's authority derives from the intensely forced vision of one wearing blinders. Everything declares itself to her in a single pattern. Thus her prose, reiterating her simplified view, has an awkwardness produced by the tension between its professed objectivity, the depersonalization of truth-telling, and the strong emotional bias that underlies it.

A representative bit of Millett argument: "And since both masculine vanity and masculine uneasiness lest 'femininity' be lost (and with it, the only kindness either men profess to see in human beings) prevents the male from acquiring the humanity attributed to woman, or woman from transcending her politically and socially powerless role, Erikson is as unlikely to realize his hopes as Ruskin's queens were powerless to abridge the evils of industrialism." The sentence has more than the usual quota of grammatical difficulties, which reflect the deeper problem of intellectual clarity. Miss Millett's subject is Erik Erikson's declared belief that women may be expected to have a "moral," civilizing effect on men, a belief that offends the feminist because, reflecting the view that men and women have fundamentally different natures, it can be used to justify the existent structure of inequality. The most convincing phrase in Miss Millett's critique is "politically and socially powerless." Here she is on sure ground; the phrase rings with conviction if not with individuality.

But the explanation of Erikson's fallacy depends most heavily on the unsupported attribution of inhibiting emotional patterns ("vanity" and "uneasiness") to "the male" in general: a mode of argument appallingly like the one she attacks. And the comparison of how "unlikely" Erikson is to realize his hopes with how "powerless" Ruskin's queens were is both linguistically and logically fuzzy. It lacks analytical clarity and the note of genuine belief.

The forms of assumed authority are not sufficient basis for argument. Miss Millett's sentences, in this political treatise, are declarative, pervaded with superficial energy, provided with the trappings of logic. She writes as an impassioned partisan, exploiting the anger that pervades her version of history, her accunt of modern psychology and sociology, and her literary criticism. But she writes badly, making herself an easy target for Norman Mailer, who observes that her "style is suggestive of a night-school lawyer who sips Metrecal to keep his figure, and thereby is so full of isolated proteins, factory vitamins, reconstituted cyclamates, and artificial flavors that one has to pore over the passages like a business contract. What explosions are buried in those droning clauses, those chains of familiar aggregates (of words)." It's tempting enough to attack Mailer, but no one could ever accuse him of sounding like a lawyer, with or without cyclamates: he sounds always like his irritating self. Unlike Mailer, Kate Millett is unwilling to commit herself openly to the implications of her own emotion; her personal anger mingles uneasily with the night-school lawyer's pomposities; her book implies the necessity for a reconciliation of the personal and the impersonal which it is unable to achieve. One can be far more sympathetic to her views than Norman Mailer is and still find great difficulty reading her prose.

Her stylistic problems appear to derive partly from intellectual vagueness. "It is at moments like this that Swinburne most reminds one of a prurient schoolboy jerking off." This sentence refers to the famous lines about the poet's desire to change "the lilies and languors of virtue/

36

For the raptures and roses of Vice." The calculated tonal disparity between the comment and the lines that occasioned it might focus attention on the decorative pretentiousness of Swinburne's verse. There *is* something wrong with Swinburne, and it involves a sense of his poetic and moral self-indulgence. But "jerking off" is an imprecise metaphor to locate this weakness. Substituting shock for exactitude, it then blurs the shock by structural circumlocution ("It is at moments like this that . . .") and by the falseness of tone in "prurient." The two modifiers, derived from different levels of diction, different points of view, cannot comfortably coexist.

On the whole, Millett has little interest in woman imaginative writers. She dismisses George Eliot and Virginia Woolf as insufficiently revolutionary; she doesn't mention Jane Austen. Charlotte Brontë, on the other hand, wins her approval, and she spends several pages in analysis of that "subversive" novel *Villette*, commenting also on the inadequacy of male critics to deal with such a writer as Miss Brontë. Her own inadequacy—inaccuracy of summary, imperception of judgment—emerges only gradually.

Since the kind of literary criticism she recommends and practices is avowedly political in orientation, it is natural that the aspect of *Villette* that interests her most is its implied criticism of the existing social scheme. The anger for which Virginia Woolf apologizes is the focus of the later critic's attention. "There is bitterness and anger in *Villette*—and rightly so. One finds a good deal of it in Richard Wright's *Black Boy*, too. To label it neurotic is to mistake symptom for cause in the hope of protecting oneself from what would be upsetting." She comments perceptively on Lucy Snowe's function in the novel as observer of society, and on the way in which Charlotte Brontë fragments points of view in order to elucidate them.

When it comes to her treatment of Lucy's odd romance with Paul Emanuel, a tyrannical fellow-teacher, Miss Millett's method breaks down.

*Escape is all over the book; Villette reads like one long
meditation on a prison break. Lucy will not marry Paul
even after the tyrant has softened. He has been her jailer
all through the novel, but the sly and crafty captive in
Lucy is bent on evading him anyway. . . . The keeper
turned kind must be eluded anyway; Paul turned lover
is drowned. Lucy is free. Free is alone; given a choice
between "love" in its most agreeable contemporary manifestation, and freedom, Lucy chose to retain the indivi-
dualist humanity she had shored up, even at the expense
of sexuality.*

"Literary criticism of the Brontës has been a long game
of masculine prejudice." Miss Millett's variety seems a
game of feminist prejudice: the book will hardly support
the description she offers of it. To say that Lucy "will not
marry Paul" is a serious falsification. His proposal contains
a delay clause: "Lucy, take my love. *One day* share my
life." Lucy accepts immediately, commenting, "Now, penetrated with his influence, and living by his affection, having his worth by intellect, and his goodness by heart—I
preferred him before all humanity." She makes no "choice"
between love and freedom, or not the choice that Miss
Millett claims for her; she explains at length that her
pleasure in her "freedom," during her lover's absence, depends largely on her commitment to him. "The spring
which moved my energies lay far away beyond seas, in an
Indian isle." "I have cultivated out of love for him (I was
naturally no florist) the plants he preferred, and some of
them are yet in bloom. I thought I loved him when he
went away; I love him now in another degree; he is more
my own." And the drowning of M. Emanuel, which Miss
Millett seems to see as Lucy's triumph of elusion, is from
Charlotte Brontë's point of view a more ambiguous matter.
Lucy describes the storm that troubles the seas, reveals
that many vessels have been wrecked in it, but fails to
specify that her lover's has been one of them. Then she offers this paragraph: "Here pause: pause at once. There is

enough said. Trouble no quiet, kind heart; leave sunny imaginations hope. Let it be theirs to conceive the delight of joy born again fresh out of great terror, the rapture of rescue from peril, the wondrous reprieve from dread, the fruition of return. Let them picture union and a happy succeeding life."

The book Charlotte Brontë wrote is even more interesting than the one Kate Millett invents. The invitation to the reader to construct his own fantasy about Lucy and Paul calls attention to the element of fantasy in the novel as a whole (which Miss Millett points out), but also to the various possibilities of relationship. The life of love may be ended by death—certainly the implication is that M. Emanuel has in fact been drowned—or it may produce union and happiness. But a third possibility is also alive in the prose: that the result of "union" is not inevitably "a happy succeeding life," that union need not produce bliss, that vexation persist in human intercourse. If *Villette* is, as Miss Millett claims, a fantasy of success which would in fact be impossible of realization for a woman in Charlotte Brontë's time (I'm not at all sure she's right about this), it is a fantasy with remarkably realistic elements; and its greatest strength is not its "political" awareness but its consciousness of emotional complexity as creating not only richness but difficulty in experience. The people in this book get on one another's nerves more than those in other nineteenth-century novels. And the novel recognizes that people who get on one another's nerves may also be happy—not *perfectly* happy—lovers. No woman here *chooses* the freedom which is finally Lucy's lot: it is the freedom of Mme Beck, the forceful French schoolmistress, a freedom thrust upon some, but impoverished by the lack of love. Love, like other human conditions, is necessarily imperfect. It is still a goal to be sought.

Lucy, despite her sharp-sightedness, is not really a revolutionary heroine. Miss Millett sees her as gradually triumphing over the impediments of her sex: the nature of social expectation, the limitation of opportunity, the temptations of masochistic self-contempt. It is true that she grows in the course of the novel, and that she is a penetrating critic of the world she inhabits. But her triumph involves also the ability to live gracefully with the existent. Confronting a difficult interview with Paul, long before he is her declared lover, she begins to mend her pens. "I knew that action would give a turn to his mood. He never liked to see me mend pens; my knife was always dull-edged—my hand, too, was unskilful; I hacked and chipped. On this occasion I cut my own finger—half on purpose. I wanted to restore him to his natural state, to set him at his ease, to get him to chide." Masochism? Maybe. But also a sharp awareness of a man's nature and how it can be turned to her advantage. Paul, proposing that she be a sister to him, invites her to manipulate him. " 'My little sister must make her own experiments,' said he; 'I will give no promises. She must tease and try her wayward brother till she has drilled him into what she wishes. After all, he is no inductile material in some hands.' " From the feminist point of view, this sort of relation between the sexes is a sign of corruption; but there is no evidence that Lucy, or Charlotte Brontë, shares this point of view. The heroine takes lively pleasure in her skill at manipulation, and the combination of this pleasure with her vivid consciousness of exactly what it is she is doing is a source of interest in the novel.

A source of interest of which Kate Millett cannot be aware. Her anger at masculine injustice forces her to believe that other women, if they are worthy of her attention, must share it; and she finds in literature the simplifications she creates. The simplifications of anger generate the energy and the intensity of focus which are strengths of *Sexual Politics;* they give a forceful, if slightly illusory, clarity to summaries of Freudian psychology or reactionary sociology; they sometimes provide refreshing moments of wit, as when Miss Millett wonders how one measures awe in a fish. But since they are simplifications, they are necessarily reductive. Commitment to anger, instead of disguise or evasion of it, creates new difficulties. The perspective it provides is at once vivid and obfuscated. Its obfuscations emerge in the muddle of individual sentences and of large analyses, the muddle which derives from confusing emotion with ideology. The sexless, impersonal voice of political utterance, derives from anger transformed if not transcended. Miss Millett's effort to employ it prevents her from often finding a note of personal utterance. She avoids charm, grace, personal style, as though they were traps —which perhaps from her point of view they are. But since her anger is manifestly personal as well as political, taking the form, among others, of a distinct animus against men (one must agree with Mailer here), it often undermines her claim of large authority. Although her approach is different from her predecessor's, she too reveals the problems of women writing about women.

So what is a woman to do, setting out to write about women? She can imitate men in her writing, or strive for an impersonality beyond sex, but finally she must write as a woman: what other way is there? Examining the problems women reveal in imaginative writing, she will necessarily uncover her own. The students in my course concluded, at the end of the semester, that there were few generalizations, if any, to be made about the forms and techniques of women's writing, but many about "women's problems." Through all literary genres—criticism as well as poetry, fiction autobiography—women demonstrate their approaches to the solving of those problems. The same consciousness of difficulty presents itself over and over.

Two

POWER AND PASSIVITY

Annihilation of the woman, before the superiority of the man she loves, must be the greatest enjoyment of self-love that a superior woman can experience.

—MARIE BASHKIRTSEFF

The Victorian woman, it is now fashionable to assume, inhabited a dungeon of hypocrisy and repression illuminated only by fitful gleams from John Stuart Mill. Her lot was particularly poignant because of its disguises. John Ruskin's essay "Of Queen's Gardens" infuriates Kate Millett by pretending to accord women superior status while revealing his belief in their necessary subordination. There is little evidence, however, that it infuriated many of his female contemporaries. The most remarkable nineteenth-century woman writers who rebelled in print against the injustices of women's lot—Charlotte Brontë; George Eliot; in America, at the century's end, Kate Chopin—assume, like Ruskin, some essential difference between the masculine and the feminine nature. They complain about what women are prevented from *doing* in the world, not about what they are capable, even in existent social conditions, of *being* as developed moral individuals. Impatient as they may be with social injustice, they concern themselves with the primacy of personal moral effort. And they dramatize a point of view now highly unfashionable: that the limitations imposed on women, like the different limitations imposed on men, may provide opportunity rather than impediment in the struggle for moral and emotional fulfillment.

My students enjoyed *The Mill on the Floss;* they agreed that it was "one of the best books" they'd read, if not *the* best book, in the course. But their most profound response to Maggie Tulliver's dilemmas was impatience, expressed by their insistence tsat her proper line of action was really simple to discern. Their characteristic responses involved insistent rejection, or avoidance, of the moral issues George Eliot poses. They called Maggie masochistic, saw her as a victim who invokes morality to explain her meaningless suffering, said that she should just marry somebody, anybody, or do something, anything—reactions suggesting that the speakers found the problem as stated simply intolerable. The girl who believed that Maggie should have married Stephen in order to have "opportunities to travel and live nicely" would not in other contexts have recommended the desirability of marrying for money. Those who insisted that Maggie's moral problems were illusory were often the most eager to describe their own personal problems in moral terms. But to face George Eliot's statement of the female dilemma—this was unendurably painful.

The Mill on the Floss concerns itself with what it means, what it *can* mean, to be a girl, a woman. It establishes for women first a relatively simple set of polarities, between feeling and form. Maggie is committed to a life of feelings; the other women in the book—her mother, her aunts, and in a more complicated sense her cousin Lucy—have perverted their natural feelings by accepting the value of the external. George Eliot carefully specifies the definitions imposed upon women, their lives quite separate, in the microcosmic society of St. Ogg's, from the vital concerns of men. Mrs. Tulliver justifies herself by the excellence of her pork pies and her housecleaning; she confesses with pride her inability to see into men's business. "A woman can do no more nor she can," she concludes, only to be reminded by her sister, "But it's all o' no use, you know, Bessy, if your husband makes away with his money." Lacking masculine money, no feminine accomplishment has value. The Dodson sisters treasure only their possessions—even their ailments feel like possessions—and their children. Mrs. Pullet's husband preserves all her medicine bottles to offer as testimony of her suffering after her death; she worries that there will be nothing to show for the pills, which come in perishable paper boxes. Lucy Deane, the model child, will stay there indefinitely if you put her on a stool: just another ornament. Maggie's intractability about being treated as an object makes her unsatisfactory to her mother and her aunts, and cause for shocked wonder in Lucy, who exercises her mental capacities little more than the china doll she resembles.

The detailed characterization of the Dodson sisters sheds a rather lurid light on the generalizations about the nature of women which George Eliot provides throughout this novel. The feminine capacity for feeling, particularly for suffering, provokes frequent authorial comment. Men have acted, women suffered. Women fill "their long, empty days with memories and fears"; men, characterized by "purpose," lose "the sense of dread and even of wounds in the hurrying ardour of action." A girl may feel that "sorrow made larger room for her love to flow in," but "no true boy feels that; he would rather go and slay the Nemean lion or perform any round of heroic labours than endure perpetual appeals to his pity for evils over which he can make no conquest." Men "do"; women "submit." Such pronouncements provide a perspective by which to assess Maggie's passionate nature, but the trivialities of the Dodson sisters reveal that George Eliot's association of female suffering with Hecuba does not deny the possibility that such suffering may be mere self-indulgence. To "submit" may display a woman's dignity or her cravenness: the question is what—or who—she submits to, why and how she suffers and loves. Maggie's mother and aunts, who seem her opposites, in fact parody her most "feminine" characteristics to suggest the danger in facile acceptance of the kind of generalization George Eliot generously supplies.

It is a pathetic sight and a striking example of the complexity introduced into the emotions by a high state of civilization—the sight of a fashionably dressed female in grief. From the sorrow of a Hottentot to that of a woman in large buckram sleeves, with several bracelets on each arm, an architectural bonnet, and delicate ribbon-strings—what a long series of gradations! In the enlightened child of civilization the abandonment characteristic of grief is checked and varied in the subtlest manner. . . . If, with a crushed heart and eyes half-blinded by the mist of tears, she were to walk with a too devious step through a door-place, she might crush her buckram sleeves too . . .

Mrs. Pullet, the fashionably dressed female in question, weeping for the death of an acquaintance, declares the sensitivity of her nature by her tears and by her care for her sleeves. Considering her weeping as ornamental as her bracelets, she puts both on and off according to social occasion. George Eliot's conspicuous ironies control the reader's evaluation of the lady's grief, making it clear that the author does not believe the feminine capacity for suffering necessarily a virtue.

The feminine capacity for suffering can be perverted into the feminine *role* of suffering—a very different matter. The Dodson women feel genuine grief only over the loss of their goods. Mrs. Tulliver, a poignant figure, deprived of the household possessions which have supplied her sense of identity, endures real suffering. But her misery is also "what's expected of women," as one of my students pointed out. The novel's action continually draws attention to the ways in which limited social expectation creates limited personality. Mrs. Tulliver's sisters, unable to participate imaginatively in her grief, treat her with insensitive contempt when she loses her tablecloths and china. So accustomed are they to assessing people by their possessions that loss of possessions mean loss of human value, a loss as inexorable in the case of a sister as of a stranger. Although they will fulfill what they understand as their re-

sponsibilities toward her, they cannot afford to feel for or
with her: sympathy or empathy would deprive them of
the moral certitudes by which they live—the certitude that
to amass and preserve is good, to lose is wicked. Their
contempt for the sin of poverty includes contempt for the
sinner. The alternative would force them to face the possibility of loss inflicted rather than deserved, loss which
might descend even on them.

Nothing in them can tempt Maggie to imitation. Maggie lives in a world that provides no female models. In this
novel of education, the protagonist can progress only by
rejection.

Her cousin Lucy provides some temptations as a model,
if only because she consistently wins approval, and Maggie's own need for approval is strong. Lucy, pretty and
docile, concurs through genuine sweetness in being treated
as an object. But she concurs also, the action suggests,
through unconscious self-interest: thus she refuses the pain
of awareness. Maggie as a child thinks "that she could
never be cross with pretty little Lucy, any more than she
could be cruel to a little white mouse": the analogy suggests Lucy's human inadequacy and its advantages for
her. Because she is so patently devoid of self-originated
will or purpose, she cannot be held responsible for anything. When Maggie pushes her into the mud, she is mystified. "She could never have guessed what she had done
to make Maggie angry with her." The same moral
obtuseness persists into her later life: the charming child becomes a charming young woman. Stephen Guest can readily fancy himself in love with her because "she was a little
darling and exactly the sort of woman he had always most
admired." But "a little darling" resembles "a little white
mouse" in moral stature. Lucy, full of "benignity," "benev-
olence," "gentle affections and good-natured offices,"
emanates a goodness produced by instinct rather than
moral choice—a fact that does not diminish her virtue, but
allows her to remain profoundly irresponsible. Unable (in
a deeper sense, perhaps, unwilling) to see what is going

on around her, she is equally mystified by being pushed into the mud and by Maggie's later betrayal. Although one admires her generosity in making a secret visit in order to forgive her friend, one also assents at the conclusion of that visit when she says, "Maggie, you are better than I am." She can't explain this statement, and Maggie herself neither understands nor agrees with it. But the reader, led through the stages of Maggie's moral development, must recognize the justice of Lucy's comment, understanding Maggie's superiority, despite her errors, in her sense of responsibility for her actions. Lucy has chosen an earlier feminine way, closely related to that of her mother and aunts, although modified by her native goodness: passivity as a principle of being. Although it gets her what she wants in the long run—she ends up with Stephen—it embodies a willingness to be less than fully human which duplicates the lack of humanity involved in turning all reality into objects to be possessed.

The first stage of Maggie's education in womanhood involves her rejection—by virtue of character rather than of decision—of the role models available to her. The second, beginning with her father's stroke, which demands of her a new kind of adulthood, includes her search for models in literature. She has long yearned for a boy's kind of education, some significant knowledge to help her in life. Proud from early childhood of being smart, she is consistently rebuffed by adults who tell her that women are not valued for being bright. "An over-'cute woman's no better nor a long-tailed sheep—she'll fetch none the bigger price for that," her father observes to his wife. When Maggie visits her brother, who is being instructed by a second-rate clergyman, she feels immediately conscious that her capacities would enable her to make better use than he can of the instruction he's receiving. But Mr. Stelling soon rebukes her, with another generalization about girls. "They can pick up a little of everything, I dare say. They've a great deal of superficial cleverness, but they couldn't go far into anything. They're quick and shallow." This voice of authority does not, of course, solve Maggie's problem.

Her passionate yearning for knowledge that might help her leads her to various experimental reading, none of it satisfactory. The dream worlds of romantic poetry and fiction cannot help: "she wanted some key that would enable her to understand, and in understanding endure, the heavy weight that had fallen on her young heart. If she had been taught 'real learning and wisdom, such as great men knew,' she thought she should have held the secret of life." The voice of her creator intervenes in Maggie's crisis, to remind the reader that many share Maggie's plight, that school does not train the soul for struggle but provides "much futile information" instead of "that knowledge of the irreversible laws within and without her which, governing the habits, becomes morality."

George Eliot's own intense interest in education for women focused on the need for knowledge and training to counteract dangers inherent in the feminine nature. She writes to a bereaved friend:

We women are always in danger of living too exclusively in the affections; and though our affections are perhaps the best gifts we have, we ought also to have our share of the more independent life—some joy in things for their own sake. It is piteous to see the helplessness of some sweet women when their affections are disappointed!—because all their teaching has been, that they can only delight in study of any kind for the sake of a personal love. They have never contemplated an independent delight in ideas as an experience which they could confess without being laughed at. Yet surely women need this sort of defence against passionate affliction even more than men.

Maggie longs for exactly what George Eliot here prescribes, and for similar reasons: the unendurable pain of emotions unqualified by ideas, the doom of one unavoidably committed to the life of feeling.

Maggie's first attempt at systematic self-education, though, involves an effort to suppress emotion. Feeling the potent temptation of sainthood, she tries to imitate Thomas à Kempis in his imitation of Christ. This phase of self-denial comes to an end as she commits herself to Philip Wakem, an act agreeably combining some element of feminine magnanimity—he is a hunchback, she is motivated primarily by pity—with Maggie's sense that this man speaks to the best in her nature: not only the giving, but the thinking part of her. He encourages her aesthetic sensibilities, her desire for knowledge, her interest in music, encourages her to believe in the possibility of a wider life of the mind, thus exercising a seductive power over her, although Maggie cannot fully love him.

The problem of feeling, for such a woman as Maggie, intimately relates to that of vocation. What a woman can do in life may affect what she can be; and no more shocking statement appears in the entire novel than Mr. Wakem's "We don't ask what a woman does, we ask whom she belongs to." Believing for a time that women's problems would disappear given more meaningful opportunities for action, Maggie rages against a social order that denies women the possibility of significant *doing*. Tom can go out into the world, work, pay his father's creditors, win the approval of the family and of society at large; Maggie, at home, must endure triviality. With his usual reasonableness, Tom explains that he knows what is right for her because he lives in that real world from which she is cut off. To be a good woman, she must learn Lucy's passivity; to attempt meaningful action denies femininity.

Unlike Charlotte Brontë's heroines, Maggie does not long for a career. Her natural vocation is to love. To be allowed to love, to help, to have the object of her affections care for her: for such fulfillment she yearns. She understands loving as of comparable importance to the masculine commitment to action. "I begin to think," she says to Philip, "there can never come much happiness to me from loving; I have always had so much pain mingled with it. I

wish I could make myself a world outside it, as men do."
In this yearning to reject her natural vocation, she reveals
its function in her life. Happiness or no happiness, loving
is, for her, equivalent to Tom's desperate industry.

So she follows her own heart's deepest need in allowing
herself to accede to the commitment to Stephen which circumstances precipitate. Previously she has loved Tom, and
been rejected by him because she is "always in extremes,"
displaying "no judgment and self-command." She has fancied herself in love with Philip, misled by pity and sympathy and by his love and need for her. Her feeling for
Stephen seems—George Eliot is very discreet on this point
—to involve the first awakening of her sexuality, and to include a strong response to his "masculine" capacity of
leading. Paradoxically, the appeal of that passivity she has
earlier passionately rejected now leads to her brief indulgence in a life of love.

My students were on the whole deeply distressed by
Maggie's feeling for Stephen—no single aspect of the book
troubled them more. The young woman who thought
Maggie should marry in order to achieve a pleasanter life
was struggling for some rationalization of a situation she
and her contemporaries found really offensive. The relationship with Stephen dramatized that separation of the
emotional and the intellectual which tempted many of
them in their own lives; seeing it objectified, they considered it intolerable.

But one student confessed, "That's something really exciting, the idea of becoming really passive and letting
somebody else open doors for you and everything."

Exciting. The adjective emerged with real conviction.
These women often think of their minds as burdens inflicted upon them which they are obligated to use. A student
once told me of her relief, after a high-school career of
straight A's, at coming to Wellesley and making C's. No
longer forced to consider herself as very smart, she could
relax into intellectual irresponsibility. My students feared

53

that a bright girl is obligated to her brightness. Shocked that Maggie should love a man she couldn't have intellectual conversations with, they were yet more appalled by their own emotional response to the appeal of passivity which lures her.

This kind of reaction, however naïve and subjective, suggests a useful way to understand Maggie's central moral perplexity. Most women feel the pressure toward separation of faculties, a problem for many kinds of people at many levels of understanding. The modern college woman's dilemma about how much to let her brains show when she's with a man can assume more complex and tormenting forms. Maggie feels challenged to use her self and her life fully against the temptation to settle for the partial: for solitary reading and public domesticity, for the suppression of feeling in virtuous action, for only taking care of (Philip) or only being taken care of (by Stephen). Maggie yearns to discover some way to combine opposites whose opposition she finds intolerable. Most painful is the clash between "feeling" and "the ties that had given meaning to duty"—those ties which, a little earlier, Stephen has referred to as "unnatural bonds." "It seems right to me sometimes," Maggie says, refusing one of Stephen's appeals, "that we should follow our strongest feeling; but then such feelings continually come across the ties that all our former life has made for us—the ties that have made others dependent on us—and would cut them in two. . . . Love is natural, but surely pity and faithfulness and memory are natural too." Surely—and they too are bonds of feeling: of the "calmer affections" which deny "the joy of love."

The hardest struggle, then, involves two kinds of feeling: the love leading to self-sacrifice and that allowing self-indulgence. Maggie, of course, chooses the former, feeling that no true happiness can depend on self-indulgence, pointing out that one cannot in any case know where happiness lies; it is wiser to attempt virtue. She consciously resigns herself to an existence of suffering, a more fully aware version of her previously attempted life of self-abnegation. Breaking the tie with Stephen, unable to resume the connection with Philip, she loses also the vital connection with her brother, who declares himself unwilling to see her. After her passionate struggle against the limitations of a woman's lot, she embraces a life of more extreme emotional and social limitation than any she has previously imagined.

Female masochism? Blindness? The failure of education?

From George Eliot's point of view, certainly, the *success* of education. Maggie's powers of psychic and moral perception steadily increase: not blindness but clear seeing leads to her final choice, precipitated by a dream with the quality of a vision. In it she sees St. Ogg, who has been blessed, according to legend, for his direct responsiveness to "the heart's need." He rows his boat, with the Virgin as passenger, but the Virgin is the injured Lucy, and St. Ogg himself becomes first Philip, then Maggie's brother Tom. Reaching out to him, she capsizes the boat in which she and Stephen sit, and feels herself sinking: sinking, of course, in her own irresponsibility, persuaded by her guilt that even her insensitive brother is, because he accepts his responsibilities to others (failing, incidentally, even to express his inarticulate love for Lucy), more truly responsive than she to the needs of suffering hearts. Lucy appears as the type of female suffering, with the suggestion that spiritual power may inhere in such suffering. The dream provides images to solidify Maggie's sense that there can be no happiness in violation.

Reminded of this fact, she appears deliberately to choose the greatest possible unhappiness. Her final sacrifice, however, restores her to happiness by restoring her union with Tom: a resolution not merely sentimental. Maggie's acceptance of a life of penance does not resolve any of her difficulties. It avoids the evil she has recognized, it provides the possibility of solitary insight, but like her earlier devotion to Thomas à Kempis, it seems a way of suppression that cannot fully use her capacities. If George Eliot were concerned only with morality, this acceptance would complete her novel. But interested in psychic as well as moral demands, in the heart's need as well as its obligations, she allows Maggie her ambiguous fulfillment at last. In rescuing Tom, his sister unites "masculine" action with "feminine" feeling, her "strongest feeling" now identical with her firmest ties, her desire to help others merged with her acceptance of Tom's superior strength, the need for independent action coinciding with the desire for relationship. The final visual image of her describes "eyes of intense life looking out from a weary, beaten face." Intensity of life is Maggie's most important achievement. Seeing his sister as if for the first time, Tom has a revelation "of the depths in life that had lain beyond his vision which he had fancied so keen and clear." Maggie, who has penetrated to these depths and survived them, is "weary, beaten," but vividly alive; and, finally, fulfilled.

As my students attmpted to evade the terms George Eliot establishes in this novel, they recurred to the problem of Maggie's relation to social convention, and the deeper problem of the relation between morality and convention. They would have been comforted to conclude that Maggie's rejection of personal happiness was simply a weak yielding to the demands of her society; but of course the novel allows no such conclusion. Finally one participant summed up what all were willing to agree about.

"She was more bound to other people than she was bound to society."

The point is crucial in understanding the difference between the attitudes of nineteenth- and twentieth-century educated women toward the problems and limitations peculiar to their sex. If one thinks in terms of social oppression, it becomes clear that Maggie is at best a sell-out, or simply a failure. Perceiving some of the injustices of women's position, she nonetheless voluntarily relinquishes her claim to a life of independent personal happiness (independent only in a restricted sense: bound to a man) and willfully (masochistically? the question keeps occurring) chooses to persist in a situation of painful lack of freedom. But to think only in terms of social oppression is itself a dangerous limitation. For Maggie, the demands of society become less real than the needs of *other people*. Her mother and her aunts live by rigorous convention; the assumptions of their society compel and restrict them, making it seem a pathetically ludicrous fate to be a woman. Real intelligence, in the case of Mrs. Glegg, real capacity for feeling, in Mrs. Pullet and Mrs. Tulliver, distort themselves into grotesque parodies. Elaborately bewigged and costumed, surrounded by their teapots and their tablecloths, these women exemplify the horror of woman's condition if she accepts society as the ultimate reality.

Maggie does not. She accepts, instead, responsibility for her own soul; she demonstrates that loving is a vocation more demanding than mill-owning; she demonstrates that the feminine capacity for suffering need not be mere self-display or self-torment, but may provide a medium for moral insight. Laboring in her vocation, she transforms limitation into moral opportunity, transcending indignation at her lot not because indignation is unjustified, but because it is too narrow.

George Eliot's feminism recognizes the social injustice of woman's position only to declare its irrelevance to the more important matter of personal fulfillment: a bold stance. Like Ruskin, Eliot seems to believe that knowledge should provide a means for women (ideally for men as well) to feel, and with feeling to judge, more usefully. In *The Mill on the Floss* she powerfully advances the argument that the most satisfying self-fulfillment for a woman—not simply the most virtuous course: the most *satisfying*—may come through selflessness; and she makes this version of an ancient and self-comforting male argument seem a dignified rather than merely submissive position for a thoughtful woman. Maggie's death is an accident of the circumstances that create tragedy. It is not willed; and it overtakes her at the moment when, reunited with her brother, she has won through to the achievement of intense life. Such intensity—of feeling and of awareness—is, George Eliot suggests, a proper goal for individual effort. But the novel's dénouement also hints at the possibility that intense life cannot long endure, that Maggie Tulliver had to die because the reality of her continued life was unimaginable. Social pressure, after all, continues despite individual revelation, and the difficulties between Maggie and Tom will not vanish just because Maggie can row a boat. "Optimistic" only in a theoretical sense, *The Mill on the Floss* promises little to the aspirations of real women.

Daniel Deronda promises little more. George Eliot seems to have thought it a novel whose interest depended on its imaginative exploration of Jewish sensibility. Twentieth-century readers, on the other hand, often find the "Jewish" parts of *Daniel Deronda* manufactured, tedious and implausible, while the study of Gwendolen Harleth, in many significant respects Maggie's opposite, remains compelling. With more opportunities apparently open to her than Maggie could dream of, Gwendolen raises further questions about feminine vocation. It is, after all, perhaps too easy to give Maggie a "vocation" for loving. What of women who do not share this admirable feminine characteristic? What are the real possibilities for a woman's doing?

The answers to these questions, as realized in *Daniel Deronda*, lead back once more to the issue of dependency. To George Eliot as to other nineteenth-century woman writers, it seems, the female's compulsion to find some strong male on whom she can rely appears almost as a fact of nature. Some fictional women, like Maggie, welcome the compulsion; others, like the heroine of Kate Chopin's *The Awakening*, loathe it. But liking and loath-

ing apart, most heroines feel driven by it, more or less
aware of what drives them, more or less able to make
valuable use of it. Gwendolen Harleth, with the great social power of her beauty, yet finds herself drawn in curious ways to passivity, her capacity for "doing" finally
oddly irrelevant to the real issues of her being.

At first encounter, Gwendolen seems one of those
women who justify their existence—for others as well as for
themselves—simply by their beauty: one of the charmers
who recur frequently in nineteenth-century novels by
women, suggesting a persistent feminine fantasy of effortless achievement. The nature of the species is perhaps best
defined by Mrs. Gaskell, in *Wives and Daughters*,
describing the heroine's stepsister Cynthia, who "exerted
herself just as much to charm the two Miss Brownings as
she would have done to delight Osborne Hamley, or any
other young heir. That is to say, she used no exertion, but
simply followed her own nature, which was to attract everyone of those she was thrown amongst." "It was part of
the charm of her soft allurement that she was so passive."

Lucy Deane, in *The Mill on the Floss*, bears some relation to this figure; and Mrs. Ratignolle in *The Awakening*
and Georgiana Reed in *Jane Eyre* may seem to parody
her. Sometimes such charmers turn out rather well, making prosperous marriages which satify their needs. But the
emotional trap lying in wait for them all is narcissism.
Even Lucy, whose role as charmer is modified by her real
concern for others. has an inclination toward "personal
vanity" which makes her look at herself in the mirror as
soon as Stephen, in his role as her lover, leaves her; Gwendolen's association with mirrors is persistent and powerful.
At a European gambling resort with friends, at the beginning of the novel, she receives a letter from her mother
announcing the family's financial ruin. Gwendolen herself
has just lost all her own money at roulette. She spends
most of the night packing for her return to England; at
dawn she studies herself in the mirror:

She had a naïve *delight in her fortunate self, which any but the harshest saintliness will have some indulgence for in a girl who had every day seen a pleasant reflection of that self in her friends' flattery as well as in the looking-glass. And even in this beginning of troubles, while for lack of anything else to do she sat gazing at her image in the growing light her face gathered a complacency gradual as the cheerfulness of the morning. Her beautiful lips curled into a more and more decided smile, till at last she took off her hat, leaned forward and kissed the cold glass which had looked so warm.*

Gwendolen's delight in herself, sustained by the consistent approval of others, contrasts with Maggie's fits of self-hatred, anger, defiance, precipitated by external disapproval. Lacking proper ladylike appearance, Maggie must contemplate and question those standards of feminine propriety to which she can never hope to conform. Gwendolen's flawless appearance, on the other hand, seems, to herself and to others, to solve all problems. Like Belinda in *The Rape of the Lock*, Gwendolen perceives and values beauty as power. But her lack of self-questioning in such matters creates personal difficulties as grave as those generated by the total dominion of self-doubt. The woman who enchants others will enchant herself: the resultant state has only ambiguous advantages.

The Sleeping Beauty seen from a searching feminine point of view, her enchantment self-imposed, but sustained by all the social forces of her world, Gwendolen is both victim and agent in her own drama. No prince's kiss will break her moral sleep; the dream of a prince is part of it. Gwendolen must rescue herself, and, like a fairy-tale prince, must perform a series of moral tasks to prepare for the rescue. George Eliot creates a distinctly antiromantic version of the romantic legend.

The mixture of dependence with self-reliance is crucial in Gwendolen's achieved character. Her progression toward self-knowledge involves learning not to rely on mirrors. From the complacency of her first encounter with the looking glass she goes through a series of similar episodes in which mirrors bolster her self-esteem, confirming her sense that no more than beauty can be required of her. "That is a becoming glass, Gwendolen," her infatuated mother tells her, seeing the mirror as in existence for the sake of her daughter's beauty. The remark, which Gwendolen takes as her due, causes her to reflect that she would make an admirable Saint Cecilia but that her features are not suited for tragedy. Evading her rich suitor, she briefly confronts her family's poverty, bewildered that her beauty suddenly has "no magic" to make all right. She has come to believe in her own divinity, George Eliot observes; now she is like Belinda deprived of worshippers, able to "confront" reality only by making mental pictures of how poverty might affect her appearance. Although such pictures cause her first movement of sympathy toward her mother, whose looks have been affected by hardship, they also underlie her acceptance of Grandcourt as a husband despite her knowledge that such acceptance will wrong others.

What she does not realize is how much it will wrong herself. Arriving at her new mansion on her wedding night, feverishly excited, she anticipates life as "the heroine of an admired play without the pains of art." Her existence for the past three months has been only "a show, in which her consciousness was a wondering spectator." Now she flings herself into a chair and sees "herself repeated in glass panels with all her faint-green satin surroundings." For the moment she can see her surroundings simply as adjuncts to her beauty; soon she will discover that they symbolize her oppression. The "admired play," the "show" she has only watched, turns tragedy: no use to protest that the role is not becoming. Aware of her own misery, reflecting that the admiration of men will not after all sustain her, she thinks of turning to Daniel Deronda for moral support. In another encounter with the mirror, she looks at herself, for the first time, "not in admiration, but

61

in a sad kind of companionship," beginning to recognize herself as a human being.

Her marriage demands external modes of self-representation; she plays a part under the "exacting eyes of a husband" (replacing her mirror) who values only appearances. Her hatred and fear of him help shape her growing disgust for her superficial life. As her distress increases, she walks "about the large drawing-room like an imprisoned dumb creature, not recognizing herself in the glass panels, not noting any object around her in the painted gilded prison." "Hardened" by living under eyes that see her always in terms of her lowest motives, she becomes less recognizable and less satisfactory to herself, hers self-preoccupation yielding to vague and sinister fantasies which move "within her like ghosts . . . : dark rays doing their work invisibly in the broad light." Grandcourt, pleased to make his wife lead her life as a "representation" of luxury, looks at her as though she were part of the yacht, thinks of her as an expensive appurtenance. Reduced to the status of object, like Lucy Deane in *The Mill on the Floss*, Gwendolen no more than Maggie can rest content in passivity. She blames her husband for her state; he condemns her to vision as through "a piece of yellow and wavy glass that distorts form and makes color an affliction. . . . Gwendolen had that kind of window before her, affecting the distant equally with the near."

To progress from contemplation of mirrors to vision through windows, however yellow and wavy, marks an advance in human possibility. Gwendolen sees horrible "phantasms" of guilt derived from her longing to do away with her intolerable husband, visions more real to her than anything in the external world. Her awareness of Daniel's reality, however, protects her from the consequences of her anger. Her vision of him depends on fantasy—no one could be as good and wise as she believes him to be—but it grows through moments of genuine contact, and it represents (among other things) a willingness to seek a center outside herself: a first movement toward dependency. The belief that she can remain emotionally independent, sustained by self-worship, has brought her only misery.

George Eliot's view of human nature, often too complex to lend itself to easy categories, and her attitudes toward the special problems of women, betray extraordinary ambiguities of feeling. Gwendolen's initial situation is itself surprisingly complicated. A society corrupt in its values has encouraged her to turn herself into an object, but, not a passive figure, she must finally be her own rescuer, as earlier she had been her own exploiter. The novel shows her first at the gambling tables, where she has won extensively but, under Daniel Deronda's eye, now begins to lose. "Was she beautiful or not beautiful? . . . Why was the wish to look again felt as coercion and not as a longing in which the whole being consents?" The second question judges by implication Gwendolen's gaming, which symbolizes her orientation to life. Deeply a capitalist, imbued with a commodity view of value, Gwendolen gambles in the same spirit with money or with herself, her own highest stake. In a capitalist society, money is power. Gwendolen, vividly aware of this equation, obsessively strives, constantly gambles, to gain and increase her power.

She understands only power relationships, tyrannizing over her mother and sisters by virtue of her beauty, which they recognize as giving her the right to her own way. Her pragmatic uncle immediately acquiesces in her demand for more advantages than his own daughter, never allowing himself quite to realize how fully he participates in the commodity view of marriage. She has no interest in relationships with other women, because "women did not give her homage"; and her understanding of possible relationships with men is limited to the receiving of homage.

In the nature of its examination of marriage, *Daniel Deronda* is perhaps unique among nineteenth-century novels. *Middlemarch,* of course, takes up the problem of the young woman badly married, and connects it with that of female vocation. But it rests (uncomfortably enough) in the assumption that the nineteenth-century woman can probably find no vocation outside marriage. *Daniel Deronda* timidly explores fresh possibilities. The very exploration seems vaguely guilty: a guilt reflected in the fact that the only alternative occupation Eliot allows herself to imagine is theatrical performance. If the woman will not accept passivity in relation to a man, she dooms herself to indulged narcissism. Yet the fact that one woman in the novel deliberately chooses career before motherhood, however the choice is criticized, suggests the unusual seriousness with which *Daniel Deronda* challenges marriage as a universal institution.

Sometimes—often—Gwendolen thinks of marriage as an arena of power. Other women may yield their freedom when they marry; she proposes to enlarge her own. Her interest in Grandcourt derives from her conviction that she can control him; his apparent lack of passionate self-motivation suggests that she might provide motives for him. Ironically, of course, Grandcourt's interest in Gwendolen is also an interest in power: over a creature with a spirit worth the breaking.

Gwendolen, unaware of this crucial fact, cannot altogether avoid knowing that other women's marital experience differs from that she envisions for herself. To imagine marriage as a state of freedom, she must imagine herself as unique. Although she says to her mother, "I see now why girls are glad to be married—to escape being expected to please everybody but themselves," she expresses the opposite opinion to her cousin and would-be lover Rex: "Girls' lives are so stupid: they never do what they like. . . . I never saw a married woman who had her own way." In the same sequence of dialogue, she announces her intention to be married but not to "do as other women do." Despite repeated declarations of this sort, to herself and to others, her deeper perception tells her that marriage is always "bondage."

This description of the married state occurs to her only at the point where she seriously considers the possibility of some alternative vocation. "The inmost fold of her questioning now was whether she need take a husband at all—whether she could not achieve substantially for herself and know gratified ambition without bondage." She fantasizes becoming an actress—she is so much an actress already!—or a stage singer, finding her singing so much admired in drawing rooms. Understanding such activity only as another form of display, wishing to gratify ambition rather than to *do,* conceiving physical attractiveness an adequate substitute for hard work, she can hardly succeed in a stage career. Herr Klesmer, a musician devoted to his art, tells her so unambiguously. She yields at once to his judgment, humiliated by it but lacking any basis to challenge it. Gwendolen has never had to work, never been taught to work, never been allowed to work. Her extreme narcissism could make her a repellent figure in her relentless self-obsession and the moral and psychological obtuseness it implies, but George Eliot perceives her, thus far, as a victim of her own beauty, of the limitations of her education, and of her society. Yet, like Maggie, she must be responsible for her own fate.

Mirah, whom Daniel loves, and the mother whom he discovers only in his manhood have alike experienced the reality of that stage career which is Gwendolen's fantasy; both characters suggest further questions about female vocation. Mirah, with her tiny feet, her doll-like air, her relentless sweetness, is the novel's least satisfactory fictional creation, a puppet to make the author's points. She enables Daniel to demonstrate his perfect chivalry toward damsels in distress, exemplifies proper attitudes of filial piety, fulfills all requirements of the "good woman," even supplies what passes in George Eliot for sexual titillation, with her tale of a narrow escape from a would-be ravisher. She sings beautifully—beautifully enough to win the approval of the rigorous Klesmer—but lacks a voice strong enough for a successful stage career. In her early years she has sung and acted, at her father's command, always hating the falsities and displays of the theatrical world. Yet she has a genuine concern with excellence, she wishes to be independent in the sense at least of earning her own bread, and she possesses a sharp sense of her limitations ("She liked the look of Klesmer, feeling sure that he would scold her, like a great musician and a kind man")—contrasting, in all these respects, with Gwendolen.

Various people at various times perceive Mirah as an "angel," and indeed she often seems too good to be true. But as a model she raises some disturbing questions. Should the ideal woman be as passive as is compatible with the immediate demands of her life, accepting rescue or occupation as it comes, but depending on the notion that others will form her destiny? Must she be incapable of criticism? Should she have only limited talent—not so much that it creates its own demands? What is to be done with the obvious reflection that Gwendolen, although morally reprehensible in comparison with Mirah, affects us as much the more interesting human being? Which raises the fundamental question in its bluntest form: Must the ideal woman be uninteresting?

Daniel's mother appears late and briefly to state a woman's need to follow the demands of her career even at the cost of family ties. She has abandoned her infant for her art—making sure he would be carefully reared, but rejecting all further contact with him. Some eloquent speeches explain her course. "I wanted to live out the life that was in me, and not to be hampered with other lives." "I did not want to marry. . . . I had a right to be free. I had a right to seek my freedom from a bondage that I hated." "Every woman is supposed to have the same set of motives, or else to be a monster. I am not a monster, but I have not felt exactly what other women feel—or say they feel, for fear of being thought unlike others. When you reproach me in your heart for sending you away from me, you mean that I ought to say I felt about you as other women say they feel about their children. I did *not* feel that. I was glad to be freed from you." "You are not a woman. You may try—but you can never imagine what it is to have a man's force of genius in you, and yet to suffer the slavery of being a girl." These are extraordinary utterances in a Victorian novel. Their passionate authenticity challenges the complacencies of automatic assumptions about woman's role and nature. True, George Eliot indicates the disagreeable aspects of this mother, hard and unresponsive to her son's emotional needs. She suffers from the mysterious wasting disease that punishes the sins of so many nineteenth-century fictional women-gone-wrong: a signal of the moral evaluation to be made of her. It is impossible to like her.

But, in a different way, it is also impossible really to like Mirah: that long drink of sugar and water.

And impossible to believe that George Eliot liked her.

The apparent ambivalence of feeling that made the novelist depict the perfect woman as a pallid automaton and give the best lines to the "bad" woman expresses itself also in the book's resolution, inasmuch as that concerns Gwendolen. If Mirah raises questions in the reader's mind, particularly in conjunction with Daniel's mother, the novel's way of disposing of Gwendolen also provokes some doubts. In fact, Gwendolen is not disposed of, nor can she be. Like Maggie, she poses a final dilemma for her creator. Her education has proceeded by a steady sequence of events; she has learned through suffering the inadequacy of self-absorption, learned that a woman's confidence in her ability to control others for her own purposes is unlikely to be justified, that appearances are not to be trusted, that one does not harm others with impunity—all negative lessons. Learning what she must not do and be, she has learned almost nothing of what she *can* do and be. Daniel has instructed her in the necessities of self-control and of awareness of consequences. He suggests that she should read some good books; she makes a stab in this direction, but cannot absorb herself in the literature she has never been trained to read. Her husband conveniently drowns, freeing her from obvious restriction. But freeing her for what? Only capable of imagining dependence on another man, she turns to Daniel with full trust that he will continue as her guide. When he announces his approaching marriage, she cries, "I said I should be forsaken. I have been a cruel woman. And I am forsaken." Then she rises to nobility, assuring him, "I will try—try to live. I shall think of you." On his wedding day she sends him a comforting letter, declaring her intention to try to fulfill his prophecy that she may live to be "one of the best of women, who make others glad that they were born." "If it ever comes true," she adds, "it will be because you helped me."

To be forsaken remains the most desperate of fates; to be saved depends on another. Gwendolen envisions a future life of vague but noble self-sacrifice; nothing has taught her how to achieve it. Daniel dedicates himself to a splendid cause; Gwendolen has no opportunity to find one. Daniel grows through being depended upon: "Those who trust us educate us." Gwendolen's "growth" means acceptance of narrowing, the consequence of her dependency. She has no demonstrated capacity for love or for action. What is she to do? She has achieved some enlargement of vision. From seeing only herself in the power of her beauty, she has progressed to awareness of large contexts: now she knows how little she can expect. She may hope for virtue, having relinquished the dream of happiness. Mirah, expecting little out of life, gets both virtue and happiness. Daniel's mother, demanding much, achieves only temporary satisfaction, left with the taste of dust and ashes. Gwendolen, wanting a great deal, ends with almost nothing. Is it better for women not to want? Wrong for a woman to try to achieve happiness, since, as Maggie Tulliver says, virtue is within our power but happiness not? Must a woman's happiness depend entirely on the luck of being chosen by the right man? Is Gwendolen with her enlarged vision better off than Gwendolen obsessed with her mirrors? The Victorian pieties that answer such questions may be obvious enough; but *Daniel Deronda*, by its structure and its characterizations, makes those pieties inadequate. Demonstrating the power of a woman's need for dependency (even when the woman believes her need is for dominion) and the satisfactions dependency can bring, demonstrating even that dependency can be a means of moral instruction, it reveals also the inadequacy of reliance on others as the only center to a woman's life.

We didn't read *Daniel Deronda* in my course: too long. But the question about the relation of virtue and happiness, a question raised somewhat less disturbingly by *The Mill on the Floss*, recurred all semester. Virtue now comes in two varieties: intellectual and moral. And my students were full of doubts about the value of both. The old question about whether one would prefer the fate of happy pig or unhappy Socrates has special poignancy for young women, who see that, even given Socrates' wisdom, they are unlikely to find much chance to use it. To study the situation of women as recorded in literature is to open one's eyes to painful truths; and to what advantage after all, my students kept asking, this seeing? Intellectual virtue consists in a commitment to clarity and enlargement of vision. But Gwendolen Harleth exemplifies one possible consequence of enlarged vision: she sees more clearly the meaninglessness of her life, able only by a blurring of vision to make the future rosy. Women rarely feel it possible to control their destinies; they are often correct. Gwendolen ends by accepting a straitened life; girls fearing they must do the same wonder about the advantage of knowing life's narrowness.

As for moral virtue—the value of that, in terms of traditional expectations about women, is no longer clear either. One of my students told a story about crossing the street in Harvard Square, suddenly finding herself accompanied by a large young man with several tattoos.

"Let's you and me make music together, baby," he remarked.

And she found herself replying, "No, thank you."

She was comically embarrassed by that, and the point of her embarrassment—instantaneously understood by all her contemporaries—was that the standards of propriety she had been taught, the notion of politeness considered proper for women—these were now handicaps rather than assets in her life. Feminine virtue, as *Daniel Deronda* makes painfully clear, is largely a matter of feminine repression.

But on the individual level what alternative can be found?

At the end of the course many students wrote comments about their experience in it. One remarked, "Also, Mrs. Spacks, I would have enjoyed hearing your opinion more often; you seem to lead a very enjoyable, worthwhile life and are not hindered by being a woman."

The result of this student's experience of literature by women had been to convince her that the state of womanhood is a handicap which may occasionally be overcome.

Daniel Deronda does not assume that the connection between feeling and morality in women is quite so natural as Ruskin believed. Daniel declares the need for women to be better than men in order to provide inspiration; but when Gwendolen replies that women need for men to be better, for the same reason, her companion admits the point. Mirah finds a "natural" connection between emotion and virtue, her feelings leading her where she should go. Daniel, always seeking and responding to human ties, uses his relationship to help clarify his ideological and moral commitments. But for Gwendolen (and for Daniel's mother) the connection is not so automatic. George Eliot, taking feelings seriously, recognizing their personal validity even when they lead toward wrong action, sympathizes with Gwendolen's passionate feelings even while condemning her wrong actions. The girl must be *taught* to feel properly: to feel for others, not only for herself—thus discovering that her emotions may lead her toward good rather than bad courses. But this teaching is partly teaching in repression (she must suppress "bad" feelings, encourage "good" ones); and the novel does not evade the point.

The remarkable quality of Eliot's respect for feeling becomes more apparent when one compares her novels with those belonging to more simple moralistic traditions. A particularly vivid example—understandably not much read today—is Maria Edgeworth's *Belinda*, first published in 1801. It too belongs to the tradition of feminine novels of education, conducting a girl safely through the evils of society to a proper marriage. One of its characters, Lady Delacour, a fashionable married woman who turns out to have made a loveless marriage, appears to have breast cancer, apparently as punishment for her responsibility in the death of a young man in a duel. It turns out, though, that she is only suffering the aftereffects of a wound acquired when she dressed in man's clothes to fight a duel herself. Her friend Mrs. Freke (splendid name!), more wild than she, is punished by moral exposure and serious injury for her indulgence in male apparel. Lady Delacour, however, suffers only until she is reconciled with her husband, having achieved some education herself.

However comic in summary, the novel is nothing of the sort in its insistence that a woman must be either womanly or not-womanly; and if not womanly, must be punished. One may sympathize with the sufferings—the quite appalling sufferings—of the sinners, but never with their motives and feelings, assumed to be bad, to lead them to bad actions: no ambiguity.

Ambiguity is the stuff of George Eliot's fiction, despite her extraordinary moral clarity. No question about what sort of action is right or wrong, and no problem about judging action. But long before Freud she understood that feelings have no morality. Her capacity to separate feeling from action, to understand that feelings cannot and must not be judged, that genuine emotion must be respected, produces the complexity in her characters, enabling her to share the conventional Victorian views of a woman's proper role, without affecting her sympathetic understanding of women uncomfortable in such a role.

"I think more and more correctly than milkmaids in general do; consequently, where they would often, for want of reflection, act weakly, I, by dint of reflection, should act judiciously."
"Oh, no! you would be influenced by your feelings. You would be guided by impulse."
"Of course, I should often be influenced by my feelings: they were given me to that end. . . . I hope . . . all my impulses will be strong in compelling me to love [my husband and children]."

This rather stilted bit of dialogue from *Shirley*, between the sub-heroine Caroline and the domineering Mrs. Yorke, suggests Charlotte Brontë's credo. The admirable woman, in her novels, will think correctly and claim to be guided by reflection; but she believes in the primacy of feeling and the value of impulse, believes, finally, emotional capacity an index of worth. St. John Rivers hesitates to tell Jane Eyre that he believes her "impassioned"; expecting her to be displeased by the word, he glosses it, apologetically, as meaning "that human affections and sympathies have a most powerful hold on you." But Jane, passionate in every sense of the word, like Rochester, finds in Rochester for this reason above all her natural mate, and St. John's lack of passion, his ability to imagine a wife as nothing more than a comrade in a good cause over whom he can exercise legal control, makes him repellent, even frightening, to Jane.

The value of emotion, in Charlotte Brontë's scheme, is not that it leads to proper action. On the contrary, strong feelings in women and men alike often produce wrong conduct. Rochester, motivated by passion, tries to deceive

Jane into becoming his mistress; Jane's intense feelings produce her childish fits of violence; Robert Moore, in *Shirley,* following his feelings, ignores the emotional needs of his workmen; Caroline must be restrained from rushing to Robert at a moment when she could only seem an intruder. On the other hand: Jane's emotions keep her from accepting St. John's cold-blooded proposal; we applaud. Shirley's feelings lead her to the right man and enable her to defy social disapproval in marrying him. And *lack* of feeling invariably produces wrong: St. John's blind self-sacrifice (noble in a limited but not an ultimate sense), the cold self-seeking of the Reed sisters in *Jane Eyre;* Helstone's emotional destruction of his wife, in *Shirley;* Robert Moore's proposal to Shirley, based on need for money rather than on love.

The moral scheme implied by such episodes seems considerably more complicated than Ruskin's, with perhaps richer possibilities for feminine self-expression. Yet, despite the fact that Kate Millett claims Charlotte Brontë as an ally, the result of these novelistic investigations of feminine feeling is to enforce a view strikingly similar after all in its implications to the conventional masculine Victorian view of woman's place. In these books, too, women discover their dependency; although they also discover that dependency need not imply total relinquishment of power.

More than any other book we read together—and much to my surprise—*Shirley* provoked my students to display their own beliefs about the nature of women and of men and about the social assumptions that govern them.

"It's more that she's dying of total boredom than that she's dying of a broken heart. God, think of having both those things!"

"Don't men sometimes think it's kind of cute for women to manipulate them?"

"Shirley is sort of manlike, because she *can* speak what she's thinking."

"When she deals with men, she always takes the

73

pseudo-role of inferior. She *knows* she's maneuvering them. . . . She sees that a man has to think he's dominant in a relationship, she doesn't have to stop to think about it."

Most of these remarks suggest that the speakers see the question of power as the fundamental issue between men and women. They resent masculine power and the necessity for women to disguise their own attempts to counteract it, and they envy the situation of the woman who is able to "maneuver" men without thinking about it, without having to realize what she's doing.

Unlike Gwendolen Harleth, the women in Charlotte Brontë novels do not recognize their desire for control: my students envied this innocence. Jane Eyre wishes only to live as full a life as she can manage. Lacking in obvious sexual power, but rich in intelligence, moral clarity, force of will and determination, she has mental powers to compensate for her physical and social limitations, the energy of fantasy overcoming the restrictions of her actual experience. Caroline, in *Shirley*, accepts her emotionally impoverished existence as necessity and struggles, with a spirit Ruskin would approve, only to be "good." True, as my student pointed out, when she falls into the decline characteristic of suffering Victorian ladies she seems to express boredom as much as heartbreak—but she herself remains unaware of this fact. And Shirley, who, with a masculine name, fantasizes that she is a man, referring to herself as "Captain Keeldar"; Shirley, whose wealth and beauty subordinate most males; who claims that she cannot bear the prospect of marriage because "I could never be my own mistress more. A terrible thought!—it suffocates me!"—Shirley announces at last, "I will accept no hand which cannot hold me in check," and marries the man able to control her.

Yet all these women yearn for and finally achieve power over others and a way of life that allows them to exercise it. Caroline, apparently almost flawlessly passive, makes

74

the point most complexly. (*Shirley* is an interminable, often boring novel, artificial in structure, stilted in manner; but as a treatment of the feminine situation, truly compelling.) What her uncle orders her to do, she does, without complaint. She accepts Robert's arbitrary changes of manner as though they embodied laws of nature. She submits to Hortense's educational tyranny; she submits to everyone. But she asks some questions, largely interior, and her questions center invariably on how—even whether—people should help one another.

Early in the novel, she feels and expresses her frustration at having no meaningful occupation. She would like to be apprenticed to Robert Moore, she tells him.

"I would do the counting-house work, keep the books, and write the letters, while you went to market. I know you greatly desire to be rich, in order to pay your father's debts; perhaps I could help you to get rich."

"Help me? You should think of yourself."

"I do think of myself; but must one for ever think only of oneself?"

Her desire to help Robert derives from her love for him; when she contemplates the possibility of helping others in a different context, she expresses very different feelings. Perhaps, she thinks, she must be an old maid, since Robert doesn't care for her; she will "never have a husband to love, nor little children to take care of." What, then, is she to do with her life? This problem must plague all old maids:

Other people solve it for them by saying, "Your place is to do good to others, to be helpful whenever help is wanted." That is right in some measure, and a very convenient doctrine for the people who hold it; but I perceive that certain sets of human beings are very apt to maintain that other sets should give up their lives to them and their service, and then they requite them by praise: they call them devoted and virtuous. Is this enough? Is it to live? Is there not a terrible hollowness, mockery, want, craving, in that existence which is given away to others, for want of something of your own [my italics] to bestow it on? I suspect there is. Does virtue lie in abnegation of self? I do not believe it.

Given "something of your own," you are benign, even sacrificial for it. But "something" of your own" as a formula to designate husband and children has an ominous ring of possessiveness; and a good deal in Caroline's character supports these disturbing implications. Her lack of occupation to some extent only apparent, she knows she's supposed to educate Robert, an industrialist, who runs his mill without regard for the human implications of his activity. Caroline, with no comprehension of what goes on in the countinghouse, much less the business world at large (she differs in this respect from Shirley, who has considerable grasp of financial affairs), feels confident of her capacity to understand the human issues involved in mill ownership. She never neglects an opportunity to tell Robert what he should do. He should not come home after dark, he should take a different route, be kinder to his workmen, allow the men to see more of his true character. By the novel's end, her role emblemizes the Victorian woman's elevating function.

"*If you get rich, you will do good with your money, Robert?*"
"*I will do good; you shall tell me how.*"

"*I can double the value of their mill-property: I can line yonder barren Hollow with lines of cottages, and rows of cottage-gardens—*"
"*Robert? And root up the copse?*"
"*The copse shall be firewood ere five years elapse: . . . and my mill, Caroline—my mill shall fill its present yard.*"

"Horrible! You will change our blue hill-country air into the Stilbro' smoke atmosphere."

"Such a Sunday-school as you will have, Cary! such collections as you will get!"

Taken out of context, such passages seem almost parodic in intention; but nothing in the novel indicates that the author takes any but a serious view of Caroline's concern with nature and morality. The woman, given "something of her own," can occupy herself with trying to shape it according to her desire. Robert may not allow her concern for pure air to interfere with his desire to expand his factory; he feels her proper sphere to be the Sunday school. But the effort to exercise her influence is her most significant outlet, the avenue of expression she wants and finds most natural.

Robert runs the mill; but women run the world.

Men have all the public power, in the novel as in nineteenth-century England. They constantly make decisions about how they will act; women can only make decisions about how they will accept. The effort to accept often generates suffering; Caroline suffers spectacularly and at length. But the antithesis between action and suffering does not define the lines of power. Mrs. Yorke is a satiric target in *Shirley* because of the rigidity with which she manages her household and tries to manage the world at large, mocked for her lack of subtlety. Caroline's kind of "managing," far less apparent, consists mainly in "helping" people. There is no indication that Charlotte Bronte disapproves, despite her outbursts about the limitation of social possibility for women. She depicts a world in which women constantly and cleverly manipulate men. Men command women, but they cannot in a deeper sense control them. The "declines" in which Victorian heroines display their disappointments in love by dying, if necessary, reveal the lengths to which women will go to escape domination. Men can refuse to love them, but cannot force them to live. Granted the ultimate, universal freedom to die, this particular mode of dying seems peculiarly and significantly feminine, a dramatization of passivity which declares the woman's perfect virtue and perfect acceptance in the very act of defiance. Caroline need not go so far. Her dependency finds fulfillment in marriage to the man she wants; in her dependency, she can help him, educate him, improve him . . . control him.

Jane Eyre reveals a more fiery spirit, but the course of her love bears some similarities to Caroline's. By no means naturally passive, she is forced into at least an imitation of passivity by the limitations of her social roles: dependent orphan, dependent schoolgirl, dependent governess. The end of her passivity is marked by her helping Rochester, in her first sight of him, after he has sprained his ankle. She finds herself exhilarated by the episode: "My help had been needed and claimed; I had given it: I was pleased to have done something; trivial, transitory though the deed was, it was yet an active thing, and I was weary of an existence all passive." Her relationship with Rochester develops through her perfect willingness to do whatever he asks of her. She has two more conspicuous opportunities to "help" him: she saves him from being burned to death in his bed, and she aids him with his wounded visitor, Mason. She feels herself dependent on his goodwill, dependent on his existence for her own happiness. But Rochester sees matters rather differently: "Jane: you please me, and you master me—you seem to submit, and I like the sense of pliancy you impart, and while I am twining the soft, silken skein around my finger, it sends a thrill up my arm to my heart. I am influenced—conquered; and the influence is sweeter than I can express; and the conquest I undergo has a witchery beyond any triumph I can win." In displaying her weakness and passivity, Jane manifests her strength. Once betrothed to her employer, she delights in manipulating him, teasing him to the point of anger because she thus maintains his interest and suits his taste. "I can keep you in reasonable check now," she reflects, "and I don't doubt to be able to do it hereafter: if one expedient loses its virtue, another must be devised." Such reflections do not in the least interfere with her sense of her own deep submissiveness and dependency.

She checks his will most decisively by her flight from him after discovering the impossibility of their marriage. Her retreat into conventional morality at this point does not altogether surprise us, since matters have not been going well between her and Rochester even before the morning of the wedding. In fact, their betrothal has seriously disturbed the balance of power. Although she teases him with increasing desperation, keeping him "cross and crusty" because she believes that "a lamb-like submission" would not truly please him, she suffers increasingly from "a sense of annoyance and degradation." Rochester treats her like an object, a poppet, a member of a seraglio; he dresses her like a doll, heaps her with jewels, anticipates attaching her to him with a chain and wearing her in his bosom. She can hardly "endure" the sense of being "kept" by him; as a direct result, she initiates the inquiry about her Madeira uncle which eventuates in the marriage's frustration. When an external force prevents her becoming Rochester's bride, it interrupts a relationship that seems already seriously marred.

The "external force" is the mad wife lurking in the attic, a melodramatic figure epitomizing one of the novel's central concerns. Jane Eyre's problem, like Maggie Tulliver's, centers on what to do with her feelings—not all benign. The novel begins with an image of her childhood rage at a male oppressor: she physically attacks her pseudo-sibling John Reed when he persecutes her. Suffering a dreadful punishment for her violence, she relearns the lesson that emotions—particularly hostile emotions—must be repressed. Her experience at Lowood School elaborates the same lesson (a version of Tom's lesson to Maggie), providing models of Christian piety and self-control. Jane practices these virtues, but only superficially. She leaves Lowood explicitly to seek fuller emotional life: "I remembered that the real world was wide, and that a varied field of hopes and fears, of sensations and excitements, awaited those who had courage to go forth into its expanse, to seek real knowledge of life amidst its perils." At Thornfield Manor, both before and after Rochester's arrival, her emotional gratification derives not from "real knowledge of life" but from indulged fantasy. She wanders around the third floor daydreaming, allowing her "mind's eye to dwell on whatever bright visions rose before it," contemplating the plight of her sex: "Women are supposed to be very calm generally: but women feel just as men feel; they need exercise for their faculties and a field for their efforts as much as their brothers do." In the distance she hears the goblin laugh and "eccentric murmurs" of the maniac she thinks is Grace Poole, the woman who objectifies the dangers of that anger which Jane somewhat precariously controls. The façade of womanly calm conceals the reality of womanly rage—directed at all who limit female opportunity. Rochester would be its logical immediate target, but Jane cannot allow herself to express her anger at him directly. It emerges indirectly, in her depression and annoyance, the mad wife her surrogate for more dramatic, more accurate expressiveness. The magnitude of unexpressed female anger implies the danger of madness: once a woman allows herself to reveal her rage, where will it ever stop? Better to keep it underground, emerging only in occasional wisps of smoke.

When Jane leaves Rochester, she takes refuge with St. John Rivers, who tempts her by offering that exercise for her faculties and field for her efforts that she has declared women to need. Unlike Rochester, he recognizes her special capacities for achievement, finding her not only "docile" but also "diligent, disinterested, faithful, constant, and courageous; very gentle, and very heroic"—if not lovable. He demands that she control passion in order to participate in heroic action as a missionary; he takes her seriously—far more seriously than Rochester does—as a fellow human being. He also dominates her utterly. Rejecting him and the relationship he offers, she chooses passion over action.

The mad wife is dead by now—no longer needed as a symbolic embodiment of female anger since that anger has been satisfied, the balance righted, by Rochester's maiming, a shocking accident which provides a masculine equivalent for the wasting disease that punishes women's moral flaws. Rochester has paid the penalty for his efforts to control Jane (although it is disguised as punishment for his wishing to lead her into a life of sin): he has lost his hand and his sight, symbolic castrations both; fire has scarred his forehead. The last pages of *Jane Eyre* dwell almost obsessively on dependency. Conscious of his physical handicap, Rochester feels he can no longer be attractive to a woman because he must depend on her. Jane tells him that she is now an "independent woman," meaning by that mainly that she has enough money for her needs, but meaning also that as a consequence she can lead whatever life she wishes. She also sadistically duplicates Rochester's earlier technique of taunting her with a glamorous alternate lover: St. John plays the role that Blanche Ingram had previously filled. Rochester suggests that only a desire for self-sacrifice can motivate her interest in him; she responds that his mutilations are pitiful, "and the worst of it is, one is in danger of loving you too well for all this; and making too much of you." Despite the reality of her pity, she seems almost to gloat over his afflictions, turning over in her mind the fact that now he really needs her. "His countenance reminded one of a lamp quenched, waiting to be relit——and alas! it was not himself that could kindle the lustre of animated expression: he was dependent on another for that office!" As they move toward marriage, she declares explicitly that his need to be helped makes him appealing. "I love you better now, when I can really be useful to you, than I did in your state of proud independence, when you disdained every part but that of the giver and protector." He resigns himself to relative helplessness, their marriage founding itself on his dependency. "He loved me so truly, that he knew no reluctance in profiting by my attendance: he felt that I loved him so fondly, that to yield that attendance was to indulge my sweetest wishes."

Unlike *Shirley*, *Jane Eyre* makes few overt claims to realism. Its plot of insane wives, unexpected inheritances, surprising discoveries of relationship; its Cinderella-heroine and Byronic hero; even its emphasis on Jane's imaginative life—all suggest that the author here shapes a world closer to her heart's desire rather than tries, as in *Shirley*, to deal with realities of the world she inhabits. In this fantasy atmosphere, the physical metaphor that expresses the feminine equation between helping and controlling takes on significance. Rochester must be crippled to punish his sins; but also so that Jane can help him and, helping, substantiate her power to govern.

The dependency, however, is not altogether one-sided. When Rochester complains about his sense of uselessness, Jane replies, "You are no ruin, sir—no lightning-struck tree: you are green and vigorous. Plants will grow about your roots, whether you ask them or not, because they take delight in your bountiful shadow; and as they grow they will lean towards you, and wind round you, because your strength offers them so safe a prop." Again, she observes, "To be privileged to put my arms round what I value—to press my lips to what I love—to repose on what I trust: is that to make a sacrifice?" These remarks, dictated by her desire to reassure her lover, echo some of Jane's earlier observations about Rochester. The maimed husband, in this fantasy version of experience, makes possible a marriage of ideal reciprocity: a disturbing resolution for the novel's clearly defined emotional issues. Jane emphasizes the closeness of their relationship in marriage, and speculates "perhaps it was that circumstance [Rochester's blindness] that drew us so very near—that knit us so very close! for I was then his vision, as I am still his right hand." Rochester, even crippled, remains the strong male on whom a woman can safely and happily depend, to whom she will willingly submit. But to deprive him of physical power helps to equalize the situation, expressing the feminine need to be needed and revealing again the intimate connection between helping and controlling.

One must note the pathos of this particular version of feeling. To fulfill Jane's need, it is necessary to handicap her lover: thus an indirect expression of her anger allows some parity to be achieved between man and woman. Rochester, a fantasy figure of brooding strength, his independent confidence, we are explicitly told, as the source of his appeal. A man at once strong and weak: Charlotte Brontë manufactures an ideal realization of a female fantasy.

Caroline, Jane, and Shirley form a continuum of female types. Caroline conforms to the most conventional notions of femininity with her gentleness, compliance, passivity, her longing for a mother, her heartbroken decline, her determination to be good. Jane is strong-willed, passionate, not conventionally attractive; but prevented by external forces from following her own will. Shirley has every feminine advantage. She shares Jane's forcefulness, but possesses social position, wealth, and beauty, as well as intelligence and imagination. Although orphaned too, she has a kindly mother-surrogate on the scene: a woman who provides guidance, affection, comfort, but who never interferes with what Shirley wants to do. Like the other two young women, she wishes to unite herself with a man on whom she can depend, but whom she can also "help." Her apparent passion for self-abnegation reminds one of Marie Bashkirtseff's dictum that the woman's total yielding is the triumph of her self-love.

My students admired Shirley—"Anger doesn't make her completely impotent"—as she displayed her power through most of the novel. She seems a character unusually free to recognize and express her own emotions, and able to deal even with her own anger without being destroyed by it.

Most modern female college students believe anger a totally unacceptable emotion to express toward others. (One girl told me that when she gets angry, she yells at herself in the mirror.) To read about a woman capable of ordering a rude man to leave her house filled them with wonder and admiration. But they understood this emotional freedom as the result of being "really pretty and really rich." Lacking confidence in their own possession of such socially viable virtues, they could not imagine behaving likewise.

And they were troubled by Shirley's attitude toward the man she loved.

"She's *making* him dominate her, it's sort of like having her cake and eating it too."

Exactly. In fact for many reasons *Shirley* deserves a second, more searching interpretation.

When Caroline first sees Shirley, the heiress is standing "bending slightly toward her guest, still regarding her, in the attitude and with something of the aspect of a grave but gallant little cavalier." The masculine superiority, masculine spirit, and masculine style of courtesy implicit in this description characterize Shirley throughout the novel. Her wealth and beauty make it possible for her to exercise overt control over her own destiny; her cleverness enables her to manipulate men to her own purposes, as when she arranges for the local rectors to participate in the distribution of charity; her penetration reveals to her much of the truth about men's dealings with women. Arranging for herself and Caroline to watch a confrontation between Robert Moore and his dissident workers, she enjoys her demonstration of women's superior cleverness. "They imagined we little knew where they were to-night: we *know* they little conjectured where we were. Men, I believe, fancy women's minds something like those of children. Now, that is a mistake." Yet the intrigue and manipulation she indulges in are in fact very childlike.

Shirley's vision of feminine possibility appears unrestricted by social reality, her awareness of essence protecting her from feeling the indignities of the feminine lot. Her fantasy about Eve, the first woman, claims women as the ultimate source of power. "The first woman's breast that heaved with life on this world yielded the daring which could contend with Omnipotence: the strength which could bear a thousand years of bondage ..." She identifies Eve finally with Nature itself; and Charlotte Brontë, throughout the novel, associates women with nature, men with industrial life. The contrast exemplifies the different sources of masculine and feminine power, feminine strength being deeper, instinctive, independent of external circumstance. Feminine power includes the power to "endure without a sob" the greatest suffering, to close the hand upon a scorpion without crying out. It also includes the profound wiliness that Shirley consistently displays.

Yet Shirley rhapsodizes about the worth of men: "Indisputably, a great, good, handsome man is the first of created things." Her panegyric bewilders Caroline, finally driven to inquire, "But are we men's equals, or are we not?" Shirley evades the question: "Nothing ever charms me more than when I meet my superior—one who makes me sincerely feel that he is my superior." Responding to further questioning, she implies that she has never actually met such a being: she believes in his existence, but finds actual examples of the species "false gods" at best. Despite the theoretical superiority of the best of men to the best of women, in practice women more than equal the men they encounter, although social convention declares otherwise. Shirley expertly has her cake and eats it too: her theoretical pronouncements counteract any suspicion of unwomanliness that might be created by her freedom in living her life.

Shirley recognizes the emotional danger of her freedom. Having taken full advantage of her independence, in the nineteenth-century sense of financial self-sufficiency, to create independence of a more metaphysical sort, she must find the way to fulfill the other side of her nature, her need for dependence. She does so, as my student pointed out, by *making* her lover dominate her.

Louis Moore, her financial and social inferior, since he is a tutor in her uncle's household, has intellectual and emotional strength of his own, demonstrated in his resistance to Shirley's early overtures and most strikingly in his response to her fantasies of hydrophobia. The curious hydrophobia episode seems almost to be inserted for the purpose of suggesting that every woman is after all a fool. Shirley, bitten by a dog which she believes mad, immediately declares herself doomed to die. Instead of confiding her fears to anyone or seeking medical advice, she resorts to the tactic that Charlotte Brontë has earlier declared necessary for women: she shuts her hand silently on the scorpion, pining mildly away, waiting for death. Louis penetrates to her secret, takes the immediate practical course (why didn't she?) of ascertaining that the dog was not mad, relieves her mind, and reverses the decline. He thus declares a kind of ascendancy over her which she eagerly accepts.

But if the hydrophobia gambit was contrived to demonstrate Louis's power, the contrivance seems Charlotte Brontë's rather than Shirley's; or if Shirley's, hers only on an unconscious level. Her conscious contrivances come later, after she has accepted Louis's proposal.

"Teach me and help me to be good," she begs him, ". . . be my guide where I am ignorant: be my master where I am faulty . . ." Louis describes her in terms similar to those Rochester uses of Jane: "Pantheress!—beautiful forest-born!—wily, tameless, peerless nature! She gnaws her chain . . . ! She has dreams of her wild woods, and pinings after virgin freedom." ("One thing that's different about this book," remarked one of my students, "is that Shirley's tameless, like they say, but she isn't a bitch.") Shirley, yielding her freedom, demonstrates her power most in appearing to yield that as well. She refuses to set a date for the wedding, procrastinates until Louis insists. Then the author comments, "there she was at least, fettered to a fixed day: there she lay, conquered by love, and bound with a vow. Thus vanquished and restricted, she pined, like any other chained denizen of deserts. Her captor alone could cheer her; his society only could make amends for the lost privilege of liberty ..." The next paragraph suggests that this extravagant imagery of bondage and lost liberty represents masculine fantasy, Louis's view of things, rather than reality. It turns out that Shirley has yielded all control of her household to Louis, before the marriage. She refers every request to him, forces him to make all decisions. "In all this, Miss Keeldar partly yielded to her disposition; but a remark she made a year afterwards proved that she partly also acted on system. 'Louis,' she said, 'would never have learned to rule, if she had not ceased to govern: the incapacity of the sovereign had developed the powers of the premier.'"

Shirley demonstrates her power most fully by making her lover exercise power. She indulges herself as an actress, preparing an elaborate display of maidenly passivity which proves its own falsity. Much more ostentatious than the gentle Caroline in her yielding, Shirley also controls more forcefully, her self-love triumphant in the arrogance of her performance. The social inequality of the marriage alone makes the situation possible. Rochester is crippled in order to equal things out between him and his bride; poverty-stricken Louis Moore marries a rich wife. She therefore has initial social power, free to act the charade of tamed pantheress because her wealth gives her security. From this position of security—equivalent to Jane's clear vision and strong hands—she can vividly demonstrate her willingness to yield, her dependence the ultimate sign of her independence.

From a twentieth-century point of view, it is possible to recognize the pathos of the Brontë contrivances for giving her women power. Shirley and Jane require some stacking of the deck before they can get what they want; Caroline, who takes a more orthodox way, marrying a man neither her social nor her physical inferior, seems unlikely to exercise as much real control as she wishes. *Shirley* ends with a vision of the wild hollow, where fairies used to roam, now occupied by industrial plants; it would seem that Caroline's wish to preserve woods and clear air has no effect at all. Charlotte Brontë recognizes the difficulties of woman's lot; but her sensibility is not revolutionary. With her profound faith in the value of emotion, she appears to accept as given the woman's psychic need for dependency and for control, and the close relation between them. Her fantasies provide images of how these needs can be fulfilled; but she implies no criticism of their existence.

Charlotte Brontë sees the relations between men and women as necessarily involved with issues of power. Shirley is a tameless panther; Rochester describes Jane as a "resolute, wild, free thing . . . , defying me, with more than courage—with a stern triumph. Whatever I do with its cage, I cannot get at it—the savage, beautiful creature!" M. Paul, in *Villette*, says to the heroine Lucy, "You remind me, then, of a young she wild creature, new caught, untamed, viewing with a mixture of fire and fear the first entrance of the breaker-in." The similarity of imagery in the three novels underlines the point: a man wins a woman by capturing her; she defies him with subtle and devious sources of power, the resources of the captured wild creature.

Charlotte Brontë also succeeds remarkably—far better than George Eliot, for example—in depicting noncompetitive relationships between women. Although Shirley has more social power and far more obvious aggressiveness than Caroline, the friendship between them is one of equals. They are in many ways more harmonious than sisters.

Two women together are likely to talk about men. Shirley and Caroline, discussing their yearnings and their fears, trust and support one another. Shirley restrains Caroline from excessive emotional display, encourages her confidence, never betrays her. Caroline does not interfere with Shirley's love life, even when it may destroy her own happiness. Although Caroline feels Shirley to be her superior in many respects, their social and emotional inequality does not govern their interchange. Similarly, Jane Eyre's school tie with Helen, a girl older and wiser than she, is one in which all the guidance comes from one side, in which Helen's superiority is clearly acknowledged; but the problem of power in no way intrudes into the relationship. The image of the two girl lying in a single bed—Helen dies in Jane's arms—with all its sexual ambiguity suggests the special intimacy of the bond between women. It is of course outside the conventions of the Victorian novel to hint that a man and a woman might inhabit a single bed, but more than convention seems involved here. In many ways Charlotte Brontë conveys her conviction that intimacy between women may be more profound, more *balanced*, than any union possible between the sexes.

Charlotte Brontë's novels display a theoretical optimism not unlike George Eliot's. Despite their clear view of how women suffer, both authors seem to believe it possible for women to find emotional and moral satisfaction—not without difficulty, to be sure. But George Eliot reveals that men encounter similar—although by no means identical—difficulties in their struggles for fulfillment; and Charlotte Brontë, with no apparent interest in the struggles of men, hints that the superior emotional capacity of women compensates for the difficulties of their lot. Kate Chopin, sharing the recognition of her English predecessors that the need for dependency is powerful in women, conveys in *The Awakening* a darker vision of the implications of that need.

As the title suggests, *The Awakening* records a woman's self-discovery. Edna Pontellier bears some resemblance to Gwendolen Harleth, although the lack of satisfaction in her marriage is not initially so apparent to her as marriage's frustrations are to Gwendolen. Gwendolen reflects, early in *Daniel Deronda*, "Other people allowed themselves to be made slaves of, and to have their lives blown hither and thither like empty ships in which no will was present. It was not to be so with her; she would no longer be sacrificed to creatures worth less than herself, but would make the very best of the chances that life offered her, and conquer circumstances by her exceptional cleverness." Edna similarly opposes the idea of self-sacrifice. She "had once told Madame Ratignolle that she would never sacrifice herself for her children, or for anyone." As she elaborates, her sense of herself seems nobler than Gwendolen's: "I would give up the unessential; I would give my money, I would give up my life for my children; but I wouldn't give myself." But the mixture of reprehensible selfishness with an altogether admirable awareness of her own worth as a human being resembles Gwendolen's, the apparent difference perhaps deriving from the difference in the authors' attitudes toward their characters.

Kate Chopin, unlike George Eliot, does not claim to be a moralist. Eliot's sympathetic understanding of the irrationality, the power, and the value of emotion exists in the context of her fundamental assumption that right action must be the goal of every decent human being. Charlotte Brontë, even with her greater emphasis on the self-sufficient value of feeling, shares that assumption: Jane cannot live a life of sin with Rochester. *The Awakening* depicts a world of emotional needs and social commandments in which morality must be discovered, not assumed. Edna wishes to behave "rightly"—but rightly in relation primarily to her own needs. She feels responsibility finally only to herself, facing therefore a problem of self-discovery more intense and more painful than that of her fictional predecessors.

First of all, she must separate reality from fantasy. Edna's youth has centered on a series of fantasies about ideal men whom she loves from afar. Although she considers that her marriage to a businessman has put an end to these dreams, in fact she immediately transforms that marriage into yet another version of dream: "As the de-

Three

TAKING CARE

> What I dislike is feeling that I'm always
> taking care, or being taken care of. Never
> mind—work, work.
>
> —VIRGINIA WOOLF

A friend of mine, a professional woman, bore her first child in her mid-thirties. Her mother was delighted—not because of her daughter's obvious joy, or because she herself now had a new grandchild, but because she had never expected that daughter to follow the normal course of women. The girl was selfish, her mother had concluded long before; interested in her own career; self-obsessed. But she had finally proved her unselfishness, vindicated her mother's training, simply by giving birth.

This episode embodies, as a fable might, one way women feel about women. The notion of childbirth as justification persists with extraordinary vitality, in literature and in life. Connected with some crucial assumptions about feminine capacity, it is also allied with powerful traditional attitudes about the meaning of marriage. To take care of a child, to take care of a man—these activities, alternate or simultaneous, reflect similar self-images in the women who perform them. And the women who write about them—whether or not they have performed them—often illuminate the shape of such self-images.

They may be quite flattering, these images. It seems easy (the historical reasons are all too obvious) for women to take an attractive measure of themselves, or of one another, in the role of wife and mother. George Eliot and Kate Chopin may dissect marriages that prove means to feminine self-destruction, but even they appear to be at least vaguely aware of alternative versions in which women—*some* women—are enabled to fulfill themselves through happy service to others: the Garths' marriage in *Middlemarch*, the Ratignolles' in *The Awakening*. Nineteenth-century woman novelists, like their eighteenth-century predecessors, like even some of their twentieth-century followers, more characteristically imagined marriage as a state of moral possibility, the successful marriage both reward and arena for a woman's goodness.

"We would not be 'Yale wives' or much of anything else without our Yale men" (letter in *Yale Alumni Magazine*, November 1973).

That Jane Austen is far from naïve about the concept that marriages are made in heaven is clearly indicated by the famous first sentence of *Pride and Prejudice*. Her ironic observations of the marriage of convenience and how it happens occupy considerable space in all her novels; yet the usual reward of hard-achieved virtue for her heroines is a marriage imagined as offering the opportunity for self-expansion through devotion.

The central moral issue of *Persuasion*, as the title suggests, is how much a woman should subordinate herself to the needs and desires of others. In this context, marriage, with its pressure toward feminine subordination, might seem for women an ambiguous good. Yet for Anne Elliott it represents a triumphant moral achievement. Her tragic mistake as a girl was to allow herself to be persuaded that the marriage she wished would not be prudent. Eight years later, she still believes that she could not have done otherwise than accept the arguments of Lady Russell, considering her age (nineteen) and the manifest justice of the claim that her lover had not yet won a place in the world that would enable him to support her. But she knows that in her maturity she might see matters differently, be more willing to take a chance; and she would not urge another girl to behave as she has had to. From her lover's point of view, the issue is clearer: he believes that she has been overpersuaded in the first place, and that her willingness to yield to Lady Russell indicates lack of character. Having thought extensively about the traits of the satisfactory woman, he declares—his fortune made, his desire for a wife explicit—that the woman he wants must combine "a strong mind, with sweetness of manner." Anne, he believes, lacks the first of these requirements; *Persuasion* investigates in detail what "a strong mind" can and should mean in a woman.

It means, among other things, a mind that balances the claims of reason and emotion. Excessive feeling (as in Captain Benwick) is the enemy of self-control; excessive rationality (exemplified by Anne's cousin Walter Elliott) leads to narrow self-interest. The ideal compromise would involve a healthy and disciplined self-concern combined with rich awareness of the needs of others. Women, trained to subordinate their wills, face the temptation of allowing their responsiveness to others to determine the course of their lives. The woman who rejects this temptation entirely, as Anne's two sisters do, seems ridiculous at best, monstrous at worst. But when Anne yields to it, she gradually loses her vitality, her looks, and her capacity for joy.

The principal target of irony in *Persuasion* is the blindness of self-obsession, a weakness shared by both sexes. Sir Walter Elliott, Anne's father, makes himself the standard of universal judgment, without distinguishing between his deficiencies and his virtues. Physically vain, he finds other men and women inadequate by comparison to his own image in the mirror. No woman in the novel displays such narcissism as he: Admiral Croft, when he rents Sir Walter's house, has to remove the enormous number of looking glasses which line the bedroom. But Sir Walter's obsession with personal appearance and with rank is only a dramatic form of that self-concern shared by most inhabitants of his world. Anne's sister Mary Musgrove spends much of her time seeking occasions to be insulted and most of the rest making sure that she has as many privileges as anyone else. Her sister Elizabeth, rather sketchily depicted, shares her father's disposition in milder form. Louisa and Henrietta Musgrove, in search of husbands, believe that the rest of the world should share their concentration on how they are to achieve that state in life they deserve. Mr. Elliott wishes only to preserve his inheritance of rank, thus to prevent Sir Walter from marrying again. Even Anne's invalid friend Mrs. Smith is deterred by self-interest from informing Anne that she seems about to engage herself to a villain.

Jane Austen jokes gently about many of these displays of self-concern and about the problems they present for her heroine. When Anne goes to visit Mary at Uppercross, the realizes how unimportant even to other members of the family are the issues that have been central to her own life at Kellynch Hall. "She believed she must now submit to feel that another lesson, in the art of knowing our own nothingness beyond our own circle, was become necessary for her—for certainly, coming as she did, with a heart full of the subject which had been completely occupying both houses in Kellynch for many weeks, she had expected rather more curiosity and sympathy than she found. . . . She could only resolve to avoid such self-delusion in future, and think with heightened gratitude of the extraordinary blessing of having one such truly sympathising friend as Lady Russell." Because of Captain Wentworth's arrival, her visit to her sister changes the current of her life and her thoughts so that when she returns to Lady Russell, she discovers new difficulties. "She had lately lost sight even of her father and sister and Bath. Their concerns had been sunk under those of Uppercross, and when Lady Russell reverted to their former hopes and fears, and spoke her satisfaction in the house in Camden Place which had been taken, and her regret that Mrs. Clay should still be with them, Anne *would have been ashamed to have it known* how much more she was thinking of Lyme, and Louisa Musgrove, and all her acquaintance there. . . . She was actually forced to exert herself to meet Lady Russell with anything like the *appear-*

ance of equal solicitude, on topics which had by nature the first claim on her" [italics mine]. The "truly sympathising friend" in this new perspective seems as unconcerned with Anne's central interests as even her selfish sister Mary. The irony is partly at Annes expense: she should know better than to expect "true sympathy" from those she knows. But it also focuses on the narrowness of most human interests: even the most generous men and women are bound by the limitations of their own experience.

"Ashamed to have it known" what she was truly thinking of, Anne exerts herself to create the "appearance" of being more interested than in fact she is in Lady Russell's preoccupations. The author's tone implies no criticism of this procedure, which exemplifies Anne's way of conducting herself throughout the novel. "Taking care," for the unmarried woman, often implies taking care of one's own conduct. Anne cannot eliminate her feelings. She is still in love with Captain Wentworth, she shares the universal desire to have attention paid to her, she feels insulted or slighted when she overhears condescending or derogatory remarks about herself, she wishes to be valued, she is often lonely, even isolated. All of these feelings she successfully conceals: she would be ashamed to have them known. Despite her unfailing charity in action, she inwardly condemns her family's preoccupation with external appearances; yet her life too is primarily concerned with manipulating appearances—not physical, but emotional. Her moral endeavors are serious and sustained; but her most consistent moral triumph is successful *concealment*.

The close connection between self-control and concealment for a woman is a persistent theme in eighteenth- and nineteenth-century novels, particularly apparent in the work of novelists who concern themselves with the relation between manners—which imply manipulation of appearances—and morals. Fanny Burney, far less dexterous than Jane Austen in her own concealments, shares with her successor the conviction that manners reflect morals. For

Fanny Burney's heroines, too, marriage is the reward for virtue, but marriage and virtue are both imagined in fairly crass terms. The "good" marriage must elevate the heroine's social rank; in *Evelina,* it also brings wealth. What it rewards is "pleasing" manners. Good breeding is good character; Evelina's social mistakes endanger her moral status.

Early in the novel, Lady Howard writes Evelina's guardian, characterizing the young and inexperienced girl. "She has the same gentleness in her manners, the same natural graces in her motions, that I formerly so much admired in her mother. Her character seems truly ingenuous and simple; and, at the same time that nature has blessed her with an excellent understanding, and great quickness of parts, she has a certain air of inexperience and innocency that is extremely interesting." The observation is particularly revealing in conjunction with one made much later by Evelina herself, now the beneficiary of considerable experience, about Mrs. Selwyn, to whom she has temporarily been entrusted: "She is extremely clever; her understanding, indeed, may be called *masculine;* but, unfortunately, her manners deserve the same epithet; for, in studying to acquire the knowledge of the other sex, she has lost all the softness of her own." Both comments imply the same value system. Understanding, quickness, cleverness, are admirable; but in a woman they should ideally be concealed under a manner ingenuous, gentle, simple. Evelina feels Mrs. Selwyn to be her moral inferior because she lacks "femininity" in her manners. Consequently, as Evelina points out, she makes "many enemies": a woman's ultimate failure. Women must be pleasing. Evelina shares with her creator the belief that women should be intelligent, that they should not concentrate on dress and frivolity, that they should cultivate virtue; but most of all that they should please men. What will not please must be concealed: the heart of manners and of morality.

The same point is explicit in Fanny Burney's later (and less entertaining, more Johnsonian) novel, *Cecilia, or*

Memoirs of an Heiress. Cecilia, as the title suggests, is rich already, so she need not marry for money. (As the plot works out, however, she voluntarily sacrifices her wealth before marrying, specifically in order that her husband should not feel inferior, since her inheritance depends on her husband's assuming her name.) Like Evelina, though, she achieves and values social advancement through marriage. Through all the vicissitudes of an elaborate plot, she concerns herself obsessively with what others think of her: her principal guide to morality. The frivolous woman, Lady Honoria, who exists only to provide contrast with Cecilia, "had quick parts and high spirits, though her mind was uncultivated, and she was totally void of judgment or discretion: she was careless of giving offense, and indifferent to all that was thought of her." Such carelessness, such indifference, are likely to destroy any woman: at any rate, they will stand in the way of successful marriage.

The concept of successful marriage is richer in Jane Austen, and so is the notion of successful concealment. The younger Musgroves' marriage, in *Persuasion,* epitomizes the average way-of-the-world partnership, in which some genuine affection and interest link man and woman, but the course of their life together is dictated mainly by the desire of each for self-indulgence. Given a better woman, Anne believes, Charles Musgrove would have been a better man: "a woman of real understanding might have given more consequence to his character, and more usefulness, rationality, and elegance to his habits and pursuits." The good wife "takes care" of her husband's moral life and his activities; Mary's failure to do so reflects a moral weakness. In contrast to the Musgrove marriage, the Crofts' totally unfashionable union embodies true partnership. "I can safely say," observes Mrs. Croft, "that the happiest part of my life has been spent on board a ship. When we were together, you know, there was nothing to be feared." As she and her husband drive together in a carriage, she notices their imminent danger of colliding with a post. "But by coolly giving the reins a better direction herself they happily passed the danger; and by once afterwards judiciously putting out her hand they neither fell into a rut, or ran foul of a dung-cart; and Anne, with some amusement at their style of driving, which she imagined no bad representation of the general guidance of their affairs, found herself safely deposited . . ." Matter for amusement such driving may be, but a serious emblem of happy marriage. Mrs. Croft's technique is notably self-effacing: she does not claim the right of control, but unobtrusively exercises it when necessary. Such combined assertion and concealment is the feminine ideal.

Anne has not felt the special power of pleasing anyone since her brief love affair with Captain Wentworth. "She knew that when she played she was giving pleasure only to herself; but this was no new sensation." Lacking special admirers, she has no encouragement to self-indulgence; it seems natural that she should play for others to dance. She makes herself useful—to her sister, to her friends, to her father—though she is inadequately appreciated. This is one mode of her self-concealment, important because it involves moral effort toward "good" conduct, only partly in the service of covering up unacceptable feelings. She is also practiced in simpler forms of concealment, having trained herself in restraint. Thus, when Mrs. Croft comments on Wentworth's acquaintance with her, "Anne hoped she had outlived the age of blushing; but the age of emotion she certainly had not." She has learned how not to blush, how to control appearances, but not how not to feel. Yet she believes also in the possibility of controlling feelings, as she demonstrates in her colloquy with Captain Benwick, on whom she urges "a larger allowance of prose" instead of exclusive preoccupation with romantic poetry: "the strong feelings which alone could estimate it truly were the very feelings which ought to taste it but sparingly." And she participates generously in the feelings of others, even when the others are as silly as Henrietta

106

Musgrove: another means of keeping her own emotions in check.

Captain Wentworth declares to Louisa (and is overheard by Anne) the special value of "firmness." "My first wish for all whom I am interested in, is that they should be firm." Soon afterwards, Louisa demonstrates the ambiguity of this virtue by firmly persisting in her whimsical desire to be jumped down the steps, thus knocking herself insensible. Captain Wentworth has not entered far enough into the question: the issue is not whether one should be firm (who could be firmer than Sir Walter Elliott?), but what one should choose to be firm about. The dénouement of the novel is precipitated by Anne's claiming for her sex the exclusive possession of one sort of firmness: steadiness in loving when all hope is gone. Earlier, Captain Wentworth has implied his own possession of equivalent faithfulness when he reproaches Captain Benwick for turning to a new love after his fiancée's death: "A man does not recover from such a devotion of the heart to such a woman!—He ought not—he does not." Hearing Anne's claim, he proposes to her once more: having proved her moral equality, she deserves to live happily ever after.

Anne's elaborate justification of her sex makes a rather unusual sequence. Generalizations about the sexes emerge in Jane Austen's novels usually by indirection. Here, though, Anne not only generalizes about the nature of women, she persists in her assertions (firmly) despite masculine opposition. She and Captain Harville are discussing Captain Benwick's shift of affections from Harville's dead sister to a less worthy object. When Harville says that Fanny would not have forgotten her lover so soon, Anne agrees that such "would not be the nature of any woman who truly loved." The captain's smile at this claim provokes her to elaborate it: "It is, perhaps, our fate rather than our merit. We cannot help ourselves. We live at home, quiet, confined, and our feelings prey upon us. You are forced on exertion. You have always a profession, pursuits, business of some sort or other, to take you back into the world immediately, and continual occupation and change soon weaken impressions." Harville claims an analogy between man's superior physical strength and his strength of feeling; Anne, making the analogy more precise, points out that man is more robust, woman longer-lived: so with their affections. When Harville adduces literary evidence of masculine faithfulness, Anne observes, like a modern feminist, that books are written by men. She concludes by claiming for her own sex only the unenviable privilege "of loving longest, when existence or when hope is gone."

The implications of this argument, significant for the novel as a whole, not only emphasize Anne's own faithfulness but illuminate the moral significance of her entire course of action. Anne struggles to be "good"; yet in a real sense it is her fate rather than her merit to be so. It is true—and elaborately demonstrated by all the Austen novels—that the restrictions of women's social condition, the necessity for them to live confined at home with their feelings preying on them, become the occasion for the exercise of virtue. Men, too, must work to be good, and the criteria for goodness in men and in women are not necessarily dissimilar: as Evelina's guardian puts it, "the right line of conduct is the same for both sexes." But men do not face the same kind of pressure from others that women confront in the ordinary course of their existence. Mr. Elliott and Mrs. Clay reveal equivalent moral flaws: both are "too generally agreeable." They adapt their verbal responses to the desires of their companions, have no clear sense of personal identity, no apparent ethical standards beyond mere expediency. Anne, whose viewpoint often embodies Jane Austen's, is critical of them both. Both are hypocrites: hypocrisy is the obvious danger implicit in total commitment to the art of pleasing. But Mrs. Clay is the object of less severe criticism than Mr. Elliott because of her dependent state: she *must* please in order to survive in the social world, lacking as she does both money and position. Anne fears her father's potential romantic involvement with so unworthy an object, dislikes Mrs. Clay for her lack of moral substance, but never condemns her as strongly as she does Mr. Elliott, whose effort to please everyone is not a response to social pressure but a more gratuitous form of self-seeking than Mrs. Clay's. Mrs. Smith fails to tell an unpleasant truth for fear of being disagreeable: she must be agreeable, she believes, in order to maintain her single precarious tie with the world of social power. But Mr. Elliott fails to tell the truth because he wishes to enlarge the considerable power he already possesses. All three are reprehensible—but the women have more obvious excuses for their moral weaknesses.

Like all who successfully make pleasing an aspect of goodness, Anne avoids hypocrisy by involving herself with action as well as appearances. For women, whose sphere of action is limited, the possibility and the necessity of acting so as to be useful to others are more pressing than for men. This is perhaps the explanation for the traditional feminine role as guardian of morality: women occupy themselves with being good not because men force them toward virtue, but because the struggle for goodness is the most viable alternative to simple passivity.

This situation is not necessarily a matter for cynical reflection, or even for irony. In Jane Austen's rendition, it is merely a recognition of actuality to understand exactly why Anne Elliott comes to be so virtuous. And the reward of her virtue is quite appropriately a marriage in which she too may hope to guide the carriage away from posts, to avoid ruts and dung carts by judicious extensions of the hand, to help, and be valued for helping, her husband, without ever claiming leadership. By "taking care" of her own conduct and of the appearances she creates, she wins the privilege of taking care of a husband.

About twelve years ago, a group of Wellesley students invited me to have lunch with them to talk about how and whether one could combine marriage with a career. They were all seniors, suddenly afraid of turning into mirror images of their suburban mothers, yet half-yearning for exactly that fate. I spoke passionately, and, I thought, eloquently about the richness of life committed to various kinds of endeavor. The students remained conspicuously unconvinced. Finally one girl burst out, with real passion, "But do you ever send your daughter off to school with dirty underwear?"

That's become a family joke for us, but it was no joke at the time. I still remember the odd intensity with which that young woman spoke. What did dirty underwear mean to her? Hidden, intimate, protective: it symbolizes a whole range of feminine responsibilities. To keep someone else's underwear clean, though no one ever sees or knows, is to *take care*. The woman makes and preserves the order of the intimate. If she allows it to lapse ... chaos is come again.

The power of this notion of "taking care," for those apolitical students more than a decade ago, was greater than the glamour of career or the pull of the superwoman self-image. The concept itself combines a rather precise suggestion of hidden control with the appeal of selflessness. Every woman, traditional teaching and literature tell us, has it within her grasp to be a kind of saint. The temptations of sainthood are difficult to resist.

I became very defensive when accused of neglecting Judith's underwear. I said my child never suffered dirty underwear. I felt as though someone were inspecting my bureau drawers. My credentials as a good woman had been challenged.

Novelists less tactful than Jane Austen make even more vivid than she does the necessity and the charm of a woman's "taking care," the arduousness with which she trains herself, and is trained, for proper self-forgetfulness in the role of wife and mother, the degree to which the promise of that position compensates for all the hardships of girlhood.

Elizabeth Gaskell—a novelist seriously underrated in the twentieth century—wrote several novels dominated by a vivid, although perhaps not entirely conscious, awareness of the plight of women. There are many useful ways of examining a Jane Austen novel; generations of critics have explored them. To look at *Persuasion* from the point of view of its assumptions about women sheds light on some but by no means all crucial aspects of the novel. But to examine *Wives and Daughters* (or *Mary Barton*, or *North and South*) as a treatment of the special dilemmas of femininity is to reveal unexpected depth and subtlety of conception and structure—far more than emerges from attempts to place Mrs. Gaskell in the "realistic tradition" of the novel or to compare her plots and characterization with George Eliot's.

Like Jane Austen, Mrs. Gaskell specializes in social observation: she speculates on the emotions of a governess or a countess with equal aplomb. In the novels I've mentioned she displays little of Jane Austen's capacity for irony, little wit or lightness of tone; her tone in general seems a trifle solemn. And she lacks Austen's economy of touch. Her characterizations depend on accumulated detail, her own voice lacks individuality, she rarely provides flashes of sharp perception. Not even an enthusiast could claim that she is Austen's equal. Yet her special quality is compelling: a steady integrity of observation that creates the sense of penetrating accuracy. Often she treats female dilemmas in the perspective of large social issues. In *Mary Barton* and *North and South*, the nominal center of concern is relations between master and man in the factories. Hidden analogies between the plight of women and of workmen surge beneath the surface, never quite explicit. In *Wives and Daughters*, her final novel (left unfinished at her death), she avoids the industrial scene; but here too she displays quite specific awareness of what it is men *do* with their time. The contrast between necessary male occupations and unnecessary female ones, hinted in Jane Austen, is developed in *Wives and Daughters*; it forms the novel's perspective on female problems.

*Her days at Hamley were well-filled up with the small du-
ties that would have belonged to a daughter of the house
had there been one. She made breakfast for the lonely
Squire.... She read the smaller print of the newspaper
aloud to him.... She strolled about the gardens with him,
gathering fresh flowers, meanwhile, to deck the drawing-
room against Mrs. Hamley should come down. She was
her companion when she took her drives in the close carriage; they read poetry and mild literature together in
Mrs. Hamley's sitting room upstairs. She was quite clever
at cribbage now, and could beat the Squire if she took
pains. Besides these things, there were her own independent ways of employing herself. She used to try to practise
an hour daily on the old grand piano.... And she had
found her way into the library, ... sitting on the steps for
an hour at the time, deep in some book of the old English
classics.*

This is an unusually detailed rendition of how a well-
bred nineteenth-century girl filled her time. Pleasant
enough, perhaps, yet the relentless triviality of endeavor
(except for the "old English classics," which merit an hour
at a time) contrasts poignantly with Roger Hamley's
development toward a scientific career, on Mr. Gibson's
industry as a doctor. Molly struggles to fill her time; the
admirable men in the book struggle to find time for all they
wish to accomplish. The difference derives not from character but from fate—the divergent fates of men and of
women.

"My husband has . . . been positively supportive at
times, declaring that my working is a cheaper prescription
for my unpreditable, inexplicable depressions than psychi-
atry" (letter in *Yale Alumni Magazine*, November 1973).

There is nothing to be done about the occupation problem—no way of fighting fate. What takes its place as a
feminine preoccupation is the familiar issue of how one

should deal with feeling. *Wives and Daughters* follows Molly Gibson from the age of ten to eighteen. She is learning how to be a woman—a hard lesson, although a number of different models are available to her.

A surprisingly complicated example is Hyacinth Kirkpatrick, the ex-governess who becomes Molly's stepmother. As stepmother she is far from satisfactory: selfish, hypocritical, devious, insensitive. To be sure, her high regard for appearances makes her scrupulous in treating Molly as well as she does her own daughter, Cynthia, and she has moments at least of impetuous good feeling. An easy target for satire, she is the focus of Mrs. Gaskell's rare moments of comic observation. One of the remarkable aspects of *Wives and Daughters*, though, is the sympathy with which it treats Mrs. Kirkpatrick's real dilemma. Mrs. Gaskell never relents in her perception that the woman is a less than admirable human being, but she is nonetheless a subject for sympathy—partly for her very unworthiness.

Hyacinth Clare (her maiden name) has started adult life as governess in a noble family, forced into hypocrisy (like Austen's Mrs. Clay) by the pressure to seem agreeable. Her livelihood depends on her compliance. She eagerly accepts her first suitor, glimpsing the possibility of a more satisfying life. Shortly after she bears him a daughter, Mr. Kirkpatrick dies, forcing her back to the necessities of earning a living. She opens a school, unsuccessfully. Unintelligent, lacking business acumen and professional dedication, her values formed by her early employers, she yearns only for the comfort, luxury, ease of the rich. On a visit to the household of Lord and Lady Cumnor, where she used to work, she appreciates every detail of wealthy life, and pays for her comfort once more by being agreeable. Looking at a decorated mirror, she thinks about how difficult it is for her to achieve the grace easily assumed by the prosperous: "Ah! it would be different if they had to earn every penny as I have! They would have to calculate, like me, how to get the most pleasure out of it. I wonder if I am to go on all my life toiling and moiling for money? It's not natural. Marriage is the natural thing; then the husband has all that kind of dirty work to do, and his wife sits in the drawing-room like a lady. I did, when poor Kirkpatrick was alive. Heigho! it's a sad thing to be a widow." When Gibson proposes to her, "she burst into hysterical tears: it was such a wonderful relief to feel that she need not struggle any more for a livelihood."

Such passages indicate the governess's selfishness, her lack of responsive feeling, her calculation. But they also recognize the pathos of her situation: the felt limitation of possibility, the unsuitableness of her position to her talents, the forces pushing her toward any marriage at all as the only feasible solution to her problem. Gibson's proposal is motivated by equally practical considerations. Lord Hollingford has recommended, "If you found a sensible, agreeable woman of thirty or so, I really think you couldn't do better than take her to manage your home, and so save you either discomfort or wrong; and, beside, she would be able to give your daughter ... tender supervision." He articulates exactly what is in Gibson's mind. The doctor marries without love in order to give his daughter maternal care, then protects himself from the consequences of a bad marriage by keeping very busy. His wife's opportunities for busyness, of course, are more limited; her emotional frustration expresses itself in her manipulation of her daughter and her stepdaughter. One rarely encounters in literature so sympathetic an understanding of a woman who marries for money: not, like Gwendolen Harleth in *Daniel Deronda*, for wealth and power, but for money as creating the only possibility for relative freedom. The reader is not allowed to feel simply scorn for the new Mrs. Gibson, unattractive though she is. Her predicaments, emotional and financial, are real; her solution for them is the only one available to her.

To Molly she exemplifies feminine selfishness, and all the moral evils selfishness in a woman brings in its wake. Her empathic capacities, if ever she had any, have atrophied; she can now feel only for herself. But Molly can also see in her the advantages that selfishness brings. Mrs. Gibson is not "punished" in the action of the novel, except by the gradual alienation of her husband, on whom, in any case, her emotional dependency is limited. She gets most of what she wants—ease, power, freedom—and if she does not seem happy, neither does anyone else.

Cynthia, Mrs. Gibson's daughter by the earlier marriage, exemplifies other emotional possibilities. Although she retains her mother's self-seeking orientation, she is far more generous, feeling real affection for Molly and wishing to feel more. Her self-described problem is severe emotional incapacity: she calls herself "a heartless baggage" and means it. She is unable to love: Mrs. Gaskell tells us, perceptively, that this incapacity derives from Cynthia's lack of received love. When Molly asks her if she loves Roger dearly, she replies, "You know I've often told you I've not the gift of loving ... I can respect, and I fancy I can admire, and I can like, but I never feel carried off my feet by love for any one, not even for you, little Molly." Lacking the capacity to love, she has instead an endless desire to be liked and admired; consequently when circumstances reveal her meretricious behavior, she leaves home to marry an attractive, rich, but superficial young man—no penalty for her sins, exactly what she wants. She explains that she cannot stand the possibility of being criticized by those whom she wishes to love and admire her. Her inability to love truly, her desire only to be loved, comprise a moral weakness which accounts for all her evil acts. Molly first admires, then pities her, yet cannot choose to be like her, even if she had the power. The fate of the "charmer" is another trap of women's social condition.

A more viable possibility for Molly, strongly urged upon her by example and by precept, is the familiar solution of totally suppressing inconvenient emotion—a pattern related to the acceptance of feminine responsibility to others. The principal exemplar of the technique is Mrs. Hamley, who loves her husband but shares no interest with him. He is willing to indulge her in her desires, but not to participate in her activities. "She gave up her visits to London; she gave up her sociable pleasure in the company of her fellows in education and position. . . . Deprived of all her strong interests, she sank into ill-health; nothing definite; only she never was well." By the time Molly knows her, she has a real, if unspecified, disease, of which in due time she dies. She is a charming, appealing woman, who brings the missing maternal element into Molly's life. Because she is so tender toward Molly, her model of the woman who sacrifices everything for the men in her life has real power over the girl.

It is heavily reinforced by Mr. Gibson, characterized almost to the point of tedium—except that it is such an unusual idea to find spelled out in Victorian fiction—by his effort to suppress his own emotions so that he won't have to examine them. He "was truly sorry for his little girl; only he thought that there was a greater chance for the future harmony of the household, if he did not lead Molly to define her present feelings by putting them into words. It was his general plan to repress emotion by not showing the sympathy he felt." "He never allowed himself to put any regret into shape, even in his own mind." He is briefly forced to recognize Molly's unhappiness and her deep affection for him: "But in a moment he began to whistle an old Scotch air he had heard in his childhood, and which had never recurred to his memory since; and five minutes afterwards he was too busily treating a case of white swelling in the knee of a little boy, and thinking how to relieve the poor mother, who went out charring all day, and had to listen to the moans of her child all night, to have any thought for his own cares, which, if they really existed, were of so trifling a nature compared to the hard reality of this hopeless woe." "It was better for them both that they should not speak out more fully . . . but he walked away from her with a sharp pang at his heart, which he turned into numbness as soon as he could by throwing himself violently into the affairs and cares of others."

Numbness is what this technique inevitably produces. Molly half-recognizes this fact, as she recalls her passionate unhappiness at the news of her father's approaching marriage and compares it with the emotional state she has learned to achieve: "Was it goodness, or was it numbness, that made her feel as though life was too short to be troubled much about anything? Death seemed the only reality." Mrs. Hamley perseveres in self-suppression to its natural conclusion in death; Molly finds the course finally impossible, given her deep emotional vitality. Her lack of real occupation contributes to her difficulty about repressing all feeling. Even the few examples quoted above of her father's successful evasions of feeling may suggest how heavily he relies on his work to help him avoid his emotions. Only in brief intervals, on the other hand, does Molly have any real work. Most of the time, she has only her feelings; if she denies them, there will be nothing left—except the ultimate reality of death.

Suppression as a legitimate form of self-control has long been recommended to women; literary recognition of its dangers as early as Mrs. Gaskell's time is unusual. By associating the technique with a man as well as with women, the author suggests that it represents a universal temptation; by associating it with death, she unequivocally condemns it. She is more ambiguous in her treatment of the other traditional feminine way of dealing with emotion by the more complicated repression involved in giving up one's life to the service of others.

It is Roger Hamley who recommends selflessness to Molly, when he finds her weeping over her father's approaching marriage. He tells her a story about "Harriet," who, deprived of her mother, "gave herself up to her father, first as his comforter, afterwards as his companion, friend, secretary—anything you like." When her father remarries—Harriet being then in her twenties—the new trio is remarkably happy. How did that happen? Molly inquires. "'Harriet thought of her father's happiness before she thought of her own,' Roger answered, with something of severe brevity. Molly needed the bracing." Roger, in his "severe brevity," seems something of a prig, but Molly eagerly incorporates his lesson. Henceforth, she tries to devote herself to others, to "give herself up," in Roger's revealing phrase. At an evening party with Cynthia, she talks to two unattractive, shy girls; consequently, Cynthia captivates Roger. Cynthia exploits her, her stepmother exploits her, she castigates herself for every fleeting bad thought she has about others and warns herself ceaselessly about the danger of selfishness. She becomes very good, people are always telling her how good she is. But she is not happy; and finally she falls into the familiar Victorian decline, brain fever this time, consequence of her labor for Osborne Hamley's widow and child and of her own unrequited love. She survives, of course, and it is clear enough—the last chapter was never written—that she is to marry Roger in the end.

But it is perhaps the triumph of the novel that one wonders about this marriage as the reward for Molly's virtue. There are three established marriages in the book: the Gibsons, the Hamleys, and Lord and Lady Cumnor stand as representative couples on different social levels. All three are, as the world goes, "happy" marriages. None offers the wife any apparent real fulfillment, although all provide what she believes she wants. Only Squire Hamley, of the men, seems really happy in his marriage, and his is the happiness of blindness and total dependency: he refuses to recognize his wife's needs; when she dies, he disintegrates. What will the marriage between Roger and Molly be like? Roger, a brilliant career in progress, has already demonstrated some interest in educating Molly, who is highly responsive to his teaching. But what is she to do with him, how is she to live? The good marriage is only a hypothesis in this book; hardly that, even: a vague fantasy. It is a fantasy of enlargement, of greater freedom—exactly what Mrs. Kirkpatrick sought in marrying Gibson. She found what she sought, but not happiness. Molly's life, too, will surely be enlarged through marriage; and she is no Mrs. Kirkpatrick. She has real emotional capacity, she recognizes her emotional needs, she yearns to love as well as to be loved, and to find a larger sphere of action rather than of indulgence. Still . . . there are questions to be asked.

The measure of worth, in *Wives and Daughters,* is the capacity for feeling and for awareness of feeling in others: Molly's most serious criticism of a man she dislikes is: "He never seems to know what one is feeling." The various marriages arranged in the course of the novel illuminate various modes of feeling and fantasy. This fact is important in understanding what ma may seem the facile romanticism of Mrs. Gaskell's plotting. Her marriages do not merely dispose of the characters; they have individual and specific meanings. Mrs. Kirkpatrick's marriage to Gibson exemplifies the distortion of human relationships to serve narrow self-interest. Osborne's marriage to the French girl expresses romantic impulse, but his failure to acknowledge the marriage, his insensitivity to his bride's emotional needs, show the consequences of emotional irresponsibility. Cynthia's marriage is an attempt to escape moral demands, as her mother's has been an attempt to escape economic restrictions. And Molly's—Molly's is an effort to fulfill herself and another, both morally and emotionally, an effort made with full responsibility, but with limited awareness of what the possibilities of marriage may be.

The fact that the book is unfinished adds strangely to its effectiveness, by underlining the questions about the "happy ending" clearly in store. Despite the romanticism of her plot, Mrs. Gaskell has managed to pursue a rather searching investigation of the feminine situation. It is not at all apparent what the answers are to the dilemmas she reveals. Her model young woman, like the model young women in other novels, occupies herself by "taking care" of others and wishes only for something of her own to take care of; but we are enabled to ask whether this must be all there is, whether it is in any sense enough.

"When I was in fourth grade I was a horse. I was a stallion, I was the one that led the herd and everything. The thing was, I always thought of myself in the masculine position. A year or so later I started to write a book about being an Indian, and I was the boy. I just thought could get more accomplished that way."

That was a characteristic response to reading *Little Women*, which about half my students had first encountered as children. Some confessed to weeping again over the death of Beth, some professed to be cynical. Some thought it was "a really good book," at least for children, some thought it sentimental, or too moralistic. But all agreed that they had identified with Jo. Not with noble Beth, or domestic Meg, or artistic Amy on her jaunt to Europe, but with boyish Jo, striving for masculine achievement, yearning for masculine freedom. I never asked my students how many of them wished they were men, or had wished it, but their reaction to *Little Women* suggested that all of them yearned somehow to be boy and girl simultaneously. Who can blame them?

The difference between boy and girl is strongly marked in *Little Women*. It is spelled out in an account of Meg's twins, a boy and a girl, who from infancy define themselves according to sex:

At three, Daisy demanded a "needler," and actually made a bag with four stitches in it; she likewise set up housekeeping in the sideboard, and managed a microscopic cooking stove with a skill that brought tears of pride to Hannah's eyes, while Demi learned his letters with his grandfather. . . . The boy early developed a mechanical genius which delighted his father and distracted his mother, for he tried to imitate every machine he saw, and kept the nursery in a chaotic condition, with his "sewinsheen". . . ; also a basket hung over the back of a big chair, in which he vainly tried to hoist his too confiding sister, who, with feminine devotion, allowed her little head to be bumped till rescued. . . . Of course, Demi tryannized over Daisy, and gallantly defended her from every other aggressor; while Daisy made a galley slave of herself. . . . A rosy, chubby, sunshiny little soul was Daisy, who found her way to everybody's heart, and nestled there.

This distribution of virtues seems invented for the purpose of being attacked by feminists: a textbook example of damaging assumptions aboutt he nature of the female, and of the way a girl learns to be charming because she's not allowed to be intelligent or inventive. The patterns of life for bigger girls and boys in the book are what one might predict from this version of babyhood.

Little Women is usually remembered, sometimes even referred to in print, as a study of four girls with an absent father. In fact, the father is on hand for half the narrative. He provides spiritual advice to his daughters (his tone and language eerily identical with his wife's), confiscates the wine at Meg's wedding, teaches his grandson the alphabet: guide, rebuker, pedagogue—man. Yet he seems invisible: in a deep sense this is a women's world. On the other hand, there is no doubt about which sex really *does things.* The novel—one hesitates to call it that, since the narrative complexity is on the level of a child's story: all, of course, it purports to be—exhaustively examines the feminine role of "taking care," yet makes clear from the outset that the masculine kind of taking care—providing financial and serious moral support—is the kind that counts. The girls dispute about who is to have the privilege of buying their mother some new slippers. Jo wins, saying, "I'm the man of the family now papa is away, and *I* shall provide the slippers, for he told me to take special care of mother while he was gone." Unfortunately for her psychic well-being, she can only temporarily occupy the comforting role of "man of the family"; her father returns to supplant her.

The book is not one an adult is likely to reread with pleasure, yet children—even college students—still respond strongly to Jo as a fictional character. And the pure didacticism that governs the narrative gives it special clarity as a revelation of nineteenth-century feminine assumptions about feminine nature and possibility. Louisa May Alcott's ideas about what women should and can be, and what men naturally are, shape the simple narrative structure, which moves from one "lesson" to another. These pieces of didacticism reveal how completely women can incorporate unflattering assumptions about their own nature, using such assumptions as moral goads. The assumptions, and the lessons drawn from them, are only cruder in presentation than Mrs. Gaskell's: at core they are virtually identical.

The nature of women, this book suggests, is to be frivolous, foolish, vain, and lazy. They must be laboriously taught to be otherwise. Only in relative isolation can they learn to be good, since female society is thoroughly corrupt. Confining themselves within the family, learning at the knee of a virtuous mother, controlled from afar by a vague but stern father, they may hope to acquire goodness, which will be rewarded, at best, by marriage or at least by the opportunity to exercise positive influence on a man. Boys, on the other hand, are naturally enterprising, gay, and bold. Masculine society may lead a young man to play pranks; such boyish high spirits will be admired and envied by young women, who beg to be told of them. At worst, such society leads the man to drinking—but a word from a good woman will make him swear off. A man may fall into depression; a woman can bring him out of it. Such power is her highest achievement. In most cases her other nondomestic accomplishments represent only ways of passing time until she is married. It is true that Jo writes successfully—but Jo is a special, and complicated, case.

Given such unpromising raw material as four daughters, the virtuous mother (who has presumably received rigid early training from *her* mother, and who at one point explains how her husband has helped to train her) must struggle to inculcate the proper values. Beth is a saint, rewarded by dying young. The other three, left to their own devices, will glory in laziness, valuing a vacation week of no responsibilities. They are of course wrong: Beth's canary dies as a result (even she succumbs to inertia and neglects her bird) and everyone agrees at the week's end that it's really more fun to have little tasks to do. Meg shows a reprehensible interest in finery, regretting the poverty that deprives her of clothes as attractive as her peers': but she learns that there are more important things in life. Amy, at a school where all the other girls trade pickled limes, wants to have contraband pickled limes too. She is discovered and punished, thus learning that one is not to value pickled limes. Jo's special lessons are more interesting—all lessons in self-control, a virtue highly valued for everyone. Because she says what she thinks, tactlessly, she is deprived of a trip to Europe. She learns that one should be careful about saying what she thinks.

"To be loved and chosen by a good man is the best and sweetest thing which can happen to a woman; and I sincerely hope my girls may know this beautiful experience. . . . I'd rather see you poor men's wives, if you were happy, beloved, contented, than queens on thrones, without self-respect and peace." So speaks the mother: the first and great commandment for girls is to value the love of a good man. The problem is, how to win it. Ignorance is the first article of virtue. No matter that Meg is ill equipped, as a result, to deal with the malice of acquaintances who accuse her and her mother of plotting to ensnare a rich husband—her total ignorance, which her mother would call innocence, makes her automatically the moral superior of those who accuse her. Such superiority demands no effort on the part of its possessor, and this is part of its attraction. Passivity in sexual matters is highly valued. "Better be happy old maids than unhappy wives, or unmaidenly girls, running about to find husbands." Like Molly in *Wives and Daughters*, Miss Alcott's heroines learn that they must sit at home and wait.

And they too must learn to repress emotion, specifically anger. The expression of anger, it seems, is always unforgivable. When Meg's husband brings home an unseasonable guests, she reveals her anger and frustration in an explosion. He conceals his, so he wins: she apologizes. When Meg is extravagant with her husband's money, he says almost nothing, but quietly sacrifices his winter overcoat. He wins. Mrs. March has learned almost total repression of hostile emotions: this is a source of her power. She urges the lesson on Jo particularly, whose curse is a temper. Girls are not expected, not *allowed*, to have tempers. When a boy, their neighbor Laurie, has a fit of temper, Jo goes over to soothe him and his grandfather and bring them together by feminine wiles. No one objects to the boy's directly expressed resentment and hostility. When Jo has a fit of temper, her sister almost dies as a result. Her mother reveals that she has once had the same fault, but "I've learned to check the hasty words that rise to my lips and when I feel that they mean to break out against my will, I just go away a minute, and give myself a little shake, for being so weak and wicked." It is "weak and wicked" for a woman ever to express hostility ... ever to express even vitality, except in limited prescribed forms. Jo's mother has learned from her husband to be good. "He never loses patience—never doubts or complains—but always hopes, and works, and waits so cheerfully that one is ashamed to do otherwise before him." For men virtue seems natural; for women, in most cases, it must be bitterly acquired.

If girls are to be passive in their relations with men, repressed in their emotional lives, they yet are allowed that familiar sphere of service to others. The glorification of altruism as feminine activity in *Little Women* reaches extraordinary heights. The good woman *serves,* she subordinates herself always to the will of others—to husband, to employer, but also to the poor family down the street—she demonstrates her worthiness by sacrificing her self, in the most literal sense: one comes to feel that no *self* remains for the book's ideal woman. Beth, exemplifying the ideal, quietly fades away. As she points out soon before her death, she has never had plans for the future, as the other girls have: she is a model of selflessness. What can she do but die? True, the most powerful explicit argument for altruism is that it generates a sense of self: "Work is wholesome, and there is plenty for everyone; it keeps us from ennui and mischief, is good for health and spirits, and gives us a sense of power and independence better than money or fashion." But such language does not correspond to actuality. Although service to others may make the server smug, it seems ill-adapted to generating real power and independence—or even a convincing illusion of their presence.

In the context of these precepts and assumptions, Joe is remarkable. She is of course a version of the author herself: if we didn't know that, we'd be forced to surmise it. Her fictional vitality comes from the fact that she alone is in essential conflict with herself. The other girls, with superficial conflicts, deeply accept the values inculcated by their mother. Jo, more ardent than the rest in her resolutions to do good, her professions of virtue, her efforts to control her temper, cook dinners, be agreeable to her disagreeable aunt, fails no more often than anyone else. Still, she is different. The difference is exemplified by her reservations about being a girl. At the very beginning, she observes, "It's bad enough to be a girl, anyway, when I like boys' games and work and manners! I can't get over my disappointment at not being a boy; and it's worse than ever now, for I'm dying to go and fight with papa, and I can only stay at home and knit, like a poky old woman!" Her rebellion, childish and ill-considered in articulation, is yet profound. She learns to behave more like a girl; her father congratulates her at length, when he returns, on having become more womanly. But her preference for boys' work and manners stems from a deep awareness of how the limitations on feminine possibility make it difficult for her to express what's in her. Indeed, she is, as a girl, constantly being told that she is not supposed to express what's in her—yet her vocation is to be a writer.

Next-door Laurie, in a bad tamper, tempts Jo to run away with him. She wants to do so, longing——as well she might—for "liberty and fun"; but she observes, "If I was a boy, we'd run away together, and have a capital time; but as I'm a miserable girl, I must be proper, and stop at home." *Miserable* is precisely the right adjective. She means by it something like "worthless," a valuation that she applies by implication to her sex in its entirety—girls are generically worthless by comparison with boys. But she also conveys the dull suffering, the consciousness of always being in the wrong, that seems the very foundation of the girl's lot in life. Boys are allowed to "have a capital time": girls are not. Seeing the division of roles in this way, Jo is necessarily doomed to suffering.

Writing provides the promise of escape. She justifies the activity on altruistic grounds—if she earns money by her writing, she can help her parents and the other girls—but the need for it is far deeper than the need to earn money. It appears to be a quite genuine vocation, although Jo has no guidance about how to develop it and promptly falls into the corruption of writing sensational stories, a trap from which she is rescued, of course, by a wiser man. The writing of trash appeals to her because she is paid for it—and to be paid is to be valued. She is interested in the occupation in itself, unlike Amy, for example, whose narcissistic desire to paint disappears promptly when she is married. But she is also interested in being valued. To be valued for expressivity contradicts what she has been taught at home: the conflict becomes ever more intense.

My students resented the way Jo is finally disposed of Meg marries the tutor next door, and bears the charming twins, acquiring a new and attractive identity in marriage and motherhood. Amy marries the wealthy, handsome neighbor who has previously proposed to Jo and been rejected. Her mother provices the rationale for the rejection explaining that both Laurie and Jo have strong temper and will therefore constantly clash—an impossible basis for marriage. In other words, Jo's failure at self-repression

126

makes a glamorous marriage out of the question for her. Instead, Miss Alcott assigns her to a poor German professor more than twice her age and allows her to open with him a school (for boys!) and to be very happy. But my students felt—rightly, I think—that this was something of a sell. Why, after all, shouldn't Jo have charming, rich Laurie? Why should she be subjected to a father figure? Would she really be as happy as the author claims?

It seems, in an odd way, despite all the professions of happiness, a punitive marriage. Jo's "problem" is self-control . . . repression. If she is so bold as to continue yearning for a man's freedom, a man's happiness, a man's possibilities, if she insists on expressing herself, will not settle down in a predictable role—if she is like this, she must be given a man who can control her. She "proves" her womanliness by nursing Beth tenderly until her death, then remaining at home to comfort her parents. Then Professor Bhaer shows up once more, and marries her, providing from without the authority she needs to keep her in check.

Louisa May Alcott does not enter deeply into the problems of marriage, although she examines Meg's match on a ladies' magazine level (what do you do when your currant jelly refuses to jell? what do you do when your husband starts spending the evening elsewhere?). She, like the other authors here examined, sees marriage as reward for virtue and as enlarged sphere for feminine activity; but she also sees it as discipline. Mrs. March's husband helps her control her temper; Meg's husband by example teaches her the beauties of self-sacrifice and self-control; Amy's husband insists that she help him spend his money doing good; Jo's husband, after all, is a middle-aged professor who has begun his relationship with the girl by showing her that she is wrong to write newspaper fiction. Discipline, *Little Women* suggests, is that women little and big require. They must be controlled or their passion for pickled limes and finery and freedom will precipitate chaos. Jo is a dangerous figure. She reveals her creator's awareness that women have needs deeper than Mrs. March allows herself to know.

CHATTERS—Can I pen a picture of someone very special to me? Only after fishing the pockets of a shirt to be washed and finding a salary stub and some tablets for an upset stomach, did I realize how unselfish and undemanding he is.

He never picks up his soiled clothes, or puts the towel back in the proper room, never mind the towel rack, he doesn't empty the trash or wash the windows, but neither does he complain if the dishes are left in the sink or his brown lunch bag isn't made on time, or when he's down to his last pair of socks or reaches for a handkerchief and none are there.

Nor does he complain when our 2-year-old decides to get up at 3 a.m. and wants to play with Daddy. . . . And to keep me home he puts in an inground pool with all the trimmings (he doesn't swim).

So, I don't mind when I have the so-called man's chores to handle—washing and changing those screens and storm windows, mowing my share of the lawn and shoveling the driveway in the winter and numerous other things . . .

My world stops when he leaves in the morning, but starts when he comes home again.

Think I'll try to find something else to help him with. I would prefer not to see those indigestion tablets in his pocket. Look around, girls—how would you like to go to work every day—all of your adult life?

His Lucky Girl
(From the "Confidential Chat" section of
The Boston Globe, 8 August 1971)

The other side of the myth of feminine weakness (frivolity, foolishness) is the myth of feminine heroism. Women writers, like men, inculcate both——but with perhaps a special energy of self-castigation in rendering the one version of female experience, and a special, if not always conscious, awareness of the cost of the other. Ellen Glasgow, displaying a sensibility hardly more subtle than Louisa May Alcott's, is a woman novelist who carries into the twentieth century the preoccupation with the glories of wifehood and motherhood and the heroic vision of the woman who achieves them. Her own life, like Miss Alcott's, adds poignance to her narratives. In her autobiography she tells of an early trip to New York to try to market her first novel. Price Collier, of Macmillan's, takes her to lunch but offers her no encouragement: "He told me frankly that there was no hope for me with Macmillan. No, it would not do the slightest good if he read my manuscript; he could tell, without reading it, that there was not a chance of Macmillan's accepting the book. 'The best advice I can give you,' he said, with charming candor, 'is to stop writing, and go back to the South and have some babies.' And I think, though I may have heard this ripe wisdom from other men, probably from many, that he added: 'The greatest woman is not the woman who has written the finest book, but the woman who has had the finest babies.'"

Miss Glasgow, who did not dispute this observation when it was made, remained unmarried but wrote novels supporting the Collier view. In *Vein of Iron* she sketches two cartoonish "bad girls"—seductive Janet, seductive Minna—and one "bad" woman, Ralph's mother. The other women are unfailingly heroic in their care for others. There is Grandmother Fincastle, working ferociously into her eighties for the welfare of her family; Ada's mother, physically frail, spiritually indomitable; Aunt Meg, unmarried herself, but devoted to her brother's family; Mrs. Rawlings, the neighbor dressmaker, preoccupied with her son's welfare. And Ada, the child whose first spiritual revelation is that she doesn't "like to hurt things"; the woman who realizes with deep gratification, after years of bitter hardship, that her husband "depended upon her," so that it doesn't matter "if his flesh had ceased to desire her, or desired her only in flashes."

Such dependency, laboriously achieved, is the ultimate triumph of feminine heroism. Women, doggedly taking care of their men, form men who need to be taken care of.

The nineteenth-century novel reveals ways in which women may achieve power through passivity. Allowing herself to be taken care of, Shirley discovers subtle ways of exerting force; Lucy Deane through her sweet compliance usually gets what she wants; Gwendolen Harleth, making herself merely a beautiful representation, exacts worship from the beholders. Fictional treatments of female altruism uncover the opposite, equivalent truth: a truth particularly vivid in a minor novel like *Vein of Iron*, which lacks textural richness and psychological complexity to obscure its central emotional thrust. Women discover the potential for exercising control at both extremes of submissiveness: by allowing themselves to be dependent, taken care of, and by taking care of others. Both versions of the traditional female role suggest the devious ways an oppressed group may find to make an impression on the world.

Even as a girl, Ada takes full moral responsibility in her relationship with Ralph. When she becomes pregnant as a result of their two nights of love before he goes overseas as a soldier, she keeps her pregnancy a secret so as not to worry him. When he returns from the war, she keeps the job she already has—not a fulfilling job, just a money-making one—to help the family. An automobile accident leaves him paralyzed; she is rather disturbingly delighted to continue supporting the family. He tells her, unconvincingly, that he'd rather die than be a burden; she responds, convincingly, a modern-day Jane Eyre, "you know it isn't a burden for me to take care of you." She feels totally responsible for her husband's psychic state. When he suggests that he has lost his knack for selling cars, she responds, " 'Oh, no, you haven't. It will all come back to you.' Merely to say this was not enough; she must believe it. All her strength was poured into an act of faith, into a glowing affirmation of life." A bit later she observes, " 'But think how well we were doing before that accident. If nothing had happened, we'd be in our own home by this time, and we should have put by enough for a rainy day.' For she must find and give back to him what he had lost, his pride in himself and his masculine vanity."

She appears to think that she's Ralph's mother.

A certain hollowness of diction marks these glowing affirmations of life: Glasgow's dialogue is not always so stiff. The effort of denial involved in the woman's insistence that matters are not what in fact they are betrays itself in an increasing distance between the rhetoric describing femininity and the actuality described. Over and over the author asserts "the fearless gaze beneath the dark winged eyebrows, the wine-red in the cheeks, the glow of sanguine vitality"; "the image in the lighted mirrors . . . , strong, erect, undefeated"; "that strange happiness which seemed always to mean something more than itself. . . . As long as he depended upon her, she could face anything"; the "nameless wives and mothers still baking and scrubbing and washing in the hope that imperfect human ties might remain linked together." The notion of feminine heroism is largely defensive—protecting not so much against the sense of natural unworthiness so marked in Alcott as against a sense of inadequacy to the demands of real life. Much of the interest of *Vein of Iron* (which is not, however, a very good novel) comes from its author's effort to render and respond to thirty years of social change, from the beginning of the century to the early thirties. But the most significant response is denial, refusal to accept actuality though one must endure it, a reaction shared by heroine and author.

The significant men in this novel are pessimists, the women are optimists. Largely controlled by the women who insistently mother them, the men find life dubiously worth living. Ada's father is a philosopher, a clergyman who has lost his faith and taken to writing profound books which his daughter never reads. His happiness centers in his intellectual activity; despite his devotion to his wife, he feels that solitude is the natural way, the happier way, for the thinker. The philosopher intermittently regrets that he has never supported his family properly, recognizing that the masculine form of "taking care" is only economic. His single great achievement is his death; he struggles home, with truly feminine fortitude, to save his family the expense of burying him in the city.

John Fincastle, the father, is an unworldly man; Ralph, Ada's husband, is a cynic, as a result both of his war experiences and of the bad marriage earlier thrust upon him by public opinion. "When I look about me," he says, "in spite of all the good times, misery is the only thing that is real. Hunger and cold and disease and physical agony and meanness and rottenness inside and out human nature. . . ." Ada takes this outburst as manifestation of his "dark mood," which has unaccountably continued for years. It is women's function to affirm life; they are grieved but tolerant when their men deny it.

It is also women's function to be strong; men may be permitted their weaknesses. Ada breaks down only once in the book, in response to Ralph's drinking. Ralph, on the other hand, has a number of specified faults; it is also specified that they are lovable. Moreover, they are hardly Ralph's responsibility; his mother is consistently blamed for whatever is wrong with him. A woman of narrow sympathy and stern religious convictions, she is asserted to have "broken his will." Since women have the enormous responsibility of taking care of the entire masculine world, they are manifestly responsible if anything goes wrong. Men are not to be blamed for anything.

Like Jo and Laurie, Ada and Ralph are asserted to share the fault of quick temper, although no evidence of Ada's temper is ever provided. Ralph's quick temper is part of his charm; Ada's must be controlled. "It's a pity you are both quick-tempered," her mother tells her. "But you will have to be patient. Women always have to be patient." Women have the full burden of repression, both a cost and a manifestation of their stature. But they pay for their repressions, their bearing of burdens, their efforts to deny actuality. The most obvious cost is loss of physical attractiveness. Ralph remains handsome through his hardships: "All women ran after Ralph. What was there about him that made them, young and old, feel that he attracted them?" Old John Fincastle, removed in his philosophic reveries, grows gaunt and spiritual, but is always described as attractive: "His faint autumnal smile, like light that is ebbing away, softened the carved severity of his lips." But Ada sees the firm contour of her face break up "into sagging lines," develops deep furrows between her eyebrows, is described by her aunt as "real hollow-eyed," has "withered hands" and "faded cheeks": she shows all the physical signs of strain. Meanwhile, she keeps tossing out her gay affirmations. The last words of the novel are: "Never, not even when we were young, she thought, with a sudden glow of surprise, was it so perfect as this." The reader, forced to come to terms with this sort of meditation (Ada's father has just died, she's out of work, her neighbors have committed suicide, her husband is endlessly depressed), has a choice between believing Ada demented, dismissing her creator as sentimental, or accepting the woman's summation as a triumph of the spirit over sordid circumstance. The novel asks for the last judgment, the judgment Ada seems to make of herself: there is a certain smugness in all this affirmation. The difficulty of participating in it exemplifies the problem of the feminine heroism glorified by *Vein of Iron*—the heroism that consists in the assumption of total responsibility for one's family and the refusal to recognize the misery of actuality. It *is* heroism of a sort, and its limitations are peculiarly feminine. But it is also the product of sentimentality, a glorification of the restrictions of a woman's life to pretend that they are not restrictions but opportunities, and it embodies a special feminine form of pseudo-dementia. Masculine heroism involves altering circumstance; feminine heroism depends on endurance and denial. It represents the highest emotional possibilities of the commitment to "taking care" of others.

Jane Austen and Elizabeth Gaskell define in fictional terms the delicate emotional balancing point on which women must poise between commitment to others and preservation of their selves. Both authors necessarily accept the paucity of vocational opportunities for women of their time and recognize that service to others may be the best available feminine vocation; but both insist that a woman must not be endlessly compliant and self-repressive. Louisa May Alcott and Ellen Glasgow, less aware of emotional intricacy, demonstrate between them the divergent moral possibilities of the vocation to service: it may be a learned and willed compensation for woman's natural frivolity, or a manifestation of her natural goodness—but the great cost of even "natural" goodness ironically qualifies the view that it is the *nature* of women to devote themselves to others.

For all four of these novelists, different as they are, feminine altruism creates a moral issue. It is "good" to help others, "bad" to be selfish and vain. Although the consequences of action are emotional as well as moral, the dominant assumption of such novels as have been examined is that conduct can and should be *judged*.

Virginia Woolf, writing in the late twenties, investigates from an aesthetic rather than a moral point of view the woman whose vocation is taking care of others. *To the Lighthouse* recognizes the existence of various forms of feminine activity. Juxtaposing Lily Briscoe, an aspiring artist, with Mrs. Ramsay, contented mother of eight children, it uses the juxtaposition for analogy as well as contrast. Mrs. Woolf creates a metaphysics of female altruism; in the process she declares the irrelevance of moralizing about what women should and should not do.

What my students said about *To the Lighthouse* often

had little to do with the book: this was the most interesting aspect of their response. They took Mrs. Ramsay as a sort of inkblot, seeing in her the shapes of their own anxieties, the shape of the woman they feared to be. They found her power sinister, saw her as a puppeteer, were unable to believe in her real feeling for her husband. Why is Mrs. Ramsay such a troubling figure?

It is true, of course, that she manipulates others, is an incurable matchmaker and plotter. The fairy tale she reads to her son in the novel's early scenes is "The Fisherman and His Wife," a story about a woman's need for power: given a magic flounder, the fisherman's wife wants ever more, until she finds herself with nothing, having yearned at last for divine status. Mrs. Ramsay's own desires seem, from most points of view, hardly excessive. She wants happiness around her—certainly a benign wish. In the service of that happiness, she would like to change the weather: if stormy skies interfere with her son's long-anticipated trip to the lighthouse, she will declare in the face of all evidence the possibility that the day will be fine, enraging her husband, with his philosophic commitment to truth. That commitment seems to her a horrible "outrage of human decency" when it involves pursuing truth "with such astonishing lack of consideration for other people's feelings." Feelings, to her, are far more important than truth.

The declaration that feeling is more vital than truth, that the family's happiness should supersede all other goals, conceals presumption not unlike that of the fisherman's wife. Mrs. Ramsay, too, yearns to go beyond human limitations. Her yearning is focused on others, at least one of whom, Mr. Carmichael, sees its sinister aspects.

Mr. Carmichael is an ambiguous figure. Declared to be a poet, he is an old man in the background at the beginning and the end of the narrative. He hardly speaks, he only exists. But he is Mrs. Ramsay's antagonist, simply because he refuses to be helped. Mrs. Ramsay suffers from the sense "when Mr. Carmichael shuffled past, just nod-

ding to her question, with a book beneath his arm, in his
yellow slippers, that she was suspected; and that all this
desire of hers to give, to help, was vanity. For her own
self-satisfaction was it that she wished so instinctively to
help, to give, that people might say of her, 'O Mrs.
Ramsay!dear Mrs. Ramsay ... Mrs. Ramsay, of course!'
and need her and send for her and admire her?" Toward
the end of the novel, Lily reiterates the point, recalling
how Mrs. Ramsay would try to get Carmichael to declare
a want she could gratify, and how he resisted her by refusing to want. "There was some quality in her which he
did not much like. It was perhaps her masterfulness ..."

The need to help and the need to control are closely allied—a fact apparent in the characterizations of *Vein of
Iron,* whose author seemed strangely unaware of the connection. Virginia Woolf, on the other hand, is sharply conscious of it. Lily, too, sees and resists the manipulative
aspect of Mrs. Ramsay's desire to help. She knows as if by
instinct that the older woman "could not take her
painting very seriously; she [Lily] was an independent
little creature, and Mrs. Ramsay liked her for it." Mrs.
Ramsay decides that Lily should marry Mr. Bankes, but
Lily succeeds in maintaining instead her primary devotion
to her art, despite her realization that its aesthetic merit is
not great and that it will never be highly valued by others.
And she resents Mrs. Ramsay's effort to control her.

On the other hand, she also responds to her with passionate intensity, aware of the grandeur as well as the
threat in the woman. My students saw the threat, but denied the grandeur: the sophisticated complexity of Virginia Woolf's view is difficult for the young. And perhaps
the absence of clear moral guidelines is difficult, too. *To
the Lighthouse* does not declare itself concerned with feminine goodness; it leaves the question of the good woman's
nature confused. The young yearn for clarity. Although
they resist making moral judgments about one another
(everyone has the right to his own opinion, his own way
of doing things; it may not be *my* way, but it's okay),

they seem comforted by them in literature. And perhaps they are right after all in finding *To the Lighthouse* a disturbing book.

It is a book that makes judgment difficult even when the issues are not moral. As their comments revealed, my students found Mrs. Ramsay's attitude toward her husband particularly perplexing. She declares explicitly that she reveres him; yet the inadequacy of that statement as a description of her feelings is manifest. "She had the whole of the other sex under her protection; for reasons she could not explain, for their chivalry and valour, for the fact that they negotiated treaties, ruled India, controlled finance; finally for an attitude towards herself which no woman could fail to feel or to find agreeable, something trustful, childlike, reverential . . ." A student suggested that Mrs. Ramsay's reverence for her husband was a reverence for competence; but in fact she finds masculine competence a reason for protectiveness, not for admiration. "She pitied men always as if they lacked something—women never, as if they had something." Giving her husband "of her own free will what she knew he would never ask," Mrs. Ramsay calls to him, goes to him: "For he wished, she knew, to protect her." Masculine protectiveness, even masculine reverence toward woman is, from the point of view of the reverenced and protected woman, cause for reciprocal protectiveness. The woman's psychic triumph comes from responding to man's needs. Men always, from the feminine point of view, lack something. Fundamentally, they lack understanding, are simple creatures even in their intellectual accomplishments; and they must have something, someone, to protect. So the wise, benevolent, controlling woman, the eternal mother, who comprehends even if she cannot communicate the meaning of experience, in her mind reduces all masculine accomplishment to the level of child's games. She is never openly contemptuous, only patronizing; she does what is expected of her, functions vigorously—to my students' dismay—as "perfect hostess," making everyone happy, but realizing at every point exactly what is going on.

All this with a mind totally untrained, with only emotional capacities, no skills, no genius except at human relationships.

She is an impossible fictional model for young women of today; but a model they have trouble rejecting with sufficient vigor to feel safe; a very old-fashioned woman, inhabiting a novel that places her side by side with more up-to-date figures and allows her to reduce them to helplessness.

Lily, firmly choosing another way of life, is the only character who seems to have a full sense of what Mrs. Ramsay is like. Long after Mrs. Ramsay's death, Lily realizes the extent of her giving, and of the demands that her husband has made on her; by extension, of the demands all men make of all women. What men want, she realizes, is sympathy. "Look at him, he seemed to be saying, look at me; and indeed, all the time he was feeling, Think of me, think of me . . . A woman, she had provoked this horror; a woman, she should have known how to deal with it. It was immensely to her discredit, sexually, to stand there dumb." "That man, she thought, her anger rising in her, never gave; that man took. She, on the other hand, would be forced to give. Mrs. Ramsay had given. Giving, giving, giving, she had died—and had left all this." It is with great effort that Lily brings herself to praise Mr. Ramsay's boots, thus giving him what he seeks: admiration, that version of sympathy particularly acceptable to men when offered by women. For her it is difficult to offer such praise; and she remembers seeing on Mrs. Ramsay's face at such moments "the glow, the rhapsody, the self-surrender," and realizing that the giving of sympathy evidently conferred on such women "the most supreme bliss of which human nature was capable." It is a bliss she cannot feel herself, a mystery at the heart of Mrs. Ramsay, and of the novel she inhabits.

Mrs. Ramsay's small son, James, also recognizes his father's endless demand for sympathy. Watching his mother fill it, he sees that she seems "to pour erect into the air a rain of energy, a column of spray, looking at the same time animated and alive as if all her energies were being fused into force, burning and illuminating . . . , and into this delicious fecundity, this fountain and spray of life, the fatal sterility of the male plunged itself, like a beak of brass, barren and bare. He wanted sympathy."

This insistent natural imagery (repeated in three passages) evokes and helps to define the mystery. It suggests the doubleness of the feminine response—the degree to which the demand that drains the woman's energy also creates it. It declares Mrs. Ramsay's role as provide of "illumination" for her family and friends. Most important, it indicates the degree to which the woman's taking care of others, in this novel's mythology, is a manifestation of natural force. The point is not, as in *Vein of Iron*, that women are naturally good or noble or even enduring; rather, that their responsiveness to others, their capacity to offer help and sympathy, may be an essentially impersonal flowering of their natures, a manifestation of their own needs, not merely a reaction to others. (The charwomen's rescue of the decaying house is a more mundane version of the same pattern.) The masculine role, given this interpretation, remains problematical. James's angry perception of his father as arid, metallic, destructive, is not necessarily accurate. If woman's taking care is a natural force, it must follow that man's need for care is equally a part of the order of things; and Mrs. Ramsay's attitude toward men suggests this view. The light-house, which from a distance seems a glamorous, soft, "feminine" source of illumination, and from close up presents itself as stern, phallic, unambiguously black and white, unites masculine and feminine symbolism; the Ramsay marriage—in which Mrs. Ramsay's love for her husband is in fact indubitable, although complicated—is a comparable union, which appears to represent the highest form of human fulfillment.

But that leaves the question of Lily: What is the value of her kind of effort and achievement?

An ultimate value judgment, once more, is impossible; but clearly the artistic endeavor is also vital, it too embodies natural expressiveness, although it too demands great energy and striving. And clearly the significance of the endeavor has little to do with the quality of the results. Mrs. Ramsay devotes herself to her children's welfare; two of these children die shortly after she does. But the truncation of their lives in no way denies the quality of her care for them; and the fact that Lily's painting "would be hung in the servants' bedrooms. It would be rolled up and stuffed under a sofa" is of comparable irrelevance. What matters is the quality of *her* care, her attentiveness to the "space" she creates, to the "truth," the "reality" that she is trying to render. She attempts to bring order to her experience by depicting it; Mrs. Ramsay gives order to her experience by offering love. As she reads to her little boy, Mr. Bankes feels that "barbarity was tamed, the reign of chaos subdued." Serving the boeuf en daube, Mrs. Ramsay realizes that "there is a coherence in things, a stability"—expressed for her in being a hostess. Life is full of small illuminations; and Lily realizes finally that Mrs. Ramsay and she equally communicate its meaning. "Mrs. Ramsay saying, 'Life stand still here'; Mrs. Ramsay making of the moment something permanent (as in another sphere Lily herself tried to make of the moment something permanent)—this was of the nature of a revelation. In the midst of chaos there was shape; this eternal passing and flowing (she looked at the clouds going and the leaves shaking) was struck into stability."

The feminine function, then, this novel suggests, is to give form to experience. It is an aesthetic formulation of what earlier novelists considered a moral issue; but a formulation that can be applied, with surprising accuracy, to the activities of a Gaskell heroine or an Ellen Glasgow lady. Mrs. Ramsay as heroine and Lily Briscoe as subheroine suggest a powerful justification for the feminine habit of taking care of others. It is a way of thinking that, avoiding the social and moral issues implicit in women's self-subordination, recognizes the effective power of apparent humility, suggests that the repressions implicit in self-sacrifice may provide rich sources of energy and fulfillment, and that the choice of "family" or "career," when social conditions make such choice possible for women, may be a choice between different versions of identical experience.

Four

THE ADOLESCENT
AS HEROINE

Boys grow up and have to kill their fathers,
girls can be made to understand their place.

—SALLY KEMPTON

What is the girl's proper place?

"Before marriage a young girl was brought up to be perfectly innocent and sexually ignorant," Martha Vicinus writes of nineteenth-century England. "The predominant ideology of the age insisted that she have little sexual feeling at all, although family affection and the desire for motherhood were considered innate." That ideology had survived virtually unchanged for several hundred years. Innocence and ignorance are the virtues of young fictional heroines throughout the early years of the novel's development; and if Pamela's "innocence" is slightly suspect, her tears and faintings and strange lapses of awareness apparently tactical on occasion, one can never be quite sure how fully Samuel Richardson understood this fact. Woman writers, on the other hand, were often strikingly conscious of the ambiguities of adolescent innocence. They depict girls who understand their subordinate place but also understand how to exploit its hidden opportunities.

Adolescence, that notoriously difficult time of life, appears also to be a difficult subject for fiction. The female variety offers special perplexities. Some emerge, for example, in *The Mill on the Floss*, which presents Maggie's adolescence as a period of intense conflict occurring between the semi-articulate miseries of her childhood and the unsatisfactory resolution of her brief young adulthood. Writers who concentrate on the adolescent heroine (there are not a great many of them) confront tangled psychic issues. In adolescence, the woman makes her crucial

145

choices—the choices that must precede her working out of the ambiguities of dependency, her commitment to "taking care." Marriage, obviously, is the "normal" conclusion, the orthodox way for a girl to declare herself adult. Is adolescence, then, the young woman's single period of freedom, released from the restrictions of childhood, not yet experiencing those of wifehood and maternity? Only in fantasy— and the clash of fantasy and reality is intense at this time of life.

If conflict is the essence of fiction, adolescence provides rich material. The severe opposition of fantasy and reality in this stage of life derives partly from the adolescent's central problem: to find the proper balance between self and others. The self can dwell in fantasy, but others represent unevadable reality. To discover the right relation between the individual consciousness and the world outside, a problem by no means confined to the female sex, may be especially difficult for girls because of the pressures women in Western society endure to orient themselves toward the needs of others: a denial rather than a resolution of conflict. Maggie Tulliver's "vocation" for loving solves none of her problems; it only makes her extraordinarily vulnerable to the social pressures (often disguised as moral or religious) directed at her sex. Young women with other vocations, those who have yet to discover their vocations, experience other avatars of her conflict. Fictional presentations of their dilemmas often convey a sense of hopelessness. Any adolescent is likely to feel, in bad moments, that there's no place to go. Women have particular reasons for feeling so. In many ways, they are not encouraged to grow up. Admiration and indulgence may reward their extension into their chronological maturity of the narcissism, irresponsibility, unpredictability of their adolescence. To call a grown-up woman "cute," in some circles, connotes approval. A woman may come to believe that lack of thought is her only viable recourse; to think about adulthood is to confront despair. Again, the same feelings occur in men; but the external evidence to justify despair seems more largely apparent for women.

These generalizations about adolescence might be based upon observation of the teenagers who populate our universities (and our homes), but in fact they derive directly from eighteenth-, nineteenth-, and twentieth-century novels about young women. The notion, for example, that narcissism is the hallmark of adolescence long predated modern psychological theory; earlier fiction consistently explores the ways in which young women exploit, escape, transcend, or merely struggle with their narcissistic impulses. The problems of adolescent women are those of all women writ large. The continuities and diversities with which their patterns of conflict or despair shape novels of adolescence delineate vividly some crucial female dilemmas.

One problem is how and whether to relinquish the advantages of childhood. Jane Austen—to start with a complicated example—clearly believes that it's a good thing to grow up. Yet her adolesscent heroines, battling with their own impulses and with the social permissions that encourage female regressiveness, pay lip service to the values of maturity while clinging to some privileges of the child. Paradoxically, their childishness disguises itself behind a plausible adult façade. Elizabeth Bennet, at the beginning of *Pride and Prejudice*, seems a self-assured young woman; she is less sure of herself at the end—but she has grown up.

Jane Austen's heroines are the first in English fiction to undergo serious moral change. Moll Flanders remains reprobate, despite her protestations, from beginning to end; Clarissa never deviates from her virtue, even given severe inner conflict. Pamela expands in personality but does not alter; Fanny Burney's Evelina and Cecilia follow similar patterns. But Elizabeth Bennet's inner life changes; her new knowledge, of herself and of the world, affects her way of being as well as of acting. She finds a personal answer to the large questions implicit in the superficialities of her social world: particularly, the tempting superficialities of marriage.

Jane Austen's central characters are girls on the brink of full citizenship in the social world. They display various degrees of foolishness, believing in ghosts because they've read too many Gothic romances, interfering frivolously in the lives of others, failing to discriminate properly between real and apparent value. Eventually they get married: success not because it's a socially acceptable course, but because marriage genuinely marks—for them though not for everybody—their relinquishment or subdual of their childishness. The task of the adolescent is to put adolescence behind her. The Austen heroines, marked by their spirit and enterprise, their capacity to stand alone if necessary, may actively defy social convention in fulfilling this task; their acceptance of conformity is never automatic. True, their sexual feelings, unspecified, may be assumed to exist only beneath the level of consciousness; true, they never behave with a degree of impropriety that would catapult them out of their proper social sphere. But they are not ignorant or required to appear so, and their presumed sexual innocence does not prevent them from developing considerable knowledge of the world, including the world of sexual misconduct and danger.

Are they, then, really disguised adults in the first place? I think not; Elizabeth struggles with her narcissism, needs to please others and rebels against the need, suffers from self-consciousness and exaggerated embarrassments; and survives all these feelings to learn humility and restraint as well as the full value of self-assertion. In short, she survives the complexities of adolescence as a transitional stage in a complex and rigidly rule-bound social context.

Pride and Prejudice centers on marriage. In the society it depicts, marriage measures a woman's success; mothers value themselves for marrying off their daughters; girls value themselves and are valued for their ability to attract and hold eligible men. Bad marriages are thought preferable to no marriage at all. Charlotte Lucas accepts the proposal of the ridiculous Mr. Collins: "Without thinking highly either of men or matrimony, marriage had always been her object; it was the only honourable provision for well-educated young women of small fortune, and however uncertain of giving happiness, must be their pleasantest preservative from want." Her parents and her siblings are delighted; Mrs. Bennet envies her good fortune; Elizabeth alone explicitly questions the advantages of such a match. Elizabeth's frivolous sister Lydia elopes with worthless Wickham; after considerable intervention by family and friends, her lover consents to marry her. Even this match of "a couple who were only brought together because their passions were stronger than their virtue" leaves Mrs. Bennet overjoyed, though several wiser observers this time display some skepticism. But Mrs. Bennet is not alone in her folly; general assumption testifies that any marriage is better than none. Men are assumed to be more reluctant than women to embark on matrimony, women the covert or overt pursuers. The drama of female existence centers on the effort to achieve and maintain marriage as an index of social status, financial security, and moral virtue.

Yet the universally acknowledged truth "that a single man in possession of a good fortune must be in want of a wife" (a truth acknowledged, in fact, mainly by women, those guardians of social continuity) conceals a deeper truth which *Pride and Prejudice* gradually uncovers. The goal of the novel's characters is to make a good marriage, for themselves or for others. Even Mr. Bennet, that pattern of passivity, seems willing to exert himself a bit when he fears his favorite daughter may have accepted the wrong man. He would not go to any trouble to engineer a better match, but his knowledge of bad marriage is profound and he recognizes, more acutely than most, what is at stake in the choice of a spouse. The novel depicts characters at many levels of awareness, but all share the correct perception that marriage is a vital matter, though many also share the mistaken assumption that its primary significance is financial or hedonistic. In fact marriage focuses a concern perhaps more important even than love, one which not even Elizabeth fully recognizes. Marriage can be, and usually is, a particularly useful way of fulfilling the fundamental human need to discover and assert one's value.

To define one's value, discover identity, is a traditional undertaking of adolescence, made more difficult by the fact that many nominal adults have not achieved it. This is a truth of life and of literature. The shape of Jane Austen's novels often derives from clashes between those struggling to grow up and those struggling not to; in *Pride and Prejudice* no significant adult embodies achieved maturity by the standards the novel implies (the Gardiners probably do, but their function in the plot does not vividly stress the point), and Elizabeth flounders in her adolescence, as Maggie Tulliver was to do, without adequate external guides.

She sees around her the different levels at which marriage can seal self-worth. Lydia and Charlotte of course exemplify the most superficial. Lydia values herself for her sexual power and the gaiety which contributes to it; getting her man proves her capacity. Wickham, equally shallow in his self-valuation, also sustains his self-assessment by the success of his charm in solving his financial problems through marriage. Charlotte values herself for her good sense and her adaptability. Although her "good sense" in this instance seems to the wise observer a version of folly, she feels her ability to make the best of things in marriage as a public testimony of her value. Her husband, with an even simpler sense of his own importance, believes his worth testified by the mere fact that a woman, *any* woman, has consented to be his permanent audience. Elizabeth's elder sister, Jane, a model of goodness but precarious in self-esteem, feels notably bolstered when the highly eligible Bingley proposes to her. Bingley has a comparable problem: when Darcy suggests that Jane does not care for him, he is readily convinced that he must have deceived himself in believing that he has won her love.

In Elizabeth (and probably Darcy as well, though we're not allowed to know as much about his inner workings) the question of self-worth is more complicated, and more closely examined: linked with the problem of appearance, not physical makeup but social impression, and involving the determination of how much and in what ways one can properly please others. The sense of personal value, in other words, which marriage corroborates and sustains, depends partly on the establishment of an appropriate relation between internal and external demands: a special version of the universal adolescent dilemma about self and others.

Elizabeth's personal independence, defining her specialness, seems at first to exempt her from the obligation to be pleasing. She sets off in the mud on a three-mile walk to see her cold-ridden sister, arriving with untidy hair and dirty petticoat to win the hearty disapproval of the Bingley ladies for her "abominable sort of conceited independence, a most country town indifference to decorum." This disapproval troubles her not at all. She satisfies the minimal demands of decorum during her visit, but devotes her attention mainly to expressing her genuine feelings for Jane. Not caring about the Bingley women, she doesn't care to please them. Similarly, when Darcy rejects her as a dancing partner, on the ground that she is "not handsome enough to tempt *me*," she makes of the episode a funny story for her friends, feeling that the man has made himself ridiculous, not seriously challenged in her own self-esteem. Her failure in pleasing—that central feminine obligation—troubles her only slightly. The point becomes explicit when, a fellow-guest of Darcy at Bingley's, she notes him looking at her. "She could only imagine . . . that she drew his notice because there was a something about her more wrong and reprehensible, according to his ideas of right, than in any other person present. The supposition did not pain her. She liked him too little to care for his approbation."

The danger Elizabeth fears in pleasing others is that of losing her self. She sees that the will to please is often an aspect of hypocrisy. Bingley's sisters shape their every response to their notion of its effect; they are very different when there is no one to impress. Pleasing is a means toward power or prestige. Or the commitment to pleasing can amount to a denial of the deeper self, as in Lydia, who, presenting herself as all composed of delightful surfaces, ends up being no more. Elizabeth appeals in vain to her father to stimulate in his younger daughters some impulse beyond the desire for admiration, seeing the danger that Lydia will be, "from the ignorance and emptiness of her mind, wholly unable to ward off any portion of that universal contempt which her rage for admiration will excite." That contempt will punish total yielding to the will to please is a truth vivid to Elizabeth. Guarding herself from the trap of pleasing, she is less conscious of the trap at the opposite extreme.

For narcissism can express itself as forcefully in refusal to please as in ceaseless search for approval. Elizabeth, self-protective in her refusals, is also arrogant. Her "prejudice," which makes it difficult for her to discern Darcy's merit, cuts her off from full experience. Darcy emerges as her precise counterpart (she takes a long time to realize this), although she finds his weaknesses readily recognizable—one of them his lack of a gift for pleasing. From an early authorial comment on the friendship between Bingley and Darcy, we learn that "Bingley was sure of being liked wherever he appeared, Darcy was continually giving offence." His offensiveness derives from his inflexibility, part of that pride which Elizabeth professes herself unable to laugh at because it is too serious a defect, amounting to "a propensity to hate everybody." *Her* defect, Darcy retorts, "is wilfully to misunderstand them." Both descriptions, though limited and exaggerated, suggest accurately the self-protective and self-exalting aspects of the two modes of defense. Elizabeth preserves her rather elevated self-assessment by refusing to admit challenges. Although her willingness to laugh at herself as well as others seems flexibility, it too belongs to her rigid defensive structure. She laughs, like her father, in order not to have to understand, her failure to understand amounting to an unwillingness to change.

Events force understanding upon her: such is the process of growth. She realizes that she too can be deceived: Wickham has had all the appearance of goodness, Darcy the reality. Her proud consciousness of her own high standards (she feels it an act of integrity to judge Charlotte's marriage without charity) and incomparable inner resources (only her elder sister has sufficient "rectitude and delicacy" to be a worthy companion) must be modified by the knowledge that standards may not comprise a sufficient guide to conduct—they keep one from going too far wrong but do not assure doing right. She has been afraid to take into account the reality, the power, the necessity of feeling.

Lydia's melodrama once more comments on Elizabeth's drama. The slave of every passing feeling, Lydia indulges feeling so readily that her emotions lack vitality and continuity. Elizabeth, believing in "control," eager to contemplate her own feelings as a kind of spectacle but reluctant to take them seriously, long fails to recognize, much less to indulge, her emotions. A sharp observer of the world outside herself, in which Lydia sees only officers or the absence of officers, she can regulate her conduct by social demands (she behaves impeccably on her visit to the Collinses) or defy them when they impinge too sharply on her self-esteem (even on that visit, she refuses to yield to the impertinences of Lady Catherine's cross-examination). But she does not fully acknowledge the world within. Her own formulation of how she has changed, as the action draws toward a close, focuses on this fact. "Had I been in love, I could not have been more wretchedly blind. . . . Till this moment I never knew myself." Her blindness continues:

153

one can be sure that any claims to self-knowledge in an Austen character will have an ironic edge. Elizabeth doesn't yet know that she *is* in love. But her new awareness of the necessity and difficulty of self-knowledge leads her to fuller self-encounters. As Lydia's "infamy" overtakes her, we learn that Elizabeth, "by this time tolerably well acquainted with her own feelings," now understands that her repugnance at her sister's course derives not only from high standards but from sheer self-interest, her intense, newly admitted desire to marry Darcy.

Recognition of her feelings thus increases her vulnerability. Her sense of general superiority (even in the case of Jane, whom she admires, Elizabeth's respect for her sister's "goodness" is modified by belief in her own superior wisdom, attested by her capacity to laugh) can no longer protect her against her increasing desire to please. At Pemberley, "more than commonly anxious to please, she naturally suspected that every power of pleasing would fail her"; the next day, she yearns "to make herself agreeable to all." Darcy, too, shows himself newly "desirous to please." Both readily fulfill their desires. But Elizabeth's wish to please amounts to another experience of vulnerability, attended as it is by a new fear of failure. Her developing capacity to accept her own feelings necessarily weakens her defenses: no longer can she simply laugh at a world which may threaten her purposes. Lady Catherine seems not merely ridiculous when she demands that Elizabeth yield all claim to Darcy; she must be defied with the power of Elizabeth's admitted anger, not teased or mocked. When Darcy makes himself a tempting target for laughter, Elizabeth resists the temptation, attesting her changed condition by the fact that she has grown beyond her father. "Elizabeth longed to observe that Mr. Bingley had been a most delightful friend; so easily guided that his worth was invaluable; but she checked herself. She remembered that he had yet to learn to be laughed at, and it was rather too early to begin." Her awareness of her own powerful feelings has made her more subtly conscious of the feelings of others. For the rational principles of control that earlier guided her, the rectitude of her standards, the solidity of her self-esteem, she substitutes a new tentativeness, a flexibility which demands individual emotional response to individual situations, a new basis for self-valuation.

The self whose value she will assert in marriage is in part a new self, created by as well as creating the possibility of her union with Darcy. Like other Austen heroines, Elizabeth has spelled out a paradigm of adolescent potential fulfilled. Trying to deal with the new feelings belonging to these transitional years, she triumphantly confronts them at last without the aid of rigid defenses. At the novel's end she and Darcy both transcend solipsism, uniting not only in their love for one another but in mutual love for the Gardiners, who helped to bring them together. Their marriage, a commitment of dual self-assertion, rests not on the young woman's subordination or professions of innocence but on her developed awareness, her growing knowledge of reality, the counterpart of her husband's. Jane Austen demonstrates the possibility of a girl's discovering the positive advantages of maturity over childishness, even in a society whose rigidities offer protection to the continued immaturity characteristic of most of its members.

"Emma Woodhouse, handsome, clever, and rich, with a comfortable home and happy disposition, seemed to unite some of the best blessings of existence; and had lived nearly twenty-one years in the world with very little to distress or vex her." *Emma*, too, tells of a late adolescent who needs to grow up. Her problems and her solutions differ from Elizabeth Bennet's, although she too moves by a devious route to marriage. But marriage does not in this novel measure all value. Although the encompassing society supplies the rules which every participant violates at cost ("What did she say?—Just what she ought, of course. A lady always does"), the characters now seek psychological rather than social security. As Emma explains to Harriet, "I have none of the usual inducements of women to marry.... Fortune I do not want; employment I do not want; consequence I do not want." To be an old maid, she adds, is a dreadful fate only for the poor: "It is poverty only which makes celibacy contemptible to a generous public." She herself both has and anticipates adequate social status, money, occupation, and she admits no unfulfilled emotional needs, claiming that her nephews and nieces will supply sufficient outlet for her capacity to love.

Marriage as a social necessity is thus dismissed, the dismissal reinforced by occasional authorial comments implying that it has been reduced, like other important matters, to a merely social fact. "Human nature is so well disposed towards those who are in interesting situations, that a young person, who either marries or dies, is sure of being kindly spoken of." By marriage one pays one's social dues. Mr. Elton becomes a much more interesting figure when he brings home a bride; the bride glories in the status and authority made hers by a simple exchange of vows. The strongest opponent of marriage is the selfish Mr. Woodhouse, a hater of change for whom "matrimony, as the origin of change, was always disagreeable"; he never stops referring to his married daughter as "poor Isabella," and Emma's former governess remains "poor Miss Taylor" to him even after she has given birth to a daughter. If the Eltons demonstrate the possible selfishness of marriage, each barely aware of the other as a sentient individual, Emma's father reveals the possible selfishness of opposition to marriage. Is his daughter equally self-indulgent in her complacent assertions of invulnerability? Certainly her apparent concern, in the long speech to Harriet, focuses on a limited view of her own self-interest. She is unwilling to imagine admitting another into her comfortable world, in which she possesses all the power ("I believe few married women are half as much mistress of their husband's house, as I am of Hartfield; and never, never could I expect to be so truly beloved and important; so always first and always

156

right in any man's eyes as I am in my father's"). On the other hand, she welcomes the irresponsible extension of her sway implicit in the possibility that a handsome young man may be in love with her. Given Emma's theoretical opposition to marriage, the expansion of personality necessary to make hers possible is more dramatic than Elizabeth Bennet's change of heart. Emma must learn to transcend her own kind of selfishness, which resembles her father's (Austen contemplates some subtle forms of heredity), without allowing herself to relax into partnership in dual self-congratulation, the more destructive selfishness of the Eltons. Her marriage, achieved as a result of moral insight, will itself constitute a moral discipline. Despite the heroine's comparative social freedom, *Emma* offers a more rigorous version of female possibility than *Pride and Prejudice*.

It also supplies a yet more delicate apprehension than the earlier novel of the intricacies of adolescent self-love, which feeds on every experience, yet supplies only precarious protection against the dangers to confidence inherent in a world of other people. Maturity remains the relevant standard, but the novel demonstrates once more how rarely and precariously anyone achieves it. Fools are even more abundant here than in *Pride and Prejudice*. Although the author may deal with them lovingly—displaying considerable affection for ridiculous Mr. Woodhouse, prosy Miss Bates—she unerringly recognizes their follies, hardened forms of adolescent weakness surviving indefinitely. Benign Miss Bates is governed by good intentions; Emma justifies severe rebuke by mocking her. Yet her relentless absorption with the minutiae of her existence recapitulates and parodies the self-absorption that distorts Emma's perspective. Various forms of self-concern emerge: Mr. Woodhouse's insistence that his guests eat only gruel because he's found it the best fare, John Knightley's unwillingness to participate in social gatherings, Harriet's rapid progress from one imaginary lover to another, Frank Churchill's thoughtless donation of a piano, Mrs. Churchill's exploitation of ill health. It is the vice of both sexes, all ages; but the paragon figure of Mr. Knightley— "George," his name turns out to be, used only once: so completely is he the adult that he's always "Mister"— demonstrates that proper discipline in youth may produce fully controlled self-love in maturity: there is at least one genuine adult in this novel. Always giving enough, never too much, weight to the needs and desires of others, he acts as model and mentor to youthful Emma.

The moral scheme of *Emma* may seem almost uninterestingly transparent. The process by which the heroine moves from self-will to humility, submitting finally to Knightley's guidance (he is some sixteen years older than she) and testifying to the good effects of his previous instruction, seems implicit in the moral problem lucidly defined on the first page: "The real evils indeed of Emma's situation were the power of having rather too much her own way, and a disposition to think a little too well of herself." By the novel's end, her lover has substituted for herself as the focus of her esteem: "she had never been more sensible of Mr. Knightley's high superiority of character. The happiness of this most happy day, received its completion, in the animated contemplation of his worth." All very simple, and rather uncomfortably limited, with its apparent assumption of the natural superiority of men. But the psychological dimensions of Emma's situation and her solution, more complicated than they appear, reveal that though moral laws may be simple, moral experience is always complex.

Both Emma's methods and her purpose suggest an intricate view of the relation between the individual woman and her context. Despite the considerable freedom of her actual situation, beloved only child of a nonauthoritarian father, uncontrolled by mother or companion, chief arbiter of her social circle, possessed of money, independence, and self-esteem—despite her literal freedom, Emma lives in fantasy: the traditional outlet of adolescents, who even under ideal conditions lack the strength, the knowledge, the imaginative scope to create effects in the real world congruent with their feeling of their own importance. Emma, an "imaginist," submits to "the power of fancy and whim" in all her dealings with others. For example, consider her way of embarking upon the relation with Harriet Smith. Harriet's "proper and becoming ... deference" to her readily convinces Emma "that she must have good sense and deserve encouragement." Possessed by delight in her own version of reality, she becomes a more than usually dedicated hostess, "with the real good-will of a mind delighted with its own ideas." Her plans for improving Harriet's mind never get very far: "It was ... much pleasanter to let her imagination range and work at Harriet's fortune, than to be labouring to enlarge her comprehension or exercise it on sober facts." The pleasurable ease of imaginative activity, as opposed to the arduousness of effort toward accomplishment, repeatedly lures Emma back toward her special world view, which perceives a rich population of others, but manufactures their natures in response to immediate psychic needs. Emma's version of Jane Fairfax, an exact contemporary forced by circumstance to accomplish instead of only dream about accomplishment, defines Jane solely by her "reserve," antithetical to Emma's own openness. For Emma, Frank Churchill is only her admirer, responsive to her alone; Mrs. Weston is her beloved Miss Taylor translated to a sphere that provides her no pretext to interfere with Emma's self-will; Miss Bates is simply a source of boredom: Emma never stresses the "universal good will and contented temper" noted by the narrator. It requires Knightley to point out that Miss Bates has a separate identity, a defined although lowly social position, feelings of her own; events disabuse Emma about the others. Emma's acceptance of Knightley as lover implies her relinquishment of fantasy.

But Austen suggests that Emma's commitment to the operations of her own imagination has contributed vitally to her growing up. Fantasy has supplied, first of all, the pleasure of self-indulgence: an innocent enough delight, despite its occasionally destructive effects on others. Fantasy allows for expansion of the personality, providing a secret sphere of possibility in which the young woman cut off by social restriction from full public expressiveness can test her nature in interior dialogue, interior exploration—not exploration of the self, necessarily; but imaginative investigation of others. True, Emma almost always errs in assessments based on such investigation, wrong about everyone and everything, more blind and ignorant than Elizabeth Bennet. From Knightley's point of view, wrong results discredit the activity that produces them; but Jane Austen perhaps feels less undivided. The action of the novel points to Emma's development as derived partly from her mistakes. Her real moral superiority to Jane Fairfax depends on her greater daring—she dares to use her imagination as a guide to reality to discipline it by conjunction with reality, then to use it again. Her mistake in leading Harriet to "love" Elton has results less potentially disastrous for her than her later accidental encouragement of the girl's adoration of Knightley, but the second error is genuinely accidental, not willful: she has learned to interfere less.

The life of fantasy also serves important defensive functions. It guards Emma from confrontation with the essential dullness of her limited life, creating compensatory interest; it substitutes for genuine accomplishment and reduces the necessity of recognizing her limitations of achievement; it makes possible a more attractive self-assessment than Emma might otherwise manage, and protects her from the shattering recognition of inadequacy. It provides bases for relationship where none might otherwise exist. All these functions must be relinquished so that Emma may grow; Knightley speaks against them all. But all have been necessary to her full development. She does not submit to reality until reality has become attractive enough to submit to—until a real lover can replace the figment of her fancy, and she can yield false relationships for a single true one.

Like Elizabeth Bennet, Emma formulates her internal change as an increase in self-knowledge. She recognizes her "blunders" and "blindness" of head and heart, perceiving "that she had been imposed on by others in a most mortifying degree; that she had been imposing on herself in a degree yet more mortifying. . . . To understand, thoroughly understand her own heart, was the first endeavour." She realizes that she's never cared for Frank Churchill: "This was the knowledge of herself . . . which she reached." Life, she believes, can hold no more pleasure for her, but pleasure is no longer her chief desideratum. She wishes, rather, to be "more rational, more acquainted with herself." The two ideas go together: an acceptance of the desirable supremacy of reason over imagination will lead to fuller perception of truth, about the self and the world. The acceptance of rationality, in Emma's case, also leads to redefinition of her goals; and, paradoxically, to a fuller commitment to feeling.

If the characters of *Pride and Prejudice* share a desire to assert the self, seeing the chief possibility of self-assertion in marriage, those in *Emma* unite in their drive to achieve command—a slightly more complex motivation. Marriage, though a possible means to this end, is not necessarily the best one. But the theme of domination pervades the society here depicted even in its nonmatrimonial aspects. With painful insistence people use whatever means they have available—beauty, vapidity, money, illness, parenthood—to assert their power over others. Miss Bates possesses some power in the world, despite her lack of social status: her endless talking forces others to respond, or to find the means of not responding. Mr. Woodhouse, in all his gentleness, shapes the plans of others: they cannot eat outdoors, for example, if he is to be present; and it seems, briefly, impossible for his daughter to marry; it *is* impossible for her to leave him. Mr. Elton is powerful simply by his sex: he feels sought after, and glories in the feeling. People gain power through their refusals (John Knightley, Jane Fairfax) even when they also suffer social disapproval. Hardly an act committed in the course of the novel cannot be understood as part of a struggle for ascendancy in which the stakes may be minute but the motivation no less passionate for that.

An acceptable source of female power is beauty. At a time in her life when self-love is particularly dominant, a young woman might be expected to rely heavily on, a resource that emphasizes the kind of value she can hope to have in her society. Harriet does exactly this, and rather effectively. She loves to "sit and smile and look pretty, and say nothing"; Emma emphasizes the power of her beauty and her use of it. "Till it appears that men are much more philosophic on the subject of beauty than they are generally supposed; till they do fall in love with well-informed minds instead of handsome faces, a girl, with such loveliness as Harriet, has a certainty of being admired and sought after, of having the power of choosing from among many." Knightley, warning against the encouragement of vanity, insists that beauty doesn't matter as much as Emma believes, but Emma knows that it does. She hears the world debating whether the new Mrs. Elton is a little pretty, very pretty, or not pretty at all: a crucial issue in determining her effective status. She participates with Frank in discussion of exactly how beautiful Jane Fairfax is; if he won't admire her beauty he doesn't acknowledge her power. Emma is "loveliness itself" (Mrs. Weston's characterization), and Knightley sounds like a curmudgeon in assessing how much vanity accompanies such beauty, or in equating her status as "pretty young woman" with that of "spoiled child."

But as usual Knightley speaks sense. To rely on beauty as the source of command is to accept passivity and encourage simple narcissism. Emma is more ambitious. Her encouraging Harriet to rely on her beauty is a form of condescension. She herself will engage more actively in the effort toward mastery. Her life situation helps her: motherless, for many years mistress of her father's house, she has developed habits of controlling others, her semi-orphanage in her own fantasy almost a cause for envy rather than sympathy. Supporting the habit of control is her pleasure in her skill at manipulating others, apparent in all her relationships except the one with Knightley. She "handles" her father and has "handled" her governess; she plans to mold Harriet, to marry off Mr. Elton, to circumvent Miss Bates, foil Robert Martin, titillate Frank Churchill; other lives seem at her disposal. We may see in all this further operation of her active fantasy, but Emma's penchant for command is by no means entirely a matter of fantasy. Her intelligence, wit, charm, claimed authority, enable her often to manipulate others quite effectively. If they sometimes evade her—being, after all, human beings with minds of their own, not merely projections of Emma's needs—they seldom fail to offer at least a bit of satisfactory testimony to Emma's effectual force.

When that force turns to cruelty, in the Box Hill episode where Emma, frustrated and unhappy in spite of her position at the center of attention, lashes out at Miss Bates, the time has come for the heroine to understand not only herself, but the proper limits of power. Emma articulates the crucial insight (although she does not understand its full application) in a dialogue with Frank Churchill, part of the charade of flirtation with which she attempts to mask her melancholy. "You are comfortable," she tells him, "because you are under command."

"Your command?—Yes."

"Perhaps I intended you to say so, but I meant self-command. You had, somehow or other, broken bounds yesterday, and run away from your own management; but to-day you are got back again—and as I cannot be always with you, it is best to believe your temper under your own command rather than mine."

Control, command, authority—these words of power can refer to the self as well as to others; Emma has failed to understand this fact. Blithely attempting to extend her sphere of influence, she neglects to be responsible for herself; her reliance on Knightley to tell her when she's wrong indicates her inability to depend on inner guides. (An explicitly made distinction between her and Knightley is that he's always sure he's right, she is much less confident. And not just because of male arrogance: he *is* right, she isn't.) She has to take responsibility for being and for knowing who she is: for knowing herself, among other ways, as a sexual being ("It darted through her, with the speed of an arrow, that Mr. Knightley must marry no one but herself!"), hence, like Elizabeth Bennet, more vulnerable than she has pretended—vulnerable in her feelings (perhaps motherlessness is not such an advantage after all), but capable of knowing those feelings, of using them as a guide to change, and of controlling them, consequently herself, without suppressing them. To "grow more worthy" of the man she loves, she must learn the lessons of her experience. She need not relinquish her desire to command, but she must understand where command properly begins: that true power (Knightley once more the exemplar) starts with self-understanding and self-mastery.

Adolescence as a stage in human development often challenges adult assumptions and continuities. The optimism of Jane Austen's novels, an optimism of challenge, depends on a notion of individual development which makes ridiculous the common level of social assumption about marriage, about personal possibility. Despite the novels' dependence on a firm social structure, they raise quietly revolutionary questions about the usual effects of this structure on individuals. Only great novelists are in this profound sense revolutionary. Fanny Burney (from whom Jane Austen learned a good deal) exemplifies the novelists of adolescence whose conservative imaginations lead them to a deeper pessimism than they seem to realize: pessimism specifically about female possibility. The challenge implied in a woman's adolescence, as such novelists understand it, is only a temporary product of mis-understanding. As the woman grows, she adjusts to the system. Her "growth" leads her back toward childhood; the "happy endings" of Burney novels reassert the charm and irresponsibility of the child as the greatest achievement to be hoped for by adolescents. Evelina perceives her lover, Lord Orville, as guide, instructor, pseudo-father. She seems almost a parody heroine in her need for fathers, ending up, figuratively, with three: a rediscovered real one, a foster father, and a model husband. Cecilia, in Burney's second novel, voluntarily yields the wealth that has brought her at least a temporary illusion of worldly power, and submits to a dominant husband. And Camilla—well, Camilla is worth considering at length.

Fanny Burney got rich from *Camilla* (1796). "I do not like calling it a *Novel*," she wrote: "it gives so simply the notion of a mere love story, that I recoil a little from it. I mean it to be *sketches of Characters & morals*, put in action, not a Romance." She seems to be claiming realism as well as morality for her book. Its moral purpose is manifest: like Miss Burney's previous two novels, this one concerns a young woman's entry into the world, with a liberal supply of commentators providing judgment of her every act. Camilla, like her predecessors, gets her man and embarks upon a blissful marriage at the end of volume five. Remarkably docile, she assures her mother, just before the dénouement, "I will scarcely even think, my beloved Mother, but by your guidance!", and offers comparable protestations to her fiancé: in others words, she plans to take advantage of her adolescent uncertainties even as she enters adulthood. Her docility derives partly from her consciousness of having made mistakes: incapable of dealing with money, of discriminating character, of conducting a harmless flirtation, of preserving an emotional tie she values, she knows nothing about the world. A model eighteenth-century adolescent, in short, transcendently ignorant, invincibly innocent, glorying in qualities that Emma and Elizabeth struggle to grow beyond. And satisfactorily devoid of sexual feeling: her father apologizes for using the word *passions* to her, reassuring her that she can have none of which she need be ashamed.

The claim of realism for the account of her career is a little distressing. Despite all her mistakes, the exemplifies a young woman's successful exploitation of her childishness. As a child, Camilla possessed great sexual power—the novel of course does not designate it thus—over her rich uncle: "She exhilarated him with pleasure" as he watched "the unconscious bound, the genuine glee of childhood's fearless happiness, uncurbed by severity, untamed by misfortune." The process of growing up, for a girl, is one of being curbed and tamed: of losing power. Camilla reaches her teens intact, to fall in love with her cousin Edgar, who, reciprocating her affection, proposes to her despite his tutor's warnings about women's artfulness. Her incapacity for dealing with the social world, however, alienates him to the point where she feels obligated to release him from his engagement; only after psychic anguish driving her to the edge of death are her sins purged, her soul elevated to perfect compliance, and her lover consequently rewon. No more gay unconscious bounding for Camilla: she has learned the female necessity of severe restraint. Yielding the child's freedom, she rediscovers the child's reliance on charm and innocence as resources of power and comes to understand that she dare not claim independence.

The message of the book, its attitude toward feminine adolescence, is less straightforward than simple plot summary or moralizing quotation might suggest. Its treatment of the adolescent preoccupation with physical appearance exemplifies its ambiguities. Beauty becomes an important issue here. Camilla's sister Eugenia, crippled by a fall and marred by smallpox in early childhood, physically unprepossessing though morally elevated, suffers countless miseries as a result of her ugliness. Her father assures her that evanescent beauty doesn't matter, and engineers the appearance of a decorative madwoman to prove his point, that "in every competition and in every decision of esteem, the superior, the elegant, the better part of mankind give their suffrages to merit alone." But the man she loves promptly falls in love with "a beautiful doll," while Eugenia herself, misled, elopes with a cruel ne'er-do-well who loathes her body but lusts for her wealth. In an uncharacteristically passionate, if typically pompous, utterance, Eugenia points out that to place excessive value on feminine beauty is the fault of male rather than female narcissism:

Ye, too, O lords of the creation, mighty men! impute not to native vanity the repining spirit with which I lament the loss of beauty; attribute not to the innate weakness of my sex, the concern I confess for my deformity; nor to feminine littleness of soul, a regret of which the true source is to be traced to your own bosoms, and springs from your own tastes: for the value you yourselves set upon external attractions, your own neglect has taught me to know; and the indifference with which you consider all else, your own duplicity has instructed me to feel.

Camilla, meanwhile, finds sexual attractiveness also a trap. Surrounded by would-be admirers, lacking the sophistication to deal with them, she is readily tempted into vanity and frivolity. Edgar, appalled, wonders—as if elaborating on a text from Martha Vicinus—whether her distinction will not "spoil her for private life; estrange her from family concerns? render tasteless and insipid the conjugal and material characters, meant by Nature to form not only the most sacred of duties, but the most delicious of enjoyments?" Less alluring, Camilla would not thus provoke her lover's doubts; more alluring Eugenia would not suffer so. Adolescent women spend a lot of time worrying about how they look, partly because men of all ages concern themselves with how their women look. The source of feminine misery, then, is not beauty or its lack but the debilitating standards imposed by men.

Eugenia and Camilla both come out all right in the end. Eugenia's brutal husband dies, the man she loves develops belated consciousness of her worth and solves his financial and emotional problems by marrying her; Camilla's lover decides to take over the responsibility of guiding her conduct. But the conflicts faced by both girls exemplify the plight of the adolescent woman, more vividly aware than her male contemporaries of inhabiting a world she never made, in which all the rules are devised and enforced by men, with women their occasional surrogates or instruments.

The rule that young women should be innocent and ignorant creates an even more desperate double bind than the rule that they should be beautiful while confining their beauty's effects to the single chosen male. Such descriptions as *artful* and *subtle* condemn a woman absolutely. When Camilla makes friends with a faintly disreputable woman, Edgar, appalled, complains: "She is no more the artless Camilla I first adored! that fatal connection at the Grove, formed while her character, pure, white, and spotless, was in its enchanting, but dangerous state of first ductility, has already broken into that clear transparent singleness of mind, so beautiful in its total ignorance of every species of scheme, every sort of double measure, every idea of secret view and latent expedient!" Beauty, purity reside in total ignorance. Edgar talks as though Camilla had been raped. She's only had some small experience of the world, but experience is of course the enemy of ignorance. A woman, then, can retain her purity only by seclusion. But Edgar does not wish an untested virtue in his bride. Urged on by his tutor, he distrusts Camilla's love for him but also her capacity to function successfully, in a public sense, as his wife. While Camilla's father warns her not to let Edgar know she cares for him, Dr. Marchmont encourages Edgar to equivalent concealment. The impossibilities of the conflicting demands imposed upon the young woman make it seem miraculous that she should survive all tests to win through to a marriage which she and Edgar alike appear to think of as a rescue operation. "Struggle then against yourself as you would struggle against an enemy," her father advises, advocating "strict and unremitting control." By resolute self-suppression she may maintain the appearance of total innocence—and this, after all, is what is really required.

For the "place" a pre-twentieth-century girl must come to know is above all defined by appearances: Jane Austen's heroines understand this too, though they also learn how to preserve reality. Camilla never makes any fundamental moral or emotional errors, she only falls into the appearance of error. "Simple and ingenuous," she is for that very reason readily seduced into conduct "wide from artlessness in its appearance"; for false appearances she must suffer. Fanny Burney, like Camilla, takes it for granted that the rules which dictate the girl's suffering are proper: *given*. She cannot imagine better rules, though she hints the cost of these. But the cost too is *given*. Specifying the intricate laws by which a young woman must govern her conduct, delineating the penalties of deviation, *Camilla* records a systematic sequence of suppression. The teen-age girl must learn, the book suggests, not how to be an adult but how to be a child—how to accept the absolute authority of whatever Mother says: an education in diminishment. The novel which recounts it knows no way to protest it. Accepting society's strictures, Burney seems to accept also the necessity that the laws of moral growth operate meaningfully only for men, women's morality consisting in their childlike adherence to the pronouncements of others.

Both Fanny Burney and Jane Austen seem to understand the young woman's life and problems as an intense microcosm of the adult woman's. The adolescent must struggle to preserve her narcissistic self-esteem in an environment that provides little to support her sense of worth. She must learn to deal with her feelings without being overwhelmed by them; she needs to find appropriate defenses and relinquish inappropriate ones; she must fit herself into her social setting. The adolescent crisis in a woman's life foreshadows the continuing stresses of her existence—so, at any rate, these writers present it.

Fanny Burney's despairing response to her perception of female crisis recognizes the incompatibility between the yearning for self-discovery and self-development and society's pressure toward conformity, and perceives childishness as a woman's necessary defense. Eugenia sees that men pay lip service to profound commitments while valuing women for their appearance; she can do nothing about her recognition beyond hoping that a good man will arrive. Camilla endures, without full awareness, the impossible conflict of utterly opposed demands on her; she resolves it by yielding to the authority of parents and husband. The novelistic action of *Camilla* acknowledges women's dependency on men as an absolute social fact, though it also describes the pain of such dependency in rather precise terms.

Jane Austen, on the other hand, betrays no sense of grievance. Equally aware that society's pressures on a young woman encourage her to educate herself in restriction, she acknowledges this as simply one of the facts the woman must take into account. Her heroines grow instead of diminish into marriage. They are recognizable, full-fledged adolescents, beneath their protective coloration of propriety—self-loving, self-absorbed, self-willed, full of blind confidence and blind in their efforts to understand the world, irritatingly alert to the foibles of others and sublimely unaware of their own. At the outset of the novels, their defensive structures are totally enveloping—summed up in Elizabeth's tendency to laugh at the world, Emma's to reorganize it. But they learn to yield defenses, to modify their self-love, to make room to grow. Gentleness is not a defensive posture but a human grace. Elizabeth's marriage to Darcy, despite his superiority in rank and wealth, is essentially a marriage of equals; Emma's to Knightley, though he's old enough to be her father, depends at least partly on her sense of having increased in stature enough to be worthy of him. She enjoys playing the child at the beginning of the novel, but not at the end.

Social facts, in other words, provide no excuse for a woman, from Jane Austen's point of view. Her novels are heavily populated with women who *use* them as excuse—Mrs. Bennet, Charlotte, the Bingley sisters, Mrs. Elton, Harriet Smith—but evasion indicates their weakness. It's possible, the novels assert, for human beings to develop, for female adolescence to be a time of development, not of giving up.

Giving up, as Camilla does, or growing up, as Elizabeth and Emma do, are not the only possibilities for the adolescent heroine, even in pre-twentieth-century settings. *Wuthering Heights* was published in 1847. Its heroine, Catherine Earnshaw, conforms to no Victorian standards. She is neither innocent nor ignorant, nor is she, in fact, "brought up" at all. Almost devoid of "family affection," though she weeps for her father's death, she dies immediately after giving birth, having displayed no evidence whatever of desiring motherhood. Ravaged by sexual feeling of some confusing variety, she seems an antiheroine, in every respect opposed to her century's ideal prototype of the adolescent woman. More obviously than Elizabeth or Emma, she embodies the adolescent as revolutionary, articulating a new set of values for the heroine, interesting precisely for her nonconformity, representing (despite her defeat and death) some triumph of adolescent over adult standards, articulating a kind of social criticism. Nelly Dean works, Joseph preaches, Lockwood prates. They are the adults. Edgar Linton, only three years older than Cathy, tries to live a mature, conventional life. His happiness in romantic love proves illusory; his qualified happiness finally rests in parenthood, but he is not sorry to die, all passion long since spent.

The view of female adolescence implied by *Wuthering*

Heights possesses neither the optimism of Jane Austen's conviction that young women can grow to self-sustaining adulthood nor the pessimism of Fanny Burney's assumption that they must learn contentment with the child's lot. Catherine neither is nor becomes adult, yet she is something more than child. But does she exemplify anything beyond herself? To take her as a type of adolescence is in some ways ludicrous; on the other hand, it suggests a way of thinking which helps to clarify the multiple complexities of narrative and moral viewpoint in the novel.

Wuthering Heights belongs—among other allegiances—to the almost endless series of nineteenth-century narratives detailing the education of the heart. Like Pip in *Great Expectations*, like Elizabeth and Emma, young Cathy must be taught to feel—to sympathize, to empathize, to love—and to discipline feeling. The process of education which culminates in her marriage to Hareton has begun a generation before, but the elder Catherine and Heathcliff could not accept it. They demonstrate the power of passion without control as Lockwood and Nelly Dean exemplify the much more unattractive converse. Indeed, the novel virtually diagrams a range of emotional possibilities: Isabella's self-willed and superficial infatuation, Edgar's rather passive devotion, Hindley's aggressive self-destructiveness, Linton's sickly self-absorption. Among the possibilities, that represented by Cathy and Hareton is most fulfilling, least destructive. It alone suggests a prospect of continuity. One can imagine a full family stemming from this union—a difficult fantasy in relation to any of the novel's other pairings. Victorian pieties are thus satisfied at last: the young woman learns to know her place, under the control of affection rather than passion.

But I've described a more orderly novel than I've read. Although everything in the paragraph above is plausible, perhaps even true, it doesn't account for the emotional energy of *Wuthering Heights*, which derives partly from the book's fundamental opposition to the discipline it nominally espouses. The kind of emotional education that

Cathy undergoes might also be characterized as the process of growing up—but this novel is not on the side of "maturity" as *Emma* is, or *Pride and Prejudice*. Emily Brontë goes out of her way to provide despicable examples of those who are "grown-ups": Lockwood in his absurd self-satisfaction, his dead "adult" language almost parodic in effect; Nelly Dean, equally smug in her role as worker, self-justified in all her subsequent obtuseness by the fact that at an early age she has taken on herself "the cares of a woman." Both feel beyond frivolity— as does Joseph, that grotesquely punitive figure whose very existence severely criticizes "adult" values. All three of these adults, of course, are, it is suggested, emotionally inadequate in one way or another. Edgar Linton offers a more complicated case. Nelly describes him, accurately, as "kind, and trustful, and honourable," adding that Catherine "could not be called the *opposite*, yet she seemed to allow herself such wide latitude, that I had little faith in her principles, and still less sympathy for her feelings." Unappealing as it is to share Nelly Dean's assessment, how can one avoid it? The qualities she attributes to Edgar, which he demonstrates in action, are specifically those of educated feeling. Catherine's feelings and principles, shockingly *un*-educated, can hardly be endorsed. She has profound contempt for Edgar, whom she characterizes under stress as a "sucking leveret." But even Nelly, who admires him, has to apologize for him in his portrait. "He looked better when he was animated," she explains to Lockwood, who has noted his "soft-featured face," the "sweetness" of the portrait and its resemblance to Cathy, the fact that Edgar's figure is "almost too graceful." "That is his everyday countenance," Nelly continues; "he wanted spirit in general." The verdict sounds less harsh than "sucking leveret," but it amounts to the same thing: Edgar lacks masculine force. Admirable as he may be in his selflessness, discipline, and compassion, his creator appears finally to respect him hardly more than his wife does: he does not inspire passion.

Passion, that ambiguously valued state of feeling, dictates the plot of *Wuthering Heights*, itself an outpouring of a creative passion with some analogies to the less productive emotion that dominates Catherine and Heathcliff. The plot in its complexities keeps escaping the memory: one recalls the towering figure of Heathcliff, the desperate feelings of Catherine, but easily loses track of the intricacies through which the characters develop. Catherine and her brother Hindley, with their parents and their servants, Joseph and Nelly, inhabit the old house on the moor at Wuthering Heights. After Catherine's father brings home the mysterious foundling Heathcliff, the girl and the waif form an intense, rebellious alliance, weakened when Catherine makes friends with the prosperous and conventional Edgar Linton and his sister Isabella. Heathcliff, neglected and brutalized by Hindley after his father's death, disappears; Catherine marries Edgar; Hindley, whose young wife dies, sinks toward animality. When Heathcliff returns, he encourages Hindley's degradation. Catherine's deep attention still focuses on Heathcliff; Isabella promptly fancies herself in love with him. As part of his elaborate revenge on the Lintons and Hindley, Heathcliff marries Isabella, who soon flees his brutality but afterwards bears his son, Linton. Catherine dies in childbirth, leaving the infant Cathy, who as she grows becomes devoted to her father. After Isabella's death, Heathcliff reclaims his sickly, petulant son, and tricks Cathy into marrying Linton, imprisoning both at Wuthering Heights. Hindley has died; Edgar Linton soon follows him; Cathy's husband Linton dies shortly after her father, but Cathy remains Heathcliff's victim, as does Hindley's illiterate, degraded son, Hareton. Heathcliff's desire for victims weakens, however, as his obsession with the dead Catherine augments; he dies hoping for union with her, leaving Hareton and Cathy to redeem one another through mature love.

Such bare summary ignores the powerful effects achieved through disjunctive narrative and disparate points of view, particularly through the perspectives of the "outsider" Lockwood—narrator, spectator, and listener—and of self-righteous Nelly Dean. But it suggests the central issues of the novel. The grand passion that determines the fate of Catherine and Heathcliff is intense, diffuse (vaguely involving nature as well as individuals), and sterile. We may believe the lovers in their talk of some mystical union more powerful than death, but no earthly union results from their feeling. Their connection literally produces only destruction. Catherine's incompletely heard confession of her devotion to Heathcliff precipitates his exile, which hardens him into a machine organized for revenge. When Heathcliff returns, his initial appearance causes a quarrel between Catherine and her husband; a subsequent visit produces the painful scene of her articulated contempt for Edgar during which she locks the door and throws the key into the fire; conflict over Heathcliff provokes her desperate illness; his insistence on seeing her eventuates in her death. The side effects of this passion, equally disastrous, include the undoing of Isabella. Linton would never have been born were it not for Heathcliff's plotting; but this fertility contains the seeds of its own frustration. He is born only to be used by others, and to die. The survivors issue not from grand passions but from the union of Edgar and Catherine, Hindley and his socially inferior bride; they point toward the future.

But survival is not the highest of values, nor must the reader judge causes by their effects. Results may be irrelevant; or the truly significant results may be too subtle for evaluation. Catherine is, regardless of her death (perhaps partly *because* of it), a triumphant adolescent, her entire career a glorification of the undisciplined adolescent sensibility. Heathcliff, who looks so much more "manly" than Edgar, is as much as his soul mate an adolescent; more important, he is a projection of adolescent fantasy: give him a black leather jacket and a motorcycle and he'd fit right into many a youthful dream even now. Powerful, manly, mysterious, fully conscious of his own worth, frequently brutal, he remains nonetheless absolutely submissive to the woman he loves—if that is the proper verb. Around her he organizes his life. He provides her the opportunity for vicarious aggression, dominating her husband, tyrannizing over her conventional sister-in-law; when he turns his aggression toward her, though, she can readily master him. A powerful man controlled by a woman's power: when she dies, she draws him to her in death.

Heathcliff is partly a figment of Catherine's imagination as well as of Emily Brontë's. Catherine's fantasies, far more daring than Emma's, are equally vital to her development. She focuses them on Heathcliff: if he were not there, she would have to invent him. In fact, she *does* invent him, directly and indirectly shaping his being. After his boyhood, he instigates no significant action that is not at least indirectly the result of his response to her. Because of her he goes away, returns, marries lovelessly, destroys Hindley, claims his own son as well as Hindley's, arranges Linton's marriage, finally dies. But Catherine is also controlled by her own creation, her important actions issuing from her bond to Heathcliff.

Although Heathcliff dominates the action of *Wuthering Heights,* and the imagination of its author and its other characters, Catherine more clearly exemplifies what the two of them stand for. Not yet nineteen when she dies, she cannot survive into maturity; Heathcliff, who lasts twice as long, matures hardly more. Both are transcendent narcissists. Catherine explains that she loves Heathcliff "because he's more myself than I am. Whatever our souls are made of, his and mine are the same, and [Edgar] Linton's is as different as a moonbeam from lightning, or frost from fire." Her analogies suggest the ground of her exalted self-esteem. She and Healthcliff share a fiery nature—a capacity for intense, dangerous feeling. The intensity and the danger are both criteria of value; by comparison the purity of the moonbeam, the clarity of frost seem negligible, even contemptible. Hot is better than cold: Catherine has

176

no doubt about that. The heat of her sexuality and of her temper attest her superiority to the man she marries and her identity with the man she loves; her sense of self is the ground of all her values.

The theme of justification by feeling permeates the lovers' statements about themselves and one another. Heathcliff remarks of Edgar Linton, "If he loved with all the powers of his puny being, he couldn't love as much in eighty years, as I could in a day. And Catherine has a heart as deep as I have; the sea could be as readily contained in that horse-trough, as her whole affection be monopolized by him." His quantitative assessments of feeling resemble his qualitative ones, as he complains of "that insipid, paltry creature attending her from *duty* and *humanity!* From *pity* and *charity!* He might as well plant an oak in a flower-pot, and expect it to thrive, as imagine he can restore her to vigour in the soil of his shallow care!" The qualities that Nelly Dean, like most of humanity, would identify as virtues seem vicious to Heathcliff, who, like Catherine, assumes that only passionate feeling is valuable. She is equally intense in her claims for the virtue and the power of her passion, the foundation of her being. "My love for Heathcliff resembles the eternal rocks beneath—a source of little visible delight, but necessary." As she threatens Nelly, and by extension Edgar, with her self-destructive temper tantrums, explosions of feeling so powerful that they issue in that mysterious and devastating Victorian disease of "brain fever," she expresses repeatedly her conviction of uniqueness, that adolescent burden and glory.

Catherine feels "special" not on the basis of any accomplishment, actual or anticipated, but simply for her emotional capacity, which differentiates her from everyone she encounters—with, of course, the invariable exception of Heathcliff. But Heathcliff is hardly an exception, since she considers him an extension of herself: "Nelly, I *am* Heathcliff—he's always, always in my mind—not as a pleasure any more than I am always a pleasure to myself—but as my own being." She feels, therefore she exists; feeling passionately, she exists passionately. Her feeling is all self-directed; facing the threat of motherhood, with its necessity for responsibility to another, she, like Hedda Gabler, must die. Dependent on her passion for a consciousness of worth, she depends almoost as much on the feeling of others: like Heathcliff once more, she desperately wants to be loved.

In a moment of frankness, Catherine confesses to Nelly that she has always assumed that everyone loves her; it comes as a shock—clearly she can't really believe it—to suspect that she might be disliked. The manifest defensiveness of such an assumption emerges as we realize that Catherine cannot confront even the idea of hostility directed toward her. Among her bad reasons for marrying Edgar, the strongest (though Nelly thinks it the weakest) is that he loves her. After her marriage, she observes, arrogantly, "I have such faith in Linton's love that I believe I might kill him, and he wouldn't wish to retaliate." Nelly advises her to value Edgar for his affection; she says she does, but in fact she takes it for granted, *needs* to take it for granted. Isabella accuses her of desiring "no one to be loved but yourself"; Catherine, "surprised," ignores the truth of the observation. She never feels loved enough: Edgar does not, after all, totally indulge her. Heathcliff, in the grips of emotion, will not obey her command to come to her chair; she reacts with "indignant disappointment" and typical narcissistic exaggeration, complaining, "Oh, you see, Nelly! he would not relent a moment to keep me out of the grave! *That* is how I'm loved!"

Her narcissism, however, gives her an exaggerated sense of power. Her limited sphere precludes wide testing of her influence, but within it she often feels virtually omnipotent. Even as a child, Nelly reports, she would make others cry, then demand—successfully—that they be quiet in order to comfort her. When Edgar, during his courtship, witnesses her bad temper and deceitfulness, she uses similar tactics; his proposal comes soon after. Married, she orders Nelly to tell her husband that she's in danger of serious illness. Thus far, she admits, Edgar "has been discreet in dreading to provoke me; you must represent the peril of quitting that policy; and remind him of my passionate temper verging, when kindled, on frenzy." The process of growing up, for most people, involves discovering their limits; Catherine dies in testing hers.

It goes without saying that such a girl would be impatient of all restraint. Her daughter, the second Cathy, articulates an important theme of the novel when—not yet tamed by love—she defies her tormentor, Heathcliff: "I'll put my trash away, because you can make me, if I refuse," she announces. "But I'll not do anything, though you should swear your tongue out, except what I please!" The desire to do exactly what one pleases is universal, but only the young believe it possible to fulfill. Catherine dramatizes the shape and the consequences of a life devoted to self-indulgence, and the impossibility of its continuance. Unlike her daughter, who is forced to discover that what she thinks she wants does not necessarily coincide with what she really wants and that only by enlarging her notion of what pleases her can she find fulfillment, Catherine never grows. The young woman who dies after bearing a child is morally and emotionally identical with the small girl who delighted in provoking her father and who insisted on playing mistress of everyone. Her sense of identity and of the world have acquired no complexity. She claims intuitive or mystical knowledge and awareness unavailable to others, but remains invincibly naïve. Considering physical prowess an essential measure of masculinity, she admires Heathcliff and despises her husband because Edgar will not battle with his opponent. Unable to credit the full humanity of others, she cannot assess motivation or recognize emotional ambiguity in those around her. Her anger at all failures of compliance with her will extends to the world at large; she dies after a willful display of "mad resolution" in the characteristic adolescent determination to have everything.

Such descriptions of her nature, of course, falsify the tone of the novel, which responds to the splendid more than the self-defeating elements in her adolescence. Catherine also has an aspect of pathos. Caught between a child's irresponsibility and an adult's acceptance of the consequences of choices made, she exists and dies in a miserable limbo. Early in the book, Lockwood encounters her as ghost, dream, or fantasy. Asleep in her childhood bed, he wakes, or thinks he wakes, to the noise of a scraping bough and reaches through the window to grasp "a little, ice-cold hand." Its owner, identifying herself as Catherine Linton, begs to be let in: "I'm come home, I'd lost my way on the moor!" Lockwood, terrified, "pulled its wrist on to the broken pane, and rubbed it to and fro till the blood ran down and soaked the bedclothes: still it wailed, 'Let me in!' and maintained its tenacious grip . . ." When the man finally shuts her out, the child "mourns" that she's "been a waif for twenty years!"—ever since she left Wuthering Heights for marriage.

Animals and children fare badly throughout this novel, the weak always at the mercy of the strong. Alive, though, Catherine is never for long a victim: a bulldog may bite her, but she is immediately rescued into luxury. The dream fable suggests an aspect of the heroine unemphasized yet implicit in the rest of the action. In it, the adult's response to the child's need is an effort to maim. The adult, with the purpose and the power to hurt, injures the small girl whose only weapon is her tenacity. He reduces her to an "it," denying her very humanity; and he experiences her as a terrible threat, unable to contemplate the horror of letting her in. Of course his horror responds to her ghostly nature, not to any human reality; but symbolically it means something more. Children both threaten and are threatened by adults. Catherine's image of herself as "waif" is partly a response to the impossibility of communicating with her elders. As a ghost, more than eighteen years after her death at the age of nineteen, she presents herself as a helpless child. In life, too, she never

finds her home, the home of her heart, the early loss of
her parents never compensated by subsequent emotional
security, since she cannot respond fully to the love Edgar
offers her. She is always subject to severe self-pity. How
justified is it? The conviction that the old inevitably maim
the young, not through desire but by emotional necessity,
permeates *Wuthering Heights*, providing the countercase
to the argument for disciplined growth exemplified by
Cathy. It is not a reasoned or reasonable case but a felt
one. If a young person allows herself to need what the
adult world alone can provide, she will suffer. One can
choose to be lost or to be hurt: nothing else. Catherine,
unwilling to give up the waifhood of adolescence, dies.
She never attempts entry into the grown-up kingdom, unwilling to yield the solitude of her solipsism, populated
only by the incubus-projection of Heathcliff, for the community of adult equality. Her daugher, loved in childhood,
isolated in adolescence, deliberately humbles herself with
Hareton as a first step toward adulthood, learns to share,
and anticipates a shared future. The novel's "happy ending" concentrates on her, but its emotional commitment—
and its final words—respond to the ghosts of those too
bound in their narcissism to grow beyond it. *Wuthering
Heights*, acknowledging the necessity for growing up, is a
prolonged cry of anguish at that necessity.

Catherine Linton haunts herself in life, as after her
death she will haunt Heathcliff. During her final illness
she stares at herself in a mirror, shocked by what she sees,
but immediately wishing to transfer the shock to her husband ("My God! does he know how I'm altered?"). A few
minutes later she is delirious, seeing but not recognizing
the face in the glass. "Who is it?" she inquires. "I hope it
will not come out when you are gone! Oh! Nelly, the room
is haunted! I'm afraid of being alone!" The ghost that
haunts the mirror is her solitary self; she is right to fear
her self-inflicted loneliness, which contains the seeds of
terror. Freud reports his own unnerving experience of

seeing himself, for a moment unrecognizable, in a mirrored train-compartment door. "Uncanniness," he argues, is the essence of such experience, the product of its unexpectedness, its reversal of underlying certitudes, and of the eerie perspective on the self temporarily generated. Catherine's strange perspective has deep implications. It comments on the danger, the horror, of narcissism: the danger of being finally left alone in the universe.

When Nelly convinces Catherine that she has seen herself, she is more frightened than ever. " 'Myself!' she gasped, 'and the clock is striking twelve! It's true, then, that's dreadful!' " Nelly hears in her utterances only the incoherence of derangement, but the reader aware of Catherine's perverse self-centeredness will hear more. Terrified of her isolation with herself, the young woman, close to the final solitude of death, glimpsing the sterility of her self-involvement, finds that her capacity for feeling now enlarges her dread of loneliness as it has earlier magnified her love for Heathcliff in his role as a version of herself. When Heathcliff appears in her sickroom, she clings to him desperately. But it is too late. Catherine's horror at the mirror and what it means, considered in the context of her general satisfied self-absorption, summarizes the delicately balanced emotional ambivalence that shapes and controls *Wuthering Heights* and gives it its force.

To contemplate oneself in a mirror may arouse all the ambivalence a viewer feels about himself (herself). Not only for aging women does a reflection embody danger: reflections *always* contain danger: at one extreme, of narcissism; at the other, of self-knowledge. Catherine, bound by the former, avoids the latter. She is the type of the romantic adolescent heroine, her approach to madness as she nears death foretelling the self-definition of a later generation of heroines. Madness is more fashionable now, a convenient emblem of alienation and specialness. Esther Greenwood, in Sylvia Plath's *The Bell Jar*, is a direct lineal descendant of Catherine Earnshaw Linton. Both heroines value themselves for their inability to adjust to an adult world, but unlike Camilla are also unwilling to be treated like children. They offer to society the challenge of irresponsible individualism. The novels that contain them at least tacitly glorify the iconoclastic aspects of adolescence, although neither book takes full responsibility for the glorification and *Wuthering Heights,* indeed, explicitly qualifies it.

The slightly out-of-control irony that dominates *The Bell Jar* suggests how Esther differs from Catherine, a young woman capable of anger but lacking the perspective for even the unfocused irony of adolescence. In both novels, the heroines' ways of seeing themselves determine their ways of perceiving the world. Esther, nineteen years old, often looks in mirrors.

I noticed a big, smudgy-eyed Chinese woman staring idiotically into my face. It was only me, of course. I was appalled to see how wrinkled and used up I looked.

* * *

The mirror over my bureau seemed slightly warped and much too silver. The face in it looked like the reflection in a ball of dentist's mercury.

* * *

The face that peered back at me seemed to be peering from the grating of a prison cell after a prolonged beating. It looked bruised and puffy and all the wrong colors. It was a face that needed soap and water and Christian tolerance.

These grotesque visions of the self are not stimulated by disastrous external events, although all issue from Esther's readily provoked sense of psychic disaster. When psychic tragedy produces clear external effects, her suicide attempt almost successful, she is literally damaged physically, and

183

the hospital attendants protect her from mirrors. Finally she makes an opportunity to see herself; her first reaction is "It wasn't a mirror at all, but a picture. You couldn't tell whether the person in the picture was a man or a woman, because their hair was shaved off and sprouted in bristly chicken-feather tufts all over their head." Smiling at the sheer improbability of what she sees, she drops and shatters the mirror when the image cracks into a smile. "Seven years bad luck," the nurse says.

More even than Catherine, then, Esther is alienated from herself, deprived finally even of sexual identity. Because her characteristic tone is self-punishing rather than, like Catherine's, self-praising, her narcissism may be difficult to discern; but it is as persistent and as dominant as that of her fictional predecessor, and its effects are not dissimilar. Inhabiting a more varied society than Catherine's, she feels even more isolated. No Heathcliff provides substance for her fantasies, although she briefly tries to fit a simultaneous interpreter from the UN into the role. Privileged to spend six weeks in New York after winning a fashion magazine contest, she suffers from and glories in her unlikeness to her peers, the glamorous and the wholesome alike. Back home in a Boston suburb, she lies awake all night, full of contempt for her lumpish, snoring mother. Her equal contempt for the girls who have married and produced children mingles with fear for the fate they represent. Other young people cook and eat hot dogs on the beach; she pretends to do the same, but buries her food. Scorn is her main emotion toward the man who wants to marry her; the man she finally goes to bed with (producing uncontrollable hemorrhaging) elicits no feeling at all. When she has a blind date with a handsome Chilean, he flings her in the mud. Until she encounters a sympathetic woman psychiatrist at a mental hospital, she appears incapable of relationship, so rapt is she in her own misery.

But misery can be a form of self-love. "There is," Therese Benedek writes, an "emotional state in which the object of the psychic energy is the person's own self and in which the emotion is depressive, self-depreciatory, and painful. ... we refer to this emotional state by the term 'negative narcissism.' " It is not the same as masochism. Esther does not seek suffering because she derives pleasure from it, she exists in a state of suffering partly because that defines her specialness. Her pain and depression real, and really self-destructive, she is the target of her own unconscious malignance. Her feelings set her apart, her apartness marks her superiority but also her inadequacy. She takes pride (implicit in the tone of the narrative) in the clarity with which she sees reality; the reader may question the reality of that clarity.

Its nature is suggested by what Esther sees in the mirror: the ugly, the distorted, the unlovable self, the self not even she can love. The truth in her perception is manifestly partial, but she cannot get beyond it. Similarly, when she sees a pregnant woman wheeling a baby carriage she sees horror; when her boyfriend's mother braids a rug and lays it on the floor, Esther perceives only the artifact's degradation by dirt. She watches a woman give birth. "They oughtn't to let women watch," a medical student tells her. "It'll be the end of the human race." If Esther were in charge, it would be. She notices "nothing but an enormous spider-fat stomach and two little ugly spindly legs," and the groaning which tells her this is an experience of unbearable pain: only the disgusting and terrifying.

Catherine values herself for qualities traditionally associated with the role of women: for the charm she believes irresistible, the power she exercises in relationships. Esther, as the examples of her perception reveal, hates what she sees of women's roles: the ugly rug on the floor, the compliant wife in the kitchen, even the radiant girl, her breasts spilling out as a man tosses her into the air. Buddy Willard assures her that once she gets married she'll no longer care about poetry; she believes him. She thinks herself "dreadfully inadequate" at everything a woman is supposed to do and be, although she has been good at "winning scholarships and prizes," an accomplishment irrelevant in the world of grown-up men and women as she understands it. "The trouble was, I hated the idea of serving men in any way. I wanted to dictate my own thrilling letters." If she braided a rug, she'd hang it on the wall; obviously, she doesn't know how to be a woman. More significantly, she doesn't *want* to be one; and she knows this fact and feels guilty about it—hence, partly, the ugliness she sees in herself.

Her madness, her suffering, are offered as metaphors for female normalcy. When she sees the woman give birth in pain, Buddy tells her that the mother has received a drug to make her forget her suffering. Esther reacts with further horror: "I thought it sounded just like the sort of drug a man would invent. Here was a woman in terrible pain, obviously feeling every bit of it or she wouldn't groan like that, and she would go straight home and start another baby, because the drug would make her forget how bad the pain had been, when all the time, in some secret part of her, that long, blind, doorless and windowless corridor of pain was waiting to open up and shut her in again." Equivalent corridors of pain loom everywhere for Esther, her existence one long experience of "being burned alive through all your nerves" (her description of electrocution, the book's opening image: "It had nothing to do with me," she comments). But the pain of motherhood focuses with special clarity her fear of life, representing the ultimate way in which women serve men.

The only alternative to service is solitude, or so she feels. Solitude is pain, the isolation of the bell jar. "To the person in the bell jar, blank and stopped as a dead baby, the world itself is the bad dream." Within the jar the blankness of death, beyond it only the irreality of dream, the isolated dreamer victim of his isolation, like Catherine and her mirror. Such extreme separateness as Esther endures is the special burden of the psychotic, but the difference between psychosis and "normalcy" may be arbitrary:

Esther sees a striking resemblance between the women at the mental hospital and those she remembers from college. In her view of life, psychosis is virtually a female necessity, leaving only a choice of madness. Here is Esther's vision of marriage:

> It would mean getting up at seven and cooking him eggs and bacon and toast and coffee and dawdling about in my nightgown and curlers after he'd left for work to wash up the dirty plates and make the bed and then when he came home after a lively, fascinating day he'd expect a big dinner, and I'd spend the evening washing up even more dirty plates till I fell into bed, utterly exhausted.
>
> This seemed a dreary and wasted life for a girl with fifteen years of straight A's, but I knew that's what marriage was like, because cook and clean and wash was just what Buddy Willard's mother did from morning till night, and she was the wife of a university professor and had been a private school teacher herself. . . .
>
> And I knew that in spite of all the roses and kisses and restaurant dinners a man showered on a woman before he married her, what he secretly wanted when the wedding service ended was for her to flatten out underneath his feet like Mrs. Willard's kitchen mat.

It is a less appealing form of insanity than the one Esther seems doomed to, although her own life is no less "dreary and wasted." In the arrogance of her pain she refuses to comply with the expectations of others or to recognize the conceivable validity of expectations. Catherine embraces her illnesses as evidences of her distinction—her sensitive feelings, her inability to be crossed—and her power: she will punish others by her sufferings. Esther's attitude is identical. She refuses to be like other people. Some girls manufacture collars out of cut-rate mink tails and dime store chains; Esther will not. Some girls are impressed by male sexuality; Esther, when Buddy displays himself to her, can only think of turkey neck and turkey gizzards and feels "very depressed." The reality of self-contempt only obscures her equally real self-regard. Half-conscious of her narcissism's power, she can reduce her mother to total misery simply by being crazy. Catherine brings herself to the point of death because her husband hasn't noticed that she's ill; it's easy to imagine Esther doing the same thing (although not easy, of course, to imagine her with a husband).

The Bell Jar has been read as a kind of feminist manifesto, about a poor girl driven crazy by the actual hardships of a woman's lot. Read this way, it seems to me, it becomes profoundly uninteresting: a simpleminded and self-indulgent tract. It's kinder, surely, and far more stimulating, to understand that the "ideas" enunciated in such passages as the one on the nature of marriage issue from a disturbed sensibility and help to define the disturbance. Esther overflows with self-pity, for her actual and her potential situation. The self-pity derives from her sense of distinction, the source of her distortions. She cannot make any conceivable choice—to live in the city or the country, to be a professor or an editor—because nothing is good enough for her, nothing adequate to her insatiable need, her huge, undefined capacity. So she sees, wherever she looks, the ugliness that protects her from the necessity of commitment. Her view of marriage, however neatly it fits certain political assumptions, is no more accurate than her view of motherhood: both suffer from their incompleteness. Esther, tormented victim of her narcissism, cannot move forward into the adulthood she understands as psychic deformation. Her psychosis in its regressive aspects represents an unsuccessful effort to return to childhood irresponsibility, unable to read or write or do anything at all. She embodies the essential pain of adolescence, that ambiguous state poised between childhood and maturity, that time when choices must be made and endured.

One may wonder, given the descriptions I've offered, in what sense young women like Catherine and Esther can properly be understood as heroines. Both seem in conspicuous ways unattractive and unsuccessful. They don't really know what they want, and they do not get what they think they want. Their virtues are hardly striking. Both are selfish, unstable, ungiving; neither accomplishes anything of significance. If they dominate the novels they inhabit, perhaps it is only as negative images of possibility.

I think, though, that Catherine and Esther really *are* heroines—though not, certainly, Victorian heroines. Their heroism, like their weakness, derives from their adolescence. Catherine and Esther confront the universal problem of the young: to discover and to assert the self. Unwilling to accept the dictum that girls must understand their place, they feel it necessary to *find* their place. For Catherine, in the nineteenth century, the notion of "place" must be psychic: it's not as though she had a choice of careers. But she won't just dwindle into a wife, she insists on preserving herself in her specialness, on maintaining her commitment to Heathcliff—really a commitment to her untamed self—while yet nominally sustaining the marriage bond. Her defeat, acknowledging the impossibility of existing in contradiction, is heroic: the woman contesting for a worthy goal against insuperable odds. Esther, whose possible occupations seem almost infinite, faces a similar dilemma. She, too, refuses to lapse into any given "place," demanding the right to self-discovery. To discover herself she must, like Catherine, defy assumption. What, if anything, she discovers, remains indeterminate at the novel's end; but her heroism too depends on defiance rather than accomplishment. In her "revolutionary" aspect she articulates rage at the quotidian, unwillingness to yield to a maturity that means compromise, giving up. The reader, however conscious of Esther's severe limitations of perception and understanding, may come to feel that this rage, though exaggerated, calls attention to a truth that must be respected.

Yet the refusal to compromise, to give up what must be given to make maturity possible, cannot finally be perceived as heroic. Emily Brontë, dividing her focus between two young women, recognizes this fact in depicting Cathy's painful learning, the girl's heroism of acceptance counterpointing her mother's heroism of defiance. It is necessary to grow or to die, *Wuthering Heights* implies, though not necessary to like the process. *The Bell Jar* never admits the necessity. For Emily Brontë's complex perspective, perceiving the contradictory values and appeals of the two Catherines, recognizing the atmosphere of diminishment around the younger woman's development as well as the importance of that development, Sylvia Plath substitutes simple identification with her heroine. The novel conveys the pain of madness, its dreadful transformations of the commonplace, but the novelist herself appears to be involved in madness's glamour, to feel as Esther does the doom of her specialness. Lacking the distinction of viewpoints that controls *Wuthering Heights*, *The Bell Jar* does not deal with the undeniable fact that the adolescent's heroism is likely to be only internal, a heroism of fantasy, a cowardice in action.

A friend of mine told me about a friend of hers who hated to stay up late at night. When her husband refused to stop reading and turn out the light, she became so frustrated that she bit her arm till it bled. She showed him the blood, he turned out the light.

That's not masochism, it's power politics.

It's easy to imagine Catherine or Esther doing the same thing.

Power is for adolescents an issue of peculiar vividness. Moving from the impotence of childhood, fantasizing the vast resources of adulthood, they feel with anguish the limitations on what they can do, what they are allowed to do, how much they can affect the world. Lacking social authority, they must operate by devious means. The position of the adolescent woman epitomizes that of women in general, limited in opportunity by the assumptions of society, forced toward indirection to retain any illusion of force. The theme of adolescence has special poignance for women, the fate of that defiance being, almost always, to fail at last. The failure matters, but so does the effort that precedes it. In *Martha Quest*, Doris Lessing examines effort and assesses failure. Adolescent ways of seeing differ from adult ones. Focusing on this aspect of adolescence, Lessing uses it to uncover the moral anomalies of the grown-up world as well as the hopeless impossibilities of the adolescent one.

Martha's struggle for power, like Esther's, focuses on her mother. (In nineteenth-century novels women express hostility toward their mothers by eliminating them from the narrative; twentieth-century fiction dramatizes the conflict.) Her technique has its arm-biting aspects. Often, before she leaves home (the action begins when she is fifteen), she uses her suffering as a weapon against her mother, suggesting, like the disgruntled wife, that her misery is really her opponent's fault. ("Mrs. Quest was upset, for she did not know why her daughter found her disgusting.") The deviousness of such devices is, if fiction is to be believed, characteristic of young women. Martha's attempts to use direct tactics against her mother are always foiled, if only by the older woman's refusal to admit that any conflict could exist. Each generation, the novel insists, develops different patterns of denial and defense; the hopelessness of imagining possible understandings between age and youth derives partly from this fact.

Twentieth-century adolescents differ from their predecessors. Martha believes this statement to be true, and Lessing demonstrates its partial truth. Martha shares with Esther Greenwood two burdens inconceivable for Catherine Earnshaw or Elizabeth Bennet or Camilla: the weight of a new kind of self-consciousness, and that of the infinite possibilities of *doing*. Self-consciousness, of course, has always been an adolescent affliction, but in our century its terms have changed. Young people now know that they are supposed to suffer, know the forms of predictable suffering, feel the obligation of self-analysis. Martha imagines, with envy, conceivable novelists of the future who might "write cheerfully, and without the feeling that they were evading a problem: 'Martha went to school in the usual way, liked the teachers, was amiable with her parents, and looked forward with confidence to a happy and well-spent life'!" The possibilities of confident anticipation no longer exist for her. Camilla and Elizabeth, knowing the desirable form of their future lives, need simply to achieve it. Martha sees no clearly desirable forms, no viable models, no real hope. Suffering the miseries of a transitional state without knowing what she is in transition *to*, believing that some kind of self-analysis (Marxian? Freudian?) might save her but unable to discipline herself to the rigors of any particular line of investigation, Martha feels the obligation and the impossibility of understanding: a twentieth-century heroine, she must invent the problem as well as solve it, discover the ends of life before pursuing them. Obviously, she knows too much for Catherine's recourse of romantic death: the romantic self-image is no longer available. As fully self-absorbed as any previous heroine, she cannot entirely like the self that absorbs her: like Esther in her madness, Martha in her "normalcy" is a victim of "negative narcissism."

Like Esther too, she believes herself theoretically capable of doing almost anything. But dreams cannot substitute for accomplishment, and as much as Esther she seems incapacitated for accomplishment. Her dreams, intensifying her frustration, only weaken her.

Two sources of misery—the weight of cynical awareness, the psychic difficulty of significant doing—partially incapacitate Martha in the struggle with her parents: a struggle for power, for authority over her life, and for freedom from the life of her parents and all its implications, which shapes the moral structure of *Martha Quest*. Unlike Esther, Martha follows—somewhat to the reader's surprise—the conventional pattern of success for a girl of her kind, the novel concluding with her marriage to a highly eligible young man. Yet Esther's drama of disaster, her plunge into madness defining total social failure, has a paradoxical aspect of personal success, constituting her public claim of "specialness," her public demonstration of terrible power to hurt her mother. Conversely, Martha's social success amounts to personal failure, a denial of all she has wished and dreamed. We know that her marriage will be disastrous, even *she* knows it ("She ... heard a voice remarking calmly within her that she would not stay married to him"). Although her mother has had nothing to do with bringing the marriage about, never meeting her fiancé until a few days before the wedding, it seems nonetheless her mother's victory, Martha's defeat. Mrs. Quest, in a bizarre sequence, provides the engagement ring; then, in the marriage ceremony, she pushes her daughter's arm forward to receive the wedding ring, "so that everyone was able to see how Martha turned around and said in a loud, angry whisper, 'Who's getting married, me or you?'" The girl who has felt rebellion as a vocation, in action confirms the value she defies.

In action, but not in passion. Feeling consistently opposes function throughout the novel, which in its most powerful sections comes close to creating a drama of stasis: opposing forces locked in irresolvable tension. Some of Martha's feelings are unacceptable to her, some have potential consequences that she can't bear to examine, some lead in directions where she fears to go. Her most powerful weapons in the battle for autonomy are beauty and brains, both possessing complex and dangerous emotional concomitants.

Unlike Esther, Martha likes what she sees in the mirror: her self-loathing is never physical. Admiring her own long, slim, tan legs, she resolves never to lose them, never to be a victim of the childbearing she believes responsible for the swollen, ugly legs of her mother's friends, their tans inadequately concealing protruding veins. Adult womanhood, as she perceives it (and she's not mad—only young) means ugliness: swollen breasts, lined faces, scarred bellies. Adulthood is not a goal but a horror. Martha, at sixteen, spends "much time, at night, examining herself with a hand mirror; she sometimes propped the mirror by her pillow, and, lying beside it, would murmur like a lover, 'Beautiful, you are so beautiful.' This happened when Mrs. Quest had made one of her joking remarks about Martha's clumsiness . . ." In her self-contemplation Martha attempts to make permanent a vision of herself utterly opposed to her parents' view. Seeing that she has some beauty, she learns to use it as a resource, battling her mother for months over how she should dress (her mother wishes to preserve her as a child, Martha has in mind something more like a magazine model), experimenting with the effects she can have on young men, resenting a man's responding to her body rather than her mind, though deliberately provoking such response. She wants beauty, values it, uses it, but feels the danger of her sexuality. How pleasant to be an image rather than a person: part of her yearns to avoid reality. At her first encounter with a full-length mirror, she strips and studies herself. "It was as if she saw a vision of someone not herself; or rather, herself transfigured to the measure of a burningly insistent future. The white naked girl with high small breasts that leaned forward out of the mirror was like a girl from a legend." The "burningly insistent future" confronting her in the glass relates not to any literal prospect but to a vision of beauty as salvation, protecting Martha with the imperviousness of legend. If she can confine her love to self-love, she will be safe. Lying in the bath, having left home, achieved the nominal independence of a job in town, "soon, with frank adoration, she fell into a rite of self-love. . . . Her body lay unmoved and distant, congealing into perfection, under the eyes of this lover." *Unmoved, distant, congealing:* all suggest one dimension of her fantasy, of beauty as protection against the tumult of relationship.

But these words, tonally ambiguous, hint negative as well as positive meanings; and Martha's fantasy has an opposed dimension as well. If she longs to shore herself against the potential ruins of feeling, she longs also for the fulfillment of mutuality. Her beauty in fantasy guards against but also lures toward relationship. Conscious of "that other veiled personage that waits, imprisoned, in every woman, to be released by love, that person she feels to be (obstinately and against the evidence of all experience) what is real and enduring in her," she wants desperately to be loved. Her appearance attracts first Donovan, preeminently concerned with appearances, who takes charge of her wardrobe, rebukes her yearnings for a "romantic" dress, and thinks lovemaking "disgusting." Briefly she experiments with cruder Perry, whose gestures at love amount to a "self-absorbed rite" leading to no consummation. The Jewish musician Dolly obligingly deflowers her but is too preoccupied with his own paranoia and self-pity to give her what she needs. Douglas, whom she marries, takes her beauty more seriously than the others, in a mode of adoration with some sinister aspects. "Yes, but this is not what I want, she thought confusedly; she was resenting, most passionately, without knowing that she resented it, his self-absorbed adoration of her, and the way he insisted, 'Look at yourself, aren't you beautiful?'" Participating in that aspect of her fantasy that makes her beauty something external to her self, Douglas deprives her of reality in the act of worshiping her body. With her beauty she "gets her man," behaving as she condemns others for behaving; but to get is not to achieve what she wants. She uses her beauty, in fact, to confirm her mother's stultifying view of the world.

Her brains prove an equally ambiguous resource. Like Esther Greenwood once more, Martha locates her sense of specialness primarily in her awareness of superior intellectual capacity. She has little to show for this posited gift. In an obscure act of complicity with her mother, she fails to take the matriculation examination that would entitle her to more freedom than she can otherwise anticipate. Her boss in the law firm where she works (having been prodded by a friend into taking the job), noting her special gifts, pays for her secretarial training, but she cannot manage to work steadily at the necessary tasks. She finds herself similarly unable to engage in consistent serious reading, to examine her own ideas stringently, to confront intellectual challenge. Unwilling to "go all the way" in using her mind, she remains an intellectual virgin; her belief that Douglas will offer food for her mental starvation creates the bitterest irony of her misguided marriage. Mistakenly, she believes that he shares her liberal ideas; in fact, having no ideas, he can only share her fantasies. "They continued to talk, like two children at college, about growing grapes in France, or going to America, delightedly planning half a dozen different careers at once." "He was as dissatisfied as herself with the present." Dreaming substitutes for doing and for thinking; and two can do it better than one. Martha betrays her mind through marriage partly because she fears commitment to the implications of real thought, dreaming remaining her defense against awareness. The brains which she feels differentiate her from her mother lead her—so she believes—in the direction her mother would choose. Her life, somehow, slides out of her control, as though her mother still governed her; her efforts at confrontation fizzle out in marriage: not in this novel a happy ending at all.

That twentieth-century problem shared by both sexes, the difficulty of commitment, keeps Martha from winning the battle with her mother. Mrs. Quest, lacking beauty and brains, is none the less firmly what she is. (As readers of the succeeding four volumes in the *Children of Violence* series know, Martha wins against her mother only when she's in her forties. Shortly afterward her mother dies.) Martha has no equivalent firmness: "she was resentful because he would not accept her as *herself*—whatever that might mean; for was she not continually at sea, because of the different selves which insisted on claiming possession of her?" Hers is a passion of opposition for things-as-they-are: "the swelling dislike of her surroundings ... was her driving emotion." Adolescents have always been in opposition—even Elizabeth Bennet, with her contempt for marriages of convenience and for social hypocrisy, even Camilla, with her brief assertion of her right to friendship with an unconventional woman. Martha's antagonism takes powerful, though largely internal, forms: we see her, "in an agony of adolescent misery, . . . lying among the long grass under a tree, repeating to herself that her mother was hateful, all these old women hateful, every one of these relationships, with their lies, evasions, compromises, wholly disgusting." But the intensity of her rejection does not differentiate her from her fictional precursors so much as the fact that she can find nothing to be *for*. To be sure, she knows the okay political positions and pays lip service to them; but she does not believe in them enough to act in terms of them. She is not really "for" adolescence. She does not believe in anything enough—not in herself or her potentialities, not in the possibilities of love or of life itself. Like other women before her, she turns to a man in hope that he will solve her problems, rescue her from her uncertainties; but she lacks an internal gyroscope. Her misery of rebellion has no foreseeable end. Unwilling to grow up because her images of maturity are all contaminated, unable to luxuriate in feeling (like Catherine) because she can find no adequate object for feeling, discovering no place to go, nothing to do, unwilling to test herself in any serious way, she seems doomed indefinitely to the limbo of adolescence, imagined in this novel as a painful state of soul more than a chronological period.

My students in an advanced course didn't want to talk about this book. It wasn't that they didn't like it, they were reluctant to confront it. One reason, it turned out, was that Martha Quest reminded them too much of themselves. Recognizing her dilemmas, they feared her failure. But they were also eager to condemn her: for the split between her ideals and her action, for her abject submission (as they saw it) to the pressures of her society, for her inability or unwillingness to fulfill her potential. Somehow she should have managed her life better.

She thinks so too, of course; and many of my students appear to have similar thoughts about their own lives, even in their late teens. Somehow things should be better, somehow they themselves should be better. The atmosphere of self-criticism is very familiar to late-adolescent women. It merges easily into the perverse indulgences of negative narcissism—as it does for Martha Quest. Her self-preening pleasure in the contemplation of her body and her sense of guilt and frustration at the inadequacies of her achievement derive alike from that faith in personal specialness which life slowly disciplines, in most cases, into an acceptance of mediocrity. Preservation of the feeling that one is set apart by special gifts depends often on failure to test those gifts, but the reluctance to test oneself generates guilt and disappointment. Unchallenged capacities fade away, it's harder and harder to believe in them. The world allows women not to use themselves, then denies their value because they do not function fully.

But the focus of criticism in *Martha Quest* points not only toward "the world": Martha herself is target as well as heroine of the novel. The anger that shapes the book permeates its details. Martha rages at her parents, at all her elders, at the mysterious forces that limit her opportunities; she wants someone to appear with a large sum of money to "free" her from restrictions in fact not so easily to be escaped. Doris Lessing appears to be even angrier than her heroine. The tone of anger is nothing new in fiction by women—an early example, Mary Wollstonecraft's *Mary: A Fiction* (1793), begins with an explosion of contempt at the heroine's mother for her mindless self-indulgence and ends with expressed longing for heaven as a place providing neither marriage nor giving in marriage: rage directed at men, women, and social institutions. But the total inclusiveness of Lessing's anger *does* represent something new. Wollstonecraft does not attack her heroine; Lessing does, perceiving in her an agent as well as a victim of corruption. Martha may be a pitiable figure, worthy of sympathy for her helpless misery; but so are her mother and father pitiable, equally misshapen by forces they do not understand. Jane Austen, Fanny Burney, believed that people were responsible for their own lives; even Emily Brontë expresses a similar idea through the figure of the younger Cathy. Doris Lessing seems caught between rage because people won't take responsibility for themselves and despair because they *can't*, or at least *women* can't. Rage merging with despair: Martha's state of mind too, although she deceives herself from time to time into believing that she feels softer emotions. The novel contains no viable models, although the vaguely realized Cohen brothers and their friend Jasmine embody the dimly attractive possibility of political commitment and hence seem at least theoretically more appealing than anyone else on hand. Its action, formed by its characters' futile attempts to free themselves from their pasts, has little positive meaning, seeming an imitation of an imitation. People go through motions and can do no more. The shape of the novel is the shape of despair.

If Martha Quest, then, figures as a heroine, she must be a heroine of a very peculiar sort. She stands for nothing, defies nothing successfully, cannot endure her condition without self-defeating gestures of escape. She is passive when she should be active, obtuse when she should be perceptive. Her heroism consists merely in her suffering and her rage, not in any hope or promise of effect. The hope of having an effect rarely prevails among young women.

Where is the female equivalent of *Portrait of the Artist as a Young Man?*

Many books about adolescent women are written expressly *for* adolescent women. Their titles are legion: *Campus Melody* ("Jean Burnaby tackles the problems of 'settling in' to college life—including romance"), *The New Lucinda* ("A family move provides the opportunity for a

shy, self-conscious teenager to change her personality"),
The Unchosen. My literate fifteen-year-old daughter, seeking models, ended up reading something called *My Darling, My Hamburger*. They're nonbooks, really.

Where, even, is the female equivalent of *Catcher in the
Rye?*

The point isn't that novels about female adolescence
don't exist; they do. But it is difficult to think of any
serious literary work by a woman that *celebrates* female
adolescence. *The Heart Is a Lonely Hunter?* Awfully sentimental. Writers of the past might be indulgent toward the
woman in a transitional stage of life because they saw her
clearly in terms of what she would become. Novelists of
the present preach the necessity of adjustment—"settling
in," changing the personality, managing to be chosen
rather than unchosen—or the pathos of rebellion. They
dramatize the extremely limited heroism of suffering, of
irony, of self-criticism. Their protagonists lack the aspiration of Stephen Dedalus and even the cuteness of Holden
Caulfield. Martha Quest and Esther Greenwood exemplify
their situation: their aspirations too unfocused to be meaningful, their consciousness of domesticity as trap too acute
to allow them to take the risk of charm. They are afflicted
by self-pity, and one can understand why; the self-pity is
so intense, so closely linked to the feeling of specialness,
that it amounts paradoxically to self-glorification. But
there isn't enough to glorify. Female sexuality understandably seems to many female authors to mean danger rather
than power; *male* sexuality is power. Female aspiration is
a joke. Female rebellion may be perfectly justified, but
there's no good universe next door, no way out, young potential revolutionaries can't find their revolution. So they
marry in defeat or go mad in a complicated form of
triumph, their meaning the inevitability of failure. More
vividly than older women in fiction, they express women's
anger and self-hatred and the feeling that there's no way
out. Pain is the human condition, but more particularly,
these books announce, the female condition.

The "place" that girls must be made to understand is that of their suffering. Lacking a sense of their free will, of full participation in the human franchise, they learn to know that their suffering derives from gender rather than from common humanity. The woman novelists who depict their plight find in it constant images of challenge aborted or safely contained: the general fate of female challenge.

Five

THE ARTIST
AS WOMAN

This story . . . bears witness to my desire to escape from my familiar surroundings and become an omnipotent woman, or fairy, in a supernaturally free domain.

—MARIE BONAPARTE

Art to me was a state; it didn't need to be an accomplishment.

—MARGARET ANDERSON

Like the adolescent, the artist is a dreamer and a revolutionary; like the adolescent, he often finds his accomplishment inadequate to his imaginings. But his dream, setting him apart, helps him to escape the burden of the real. To some women, as to some men, the idea of art seems to solve all problems. They may insistently describe themselves as artists without actually creating much art, using the self-designation to express wish rather than fact, trying to transform reality by refusing to accept the given conditions of life as definitive. When they write about themselves directly, as many have done, they reveal the complex purposes that the condition of being an artist—unlike adolescence, a *chosen* state—may serve.

To say that the artist has something in common with the adolescent is not to derogate the artist. The comparison suggests both the high aspiration and the characteristic frustration of the artist's life. When the artist is a woman, both the function of aspiration and the nature of frustration assume characteristic forms. In many ways woman artists' self-depictions corroborate the implications of the more indirect testimony offered by fictional accounts of female adolescence.

What artists protest resembles what adolescents find intolerable. Isadora Duncan remembers a past dominated by "the constant spirit of revolt against the narrowness of the society in which we lived, against the limitations of life." Confronting a restrictive environment while powerless to effect significant change in it, a woman may find herself driven inward, to a realm where she can assert the omnipotence life denies her. Art externalizes the inward; imagining oneself an artist, one imagines *using* precious fantasies. The woman's most potent fear is likely to be of abandonment, her most positive vision, of love: the child who fancies herself a fairy princess fancies also the throng of admirers at her feet. She dreams of herself as beautiful, therefore beloved; as powerful because beloved. Her narcissism, too, may seem more acceptable if it belongs to an artist. But what of her dreams of accomplishment? Some women imagine that accomplishment is one more means to love; some fear that it is love's enemy. Almost all seem to understand that publicly acknowledged achievement is a mode of power. The puzzle of how power relates to love in a woman's experience is central to the dilemma of the woman as artist—as it is central to Emma Woodhouse and Catherine Linton. The woman as artist may help to illuminate the woman as woman.

For Isadora Duncan, the function of art was to assert power, the function of power, to demand love. The dancer provides an illuminating example of what it means to "think of oneself as an artist," precisely because words are not her chosen artistic medium. Her writing pours forth her imaginings. A dancer with the world at her feet, she can simultaneously assert her femininity, and her artistic genius. Given her history of spectacular public success, she need not rely on her imagination for sustenance; yet her autobiography testifies that a fantasy of pseudo-divine power remains the foundation of her existence. When she bears a child, she imagines the act of procreation as defining her greatness:

Oh, women, what is the good of us learning to become lawyers, painters or sculptors, when this miracle [of birth] exists? Now I know this tremendous love, surpassing the love of men. I was stretched and bleeding, torn and helpless, while the little being sucked and howled. Life,

life, life! Give me life! Oh, where was my Art? My Art or any Art? What did I care for Art! I felt I was a God, superior to any artist.

But she describes herself as artist—twelve pages later—in equally extravagant terms:

I was possessed by the dream of Promethean creation that, at my call, might spring from the Earth, descend from the Heavens, such dancing figures as the world had never seen. Ah, proud, enticing dream that has led my life from one catastrophe to another! Why did you possess me? Leading, like the light of Tantalus, only to darkness and despair. But no! Still flickering, that light in the darkness must eventually lead me to the Glorious Vision, at last realised. Small fluttering light, just ahead of my stumbling footsteps, I still believe, I still follow you.

Art and motherhood, in Isadora's view, are alike metaphors for power. The "Promethean creation" of art defines one mode in conventional romantic rhetoric, the act of giving birth, another ("a God, superior to any artist"). Parturition temporarily generates feelings of superiority, but before long dreams of artistic triumph entice the dancer once more. Both art and motherhood involve ambiguities about control of the outer world. The mother is "helpless" while "the little being" sucks and howls; yet she claims godlike power. The artist is "possessed" by her dream, itself "proud," dominating and controlling her life; but her own pride emerges as she imagines calling new creations from earth and heaven. Such ambiguity is inherent in the concept of "genius," which possesses its possessor in unpredictable ways, and it requires little imagination to see it also in motherhood. This particular significant analogy between two forms of feminine creativity is particularly significant in Isadora Duncan's account of herself because it suggests why she could receive ultimate satisfaction from neither. Seeking always ways to control her own life and the responses of others (her childhood experience of the father's desertion, the family's bitter poverty and insecurity may hint why), she thus engages in a search destined never to achieve success. Her autobiography ends with invocation of "the dream" associated with Buddha, Christ, "all great artists," Lenin: "I was entering now into this dream that my work and life might become a part of its glorious promise." Only through dreams can she sustain her sense of possibility. She resolves the potential conflict between "art" and "life" by acts of imaginative assertion that subordinate the value of all activity to that of the actor. Gazing at Botticelli's *Primavera,* the dancer decides, "I will dance this picture and give to others this message of love, spring, procreation of life which has been given to me with such anguish. I will give to them, through the dance, such ecstasy." Her extravagant assessment of the power of art to bring "ecstasy" to all the world depends on her exalted self-image: the power, finally, is not art's but Isadora's. She sees herself as the giver of unimaginable gifts, exercising her power benevolently as dancer, mother, teacher, lover, her own expressiveness the sole focus of her attention.

"Art" and "Life" alike aid her endless self-caressing. Other women may imagine lovers who will be their own mirror images; Isadora finds one. "Here, at last, was my mate; my love; my self—for we were not two, but one, that one amazing being of whom Plato tells in the Phaedrus, two halves of the same soul. This was not a young man making love to a girl. This was the meeting of twin souls." She is speaking of Gordon Craig. Earlier, she missed an opportunity to be seduced by Rodin. "What a pity! How often I have regretted this childish miscomprehension which lost to me the divine chance of giving my virginity to the Great God Pan himself, to the Mighty Rodin. Surely Art and all Life would have been richer thereby!" Her attribution of universal significance to her own sex life is another instance of her imaginative transformation of experience. People become souls or pagan gods in her mythology, a seduction can transfigure the universe, a man does not make love to a woman—even when he *does*—but enacts a symbolic union. It is impossible for her to look at things as they are; everything must feed her sense of her own unique significance. "I could not do anything without seeming extravagantly different from other people": the boast and the doom of the artist.

The patterns of Isadora's experience lend themselves readily to her myth-making. Her difficulty in making full commitments, her inability to be satisfied, insure a sequence of constant change. Nothing lasts. One lover yields to another, or to a period of celibacy which astonishes her, so conscious is she of her seductive body. She starts a school of the dance, loves its students, leaves it. She and her siblings decide to build a temple on a Green mountain. They drink goat's milk, dress in tunics, convince the countryside of their madness. Then Isadora goes away, leaving her brother to discover the impossibility of finding water and to abandon the undertaking. The tragic death of her two children corroborates the impermanence of all her commitments. She does not, of course, see it that way—nor is there any literal connection between her inability to sustain anything but the conviction of her own uniqueness and the accident that deprived her of her children. From her point of view, she is a victim of Fate, heroine of a compelling tragic drama. The disproportion between the way she sees and the way she reveals herself creates much of the interest of her autobiography, testimony to a mind that refuses to accept the domination of external circumstance. Her vision more compelling than any conceivable reality, she declares her ultimate power to deny facts, transforming them into myth.

Her tawdry prose both defines and undermines her way of seeing herself, always demanding more interest than it justifies. Isadora, trying to control Life (and Art), cannot control language because she lacks critical capacity, capacity for judgment, capacity to deal in realities. In fact, her vocation as artist expresses her discontent with the real. Only the impossible—the perfectly expressive dance, the ideally fulfilling love, the Greek myth come to life—is adequate. Dreaming of herself as creator and apostle of perfect art, perfect life, she collides with reality, successful as an artist, constantly disappointed by life. Her self-dramatizing, self-loving writing about herself tries to heighten her experience by grandiose metaphor but repeatedly reveals the final falseness of such metaphors, the necessary unhappiness of life so fundamentally founded on a dream of uniqueness.

Dancing, realizing her art, her audience before her, Isadora experiences the arrangement of the universe for which she longs—herself at its center. Here she achieves that unity of fantasy and fact which art demands, able to sustain in action her larger than life-size imagining of herself, winning the applause that attests her stature. As a dancer she expends disciplined energy in the service of her dream. Her real artistic achievement as a physical performer contrasts with the aesthetic inadequacy of her autobiography as a verbal accomplishment. Yet however real her achievement as a dancer, it was not equivalent to her vision of herself as dancer: she may have delighted millions, but she did not bring millions the experience of ecstasy. The power of the dancer is less than that of the dreamer, who can assert and believe her universal power, universal love. As an autobiographer, Isadora Duncan is dreamer rather than observer of her life: not an artist despite all her assertions of artistry.

Although she sometimes recognizes that art and life may make conflicting demands, Isadora characteristically insists on her capacity to reconcile their claims through sheer genius. She refuses to admit that the desire for power may clash with the yearning for love; her denial probably conceals a potent fear. That fear emerges more clearly in other woman artists, less able than she to use imaginative transformation as a weapon against reality. The misery flaunted or concealed in the self-depictions of woman artists often derives from their sense of the incompatibility of their desires. Two interesting cases in point are Dora Carrington, who, after adopting various temporary expedients, killed herself when "love" no longer justified her artistic achievement; and Margaret Anderson, who resolved her conflict by rejecting "life" in favor of an art which existed only in her self-conception.

Carrington's discomfort with her female nature was loud and consistent. "You know I have always hated being a woman. I think I mind much more than most women. The Fiend [her telling metaphor for menstruation] which most women hardly notice, fills me with such disgust and aggitation every time, I cannot get reconciled to it. I am continually depressed by my effeminacy [a word which clearly implies that masculinity is the standard of excellence]. It is true *au fond* I have a female inside which is proved by ~ [her symbol for sexual intercourse] but afterwards a sort of rage fills me because of that very pleasure ~. And I cannot literally bear to let my mind think of ~ again, or of my femaleness."

Carrington had lovers, a husband, a strange prolonged relationship with Lytton Strachey, after whose death her own life seemed so meaningless that she ended it at thirty-nine. She tested the meaning of relationship and of artistic endeavor, finding it impossible to value art more highly than people, feeling that only great artistic creation could compensate for human failure, recognizing her own artistic inadequacy. Love, she believed, was the fundamental means of fulfillment, art only a kind of *pis aller*. But she was doomed to want to be an artist, and doomed to feel inadequate both as artist and as woman. She did not write an autobiography, but her letters, collected by David Garnett, attest her condition. "The pleasures of being loved and loving and having friends and the pains and sordidness of the same relations. . . . One year I would like to take an average of the days one is happy against the wretched days. Perhaps it's absurd ever to think about it. If one painted pictures it wouldn't matter and one probably wouldn't think about it. But I can't see the use of painting pictures 'as good as' those at the London Group." "Gerald [Brenan, her lover], I think I am unfitted ... to have a relation with anyone. ... The alternative is to try and be a serious artist." If she is self-dramatizing in presenting herself as hopelessly miserable, she also reveals genuine unhappiness, even desperation, for the alternatives she perceives are equally impossible. She cannot by taking thought make herself happy rather than wretched, increase the proportion of cheerful days of her own capacity for fruitful relationship; nor can she by will make herself an adequate artist by her own standards. Sometimes she claims that her painting is more important to her than anything else, though characteristically she measures it by comparison with emotional realities: "I think you know that the discovery of a person, of an affection, of a new emotion, is to me *next to my painting* [my italics], the greatest thing I care about." More typical is her moan to Rosamond Lehmann: "Your reproaches towards yourself for not writing more, make my cheeks *burn* with shame. For really I used every excuse not to do any proper painting. It's partly I have such high standards that I can't bear going on with pictures when I can see they are amateurish and dull."

Like Isadora, Carrington feels the "specialness" of the artist, the degree to which she is set apart, and she feels it as tragic. Her wish to love and to be loved conflicts directly with her wish to paint, and she is unable to resolve the conflict in fantasy or in reality. Her image of herself as artist, stressing the terrible split and its inevitability, suggests also that the emotional energies of love may be the source as well as the enemy of art.

The importance above everything [that] a work of art, and a creator of such works, has for me. And yet do you know, this morning I felt these conflicting emotions are destroying my purpose for painting. That perhaps that feeling which I have had ever since I came to London years ago now, that I am not strong enough to live in this world of people, and paint, is a feeling which has complete truth in it. And yet when I envision leaving you [Strachey] and going like Gerald into isolation, I feel I should be so wretched that I should never have the spirit to work.

To paint while living in a world of people is impossible, but it is equally impossible to isolate oneself. Carrington decided to marry Ralph Partridge largely to avoid constituting an emotional drain on Strachey, to whom she writes a heart-rending letter declaring her undying love and her determination not to allow herself the dependency of love. She can imagine avoiding dependency only by creating new dependencies. She cannot paint without loving, she cannot love in "normal" heterosexual ways (her attempt at a sexual relation with Strachey was disastrous); she finds in Strachey the homosexual lover who makes painting and life possible for her, providing love without too many associated demands; without him, quite simply, she cannot exist. "What does anything mean to me now without you. I see my paints and think it is no use, for Lytton will never see my pictures now, and I cry."

The problem she dramatizes, the conflict between the yearning for artistic expression and the desire for relationship, is not peculiar to women, but women are likely to experience it with special intensity. Feminine narcissism as traditionally defined centers on love for one's own body and involves the desire to attract men sexually. The artist's narcissim, on the other hand, connects itself with the sense of creative power, the need to express preceding the need to attract. In men, for whom ideas of conquest often mingle with those of love, artistic power, declaring the vitality of the personality, may seem identical with sexual force. Norman Mailer is sexy despite his paunch; Picasso still clicked his goat hoofs at ninety. For a women, the artist's power—assertive, insistent, dominating—combines uneasily with orthodox feminine modes of attraction. If she performs as the dancer, singer, actress, the potential incompatibility may be resolved: offering herself as artistic product, she offers herself also as sexual being. The writer who writes only of herself (we shall encounter an example in Mary MacLane) attempts an equivalent resolution—risking, however, the totality of self-absorption which shuts out rather than attracts others. But the painter, the novelist, the sculptress or composer, whose separate creation demands attention for itself, faces a cruel dilemma of opposing needs. Carrington attempted to reconcile their conflict by declaring that she painted only for the sake of another; deprived of that rationalization, she could no longer live. Her belief that the feminine role is to serve others became an obsession which had to be gratified in order to make painting possible. If Isadora is the victim of her insistent self-glorification, which attempts to deny the incompatibility of power and love, Carrington was equally trapped in her devotion to the impossible Other, again, an effort to paper over the split in her desires.

Then clash between the artist's narcissism, its need for power satisfied by creation, and the woman's need to attract others by her very nature may be resolved also by denial of an opposite kind, declaring art's transcendent importance at the cost of love's. Margaret Anderson's career—which she painstakingly records, often almost moment by moment, in three volumes—involves a systematic if not fully self-aware effort to deny her need for others or theirs for her. "My unreality is chiefly this: I have never felt much like a human being. It's a splendid feeling." "I have always had so little need of the humanity of people. Their humanity is always the same." "I can't imagine belonging to a group." The life she reports is one of increasing isolation and diminishing accomplishment: first vigorous activity in Chicago and New York, then twenty-one years in France with a beloved older woman, finally solitude, in which she sustains herself by her larger than life-size self-image. Like Isadora, she feels superior to others: "My impression was that I was one of the world's most favored beings, lifted through space from one rapturous event to another, possessing everything necessary for happiness and living like a lighted Christmas tree." And like Isadora's self-conception, her "impression" derives more from wish than from fact.

Yet she had some solid accomplishment to her credit, mainly as an editor. Founding *The Little Review* before she was twenty-one, she made it an important medium of artistic expression. Her work as editor had symbolic as well as literal significance, providing a metaphor for her orientation toward life. "I was born to be an editor," she observes. Shifting the metaphor in another volume, she makes the point clearer: "I always felt that I knew the score. From morning to night I lived like an orchestra conductor." Both images are of control. The conflicts implicit for most women in a commitment to art generate chaos, a grotesque disorder of clashing impulses and purposes. The release of this disorder drove Carrington to her death; the control of disorder was the center of Margaret Anderson's life. Her impulse, as she points out, was always toward revision—of other people's expression, and of her own. She insists on dominating experience, on dominating her own consciousness: "I tried never to let a day go by without turning it into a trance." Controlling her experience, she limits it more and more. It becomes less interesting to the reader with whom she shares it—she had difficulty finding a publisher for her autobiography after the first volume. There is pathos in her claim to have achieved self-knowledge with the aid of the mystic Gurdjieff, who helps her to see "that fixed point about which my life movement had revolved . . . : self-love." The insight is all to convincing—but insight appears to have brought no end to the self-obsession, expressed in ever more frequent claims of the author's superiority to others, her rarer sensibilities, the isolation that testifies to her magnificent difference.

An artist only in self-conception, not in accomplishment, a failure at human relations, Margaret Anderson announces defiantly, "I won't be cornered and I won't stay suppressed." But she avoids the restrictions of society only by self-constriction, depriving herself of the satisfactions both of art and of relationship, demonstrating that her editorship of her own life has produced a very cramped volume. The "power" she achieves focuses mainly on herself, and its most conspicuous result in an autobiography which, like Isadora's, testifies to the substitution of self-flattery for self-confrontation. The need to think of herself as an artist is far more intense than the need to be one.

Isadora Duncan believed that the power of artistic success was a means to love, and that she had achieved both to the highest degree. Carrington and Margaret Anderson, understandably less secure in their sense of themselves as artists, doubted whether artistic power could co-exist with fulfilled love. A third possibility is represented by Marie Bashkirtseff, who shared Isadora's conviction without her achievement and identified herself as artist at least partly on the basis of her passionate yearning for fame and love.

A young woman of Russian birth whose adolescence passed mainly in Paris, Marie Bashkirtseff died of tuberculosis at the age of twenty-four, leaving diaries (clearly intended for publication) which record her experience from the time she was twelve to a few days before her death. Both adolescent and aspiring artist, she wanted desperately to be a great painter. Early in her teens, she had hoped to be a singer, but there was little evidence that she could sing. She transferred her aspiration to the visual arts, dedicating herself passionately to her effort to achieve recognition for her artistic production, ignoring her gathering illness in her full commitment to her studies. For her the connection between fame and love seemed perfectly clear. "What is necessary to my very existence is to have it acknowledged that I possess great talent. I never shall be happy like all the world. As Balzac wrote: 'To be celebrated and to be loved, that is happiness!' And yet, to be loved is only an accessory, or, rather, the natural result of being celebrated."

Over and over, in a way that by now must seem familiar, the diarist reiterates her distinction between herself and "all the world," insisting that she is different, that she can escape from the tedious restrictions of daily life into romantic unhappiness or the equally romantic special happiness of fame. Social restrictions, she realizes, are particularly limiting for a woman. She cannot go anywhere without a chaperone, she has no freedom of movement, people talk about her if she tries to assert her difference, and she seems as fearful as Hedda Gabler of the strictures of public opinion. But if people talked about her *as an artist,* everything would be wonderful. The self-image of artist is one of freedom and of ultimate justification. It is difficult, she knows, really to *be* an artist. When she paints real pictures, she necessarily risks judgment. She can protect herself by the knowledge that she is only a student; page after page of her journal records her obsessive comparisons of herself with her contemporaries. She has had less training, less experience than they; less should be expected of her. Intensely competitive, absorbed in rituals of comparative judgment, she is subject to violent discouragement over the impossibility of adequate artistic achievement. The remedy for such discouragement is the retreat inward. She can imagine herself as flawlessly beautiful (beauty, she explains, is "everything for a woman") and control her self-presentation to impose this self-image on the world. "I take great pride in appearing radiant and proud, impregnable in every way." She is literally impregnable: her relations with men take place only in her imagination. On one occasion she allows herself to be kissed, by a cardinal's nephew; nothing comes of the relationship, and she feels humiliated by having made herself momentarily vulnerable. Far safer to dream of ideal men, confiding to her diary that she would be unable to marry a man with corns, a man possessed of actual human frailties. Her dreams of herself as artist serve a similar defensive function.

There is no way for Marie Bashkirtseff to reconcile fantasy with fact: the fantasies are too extreme. She cannot be as beautiful as she imagines herself being, no real lover will be devoid of corns, no picture that she paints will win as much fame and love as she demands. The omnipotence possible in a world devoid of real opposition is more triumphant than literal power could conceivably be. The only way to preserve an inviolable sense of power is never to test it: fantasy is the best protection against the imperfections of reality.

All Marie Bashkirtseff's fantasies—of beauty, of fame, of perfect romance, of artistic achievement—reflect her intense desire for love. But the tragic result of her dedication to a larger than life-size self-image, larger than life-size demands on the world, is necessary isolation. No lover, no mother, no friend, no art critic can satisfy her needs. She is forced finally back on herself: "I know one person who loves me, understands me, pities me, who employs every hour in efforts to make me happier; someone who will do everything for me and will succeed; someone who will never betray me again—although that happened once [when she kissed the cardinal's nephew]—and that person is *myself*." Her recognition that only can gratify herself is perhaps ironic in tone; it is nonetheless true.

Mortality, the condition in which all human achievement must be measured, the ineluctable reality, is the final enemy of fantasy. As the psychoanalyst Marion Milner puts it, "Certainly the greatest disillusion, the greatest discrepancy between one's wish and the external facts, is the fact of death." Marie Bashkirtseff, like the rest of us, was dying; but faster than most. She avoids the ultimate disillusionment by attempting to incorporate death itself into her structure of romantic illusion, dreaming of death as she dreams of love: the seal of her uniqueness. "I can not live; I am not constituted like other people. . . . Were I a goddess, and had the whole universe at my service, I would find the service bad." "I should like to see everything, to possess everything, to embrace everything, to become absorbed in everything, and to die . . . ; to die in an ecstasy of joy at the thought of solving the last mystery." In some moods she enjoys thinking of herself as romantically doomed; in others, she delcares herself "amused" by the possibility of death and unwilling to take measures against it. Although she reports symptoms of illness and worries of doctors, the threat of death is never real to her; her imagination converts it into further justification for her narcissism.

But the young woman's early death, throwing a special glamour over an externally uneventful life, also becomes a powerful emblem of the limitations against which she struggled. If she was unable fully to confront this unavoidable final limitation except through the rosy lens of fantasy, she was equally unable to confront the other limitations of her life. Her only power was the power to imagine what she wished to be, what she wished of others; to try to impose her imaginings on reality. Her artistic talent suggested the possibility of fulfilling simultaneously her yearning for love and her yearning for power; or perhaps the strength of those yearnings itself generated what talent she possessed. By thinking of herself as an artist, she could escape full relization of the world's unwillingness to take her as seriously as she took herself.

At a dinner party once I met a young woman who had kept a daily journal since her early adolescence. I asked her what sort of material she included in it. "Oh," she replied, "I lie."

She might have said that she wrote fiction in her journal, but she was too conscious of the need her fictions served: to re-create her experience in a way that made it tolerable.

Mary MacLane was such a liar: and her lies, revealing the familiar wish for power and love, reveal also the degree to which she feels confined to the world of her imagination in order to achieve them. Another adolescent, she resembles Martha Quest and Esther Greenwood in her inability to commit herself to meaningful activity. Like Isadora, she interprets her life in terms of a myth of herself. Like Marie Bashkirtseff, she offers virtually no external accomplishment to substantiate the myth. She confesses in a second edition of her account of herself that she lied in the first. A nineteen-year-old girl of no external distinction whatever, living in Butte, Montana, she remarks her experience to suit her image of a remarkable Self. What she writes is no journal but a "story": a narrative imagined in a form that substantiates her grandest claim, the claim to be an artist. Her evocation of the large personality of artist, her self-justification through sensibility, generated her extraordinary looks.

Here is the opening sequence of *The Story of Mary Maclane*, published in 1902, now long out of print, remarkably revealing of the psyche of one variety of woman-as-artist:

> *I of womankind and of nineteen years, will now begin to set down as full and frank a Portrayal as I am able of myself, Mary MacLane, for whom the world contains not a parallel.*
>
> *I am convinced of this, for I am odd.*
> *I am distinctly original innately and in development.*
> *I have in me a quite unusual intensity of life.*
> *I can feel.*
> *I have a marvelous capacity for misery and for happiness.*
> *I am broad-minded.*
> *I am a genius.*

Her first self-definition sets the tone of the book and prepares for her later claims, her description of herself as Romantic artist, comparable to Lord Byron and Marie Bashkirtseff although, she decides finally, "deeper" and "more wonderful" than her Russian predecessor. In many respects her comparisons are accurate: she is indeed Byronic in her insistence on her grand isolation and her superiority to conventional moral norms (although she doesn't actually *do* anything unconventional); and she resembles Marie Bashkirtseff in the intensity of her youthful narcissism and its focus on the self-image of artist.

Unlike the Russian woman, though, Mary MacLane is richly aware of her environment. Her triumph and her limitation as an artist derive from her need to define herself against her surroundings, animate and inanimate: to distinguish herself vividly from her mother, who, she says feels for her daughter what a hen might feel for her egg, to defy the commonplace through exact rendition of observed detail, the exactness itself declaring her superiority. She sees precisely what surrounds her, praying to the devil to deliver her from her milieu, with its lisle stockings, people who refer to a woman's "shape," fried eggplant, talk of "a nice young man." Even a toothbrush provides her with a means of differentiation. Hers has a silver handle, but it hangs in the bathroom with five more matter-of-fact brushes. When she removes it, she feels overwhelmed by the ordinary; when she lets it stay, she must contemplate evidence of her separation from her kind. Everything she sees, everything she hears, refers to her. Her literary transformation of experience fills Butte with interest while declaring her frustration, making meaningful for the reader exactly what the writer experiences as meaningless. Her meticulous examination of banality is an act of triumph over it.

Marie Bashkirtseff worked hard at the study of art, making at least that much attempt to realize her dream of herself as artist. Her Montana imitator creates nothing beyond her personality to justify her self-designation, but her personality, as rendered in prose, becomes a work of art. Toward the end of her self-portrayal, she explains the nature of that "genius" she has insistently claimed: "I am merely and above all a creature of intense passionate *feeling.* I feel—everything. It is my genius. It burns me like fire." (One may recall Catherine, from *Wuthering Heights.*) But she "would give up this genius eagerly, gladly—at once and forever—for one dear, bright day free from loneliness."

It's the familiar dilemma: does the artist, even the artist of feeling, win love or lose it? Mary MacLane is not concerned with fame, but she is obsessed with the problem of winning love. And she recognizes the alienating effect of her self-obsession. "I know I am not lovable," she confesses. ". . . There is no one to love me now." "My wailing, waiting soul burns with but one desire: *to be loved—oh, to be loved.*" Although she protects herself by irony in much of her self-description, all protection vanishes here: one cannot avoid the reality of her pain. Self-mockery returns as she expresses her desire to be loved in more specific terms, but it does not disguise her genuine emotion. Mary MacLane imagines two lovers: the devil and Napoleon. Their meaning for her is identical: *strength* makes both attractive. Her longing for Napoleon has particular poignance because much earlier she has declared, "I have the personality, the nature, of a Napoleon, albeit a feminine translation. . . . Had I been born a man I would by now have made a deep impression of myself on the world—on some part of it. But I am a woman." Unable to sustain her imagination of herself as a Napoleon, she falls back on a feminine transformation: if she cannot be a great man, let her be loved by one. But such love is punishment: "I would have you conquer me, crush me, know me." "Treat me cruelly, brutally." The ultimate fantasy demands neither Satan nor Napoleon, only "any man so that he is strong and thoroughly a villain, and so that he fascinates me." She sounds more and more like Catherine, inventing her Heathcliff, but unable to discover him.

Although she speaks of falling in love with the devil and with Napoleon, her imagery of being overwhelmed, possessed, denies her active participation in love. When she thinks of herself as feminine, her stress on being loved;

conversely, her own capacity to love seems to her masculine. Much of her anguish focuses in her feeling that she is not, after all, "a real woman"—specifically because, she says, she is unable ever to "go beyond *self*" like such noble beings as Charlotte Corday. Marie Bashkirtseff had a less self-punishing version of the same fantasy, concluding that she herself was a woman only "on the outside." She took pride in the sense of her fundamental maleness, one more fantasy of escape from the reality of social restriction. For Mary MacLane, on the other hand, the self-image of bisexuality was a tragic rather than triumphant mark on her difference from others. Unable to feel herself a real woman, she was obviously not a real man either. Lacking the satisfaction of either sex, she envied both; her desire to be an artist marked her to herself as a sexual anomaly; and it doubtless would have been scant comfort to her to learn that modern psychoanalysts find bisexuality characteristic of the artist's temperament.

Jonathan Swift's famous contrast between the spider "which feeding and engendering on it self, turns all into Excrement and Venom; producing nothing at all, but Flybane and a Cobweb" and the bee "which, by an universal Range, with long Search, much Study, true Judgment, and Distinction of Things, brings home Honey and Wax," defined the difference between supporters of the Moderns and the Ancients in *The Battle of the Books*. The spider "Spins and Spits wholly from himself" because of his pride. But many a woman has been forced by fate rather than temperament to compose like the spider, deprived of the range, search, and study made possible for the certainly masculine (this bee being metaphor rather than insect) honeybee. Feeding and engendering on herself, Mary MacLane creates her story, herself its heroine and its victim. Her subject is always herself—a compelling subject for reader as well as writer. The woman who dreams of the artist's power exercises it in describing it: she has literally become an artist of self-concentration. Her artistic energy throbs with the pressure generated by confinement.

With no subject but herself, she justifies by the force of her prose her demand to be taken seriously.

"Nothing is easier to pardon than the mistakes and excesses of self-love," Lionel Trilling has written. "If we are quick to condemn them, we take pleasure in forgiving them. . . . But we distinguish between our response to the self-love of men and the self-love of women. No woman could have won the forgiveness that has been so willingly given (after due condemnation) to the self-regard of, say, Yeats and Shaw." The observation may be out-of-date, but it certainly applies to Mary MacLane's era, when to be a woman was to be severely restricted. Allowed not even the open indulgence of self-love, the writer could escape by denying actuality in the construction of a powerful self-image. Her most trivial acts, even her flaws—like Marie Bashkirtseff, she claims to tell *everything* about herself—are glamorized or manufactured. Thus, she claims her *eating* an index of her artistic gifts. Her story converts eating into an aesthetic activity, rhapsodizing over olives, steak and onions, brown sugar fudge, maintaining that her consumption of them amounts to an artistic achievement. "I have uncovered for myself the art that lies in obscure shadows. I have discovered the art of the day of small things." Cooking, for most women a way of taking care of others, becomes for Mary MacLane a means to sustain herself metaphorically as well as literally. Avid for experience, confined in opportunity, she greedily takes in to herself what she can, savors what is available, pathetically boasts her responsiveness to a green onion as an index of her imaginative gifts. Similarly, she brags of stealing three dollars in order to buy chrysanthemums for an impoverished neighbor: thus she declares her difference from her family and acquaintances. In the second edition of her book, she admits that the entire story was invented; the admission of lying becomes another element in her vision of herself as extraordinary. But the fascination of Mary MacLane's books is not primarily that of falsification. It comes from the purity of her focus on herself, the brilliance and ingenuity with which she finds meanings and declares her right to attention, not for her accomplishments, only for herself. Mary MacLane declares the supreme relevance of only her own standards, demanding not merely to be forgiven her self-love but to be justified by it. She is her own creation, the truth or falsity of her record finally irrelevant.

Yet that record has the undeniable flavor of truth, in its obsessive concentration on external detail: it cannot be dismissed as the product only of a young woman's wishes, her daydreams of how she might be seen. For Marie Bashkirtseff, the link between the real world and that of dreams is her literal activity as an aspiring painter. By working at her art she defends against the temptation to abondon reality in favor of total commitment to the inner world. Mary MacLane does as little as possible in the real world; or so she tells us. She protests the restrictions of her female lot by going through minimal motions—making her bed, talking with a neighbor, cooking a meal—but refusing to invent more meaningful activity. Her mind, however, reflects steadily on external reality: observation is the stuff of her curious prose-poetry. Her toothbrush with a silver handle sounds like something she made up; but it is actually something she looks at. The significance with which she invests it is from within, but her commitment to the outer world remains, when she writes best, the foundation of her extravagances.

Mary MacLane's cobwebs, often compelling in their intricacy and ingenuity, become flimsy at the moments when they lose that firm connection to actuality: her writing doesn't always have the discipline of art. Her imaginings can be grandiose, empty, self-indulgent, her prose unbearably self-caressing ("My heart, my soul, my mind go wandering—wandering; ploughing their way through darkness with never a ray of light; groping with helpless hands; asking, longing, wanting things: pursued by a Demon of Unrest") when she abandons all actuality beyond her emotions, answerable to no demand for exactness. Clichés multiply as she asserts the intensity of her feeling, demonstrating the destructive paradox of self-concentration: literary obsession with the self may end by weakening the self's actuality. Mary MacLane's midnight onions are more real than all her groping with helpless hands.

Hers is, of course, a version of the dilemma faced by all Romantic artists. Alienated from their environment, possessed by a sense of their own uniqueness, they may exploit their powers of perception yet feel that their surroundings are not worthy of them. Often they are gripped by what the critic Gabriel Josipovici has called "the paralysing euphoria of the Imagination," all conceivable reality less satisfying than the contemplation of infinite possibility. Economic necessity has forced action on most men since the early nineteenth century; and one may wonder whether the lack of it was an advantage to Shelley and Byron, although certainly it was to Wordsworth. It is hard to imagine a male Emily Dickinson in any era. If our poets are also insurance executives or doctors or college teachers, their work seems not to suffer as a result; one may even posit a certain profit. For women, on the other hand, until the very recent past, inertia was a social possibility. The world might not only allow but actively encourage women—as it has never encouraged men—simply to wallow in their inner lives. Mary MacLane's fate appears to have been near-paralysis. The art of her journal remained a compelling preoccupation, but her later life, more than her early years, has an unnerving aspect of parable.

"Later," in this case, means her early thirties. She herself again provides testimony. *I, Mary MacLane* appeared in 1917, fifteen years after the first book, to which it is a sequel. A war was going on; it is mentioned once, as Mary MacLane fantasizes briefly about exchanging her "two black dresses for two white ones with red crosses on the sleeves." She is back in Butte, having left it for eight years in Boston and New York made possible by the fame of her earlier book which, as she observes in its second edition, brought her "an astounding notoriety and much good gold money." In the East she met other young women, other writers, men who were interested in her; she hints at least one love affair. But she chose to return to Montana, and she writes once more of her life of spiritual impoverishment there—a life freely elected. Now she is the old maid daughter of the family, her external life confined to housework, solitary walks, reading. She makes her bed meticulously and picks lint from her blue rug. She eats dinner with the family, but she doesn't eat much. On the other hand, she makes midnight raids on the pantry, stealing a cold boiled potato or a green onion. Her picture gallery has been enlarged to include Marie Lloyd, Fanny Brawn, Nell Gwynn, Ty Cobb, Charlotte Corday, Susan B. Anthony, Queen Boadicea: earlier, it contained only thirteen pictures of Napoleon. John Keats's image presides; he is the central object of her adoration. She owns two black dresses, she listens to the voices of children, she takes luxurious baths. She laughs at William Jennings Bryan.

The choice of Butte over Boston is the choice of fantasy over reality. It enables Mary MacLane to retreat to a life obsessively private, a woman's life of external insignificance, inner power. She still defines herself as woman—meaning now something distinctly sexual—and as artist—meaning something rather peculiar.

I am a true Artist, not as a writer but as a writing person. . . .

It is not literary but a personal art. . . .

I once thought me destined to be a "writer" in the ordinary sense. And many good people visioned a writing career for me. It has a vapid taste, just to recall it. . . .

My writing is to me a precious thing—and a rare bird—and a Babylonish jade. It demands gold in exchange for itself. But though it is my talent it is not my living. It is too myself, like my earlobes and my throat, to commercialize by the day.

From her point of view, her selfhood now *is* her writing. She cannot bear to think of herself as "a 'writer' in the ordinary sense" or to contemplate anything so "vapid" as a "writing career." The sparseness of her literary production and its total concentration on herself as subject distinguish her from the "ordinary" writer and declare the high value of the "precious thing," her writing. So she thinks of herself as a writer exactly because she doesn't write much, and her literary art has weird affinities with her rubbing cold cream into her face, her attention to the quality of her underwear. One chapter begins, "I love my shoes." The forms of self-adoration are various.

Mary MacLane's most impassioned claim is that she yearns for the real:

> I want to plunge headlong into life—not imitation life which is all I've yet known, but honest worldly life at its biggest and humanest and cruelest and damnedest: to be blistered and scorched by it if it be so ordered—so that only it's realness—from the outside of my skin to the deeps of my spirit. . . .
>
> I want to feel one big hot red bloody kiss-of-Life placed square and strong on my mouth and shot-straight into me to the back wall of my Heart.

But her language betrays her: reality is her ultimate fantasy. Her actual experience—Butte, Boston, New York—seems to her only "imitation life"; her dream of erotic satisfaction identifies itself with wider, vaguer kinds of fulfillment; her masochism emerges once more, in the eagerness to be "blistered and scorched," the yearning for the "hot red bloody" kiss: clearly no literal event will ever seem sufficiently "real" to satisfy her. Despite the fact that the book's compelling subject is her self, even that self is so manifestly an image of her dreams that the author becomes a fictional character: one finds it harder to believe in her than in her observations of external fact. Did she really pick the lint off the rug, did she really have a "picture gallery"? Such questions rarely occur to the reader of autobiography in relation to such mundane details. We may wonder whether a love affair took place exactly as described, but why should we doubt whether a woman does the housework, what could be at stake to make her lie about such matters? What's at stake for Mary MacLane is her own significance, denied by the world outside her, therefore needing to be created in the most minute detail.

Here she is, explaining why she enjoys the back of magazines:

I like the Revolvers, handsome plausible short-barreled Revolvers with pictures of ordinary people in dim-lit midnight bedrooms, and ordinary expected-looking burglars climbing in windows—Revolvers of ten shots and six, and of different calibers, and all of them gleamingly mystically desirable: ... I like the foods—of miraculous spotless purity and enticement—Biscuits and Chocolate and Figs, and Foie-gras in thick glossy little pots, so richly pictured and sung that merely to let my thoughts graze in their pasturage fattens my Heart: I like the men's very thin Watches, and men's Garters—no metal can touch you—, and men's fluffy, lathered shaving sticks, and men's trim smart flawless tailored Suits, in none of which I have use or interest until I find them in the Back of a magazine: I like the jars and boxes and tubes and glasses of Cold Cream, Cold Cream fit for skins of goddesses, fit for elves to feed on—a soft satiny scented snow-white elysium of wax and vaseline and almond paste, pictured in forty alluring shapes till it feels pleasantly ecstatic just to be living in the same world with bewitching vases of Cold Cream, Cold Cream, Cold Cream—always bewitching and lovely but never so notably and festively as in the Back of a magazine: and I like the Pencils: and Book-cases: and Silver: and Jewels: and Glass: and Gloves ...

The self-awareness of this account is as striking as its sense of detail. Mary MacLane understands that she had no "use or interest" for the appurtenances she glorifies until they are transformed into fantasy. Real revolvers, real men's suits, are tedious. The advertisements which picture them distance them, provide a kind of allegory of the transforming operations of the artist's mind. Real cold cream is alluring, imagined cold cream—like Keats's unheard melodies—more so. And of course the operations of the artist's mind are much in evidence here: in the precision of language ("notably and festively"), the comedy of conjunctions ("Fit for the skin of goddesses, fit for elves to feed on"), the irony of perspective ("ordinary expected-looking burglars"), even the delight in commercial jargon ("no metal can touch you"). Real advertisements, after all, are tedious too. Enjoying the play of her mind over what is intended only to encourage buying and selling, not bothering about the "real," the writer uncovers the poetry of the prosaic.

Here, clearly, she is not lying: her professed subject and her real one are the same, the capacity of her imagination to reconcile her to the actual by converting it to the fantastic. One admires and wonders at the force of that imagination; temporarily one may even share the author's high self-assessment. But Mary MacLane's compulsion always to transform actuality or reject it or deny its claim to reality, as when she terms her own experience "imitation life," finally limits the scope of her artistic achievement. She is alienated from her own life, as she is alienated from her fellows by her tormenting awareness of being unique. Her dilemma as an artist is that of all artists, all adolescents, all human beings: to reconcile the inner and the outer world. Her compulsive, selective eating, a primitive act of incorporation, enables her to possess what she wants from outside—though only, of course, by destroying it. Her compulsive writing, attempting equivalent incorporation, likewise risks destroying objective reality. Marion Milner remarks "the primitive hating that results from the inescapable discrepancy between subjective and objective, between the unlimited possibilities of one's dreams and what the real world actually offers us." Such hating seems the dominant fact of Mary MacLane's experience—her contempt for other people is almost total; she protects herself against the probability of receiving less love than she yearns for by declaring her total superiority to everyone who might offer love. As an imaginative woman, she faces a vaster discrepancy between subjective and objective than a male counterpart would probably endure because the possibilities of real existence are so severely limited by social expectation. In Butte, the limitation is obvious: she is supposed to sweep the floor and wash the dishes. In Boston and New York, which seem to offer relative freedom, limitation is only more subtle: she still feels herself exploited by a rigid set of conventions, even if those conventions belong to the Bohemian world. Everywhere, objective reality is a terrible threat to imaginative freedom. So Mary MacLane, like Isadora Duncan, struggles to impose her dreams on the world, working to promulgate that self-image she must treasure as the best compensation for a limited existence. Sometimes her persona is as compelling for the reader as for the author; sometimes it seems only a figment of the writer's imagination, a solipsistic avoidance of communication.

Relatively few women have asserted themselves unambiguously as shaping artists in the act of writing about themselves; even Anaïs Nin, whose self-glorification as artist and as woman parallels Isadora Duncan's, publishes diaries rather than formal autobiography. Mary McCarthy, insisting explicitly on the *art* of autobiography, masters life by describing it. In a fashion rare among woman artists describing themselves, she achieves a harmonious interchange of subjective and objective, recognizing and dealing with her own desire for an imaginative heightening of experience, understanding that fantasy precedes art but is not identical with it.

231

The fusion Mary McCarthy achieves between inner wishes and outer reality depends on artistic control. Unlike Isadora, she does not have to assert her total power over the external world or to revel in her ultimate lovability. Unlike Mary MacLane, she need not cut herself off from actual experience in order to avoid damaging her image of her own specialness. Yet "specialness" and "lovability" are important to her, too. She claims them on the basis of her literary accomplishment, and makes that accomplishment a demonstration of her life's struggle and achievement. Her awareness of herself as artist—as a writer converting her life into a work of art—is unrelenting in *Memories of a Catholic Girlhood*. It is, indeed, her fundamental subject. Unlike women whose self-definition as artist defends them from the necessity of accomplishment, Mary McCarthy shows the artist as worker. Her "work" is to control her experience not only by converting it to myth but by commenting on her own myth-making: criticism the crucial dimension.

The child Mary's early experience, shared with three brothers, was of glamorous parents who gratified every desire. When she was six years old both parents died, victims of a flu epidemic, leaving their children to a dismal existence as charges of an ineffectual, infatuated aunt and her brutal husband. A few years later Mary (but not her brothers) were rescued, moving from Minneapolis austerity to Seattle luxury, cared for by a loving Protestant grandfather and his mysterious Jewish wife. She attends now an elegant convent school run by French nuns; she "loses her faith" in dramatic fashion and "regains" it equally dramatically; she moves on to a Protestant boarding school, had daring friends, successfully tricks her grandparents. Her narrative ends with her high-school experience, although there are references to her going east to Vassar and to her first unsuccessful marriage.

Adolescence contemplated from the vantage point of maturity looks very different from adolescence being endured; it is no wonder that Mary McCarthy's account of her teen-age years bears little resemblance to Marie Bashkirtseff's or Mary MacLane's. But she shares with them, and with most other adolescents, certain problems. "It was the idea of being noticed that consumed all my attention; the rest, it seemed to me, would come of itself." To be noticed is, in youthful fantasy, to be loved—that is "the rest" that will come of itself. It is not fame that she wants, not even a single lover; she yearns rather to be loved by everyone. Achieving minor notoriety, she finds it a precarious state. The security of love eludes her, nor can she even confess directly her need for it.

The autobiographer's apparent reluctance to admit openly her deep desire for love may be accounted for by the fact that the desire conflicts cruelly with the effort to control experience by understanding it, this memoir's more explicit theme. Commitment to others decreases one's possibilities for control, yet remains vitally necessary. A child orphaned at six must feel the need for relationship, and Mary's early guardians provide virtually no emotional security. Moreover, they make "success" seem the opposite of love: Uncle Myers beats the girl to prevent her getting "stuck up" when she wins an essay contest. Successful at school in Minneapolis, admired by her classmates for her intellect and her wit, she is not loved; she feels alienated from her fellows by her pitiable condition as neglected orphan. In Seattle, burning to be noticed, she is never noticed enough; although she learns to follow the devious social laws that govern her classmates, she cannot extract emotional satisfaction from them.

When she finds temporary emotional gratification, it is often at the cost of intellectual clarity: her memoir abounds in illustrative episodes. Twelve-year-old Mary, having stained her bedsheets slightly with blood from a cut on her leg, tries desperately to explain to successive nuns that she has not started menstruating. The nuns comfort away her putative fears about "becoming a woman"; she, finally helpless, accepts the offered solace and tries in succeeding months to produce a convincing show of blood to mark the sanitary napkins inexorably issued to her. It is a comedy of mutual incomprehension permeated with pathos. Miss McCarthy sees her girlish self as pulsating with energy, "excited," forever "crying out," "chafing" to be heard, "breaking in," "fighting the convent." On the other side are the forces of constraint and paralysis. The nuns are "soothing, and yet firm." Their function is to calm, to hush, to reassure. " 'And you, Mary, have lost your dear mother, who could have made this easier for you.' Rocked on Madame MacIllvra's lap, I felt paralysis overtake me, and I lay, mutely listening, against her bosom, my face being tickled by her white, starched, fluted wimple, while she explained to me how babies were born, all of which I had heard before."

The image of the child rocked on a maternal bosom, simultaneously reminded of the loss of her real mother and provided with a substitute, is both reassuring and frightening. Its positive aspect is the ease of being taken care of. But the cost is helpless passivity, the victim forced to listen to what she already knows. How does Mary get herself into such a position? She asks the question, dimly recognizing her own concealed complicity, but she cannot answer it. "It was just that I did not fit into the convent pattern: the simplest thing I did, like asking for a clean sheet, entrapped me in consequences that I never could have predicted." "There I was, a walking mass of lies . . . ; yet all this had come about without my violition and even contrary to it." The trouble comes when she asks for help—for a clean sheet, for rescue from her pretended loss of faith. She wishes to be taken care of, to be loved, but (like everyone) she also wants the opposite: to be independent, self-sufficient. So she is repeatedly "entrapped in consequences" she cannot anticipate, forced to deceit by her internal conflict—for she cannot risk rejection by fully declaring her independence, revealing that her loss of faith has become real and irreversible, telling the nuns unequivocally that they are deluded by false assumptions. Her clarity of perception, her demanding logical faculty, clash with her yearning for love and make internal conflict perpetual. She allows the nuns to be deceived, yet feels the full horror of deception; allows them to believe her restored to the bosom of the Church while driven by logic to reject the Church's comfort. When she visits the Brent sisters in Medicine Springs, Montana, they supply an instant boyfriend—married, to be sure, but that's not the real problem. The real problem is that even as an adolescent, Mary cannot avoid the consequences of her own perception. She wishes—or thinks she wishes—only to enjoy herself. Yet, "When I saw him in the drugstore, with his white coat and ripply hair, I was embarrassed for him, just because I could see him so clearly *from the outside,* as a clerk, who would always be a clerk, limited, like his kisses, flat, like the town." Although she's excited by the fact that this particular clerk is "sweet on her," she must struggle with her perception that the man is unworthy, the situation ridiculous; there is no way to resolve the incompatibility. The spirit's capacity to see, in McCarthy's autobiography as in her novel *The Company She Keeps,* generates possible salvation, but also wretchedness.

For Marie Bashkirtseff and Mary MacLane, emotional isolation seems a proof of uniqueness; they sustain their self-images partly by reflection on how inevitably they are misunderstood. Mary McCarthy, wishing desperately to be understood, wishes equally intensely to be unique. Her self-depiction repeatedly concentrates on her difference from the rest of mankind, the subject recurring in every chapter. Such "differentness," of course, is another obstacle to love. As in classic versions of the myth of artistic specialness (Prometheus, Daedalus), the writer's story reveals the special anguish of being set apart.

The defining episode of Mary's early youth was the tin butterfly contretemps. Accused of stealing the trinket, the girl makes self-righteous proclamations of innocence which convince her aunt but not her uncle, who beats her into a false confession (promptly rescinded) when the butterfly appears pinned beneath the tablecloth at her place. Subsequent beatings elicit from her "wild cries," but no further admission of guilt. "I finally limped up to bed, with a carzy sense of inner victory, like a saint's, for I had not recanted, despite all they had done or could do to me." Years later, her brother tells her "that the famous night of the butterfly, he had seen Uncle Myers steal into the dining room from the den and lift the tablecloth, with the tin butterfly in his hand." Or perhaps he tells her nothing of the sort; perhaps the idea was suggested by a playwriting instructor in college.

Mary McCarthy's deliberate introduction of the possibility that this dramatic episode contains fiction as well as fact emphasizes the mythic aspect of the tale. Ernst Kris has documented the theory that artists' biographies often incorporate anecdotes belonging to traditional mythology of the artist: the story, for example, that the youth's talents were discovered as he drew pictures in the sand while tending his sheep. Autobiographers also draw upon mythology, recalling or reshaping events that validate their claim of perceived significance in their experience. Mary McCarthy's butterfly story closely resembles Rousseau's account of refusing to confess falsely to breaking a comb as a child. In both instances, the triumphant protagonist considers the episode a testimony of his moral superiority to those around him, who misunderstand but cannot destroy him. Rousseau generalizes the effect of such misunderstanding, claiming that the event produced his lasting hatred of injustice in all its forms. McCarthy draws no general conclusions, allowing the encounter with adult unfairness to be one among many of her efforts to come to terms with an incomprehensible world. But the real point is that she does *not* come to terms. The artist-as-hero-or-heroine never comes to terms; he defies the realm of things-as-they-are to claim his difference. If anecdotes to prove it did not exist, he would be forced to invent them. Looking back on his life, he sees a sequence of proofs that he is not like other people.

Of course no one sees himself as altogether "like other

people," but not everyone is comfortable making the assertion of superiority hidden in the claim of difference. Many who cry that they are set apart base their self-esteem on production, achievement, performance. For Mary McCarthy, the self-justifying performance is the artful autobiography itself. The form and style of *Memories of a Catholic Girlhood* largely define its meaning, as the book constantly calls attention to its own artifice, manipulating the reader's doubt about whether "true" autobiography is possible. Of course not, Mary McCarthy says, if what you mean is "literal." No one has total recall; we are far too sophisticated, in an age of analysis, to believe that memory is to be trusted without question. This author publicly questions her own memory. Did events really happen as she claims? Perhaps not. Her father couldn't really have threatened the conductor with a gun when the man wished to put his flu-stricken family off the train; Uncle Myers is probably not as detestable as his niece needs to think. Memory reforms experience; the writer reforms it further. But she is not writing fiction, which would force her to provide motives for people who seem to her adult mind as incomprehensible as they appeared to her as a child. The experience she records, however transmuted, is real; it has shaped her before she can shape it.

Similar statements could be made of all autobiographies, but not all demand them. This book makes such a demand by its form: the alternation of narrated experience with interpolated comment on both the experience and the narration. Calling constant attention to the fact of writing, the author triumphs over the arbitrary, unjust world by describing it. Thus she gives to memory more order than exists in experience. She controls her past in retrospect as she could not control it while living it; the child's helplessness yields to the domination of the adult artist, as her life turns into a work of art. An artist, she offers her specialness as a gift to the world, expecting love in return—a pattern duplicating one she describes repeatedly in her childhood, when she is declared by a nun to resemble Lord

Byron, brilliant but unsound, and takes the declaration as an indication of "the fact that I was loved by Madame Barclay"; or she defies authority in an individualistic dramatic portrayal of Catiline which emerges from and contributes to her devotion to her Latin teacher; or she loses her faith and pretends to regain it in order to capture the attention of others. As an adult, she reports with emphasis that many of her readers have written to testify that they have relatives, experiences, relationships to Catholicism exactly like hers. By reporting her unique experience, she has declared her common humanity; the reward is testimony of kinship. The dream of universal love is the center of her emotional life as it is of Marie Bashkirtseff's; but she has the power to channel it more richly into successful creativity.

Is it important that this memoir is by a woman? Some of the experiences it relates are peculiarly female: the false menstruation, the excursion into dissipation with the Brent sisters. But Mary McCarthy, never made to feel that boys can do what girls cannot, reports little suffering as a special result of her sex. The crucial problems of her life—the effort to reconcile the need for distinction with the need for relationship, the struggle to gain the understanding that offers control of experience—are not peculiar to women; indeed, the analogies I have suggested are all to men, mythical or real: Daedalus, Prometheus, Rousseau. Inasmuch as Mary McCarthy understands her experience as a sequence of efforts to gain the intellectual mastery that will defeat disorder, she denies the importance of her womanhood: her brain is meaningful, not her body. Yet her self-depiction is not really so simple as all that. The final chapter, about her grandmother, adds another dimension to the entire narrative.

"She never says anything about how she may be fabricating about her grandmother, it's different from the rest of the book."

Indeed it is: and the author wishes no suspicion of fictionalizing to touch this crucial concluding portrait, in which the intricate configuration of emotions directed toward the grandmother suggests also the intricacies of complex self-perception.

In narrative form, *Memories of a Catholic Girlhood* has stressed the theme of developing awareness, deviating from chronology in order to emphasize more complex principles of growth. (Its intricate formal pattern, a comparative rarity in autobiographies by women, itself testifies to the author's deliberate artistic intent.) The final chapter in this respect recapitulates the whole, tracing a child's increasingly complex responses to a mysterious older woman. In all obvious respects, Mary McCarthy's grandmother seems very different from her descendant. The old lady holds grudges, has an almost paranoid passion for privacy, resents the idea of being written about, has little interest in her own past. Physically vain, she spends her life in self-adornment. Totally unintrospective, she cannot even respond to questions about her feelings; her days run by truisms. She has little capacity for or interest in relationship. Most important, she is intensely feminine, treating all the world as her suitors. "Life itself was obliged to court her." Living a luxurious, highly scheduled life, the world around her responsive to her whims, she yet repeatedly suffers terrible hurt: a botched face-lifting operation mars her beauty, her daughter dies, then her husband. Against such hurt, her recourse is retreat, cutting her off from meaningful contact with others. Like Mary, she endures conflicting needs for "specialness" and for community; she resolves the conflict mainly on the side of specialness, glorifying almost to the point of self-worship the physical beauty that remains to her.

Her granddaughter's increasing comprehension moves from the small child's perception of her grandmother as a fairy princess to the grown woman's shocked realization that the old lady is senile. But the chapter's deeper principle of organization depends on the gradual, never stated awareness of some deep identity between narrator and subject and the learning that results from this awareness. Mary McCarthy's search for intellectual control, like the desire for power in other woman artists, is at least partly a response to problems inherent in being a woman. The older woman's life is more miserable than she realizes, restricted in possibility to the exercise of feminine tricks and to narcissistic self-contemplation. She makes drama out of the buying of hats and she tells funny stories in which she is always the victim. "She is always the loser in these anecdotes; she never gets the better of the situation with a biting retort, as she often did in real life. But because she is the heroine, she is usually rescued, in the nick of time." In real life, verbal dexterity can save a woman; she is none the less tempted to present a version of herself in which, dependent on others, she is rescued (i.e., loved) by them.

The same temptation faces Mary McCarthy, who, thinking of her grandmother, finds a warning of the dangers in self-definition by femininity. Her narrative has included stories of her own victimization—presentations of herself emotionally at the mercy of priests, nuns, relatives, drugstore clerks, crippled boys—in which, she, like her grandmother, asks for love by presenting herself as baffled and helpless. But now, contemplating the older woman, Mary McCarthy asserts definitively her mastery of her own past: she refuses to be only a victim. The "uncontrollable event" lies in wait for her as well as her grandmother, but she will not merely wait for a rescuer: her version of the gift for "a biting retort" is the clarity of an irony often self-directed, often directed outward, always assertive of intellectual mastery. To worship the mirror, as the grandmother does, is to declare one's beauty the primary instrument of control; but other modes of self-contemplation may create more dependable power. Mary McCarthy's grandmother has no sense of future possibility; her obsession with the mirror derives from her fearful attempt to deny the power of time. Her descendant, also engaged in self-examination, is more capable of confronting the fourth

dimension. Recognizing time as an element in the creation
of the self rather than only as enemy to the preservation of
beauty, she turns to her history for sustenance and for
self-assertion as well as for the winning of love. She has
seen in her grandmother an image of women's limited
possibilities for control and of the final futility of physical
narcissism; she escapes into narcissism of another order,
modified by the action of a cool intellect, and she asserts in
her narcissism the mind's mastery of the past if not the
present. The freedom created by her wit—"there is no wit
without freedom, there is no freedom without wit," Heine
said—allows her room for the creation of order.

Her literary accomplishment demonstrates her power:
not the power to produce that man without corns for
whom Marie Bashkirtseff longs or the environment of perfect acceptance which Mary MacLane craves, but the
power retrospectively to control experience by understanding it. And it is a means to love: the esteem and acceptance of a body of readers rather than the limitless
adoration that Isadora longs for. More fully than many
autobiographers, Mary McCarthy commits herself to reality,
dealing with the gap between inner and outer experience
by turning a sharp eye on both, disciplining fantasy by
fact. Like Isadora Duncan, she earns recognition as an artist, but she does not find it necessary to exaggerate what
"art" means. Recognizing in herself conflicting desires for
the power that elevates its possessor above her fellows and
the love that unites her with them, she simply demands—
and to a considerable extent achieves—both, reminding us
that a woman's self-image as artist need not be dramatically at odds with the facts of her experience. She shows
also that the artist can transcend her metaphoric adolescence. Like those old-fashioned fictional heroines, Elizabeth Bennet and Emma Woodhouse, she grows from
irresponsibility to control, learning (and dramatizing the
process of learning) not how to relinquish her critical perspective on the world around her but how to use it.

Six

FINGER POSTS

Bob Lloyd used to say that a Parent or other Person devoted to the Care and Instruction of Youth, led the Life of a Finger Post; still fixed to one disagreeable spot himself, while his whole Business was only to direct others in the way.

—HESTER LYNCH THRALE

"My father was a gentleman." The first words of the 1656 autobiography of Margaret Cavendish, Duchess of Newcastle, oddly foretell the concluding sentence: "Neither did I intend this piece for to delight, but to divulge; not to please the fancy, but to tell the truth, lest afterages should mistake, in not knowing I was daughter to one Master Lucas of St. Johns, near Colchester, in Essex, second wife to the Lord Marquis of Newcastle; for my Lord having had two wives, I might easily have been mistaken, especially if I should die and my Lord marry again."

The Duchess, with no children of her own, had a mother, a father, seven siblings, and a husband. The bulk of her twenty-four-page autobiography—a document remarkable alike for its vigor and its incoherence—concerns them. Her sense of identity depends on others. Such identity, she knows, is precarious: men marry more than once, so their wives may be confused; a father may have many daughters. Yet she can discover no better way to make her claim.

The psychic differences between the Duchess of Newcastle and the woman artists whose records of themselves we have investigated are rooted partly in history: a seventeenth-century woman writer, rarer phenomenon than her twentieth-century equivalent, would face more social pressure to be reticent about herself. The Duchess explicitly denies the imputation that she thinks herself remarkable. The way to renown for a woman is "worth and merit."

245

*But if our sex would but well consider, and rationally pon-
der, they will perceive and find, that it is neither words
nor place that can advance them, but worth and merit.
Nor can words or place disgrace them, but inconstancy
and boldness: for an honest heart, a noble soul, a chaste
life, and a true speaking tongue, is the throne, sceptre,
crown, and footstool that advances them to an honourable
renown.*

These virtues she claims for herself. She differs from the
rest of her sex, she says, in her "bashfulness," which she
understands as deriving rather from "a fear of others than
a bashful distrust of myself." She disapproves of women
who "jostle for the pre-eminence of words (I mean not for
speaking well, but speaking much)," of women who appear in public to plead their causes or argue their
grievances. Her mother exemplifies perfect womanhood—
that mother more beautiful than any of her daughters,
more virtuous than anyone on earth, totally devoted to her
family. The Duchess herself as a girl briefly approached
public life, becoming a lady-in-waiting at court without
being corrupted: "I neither heeded what was said or prac-
tised, but just what belonged to my loyal duty, and my
own honest reputation. And, indeed, I was so afraid to
dishonour my friends and family by my indiscreet actions,
that I rather chose to be accounted a fool than to be
thought rude or wanton." At court she met her husband,
who "did approve of these bashful fears which many con-
demned, and would choose such a wife as he might bring
to his own humours, and not such a one as was wedded to
self-conceit." She married him despite her shyness because
she loved him—but not with an "amorous love (I never
was affected therewith, it was a disease, or a passion, or
both, I only know by relation, not by experience)"; rather
with a love "honest and honourable, being placed upon
merit." As his wife, she subordinates herself to his interest
and that of his family.

This self-description testifies proudly to a life totally

other-directed. The Duchess considers herself less important than her familial ties, forms herself by external standards, worries about not dishonouring friends and family rather than fulfilling herself. She does not claim the satisfaction or the power of taking care of others; the psychological rewards of her way of life do not resemble Mrs. Ramsay's. The self-gratification implied by "amorous love" terrifies her (or so her metaphor of disease suggests): self-gratification may be self-ravaging. It is enough to be remembered by links to parent and husband.

Yet the fact that she wrote and published an autobiography promises hidden possibilities for her psychic life. This seventeenth-century self-proclaimed model of feminine virtue bears striking affinities to more recent women writers. Like her modern sisters, she suffers intense conflict about her social role. Her effort to yield to the demands of her culture cannot entirely succeed because it represents a total denial of personal needs; and in an era when feminine protest was not socially sanctioned, the Duchess of Newcastle nonetheless manages to express it. Denying all "self-conceit," she reveals its necessity.

Perhaps the most poignant moment in this autobiography (particularly in conjunction with the document's final sentence) is the author's confession of ambition. She has explained that she thinks it no crime to wish for herself the best that life has to offer (the longest life, the easiest death, the most peaceable mind, etc.), as long as she wishes no evil to anyone else. Her elaborate protestations betray some uneasiness even about this point; then she continues, "But I fear my ambition inclines to vain-glory, for I am very ambitious; yet 'tis neither for beauty, wit, titles, wealth, or power, but as they are steps to raise me to Fame's tower, which is to live by remembrance in after-ages." Immediately after, she returns to her insistence that she would never perform a base act; the subject of ambition does not recur.

In one sense, there is no inconsistency between the author's confessed desire for fame and her pervasive em-

phasis on her compliance to others. She does not admit to
wanting the wit or power that might justify fame, only the
extension to after-ages of that approval she has always
sought. Yet the inconsistency is fundamental: the yearning
for fame denies the resolute subduing of self the Duchess
believes to be her life's dominant principle. The esteem of
others supports, perhaps even creates self-esteem. How is
it to be won? It is all very well to say that women win
renown by their chaste lives and noble souls—but such
renown is unlikely to persist through the ages. The
Duchess partly recognizes, although she doesn't quite admit, her desire to achieve public as well as private recognition. Her writing is an obvious way to do so; and her
relation to her writing is the most revealing aspect of her
self-depiction.

Unlike Mary MacLane and Mary McCarthy, the
Duchess does not think of herself as "a writer." She just
writes. She contrasts her literary activity with her husband's. "Also he creates himself with his pen, writing what
his wit dictates to him, but I pass my time rather with
scribbling than with writing, with words than wit." Her
husband writes, therefore he exists; but what she asserts
of him is probably truer of herself—she discovers her
identity by manufacturing it in prose. The disclaimer that
she is only "scribbling" strikes a familiar feminine note of
self-protection. Although she claims no special importance
for her literary creation or herself, the fact of such creation
asserts its own significance.

On the other hand, the entire autobiographical essay attempts to exorcise the desire for importance. Its form is
formlessness: another disclaimer of self-assertion. The sequence of self-description demonstrates little coherent order. Successive paragraphs begin, "As for my breeding,"
"As for our garments," "As for tutors," "As for my brothers." The apparently random sequence, mingling the trivial
with the important, does not issue from any genuine
stream of consciousness; the Duchess, wondering what
someone might conceivably want to know about her, an-

swers always that her circumstances matter, not herself. She admits that she knows nothing of how her brothers were bred, since "the breeding of men were after different manner of ways from those of women," but she theorizes anyhow, as though her brothers' fencing, wrestling, and shooting obscurely justified her own more limited activity. Her rhetoric, with its elaborate repetitions, belongs to her era, but it seems always on the verge of losing control. Its metaphors are precarious: "a true speaking tongue" bears little real analogy to a "footstool"; the assertion that the Duchess is as afraid of ill-bred people as some are of spirits or devils seems extravagant beyond her intent. The essay's self-justifications turn back upon themselves. "But I hope my readers will not think me vain for writing my life, since there have been many that have done the like, as Caesar, Ovid, and many more, both men and women, and I know no reason I may not do it as well as they: but I verily believe some censuring readers will scornfully say, why hath this Lady writ her own life? since none cares to know whose daughter she was or whose wife she is, or how she was bred, or what fortunes she had, or how she lived, or what humour or disposition she was of. I answer that it is true, that 'tis no purpose to the readers, but it is to the authoress, because I write it for my own sake, not theirs."

These sentences of self-exculpation inadvertently expose a central conflict. The writer claims to be justified by precedent, masculine and feminine; but she can cite only masculine. The propriety of feminine autobiography is dubious. Autobiography is self-display, opposed to the female virtues of modesty and concealment. The Duchess's anxiety about this point emerges in her fantasy that no one will want to look if she displays herself; she takes refuge in the assertion that she writes only for herself. But in the light of her earlier confession of ambition for fame, that assertion is manifestly untrue. The conflict between the desire to show and the desire to conceal poses a bitter dilemma. How is a woman to relate to the world? The

Duchess describes herself as naturally melancholy, "addicted to contemplation," happier in the company of her thoughts than that of people. Yet she worries lest "the root of my fancies should become insipid, withering into a dull stupidity for want of maturing subjects to write on." Although her thoughts are like silkworms, spinning out of their own bowels (a more flattering version of Swift's metaphor), she recognizes the necessity of external stimulation to generate new ideas. But contact with others endangers her: she fears other people, unless the are perfectly virtuous. "Because I would not bury myself quite from the sight of the world, I go sometimes abroad, seldom to visit, but only in my coach about the town." Does she wish to see or to be seen? Her ambiguous phrasing avoids the differentiation that her self-knowledge probably does not extend so far as to make.

The self-assertions of fashion provide a conventionally acceptable way for a woman to display herself. The Duchess says that her own interest in fashion encroached on her studies. She delighted especially in "such fashions as I did invent myself, not taking that pleasure in such fashions as was invented by others. Also I did dislike any should follow my fashions, for I always took delight in a singularity, even in accoutrements of habits." All her self-adornment was "lawful, honest, honourable, and modest," she hastens to add. But Evelyn and Pepys both testify in their diaries that the extravagance and "singularity" of her dress made her an object of mockery. Her concern with fashion thus metaphorically represents her writing about herself. In both instances she tries to show herself lawfully, honestly, modestly; but a mocking world, skeptical of the propriety of feminine self-display, questions her right to display herself so conspicuously. The proper place for a woman is in her husband's shadow. The Duchess of Newcastle asserts her subservience to husband, father, mother, all whom she loves; she proclaims her "bashfulness," her disinclination to go into company; she insists on her virtue. But her will to survive as a distinct person betrays itself. Yearning for a kind of fame her immediate society denies her, she tries to wrest it from posterity. Her autobiography's revelation of the clash between the desire to assert and the need to deny the self makes it a classic document of the plight of the woman with no clear external claim to distinction, no social support of the desire to be "special," little real sense of personal possibility.

Although her satisfactions are not theirs, the Duchess's dilemma in many respects resembles that of the fictional heroines whose destiny drives them to "take care" of their own social appearance and of the needs of others. But such dilemmas as recorded in autobiography assume a different form from those described in novels. The matter of "satisfaction" is particularly relevant. Fictional form creates reconciliation, as life characteristically does not. Anne, in *Persuasion;* Molly, in *Wives and Daughters;* Jo, in *Little Women;* Ada, in *Vein of Iron:* all learn to accept the necessities and the limitations of lives oriented towards the demands of others; at novel's end, they reap the reward for acceptance. (Mrs. Ramsay, of course, need learn nothing at all; she knows.) Novels end: no possibility to question what fulfillment Anne Elliot finds in marriage or how securely Ada sustains her exhilaration. Lives, as recorded in autobiographies and journals, do not reach neat conclusions. Fiction may pretend that conflict can be resolved, or solved by repression and denial; life assures us that many conflicts never find resolution and that denial solves nothing. Women who write about their own other-directed lives describe attempts to accept, to resolve, to deny; but often, discouragingly, reveal (sometimes, it seems, quite inadvertently: thus dramatizing the inadequacy of denial) the failure of such attempts.

The Duchess of Newcastle did not know she was angry; nor, one surmises, did the authors of those novels of altruism recognize their anger at the demands inflicted on women. (Jane Austen perhaps did, dealing with it effectively by discriminating among different *kinds* of demand, expressing, through her heroines, willingness to accept some but not all.) The fictional action they invent may have anger as a hidden term but becomes often a way of transcending it: Molly's desire for self-assertion may be frustrated, but she gets what she wants at the end; the frustration, then, in some sense doesn't matter. Real women writing about their real lives seldom seem to get what they want; their frustrations teach them they're not supposed to want so much, a lesson painful to learn. The Duchess's praise of her mother and her husband, her professed willingness to subordinate herself to the demands of others, conceal her resentment of her own condition. Because she has discovered that she has no right to assert herself, her self-assertion is devious. The fantasy, more even than the fact, of the self as artist provides for some women, as we have seen, an illusion of enlargement for limited lives. Women too realistic or too self-deprecating to allow themselves such fantasies may substitute dreams of perfect goodness. To be "good," as a woman, is usually to embrace limitation. The Duchess defines the proper sphere of women in confined terms, then declares her triumph within the confinement: in this respect she strikingly resembles her fictional counterparts.

It is difficult to accept willingly a life of limitation. Men gain existential dignity by triumphing within the limits of mortality or tragic dignity by defying those limits. But *limits* and *limitations* are not identical. Although both sexes endure both, the social limitations inflicted on women have usually been more restrictive than those on men.

Limits: bounds, boundary lines; . . . one of the fixed points between which the possible or permitted . . . range of action . . . is confined
Limitation: Something that limits, as some lack in a person's make-up which restricts the scope of his activity or accomplishments; qualification; restriction (O.E.D.)

Women can accept social limitation, deny its existence, defy it or circumvent it, or merely survive it. In any event, they may well be angry. Women content to define themselves as "good," as willing finger posts pointing the way for others, are obviously less likely to leave autobiographical records than those whose narcissism, more open, focuses in their claim to uniqueness. The women of this sort who have, despite their "selflessness," written about themselves, consistently reveal an anger which creates the energy of self-castigation to prevent undue self-assertion: Molly's pattern in *Wives and Daughters*. But unlike Molly, they are unable to suppose that getting their man will solve their problems. Their anger focuses most often on the mother whose controlling rebukes of budding egotism forced the child's ego into retreat. But the ego finds devious ways of expression. Female autobiographers suggest many shapes of anger, many forms of expressive fantasy. Their anger emerges more unequivocally than anger usually does in novels, where the demands of fictional form urge resolution, the reconciliations of plot contain dangerous energies. They demonstrate repeatedly the special difficulty of female self-discovery and the temptation to ignore what it seems impossible to confront.

The eleven hundred pages of text in Hester Thrale's *Thraliana* have attracted the attention mostly of those interested in people other than the author. Rich in varied anecdotes about Dr. Johnson, Goldsmith, Fanny Burney and her father, they provide a capsule social history of middle-class life in the second half of the eighteenth century. They also compose an intricate self-portrait, probably more revealing than the author intended. Despite its voluminousness, this verbal portrait has something in common with the Duchess' miniature: Mrs. Thrale, too, suffered from conflicting desires to conceal and to reveal herself; more openly than her predecessor, she exposes her rage. "Denied a real testing ground" (a condition my students believed characteristic of women), she tried to make her family life a sufficient arena for creative activity: the result was the alienation of her children. In middle age she emerged as an author, her *Anecdotes* of Dr. Johnson (published soon after his death) highly successful, although her subsequent literary efforts won much less acclaim. Her greatest energies apparently went into the *Thraliana* and several other notebooks (some still unpublished), in which she recorded her experience and her responses to it.

Like the Duchess of Newcastle, Mrs. Thrale proclaims her utter devotion to a mother who epitomized feminine virtue. "She was for all personal and mental Excellence the most accomplished Female that ever my Eyes beheld. Her Shape so accurate, her Carriage so graceful, her Eyes so brilliant, her Knowledge so extensive, & her Manners so pleasing that it was no wonder She had such Choice of Lovers in her Youth, & Admirers in her advanced Age." Mother and daughter had never spent twelve hours apart until the young woman married; afterwards she never left her mother for more than twelve days. When Hester Thrale observes that her own daughters do not love her, she adds, "nobody ever did love their Mother as I did, unless perhaps My Father & my Uncle; but in our Affection there was little Virtue! *my* Mother was an Angel upon Earth, and is now an Angel in Heaven!" Long after her mother's death, Mrs. Thrale, thirty-seven years old, takes up a piece of needlework the mother had begun forty years before, only to comment that her sewing is not as good as her mother's, adding, "I can do nothing like her; would I could!"

Mrs. Thrale cannot speak of her mother without superlatives. She attributes to her parent the "specialness" she will not directly claim for herself. Never does she miss an opportunity to deprecate herself by comparison to her mother: perhaps an effort to conceal from herself and her readers the anger her angelic mother generated in her.

The mother's role, far clearer than in the Duchess' account, epitomizes the forces of restriction impinging on the formless ambitions of a talented, high-spirited girl. From an early age Hester had revealed literary gifts—a capacity to read, remember, and quote; quick wit; some talent at verse making and translation. Her mother encouraged her to use them to charm men, notably her rich uncle, Sir Thomas Salusbury, but also her irascible father. Her role as "my Father's Favourite, my Mother's Comforter and Companion, & my Uncle's Darling" consequently superseded any sense of personal identity. Her function was to please others. Because her father became enraged at the presence of suitors, she discouraged admirers, she reports, as assiduously as other girls encouraged them. When Henry Thrale appeared on the scene, he paid almost no attention to her; her mother, on the other hand, "fell in love" with him. Her mother wished her to marry him, so she did, never having spent five minutes alone with him before the wedding. (Her father expressed his disapproval by dying of apoplexy after a quarrel over the prospective marriage.) Mrs. Thrale's mother continued to live with her daughter, and to supervise her. She discouraged all activity outside the home: the young woman never entered a theater "or any Place of publick Resort, till my Eldest Daughter in her sixth Year was carried by Lady Lade to see the King at an Oratorio; & I went too, that I might take proper Care of *her*." The Thrales' association with Dr. Johnson and his friends stimulated Hester's imagination, "but my Mother saw none of all this with much Pleasure I think; *Her* fears were always lest I should let any thing into my heart or my Head except the Babies, which were bringing & losing every Year; and Their Father who was in Dr. Johnson's Phrase Peregrinus Domi—he came home as little as he could." Twelve times pregnant, Mrs. Thrale reared four daughters to maturity. They hated her; perhaps, she speculates, because she is not lovable. She was not invited to the wedding of her eldest daughter or informed when her youngest gave birth. Late in her life, having survived two husbands, she transferred her emotional energies to an Italian nephew, whom she adopted. He exploited her as a financial resource and gave her little affection. She died at eighty, still writing in her journal, almost to the last, of her mother's virtue.

Mrs. Thrale's various versions of her life stress her psychic subordination to others. She is proud that she always obeyed her mother, never disagreed verbally with Henry Thrale (except once when he wished to cut down some of her mother's trees), made no effort to convert Gabriel Piozzi, her second husband, from his Catholicism or to influence his choice of residence. She professes willing acceptance of her life's limitations. Yet human relations are a mystery to her. Compliant as she is, she is rarely loved as much as she thinks she deserves. What has she done wrong?

*I hear an admirable Character of all my dear Girls from every one who speaks of them—and if they have but one Fault, that of not loving their Mother, who can help Taste? I may not be amicable—probably to my Children am not: and if as Johnson says one may be lovely, yet not beloved—why should one be loved—if one is not lovely? M*ʳˢ *Cochran said they all did esteem me, and think well of my Abilities—that may be honouring their Mother perhaps: I would rather at any rate be in Fault myself, than find them so.*

It is a melancholy Thing tho', to see oneself at the Close of Life surrounded by all new Faces—while so many Relations & Contemporaries still live, though dead to me; who recollect not even at Confession, the human Being I ever injured, or I think wilfully disobliged.

Anger at injustice here jostles her professions of virtue. As she proclaims that she'd rather be wrong than find her daughters wrong, announces her total innocence of willful harm to others, she also reveals bewilderment about the world. Has she not conformed to her mother's standards? Why are there no rewards? People gossip that she didn't love her first husband; her daughters think she mistreated them because she hated their father—yet she frequently professes her devotion to Henry Thrale, whose memory she honors on each anniversary of her marriage to him.

But even a reader two centuries after her time senses discrepancies of which her daughters and her contemporaries must have been more vividly aware. For one thing, the gap between form and content. Her mother (like her society) was obsessed with forms. If the girl, the bride, the young matron acted in appropriate ways, she fulfilled her primary obligations. Feeling might contradict form, no matter; form must dominate. Through following appropriate forms, one pleased others, but Mrs. Thrale's experience frequently contradicted the dictum. Life disappointed her because others never seemed pleased enough; and she never achieved the insight of an Austen heroine. Her mother continued to complain that she did not devote herself fully to her family; Henry Thrale showed little, interest in her, liittle gratitude for her ostentatious efforts on his behalf; he clearly preferred Sophie Streatfield, a young woman famous in her sphere for reading Greek and for crying on command; Dr. Johnson, she came to believe, didn't really care for her; even Piozzi, whom she married for love, didn't appreciate her virtues. Beneath those virtues seethed rage, suspected by her daughters, surely experienced to some degree by all her acquaintances.

One feels that rage, its target sometimes vague, beneath the surface of Mrs. Thrale's elaborate denials, her protestations of entire devotion to parents, husband, children: explicit statements that her feelings conformed to the expectations of her society. It emerges sharply when others fail to consult her on important matters. Here is a revealing sequence about the approaching marriage of her youngest daughter, Caecilia:

Susanna spoke freely to Caecelia—only considering me as quite out of the Question I believe. She seems to think they do not disapprove the Match per se—but treat the Idea of consulting a Mother as too ridiculous to be talked about. The Boy comes himself tomorrow, and the Ladies are to give their decided Opinions upon his Figure &c. It would not surprize me if they hooted him to his Face; It would not surprize me if one of them fell in Love with his Person:—nothing will surprize me, that happens in this Business; unless the two young ones should keep the honest Attachment they appear to have made, & marry the Moment he comes of Age, and live decently as I would wish them to do.

Surprised she might be if anyone did as she wished, but she's furious that they don't comply; on the other hand, she obviously encourages her daughters to fuel her anger, supplying grounds for self-esteem in her consciousness of being ill-used. Expert at the self-fulfilling prophecy (in this case, the young people married, but failed to "live decently": the husband finally impregnated his wife's maid—the wife herself apparently long refused to sleep with him—and in the crisis the couple once again defied Mrs. Thrale's advice), she is also good at ex post facto explanations accounting for the misery of others by their failure to consult her. Caecilia's first child was born dead: her mother, far from the scene, knows exactly why. One sees why her daughters had trouble with her. Her mother controlled her life, even posthumously; her answering need to control the lives of others (while professing not to) met constant defiance. Her experience, like that of many women, was of helplessness, its meaning in her case never realized. As she aged, her anger at the impossibility of exercising control, the necessity of submitting to the will of others, issued in increasingly frequent prophecies of universal doom. The high price of bread, the revolution in France, a strange appearance of the moon: almost anything might provoke her to imagine that the end of the world was at hand. Feeling helpless herself, she fantasized the holocaust that might consume everyone—revenge on society at large, for which self-destruction would be a small price.

The emotional cost of constant submerged anger was diminished capacity for feeling. A student spoke of the "great hole" behind the writing of women who fail to recognize the fact of social limitation. In Mrs. Thrale's account, the emptiness appears almost at the center of her life, in her relations with others. Her first marriage, entered at her mother's direction, was essentially loveless. Although she protests when others accuse her of not having loved Thrale—after all, she always behaved impeccably toward him—she confesses that she has never experienced "the soft passion." In her second marriage, however, she pleased only herself. *Thraliana* records in melodramatic terms her struggle with her daughters over her desire to marry an Italian singer. At their insistence, she gave Piozzi up, only to convince them later that her very life might depend on her being allowed to realize her passion. Marrying in the face of universal opposition, she remained happy in the marriage. As an old woman, long after Piozzi's death, writing a new journal for her adopted son, she dwells lovingly on the high drama of her choice. Yet the marriage could not solve her emotional problems. Gradually she came to feel that not even Piozzi cared for her enough. No one could care for her enough: never believing that she had satisfied her mother, she never believed she could satisfy anyone. Most poignantly, she could not satisfy herself. Although she remained vigorous until her death at eighty, emptiness overtook her.

The most vivid expression of her sense of vacuity in relationship is an outburst written when she was fifty-six years old, occasioned by Piozzi's inquiry whether they should invite more house guests to Wales to entertain her. Her answering reflections on the meaninglessness of social intercourse reveal how she compensates for meaninglessness: by insisting that she is always right. If life is a matter of conforming to external standards, she has triumphed. Her only gain, though, is the consciousness of virtue; and her feeling that there should be more permeates her complaints, her denunciations, her self-deprecation, and her self-praise:

> *Visitants do nothing for me but at best keep my Mind in Exercise, my Spirits in Motion; & make me lash myself up—as Astley does his Horses—to find them Amusement.— All I can do to entertain them is seldom sufficient either: I must call in Company, or take them abroad—show them the Places about—at hazard of my Neck, or fetch in Society for them, as they Phrase it—at certain loss of my own Time, & hindrance of my own Comforts; else they go away lamenting the Dulness & Disagreeableness of the Time they past: & I should be very sorry for that.*

> *Life has been to me nothing but a perpetual Canvass carried on in all parts of the World—not to make Friends neither—for I have certainly found very few—but to keep off Enemies.*

> *Father & Mother Brothers & Sisters [Mrs. Thrale was an only child] are the only natural & certain Wellwishers: You must canvass your Husbands, or they will—(should you not please them)—keep a Mistress: You must canvass Your Acquaintance by every possible Method, or they will speak very ill of you, & do You infinite Mischief. . . . Life is a Toil, & Visitants increase it—a London Life, keeping up one's Acquaintance as 'tis called, I consider as setting out upon a regular Canvass:—The fatigue is the same, & the Pleasure the same, to me. I can make no Diversion out on 't,— I am forced to give up any Diversion for this Business of keeping up Acquaintance.*

> *'Tis right to do it however while one is a married Woman, & lives in the World—A Man would soon tire of a Wife who condemned him to Solitude, or who appear'd to prefer it herself:—Pretending to Delight in the Company is part of the Torment; for they do nothing to delight one, & how they contrive to delight each other in my everlasting amazement.*

To *canvass* is to solicit votes or support. Mrs. Thrale's vision of life as a perpetual canvass epitomizes her difficulty in relating to others. The question is always how one can avoid disapproval and its consequences; the answer is, by relentless effort, by lashing the self like a horse. To be sure, this description of social experience may emanate from temporary depression; no other passage in *Thraliana* provides so extensive or explicit a statement of the view that one's effort in life must focus on attempting to escape the consequences of natural human malice. It is also clear that the sequence—like most of the personal material in *Thraliana*—dramatizes the trivial, that its author enjoys a manifestly exaggerated view of herself as solitary sufferer forced by external demands to function in society. But even allowing for exaggeration and moodiness, this account of life as "a Toil" illuminates many of Mrs. Thrale's experiences and problems. Angry and mistrustful as she here shows herself to be, she could never achieve security in her dealings with others. Yet the expectations of her class and era pressed her toward demonstrating competence in relations with others: a woman's proper sphere.

Her complaints here sound rather like those of a put-upon housewife. Too much is being required of her, in an area where she feels inadequate. The solution that might be recommended to a twentieth-century woman in an analogous predicament is to retreat to some other realm of competence: if you're not a good hostess, be a brilliant Ping-Pong player, have a career, take a trip around the world. Mrs. Thrale had fewer possibilities. Although she had been (by her own account) something of a child prodigy, her gifts were not as great as she sometimes imagined them to be. Still, she managed increasingly to think of herself as a writer and to use this self-image defensively against recognition of her own inadequacies.

Because her primary function was domestic, she could also defend herself from imputed insufficiency as a writer. Not claiming to be a professional writer, she should not be held to professional standards. Boswell might devote his life to recording Dr. Johnson's *bon mots;* she had better things to do.

All my Friends reproach me with neglecting to write down such Things as drop from his [Johnson] almost perpetually, and often say how much I shall some Time regret that I have not done 't with diligence ever since the commencement of our Acquaintance: They say well, but ever since that Time I have been the Mother of Children, and little do these wise Men know or feel, that the Crying of a young Child, or the Perverseness of an elder, or the Danger however trifling of anyone—will soon drive out of a female Parent's head a Conversation concerning Wit, Science or Sentiment, however She may apepar to be impressed with it at the moment: besides that to a Mere de famille doing something is more necessary & suitable than even hearing something; and if one is to listen all Even⁹ and write all Morning what one has heard; where will be the Time for tutoring, caressing, or what is still more useful, for having one's Children about ones I therefore charge all my Neglect to my young ones Account.

The mother of a family, believing it a prime necessity to "do something," finds tasks not far to seek. Occupation wards off depression, establishes a sense of worth; the mother's self-justification is almost automatic. It amounts to a feeling of superiority over men who fill their time with less essential activities, or who, merely thinking or talking or listening, are not really "doing" anything at all. But this defensive stance is not so secure as it may seem. It leaves the mother altogether vulnerable to her children. When one of them is ill, Mrs. Thrale becomes irritated that her husband is less concerned than she. Dr. Johnson points out that the father, a brewer, has his casks to think of; if she had some interest beyond her children, she would not be so obsessed with them. Again, she complains of her husband's apparent lack of interest in her; Johnson responds, "Why how for Heaven's Sake Dearest Madam should any Man delight in a Wife that is to him neither Use nor Ornament?" He points out that she does not understand her husband's business, does not display her wit, does not use her economy or understanding in relation to his property. "You divide your Time between your Mamma & your Babies, & wonder that you do not by that means become agreeable to your Husband."

Mrs. Thrale's immediate response to this criticism is to consult her mother, who assures her that babies are a woman's proper and sufficient occupation; temporarily, the daughter assents. Later, after her mother's death, she turns to writing, having also made some attempts to be helpful in her husband's business and political activities, only to receive inadequate appreciation. Appreciation, after all, is the only issue; Mrs. Thrale as writer resembles Mrs. Thrale as mother, wife, unwilling participant in society. Her literary like her other activity focuses itself on the approval of others.

For a time her role as writer helps her to escape the limitations of being a woman. The "private" writing of *Thraliana* provides an overflow valve for her anger (that anger often hidden from herself) and her intelligence. She uses it for covert assertions of superiority, covering pages, for example, with real or fanciful bits of etymology and reflecting how crudely most people use language. Although she observes, comparing her journal keeping with that of her rival Boswell, that "Life is scarce long enough to talk, & to write, & to live to rejoyce in what one has written," she obviously derives pleasure from the act of writing. When she began to publish, the rewards seemed manifest. The spectacular success of her *Anecdotes* about Johnson gave her false assurance: not having had much testing ground, she believed she could write about anything. Next she published *Letters*—Johnson's to her and hers to him— received with less universal acclaim and provoking public comment on her egotism. *Observations and Reflections* of her trip through France and Italy, fairly successful, occasioned a revealing remark in *Thraliana:* "When People

press me to write my *Tour of our own Island* in good
Time! they say it to ensnare me: was I to act according to
such Advice I should deservedly lose the little Fame I
have already acquired. How false the Creatures all are!!!
but I *know* them." She has learned that literature is no
more secure than social intercourse as a means for gaining
love. Unlike Mary MacLane, subordinating all experience
to her vision of herself as artist, Mrs. Thrale subordinates
all else to the issue of her relation to others. Her paranoia
is the response of one who, always unable to gain sufficient reassurance, begins to believe that she's getting less
than nothing.

Nonetheless, her literary undertakings became increasingly grandiose. She reacted to the limitations of her life
by declaring intellectual limitation nonexistent. Thus, she
projected a work to be called *Retrospection*, "containing a
Summary of Events, & general Ideas of what has happened in the World during those Centuries [since the
birth of Christ]: with a Review of Ancient & Modern Ge-
ography, & a Table in English French Latin & Italian of
all the Places & their Names in those Languages." She expected, as she says more than once, to gain a thousand
pounds by this project. Her actual receipts were less than
a hundred pounds from the first year's sale of the "summary of events" which was all she completed, and review-
ers united to mock the inadequacies of knowledge and
perception she revealed. She was not a scholar, not an intellectual, not even a good writer. The energy of her
brain, which she comments on with pride, poured itself
out in undisciplined prose; her most meaningful literary
achievement was to sustain some sense of her own significance.

Ultimately though, even her success fed her conviction
of the impossibility of winning friends and influencing
people. "Mr Piozzi has his own Country Prejudice against
writing Ladies—Mr Thrale would have liked Me to enter
the Lists exceedingly;—so runs the World away. but while
Johnson lived whatever I wrote would have been attribut-

ed to *him* & I *could* not turn Author. Piozzi likes the
Money I get well enough, but dislikes yᵉ Manner of getting it; he married a *Dama* not a *Virtuosa* he says." On
the same page of *Thraliana*: "Every body—Every Thing
grows so detestable to me. nothing but Baseness, nothing
but grossness.—The World does get *too* bad." Later: "She
who would please the other Sex must certainly not
encrouch upon its privileges." Her earliest literary produc-
tions had seemed to win love; increasing depression accompanied her mature realization that putting words on
paper did not guarantee emotional return. She had not yet
found the secret of love.

In *Thraliana*, her intentions vacillate. Sometimes she
seems, like the Duchess of Newcastle, to rest on the conviction that a woman's renown must depend on her private virtue. Consciousness of her virtue is her strongest
fantasy. Sometimes, on the other hand, she betrays her
longing for a more public claim to fame, and a yearning
even that the private should become public, that the
random jottings of *Thraliana* should be published by her
executors, revealing herself truly at last to a world which
might admire and love her once she was dead. The fantasy
of fame and that of virtue thus unite: her writing, testifying
to her goodness, all win her lasting approval. Her ambiguous feelings emerge in the late journal written for her
nephew. She writes some verses about the superiority of
the laurel to the willow as an emblem of feminine endeav-
or, then comments:

*Now tho' I feel sincere in all I have said in these Verses—I
would not have you think I scorn Family Consolations; &
tho' I would not lose my own little Sprig of Laurel——or exchange it for Queen Proserpine's Golden Bough; I would
not advise you to breed your Girls to Literature: My Happiness was almost all made by it, but it is not the natural
Soil, whence Females are likely to find or form a permanent Felicity . . . No severities could make me averse
to Learning; but the very—very little Learning I obtained,*

*made many People averse to me, who I certainly never of-
fended: & tho' I was the most fortunate Woman breath-
ing—in my Husbands;—It was not for my Literature that
they loved me.*

She had outlived both husbands by the time she wrote
this, at seventy. Her conclusion that literary accomplishment alienates rather than wins others is a sad resolution
to her lifelong struggle for approval—if not her mother's,
her husband's, her readers', her friends'; if not for her self,
for her accomplishment. But accomplishment does not in
itself solve a woman's problem (or, for that matter, a
man's). In Mrs. Thrale's case, it simply points more clearly
to what the problem is: a desperate need for love, a desperate awareness of the limted modes acceptable in the
search for it. The literary interest of *Thraliana* is its vivid
revelation of a woman's psychology. The very lack of control in Mrs. Thrale's writing allows it to reveal the full ambiguity of her almost archetypal emotional experience:
anger at her fate masked by protestations of virtue, the
longing for love reinforcing the restrictions of society, since
compliance might wrest approval from the world. Although the journal reveals little depth of self-knowledge, it
delineates a self for the reader to know—a self poignantly
confused by the impossibilities of its position, making itself
disagreeable as inevitable result of experiencing the severe
limitations involved in the attempt to be agreeable.

What kind of accomplishments enable a woman to take
herself seriously, to feel that the world values her? The
Duchess of Newcastle and Hester Thrale, burdened with
an appetite for renown, could not satisfy it during their
lifetimes, and even their posthumous fame is hardly sufficient to fulfill their yearnings. Both lacked—what? sufficient talent? intelligence? drive? opportunity? to force the
world to attend. Certainly the last; and given lack of opportunity, no amount of talent, intelligence, or drive could
be enough. And neither woman expresses the sense of daz-

zling personal uniqueness so marked in the writing of Isadora Duncan or Marie Bashkirtseff.

What both *do* express is a darker aspect of female altruism than often emerges in novelistic presentations of the theme of "taking care." Neither woman found adequate outlet for her energy in caring for husband or children; both felt largely bound by the cultural assumption that a woman's orientation should be toward others. In fictional presentations of the result of this assumption, the conflicts implicit in a woman's acceptance of externally imposed demands on her time and energy usually work themselves out: Mrs. Ramsay, taking satisfaction in her power, can largely ignore its costs; Molly Gibson, in *Wives and Daughters*, is assumed to have overcome many of her youthful problems simply by achieving marriage. But life refuses to be neat. The autobiographical presentations of women who direct their energies toward the needs of others—or, at any rate, believe that such is their direction—reveal more vividly the difficulty of relationship, the cost of defensiveness, the omnipresence of anger as the corollary of "goodness." The Duchess and Mrs. Thrale both need to claim their own specialness and have difficulty finding adequate grounds for such a claim. In insisting on their virtue, they implicitly recognize their confined opportunities: virtue, under such circumstances, has a bitter flavor.

Is the feeling of "specialness" a prerequisite to outstanding public accomplishment? The question becomes complicated as one contemplates the case of Charlotte Perkins Gilman, born in 1860 (thus presumably possessed of more social opportunities than the Duchess of Mrs. Thrale), famous during her lifetime as a thoughtful crusader for woman's rights, author of twenty-five books, who expresses in her autobiography virtually no distinct positive sense of personal identity, although her life story is shaped like a novel. The Duchess and Mrs. Thrale struggle for an identity to assert; Mrs. Gilman, in another recognizable feminine pattern, struggles to avoid asserting one. Believing herself a psychic cripple, she subordinates her desire for distinction to her commitment to large causes and achieves greatly as a mysterious corollary to self-deprecation.

Charlotte Gilman's response to experienced limitation which she understood as contingent on her sex was to declare herself a psychic cripple. Facing the world courageously, she insisted on her inability really to face it at all. The form of her life, in some essential sense, emerges in her most famous short story "The Yellow Wallpaper." The first-person narrative records the descent into psychosis of a young woman in comfortable circumstances with a devoted husband, an infant, and people to help her. She has been physically ill and is "nervous"; her husband, a doctor, encourages her to take care of herself physically but believes she should think as little as possible about her psychic condition and that she should do as little as possible to occupy herself. Even writing a journal is therefore a surreptitious activity.

I get unreasonably angry with John sometimes. I'm sure I never used to be so sensitive. I think it is due to this nervous condition.

But John says if I feel so I shall neglect proper self-control; so I take pains to control myself—before him, at least, and that makes me very tired.

The emotional sequence—anger, apology, "self-control," exhaustion—supplies the dynamics of the heroine's life. Finally it takes a bizarre form, as she identifies herself with the woman she imagines behind the bars of the wallpaper. John's sister Jane, who runs the household, provides a model of femininity which the central character rejects: "She is a perfect and enthusiastic housekeeper, and hopes for no better profession. I verily believe she thinks it is the writing which made me sick!" But she is unable to commit herself openly to an alternate model of accomplishment. She feels how narrowly she is confined, limitation her destiny. Her escape is into madness, beyond self-control, in which she can dramatize her anger and its sources: " 'I've got out at last,' said I, 'in spite of you and Jane. And I've pulled off most of the paper, so you can't put me back!' "

The anger and its sources are the same in author and character, but Charlotte Gilman acknowledges it less openly in her account of herself. At the age of seventy-five she chloroformed herself, incorporating her suicide note (she was suffering from breast cancer) in her autobiography's last chapter. Having lived well into the age of Freud, she was infuriated by the presumption of psychoanalysts, one of whom dared send her a written analysis of her development, based on her published writings, which she burned unread. But her history seems designed to tempt the analyst. Central to her experience was a painful relation with a mother who steadfastly refused approval. When she brought her mother her first real poem, that formidable personage merely ordered her to put the teakettle on the stove. The maternal philosophy held that manifest affection was bad for a child; the mother hugged and kissed her daughter only when she believed her to be asleep. (Predictably, Charlotte struggled to keep awake, sticking pins in her flesh in order to remain conscious of her mother's affection. But she pretended sleep: no possibility of reciprocal love.) Charlotte developed an elaborate fantasy life to compensate for her emotional impoverishment. She felt that "this was so delightful that it must be wrong" and consequently "I arranged it with my conscience thus: every night I would think only of pleasant things that really might happen; once a week I would think of lovelier, stranger things, once a month of wonders, and once a year of anything I wanted to!" This desperate struggle between imagination and conscience persisted to the beginning of puberty. "Then, influenced by a friend with a pre-Freudian mind, alarmed at what she was led to suppose this inner life might become, mother called on me to give it up. This was a command. According to all the ethics I knew I must obey, and I did."

The note of self-pity becomes plangent as the writer tells this story. She associates all possibility of happiness with the private inner life; when such life is declared a crime, she relinquishes hope of happiness. Her antagonism to psychoanalysis becomes more comprehensible: she thinks it a mysterious doctrine which declares the beautiful ugly. The force destroying beauty, hope, and love for her is in fact her mother, whose energy, as her daughter describes her, directs itself entirely toward rejection, suppression, denial. The mother forbids recreation; the daughter obeys. She declares the reading of fiction impermissible; Charlotte gives it up. No matter how "good" the child is, she wins no approval. Her father has disappeared, for mysterious reasons. The mother never explains; blandly praising him to her children, she allows Charlotte to believe that he has vanished in order to avoid further procreation with its physical danger for his wife.

The anger produced by such a mother-daughter relationship turned against the self. Mrs. Gilman shows no trace of Mrs. Thrale's paranoia of her muffled resentment of her mother's insistence on exclusive domesticity. Although the autobiographer confesses her mature belief that her mother was "mistaken," recalling vividly her experience of emotional deprivation, she reports that her childhood response was to strive more and more desperately to be good; her story reveals that her adult response was similar. Recognizing dimly the impossibility of meeting her mother's standards, she gradually and painfully evolved her own equally rigid ones: the child who would let herself enjoy her fantasies once a year would hardly become a self-indulgent adolescent. In rigidity lay hope. The girl asserted not the integrity and uniqueness of her self, but the power of external standards. Her version of Mary McCarthy's experience with the tin butterfly, Rousseau's with the comb, assures her—as the corresponding episodes did McCarthy and Rousseau—of her personal power, but its emotional consequences are very different.

The incident has a craziness characteristic of her memories of her youth: she is blamed not for *doing* something but for *thinking* something. Her mother by this time has joined a Swedenborgian community. Charlotte, in her early teens, looks out the window to see another community member eating grapes in the back yard. The eater, seeing herself observed, claims to know, with her special psychic powers, that Charlotte is thinking "harsh things" about her: thinking that she has no right to eat the community's grapes. The girl's mother commands her to apologize, she, having had no harsh thoughts, refuses. " 'You must do it,' said mother, 'or you must leave me.' " The ultimatum issues from her conviction that absolute childish obedience is the only way for children and parents to coexist; but Charlotte refuses it. " 'I am not going to do it,—and I am not going to leave you—and what are you going to do about it?' " Her mother strikes her, but she does not care: she has realized for the first time that no one can *make* her do anything.

She summarizes the experience, "I was born," describing it as a new recognition of freedom. But it was not freedom to express the self, only to conform to new standards. The record of her adolescence is of constant moral struggle—not to escape her mother's restrictions so much as to conform to her own. The fantasy of goodness had entirely replaced earlier, more escapist dreams. She decided that her sole purpose was to help humanity. Self must be denied. She kept a diary, with the conscious aim that it should contain nothing that might not be read by anyone. She "understood a course of minor self-denials, for the sole purpose of . . . turning my mind from what I wanted to what other people wanted"; finding this procedure "to slow," she located a blind cripple to take care of. Every year she defined the traits she wished to acquire and labored till she acquired them. She became absolutely truthful; she dealt with men exactly as she did with women. "For eight years I did not do anything I thought wrong, and did, at any cost, what I thought right."

The result of this extraordinary labor of self-suppression was exactly what one might predict: total breakdown. The collapse, the victim's understanding of it and response to it, and its consequences are at the center of Charlotte Gilman's life, giving it compelling symbolic shape. At the age of twenty-one the young woman, still dedicated to helping humanity, had "a tremendous sense of power, clear glorious power, of ability to do whatever I decided to undertake." A year later she met Charles Walter Stetson, a young painter, who promptly proposed to her. She found herself in an unfamiliar state of conflict, unable to govern herself entirely by her own clear principles. Believing that women could and should marry and have children without giving up their work, caring for Stetson, and sharing with him many interests and concerns, she denied her unaccountable disinclination and married him. Immediately, something went wrong. "The steady cheerfulness, the strong, tireless spirit sank away. A sort of gray fog drifted across my mind, a cloud that grew and darkened." Her husband did the housework; it didn't help. She gave birth to an "angelic" daughter but couldn't find the strength to care for her. Her mother came to assist her; they acquired a marvelous servant. "Here was a charming home, a loving and devoted husband; and exquisite baby, healthy, intelligent and good; a highly competent mother to run things; a wholly satisfactory servant—and I lay all day on the lounge and cried." Her situation literally duplicated that of her fictional heroine.

Recovery was difficult and, the writer maintains, never complete. Her state became steadily worse: "every painful mental sensation, shame, fear, remorse, a blind oppressive confusion, utter weakness, a steady brain-ache that fills the conscious mind with crowding images of distress." She felt guilty, but could not understand how to engage her will for recovery. A trip to California brought relief, but return to her family nullified it. A friend gave her a hundred dollars to go and get cured. She consulted the famous specialist S. Weir Mitchell (an off-stage villain in "The Yellow Wallpaper"), who ordered, "Live as domestic a life as possible. Have your child with you all the time. . . . Have but two hours' intellectual life a day. And never touch pen, brush or pencil as long as you live." The prescription, rigidly followed for months—the prescription that drove the fictional heroine to madness—intensified Charlotte's distress. Finally she decided she must leave her husband, believing as she did that "mis-marriage" was the immediate cause of her collapse, although the "conditions of childhood" and her "constant effort in character-building" seemed contributing factors. In 1888, after four years of marriage, she moved with her child to California, accepting full responsibility for self-support. Her mental condition was extremely precarious; as much as possible, she ignored it. She worked very hard. Her continuing belief was that this hard work was responsible for her psychically "crippled life," her "lifetime of limitation and wretchedness"; she believed that, given "care and rest" at the time she left her husband, she would have recovered completely. True, she achieved greatly, but she might have achieved more. She suffered a terrible loss of power, never regained; and a vivid purpose of her autobiography is to insist to her readers, to the world, that she has labored under enormous difficulties, has suffered greatly, has terrible "limitation" built into her nature—all as a result of that mysteriously disatrous marriage.

The pathology of Charlotte Gilman's case of course demands expert knowledge for adequate diagnosis. From a nonmedical viewpoint, what seems interesting is the way in which her "nervous prostration" helps to solve problems inextricably connected with her life as a woman and the degree to which it expresses her anger at what a woman's life is. Dr. Mitchell's advice epitomizes the "external pressures" on talented women: devote yourself to your child, give up your claims to artistry, limit your intellectual pretensions. This is what she's "supposed to do," by society's standards, and she knows it. But her collapse makes this kind of doing impossible for her, and the prescription intensifies the disease. "Internal pressure" urges her toward her old goal of helping humanity, subordinating herself not to some demanding individual but to a grand purpose. It is as though, paying in mental suffering, she gains the right to personal fulfillment. Her desperate insistence that the suffering has been unrelenting, that she has never regained youthful power or happiness, propitiates the fates. She permits herself to do what she wants because her enjoyment of it is never complete, always angry about that fact even while using it for self-justification, and she exemplifies the remarkable devious relationship possible between a woman and her work.

Sometimes she claims that she doesn't work at all—a variation on the Duchess of Newcastle's explanation that her husband writes, she only scribbles. "The work I have done has never been 'work' in the sense of consciously applied effort. To write was always as easy to me as to talk." Often she can't read, but almost always she can write: a thousand words an hour for three hours, no more. The first draft of her book *Women and Economics* emerged in seventeen days. She wrote fiction, verse, essays, sermons, theoretical books, all at the same speed. And she lectured steadily, almost from the moment she left her husband, although she had never lectured before. Her attitude toward this phenomenon too is an odd mixture of self-deprecation and pride. Over and over she insists that she is not and never has been an artist. What she does is important, if at all, only for its effects: it earns money to support herself and her child; perhaps it does something for "humanity." She is *good*, not "special." But special, finally, in her goodness.

The bizarre aspect of the story she tells never seems to strike her. It is almost beyond belief that a young woman with an infant should leave her husband twelve years before the beginning of the twentieth century and, despite the fact that she has been for four years totally incapacitated by depression, should cross the continent and promptly begin supporting herself by making public appearances to talk about the plight of women, socialist theory, or virtually anything anyone wants to hear. At first she writes out her lectures in advance; later she speaks extemporaneously. A man introducing her announces quite the wrong topic; she improvises a speech with the title he provides. Her speaking career had begun when a woman on a bus asked her, a stranger, to address a meeting of the Nationalist Club of Pasadena; she spoke on "Human Nature." In a similar spirit, she taught painting to children, redecorated a theater, and tried to organize working women: her theory was that she would do whatever anyone asked her to do as long as she didn't believe it wrong.

Whatever anyone asked her to do. At every point she struggles to avoid recognition of the claims of her own ego: in her version of herself, she is all superego and sickness. Rejecting the traditional role of "finger post" for children, she tries to fill it for all mankind: only thus can she feel justified. Her mother joins her in California, dying of cancer. She nurses the old woman, runs her boarding-house, exhausts herself. Her doctor advises her to hospitalize her mother. She refuses, saying that she will follow this course only if told "definitely" that the alternative is to die or go crazy. "If I can possibly stand it I want to go on, I do not wish to have it said that I have failed in every relation in life." The fear of what may be said is almost identical with the fear of failure at relationship: both emanate from a sense of primary responsibility toward others. By this time in her life, Charlotte had parted from her daughter, sending the girl east to be with her father and his new wife, Charlotte's close friend. The separation was necessary, she felt, for her daughter's good; she could not offer the stability or financial security the child needed. Predictably, newspapers pounced. The "new woman" was accused of lacking maternal feeling, of rejecting fundamental claims for peripheral ones. Repeatedly, passionately, the autobiographer explains her act as a triumph of selflessness. It was, she insists, the ultimate self-sacrifice, a denial of her deepest desires for the sake of the child's welfare.

One wonders, of course, despite all the protestations (or because of them): why did she, after all, choose to relinquish her child? It is difficult not to speculate that her sense of inadequacy in personal relationships influenced the decision. Aware of the consequences of her own mother's failure—for she seems dimly to have blamed her mother for all her subsequent suffering—she must have felt and feared the enormous burden of maternity. In effect she gave it up, as she had given up marriage; her "work" encompassed mankind. She concerned herself with the plight of women in general, understanding that the right to vote was peripheral to their deeper needs. "Women whose industrial position is that of a house-servant, or who do no work at all, who are fed, clothed, and given pocket-money by men, do not reach freedom and equality by the use of the ballot." Her greatest success was with strangers, who would confide in her at sight; she explained to one bewildered old man that she wasn't really a stranger: "people were people anywhere and my service was for all. So they told me their troubles as usual, and I helped as I could, finding always that the losses and sufferings, mistakes and misdeeds of my own life gave me the key to the hearts of others."

The remarkable aspect of her philanthropic activity was not that it substituted for more intimate kinds of relation but that it continued to enable her to conceal from herself her narcissistic needs. She married again, at the age of forty, her first cousin. Bearing no children, she continued her life of strenuous lecture tours and writing. This was, she explains, a new period of personal happiness for her; but her account remains oddly impersonal. She does not understand the compulsion by which she operates. She has to write: it is as simple as that. Some people, she knows, write as artists, fulfilling mysterious demands of form as well as content. She does not. Some write to make a living, are therefore subservient to the demands of editors. She sees herself as writing only in order to express vital truths. Her compulsion to write outstripped any conceivable market for what she produced. "Think I must and write I must, the manuscripts accumulated far faster than I could sell them . . ." For seven years, therefore, she pub-

lished a monthly magazine (*Forerunner*) written entirely
by herself, each issue containing an installment of a novel
and of another book, a short story, articles, poetry, "humor
and nonsense," book reviews, comment on current events,
advertisements (of products she felt eager to endorse;
their manufacturers did not pay her). It was hardly a
money-making operation; she had to intensify her schedule
of public activity in order to provide the three thousand
dollars a year the venture cost her. Still, she continued:
seven years.

Charlotte Gilman herself understands—even insists—that
this was a noteworthy achievement. "Without any question as to its artistic merit, it was certainly a unique piece
of work, worth recording." She comments rather petulantly
on the fact that critics ignored it, then comforts herself
that in general she has met "a far wider and warmer welcome" than she ever expected. Then immediately, and
characteristically, she insists that her interest is not in personal recognition, only in the communication of her
ideas—ideas that, as she here summarizes them, all stress
the importance of the social over the personal and unvia-
ble position of the mother (an "amateur" at cooking and
child care) in modern society. Again, one wonders. Are
her social convictions entirely defensive self-justifications?
As she ages, she is less in demand, finally she is unwanted,
as a speaker. She offers her services to the League of
Women Voters, volunteering to go anywhere in the state.
One town invites her; it produces an audience of ten. Con-
necticut College, in a neighboring community, never asks
her to speak. She reports these facts, hurt feelings manifest
in every sentence, then observes, "My happiness in Norwich was in my garden, with Houghton [her husband] as
always, and with a few beloved friends." The statement, in
the autobiography's final chapter, invites the reader to
remember what, in this account of a life, the author has
claimed as happiness. Her explicit statements, stressing her
joy in child and husband, contrast the satisfaction of her
second marriage with the joylessness of her previous life;

but her tone declares that happiness lies in making speeches, talking to strangers, writing articles, publishing magazines. That's where the energy is, that's where you feel the joy. A few sentences after the description of her "happiness in Norwich," she relates her discovery that she has cancer and her plan to chloroform herself. Her justification is that she can no longer *serve.* "Human life consists in mutual service. No grief, pain, misfortune or 'broken heart' is excuse for cutting off one's life while any power of service remains."

Power. In content as well as title, *The Living of Charlotte Perkins Gilman* stresses public process rather than private achievement. This curious autobiography paradoxically denies the importance of the self; it records the life of a woman for whom power appears not to be an issue. But anger can generate power, and Mrs. Gilman's life story is a paradigm of feminine anger. Her career spells out more plainly what is implicit in such records as those by the Duchess of Newcastle and Mrs. Thrale: a female childhood that, because female, is repressed, fosters angry womanhood. The adult, disguising her anger by her insistent claims of selflessness, fantasizes her "goodness" into power. By being good she helps all mankind, she wins fame or love. She can be good instead of being gifted, or she can use her gifts in the service of her goodness, thus avoiding the guilt of self-expression. Still repressing her hostile impulses (or confiding them only to her journal), even repressing her desire for enlargement through fantasy, she can rely on a mode of fantasy so disciplined that it does not present itself to her consciousness as a product of the imagination: the compelling image of herself as guide, even savior—"finger post" perhaps for all the world; not overtly aggressive, but very powerful indeed. Like Mrs. Thrale, wishing only to do what others wanted, and the Duchess of Newcastle, wishing simply to be remembered in her relationships, Charlotte Perkins Gilman shows how selflessness can become self-expression. The desperation of her search for opportunities of "service," the compulsiveness of her need to work in larger spheres than those of wife and mother: these measure the assertive strength of a suppressed ego. The mirror image of such "positive" narcissists as Marie Bashkirtseff and Mary Mac-Lane, she directs her energy toward a similar effort to create a visionary extremity of experience as substitute for a sane, balanced acceptance of workaday reality.

"I'm always playing myself down to build him up."
"What I had gone through to make that man a sculptor!"

The first statement quoted above is by a student; the second is by Mabel Dodge Luhan, with reference to her husband, Maurice. In many respects Mrs. Luhan seems to have been a remarkable figure (we shall encounter her again shortly); but rather often she sounds like a Wellesley student. She shares with many undergraduate women, and with many other women who write about themselves, the peculiar self-image that insists on the self as powerless and dependent, while concealing the energy of anger.

Charlotte Gilman denied the implicit egotism of autobiography by insisting that self is less important than service. More elaborate denials are possible. A peculiarly feminine one is the pretense that the self is being presented only as an object of mockery—not for Chaplinesque ineptness, primarily for the personal consequences of domesticity. Erma Bombeck currently writes a syndicated colume four times a week, its insistent subject the ludicrous degradation of her plight as middle-aged housewife. She presents herself as fat, unattractive, no longer an object of sexual interest, incompetent at all activity, butt of her children and her friends for her stupidity and her middle age. The mode may have begun with Betty MacDonald, whose *The Egg and I* was a best seller of the mid-forties. She tells of her career as wife of a Washington egg farmer. Her husband does everything right, she does everything wrong. (She is, however, an excellent cook.) She can't adjust to the realities of farm life, in which people are judged by what they do, though much of it isn't intrinsically worth the doing. For example: her husband insists on making their house floor of white pine, as subject to spotting as white velvet. He then insists that it be scrubbed every day. Resenting it, she scrubs; but the floor never looks clean. She is a failure.

The fact of this summary come directly from *The Egg and I*, but the tone falsifies the author's professed intent. Resentment rarely comes to the surface. The floor-scrubbing episode, as narrated by Betty MacDonald, invites the reader to chuckle at the comic unawareness of husbands, but also to admire them for their above-it-all impracticality. It invites some sympathy for the put-upon wife, but its stress is on how ridiculous she is in her inadequate efforts. Her account of her marriage epitomizes her tone of self-deprecation:

When I was seventeen years old and a sophomore in college, my brother, Cleve, brought home for the weekend a very tall, very handsome older man. His brown skin, brown hair, blue eyes, white teeth, husky voice and kindly, gentle way were attributes enough in themselves and produced spasms of admiration from Mary and her friends, but the most wonderful thing about him, the outstanding touch, was that he liked me. I still cannot understand why unless it was that he was overcome by so much untrammeled girlishness.

Seeing her husband as physical and moral paragon, she casts herself as his opposite, with only the capacity for infinite compliance (and the temporary advantage of "girlishness") as her resources. She judges herself in relation to other women and finds herself wanting, unable to meet the standards of her immaculate mother or to achieve the devil-may-care style of her feckless grandmother, failing to equal the farm wife of her acquaintance who has done a full day's work before seven in the morning and whom she imagines smoothing her apron after finishing the dishes and wondering if she should bake an angel food cake; but unequal also to the abandon with which her neighbors, the Kettles, allow all responsibility to slip from their shoulders. Her life produces emotional impoverishment. "Bob's life was as harried, and our marriage became a halloo from the brooder house porch to the manure pile; a call for help when pulling a stump or unrolling some wire; a few grunts at mealtime as we choked down our food and turned the leaves of seed catalogues and Government bulletins.... 'Another year or two and we probably won't even use first names,' I told Bob." They rarely go to the movies: Bob sleeps through them, and she discovers that she's only interested in whether the heroine has to work hard—if the star has time for hot baths, who cares whether she gets her man? The fact that Betty MacDonald reads books becomes a subject for local gossip; it is not proper feminine behavior. She paints and draws in secret, somehow avoiding the madness described in "The Yellow Wallpaper"—unless her insistent self-deprecation amounts to madness. When a visiting brother-in-law shows some interest, she wonders what she can do just this side of human sacrifice to express her appreciation. She also hopes in vain that Bob will now take her artistic endeavors more seriously: he "had always treated my painting as a sort of recurring illness like malaria." In a rare moment of reflection, she concludes, "Husband and wife teamwork is just fine except when it reaches a point where the husband is more conscious of the weight his wife's shoulder carries than of the shoulder itself." But there's nothing she can do about it: her life is at the disposal of others. The "happy ending" of her account is her husband's revelation that he has bought (without consulting her) a new chicken farm, with electricity and inside toilets. For an ecstatic moment she thinks she'll no longer have to get up at four, but her husband disillusions her: chickens still must be fed, they're more important than wives.

I'm making Betty MacDonald sound rather like a tragic

heroine, and of course she's not at all. She sees herself, wants others to see her, as a comic figure; and the making of comedy from hard experience is a way of triumphing over the hardness. It is also a way of accepting. Anger is not far beneath the surface as she contemplates her reduction to a burden-bearing shoulder or her husband's attitude toward her painting, but she knows nothing to do with it. Self-esteem as she understands it must depend on accomplishment. Her life creates a circle: never able to do what she's supposed to do (autopsy chickens, scrub floors, entertain Indians) well enough, she can never value herself sufficiently highly to declare her determination to do something else. She asks attention for her ineptitudes and thus commits herself more firmly to them.

The Egg and I suggests a paradox central to the writing of many women who make for themselves no claim of special artistic ability or manifest significance in the world. On the one hand, writing is an escape from their life dilemma. Betty MacDonald may not be too good at ironing clothes with a sad-iron, but she's able to write a book and have it published. She has *done* something to justify herself, and in the doing is escaping from the circularity of her domestic existence. On the other hand, writing of her sort also confirms the trap. Inviting the reader to laugh at how badly she functions, perhaps even to sympathize with the husband who must put up with her (if she weren't so inexpert he wouldn't need a hired man), she declares the necessity of the choices she has made. Those who laugh also accept. The Erma Bombeck–Jean Kerr–Betty MacDonald comic tradition is profoundly conservative in its social implications, preserving the image of feminine incompetence, siphoning off anger, suggesting that if it's funny to be a bad housewife there may be some dignity to being a good one.

Women can, of course, write of the limitations of commonplace lives without discovering comedy in them. Their recourse may be to other modes of self-chastisement: as in the diary of a young wife crossing the plains in a covered wagon in an advanced state of pregnancy, berating herself for her state of "inward gloom" because it must be "unnatural and morbid." Her technique is different from Betty MacDonald's, which denies depression by offering it as a target for ridicule, but the point is really the same: both women believe that they should not permit themselves their actual feelings. Arvazine Angeline Cooper, the western traveler, perceives that writing about herself, even in a private diary, implies some claim of personal significance. After her son is born, she worries that her "narrative will necessarily be so personal as to seem egotistical," and decides therefore to write of herself in the third person—a device that enables her to refer to herself frequently as "that poor weary mother of the young babe." Her depression and weariness are understandable; she feels herself little more than a chattel, with no control over her own destiny, her powerlessness emphasized by being part of a large group. In this situation, her solution is to try to be a perfect woman. Unlike most women, she cannot see this goal as a product of *doing* much of anything: the perfect woman simply endures. Another woman in the company sticks a fishhook in her finger and complains so much about it that everyone becomes annoyed. Mrs. Cooper listens and learns. When she herself becomes seriously ill, she bears "her sufferings in grim silence" so that no one will disapprove.

This record exemplifies woman's lot at its hardest. Mrs. Cooper doesn't even have a language of her own; her experience emerges in clichés. She has no way to think of herself as an independent human being with a capacity for autonomous functioning, no way to deal with her own misery. Suppression is not only her fate but her self-defined purpose. And the act of writing about herself, an important bit of self-assertion, constantly contains denials of itself—in the secondhand diction, the effort to avoid "egotism," the recorded struggle to disappear as much as possible: the ultimate service to others being to inflict oneself upon them as little as one can.

Mrs. Cooper and Mrs. MacDonald, writing in different modes, convey a similar sense of emotional impoverishment—that hole in the center of their writings. Neither, of course, makes any claim to literary significance: Arvazine Cooper was not writing for publication, Betty MacDonald defines for herself a *Ladies' Home Journal* type of audience. They are "good women," not good writers—and perhaps there is a necessary antithesis. What I'm really talking about of course, is the myth rather than the reality of the "good woman," the compelling fantasy that possesses so many. Although it may be, as I have suggested, at least partially a fantasy of power, it is founded on apology. The Duchess of Newcastle knows she has not done anything to make her worth remembering, Mrs. Thrale fears that she is not lovable, Charlotte Gilman believes herself a failure at human relations, Betty MacDonald cannot feel adequate as a wife, Arvazine Cooper thinks conspicuousness the ultimate feminine sin. Men, too, have devoted their lives to service; many who have accomplished less than Charlotte Perkins Gilman have written proudly of their accomplishment, without explaining it as compensation for their inadequacies. But women, forced to be good because convinced that they're not talented, can never feel good enough. Their fantasies of selfless virtue—their visions of themselves as desperately devoted to the feeding of chickens, the care of children, the service of the husband or of all mankind—may partly satisfy their personal needs but do not sufficiently compensate for the frustrations involved in ways of life not freely chosen. The impossibility of full responsible choice is a striking aspect of all these lives, including the twentieth-century ones. Women choose marriage—even that, often, as a result of social pressure—and find their fates, the consequences of their choice dependent on the will of another. Only Charlotte Gilman, of these women, seems to have come close to defining her life for herself—and she could do so only at the cost of the complete psychic collapse that irrefutably demonstrated the impossibility of her focusing her energies as wife and mother.

The "hole," then, that final sense of inadequacy my students felt in so many of the woman writers they encountered, may reflect the emotional consequences of the social limitations on women's position. Modern feminists as well as nineteenth-century ones have raged about the limitation of female choices; its literary consequences can probably never be fully assessed. The point is not that women cannot be good writers; rather, that women absorbed in the obligation to commit themselves to others may feel that personal inadequacy underlies their commitment; their prose will reflect that sense of inadequacy. Only recently has it become possible for women to express directly in print the rage that responds to the world's insistence that they be "good," letting who will, be clever.

Mabel Dodge Luhan would be bewildered and displeased to find herself treated in a company of women who identify themselves through their relation to others. Unlike the Duchess of Newcastle or Betty MacDonald, she sees herself as a glamorous figure, her narcissism loud and relentless. In a four-volume autobiography (*Intimate Memories*) and a book nominally about D. H. Lawrence (*Lorenzo in Taos*), she keeps saying "Look at me!" But all her self-display reveals how completely her sense of identity depends on others. It seems oddly appropriate that she is remembered now mainly as the friend of D. H. Lawrence.

Like Charlotte Gilman, Mabel Luhan suffered a childhood lacking in maternal love. "Probably most people have some memories of their earliest years that contain a little warmth and liveliness but in my own I cannot find one happy hour. I have no recollection of my mother's ever giving me a kiss or smile of spontaneous affection, or of any sign from my father except dark looks and angry sound." Much more openly than her nineteenth-century counterpart, she hated her mother; she reports writing her father a letter, in her early adolescence, condoling him on having to live with someone so ignorant and insensitive. The most obvious result of her emotional deprivation—although she does not make the connection herself—was an apparent obsession with women's breasts. She spends most of a night fondling the large breast of a servant girl, her aunt reduces her to hysteria by calling her a baby and making a gesture as though to offer her breast, she has a teen-age relationship with another girl which she describes as a relationship with her breasts, not at all with "that cold girl," about whom she cared not at all. Her earliest and most devastating fear, she reports, was "of being alone, of being only on."

Charlotte Gilman reacted to lack of love by fear of relationship; Mabel Luhan responded with a hunger for human contact. She describes herself as having a genius for dealing with others:

I was just naturally fluctuating and flowing all the time, wherever I found myself, in and out of the people I was with. I have always been myself and at the same time some one else; always able to be the other person, feel with him, think his thoughts, see from the angle in which he found himself. This has caused me many inward conflicts, and it has always drawn people to me in the same degree that I flowed out to them and identified myself with them, and it has always made people want to kiss me, to manifest an actual nearness and union, finding it comforting and consolatory. It is the only genius I have ever had but it has been enough, and these pages are given to recording its progress.

The insistence of this self-definition, not altogether convincing, makes it a hopeful act of defiance. Certainly Mrs. Luhan's subsequent accounts of her actual relations with others suggest that her "genius" was not unalloyed, that those who wished to kiss her soon discovered the wish to knock her down. Her self-loving prose suggests her fundamental lack of insight. In an honest moment she admits, "I knew I could always win people to me if I could be near them often enough and demand, by endless silent maneuvers, their interest or affection or whatever it was I wanted of them." The issue, finally, was the familiar one of power. "My interest in men was in discovering my effect upon them, instead of in responding to their feeling for me." Lacking genius of the sort that is publicly negotiable, the woman's experience of life is often of powerlessness. Mabel Luhan saw her mother as a controlling woman, primarily interested in ordering the servants around; she herself was more interested in controlling men. She wished to affect the world at large, although she lacked obvious talent with which to demand attention.

Her maneuvers are tedious in detail, although interesting in essence. She began by manipulating men. Having made a husband into a sculptor, she became bored with what she had wrought. "It had been very degrading, really, to hold to Maurice and use him as I had all this time when I thought as little of him as I did. Making a sculptor of him had been my subterfuge, I discovered, the high motive to justify me for keeping hold of him." In Taos she abandons her husband for an Indian lover, Tony, with whom she has an enduring liaison. Tony doesn't talk much; one sometimes has the impression that his mistress manufactures his character out of her needs. At any rate, he satisfies her; he even, she says, dominates her, giving her "that submissive feeling" she's always wanted. Still, she needs Lawrence as well. In *Lorenzo in Taos* she relates how she made him come to New Mexico (he'd wanted her to meet him and Frieda in Ceylon) by sheer force of will. The mystical power she believes herself to exert, drawing others toward her, is the central subject of the book.

This need to draw others—or to think that she does so— is finally utilitarian. Mrs. Luhan needs other people to make herself real: the point becomes clear in this last of

her books. Her hope is for some collaboration with
Lawrence. For a time it seems about to be realized:

*He said he wanted to write an American novel that would
express the life, the spirit, of America and he wanted to
write it around me—my life from the time I left New York
to come out to New Mexico; . . . my renunciation of the
sick old world of art and artists, for the pristine valley and
the upland Indian lakes. I was thrilled at the thought of
this. To work with him, to give him myself—Tony—Taos—
every part of the untold and undefined experience that lay
in me like a shining, indigestible jewel that I was unable
either to assimilate or to spew out! I had been holding on
to it for so long, solitary and aware, but helplessly inex-
pressive!*

But the project never materializes—according to Mabel
Luhan, because of Frieda Lawrence's jealous opposition.
And gradually it becomes clear that Mrs. Luhan's wish to
collaborate on a piece of writing is a passionate yearning.
She feels unable to do anything at all by herself; nothing
she can do is real or meaningful. Only through someone
else can she "work."

*I was always trying to get things done: I didn't often even
try to do anything myself. I seemed to want to use all my
power upon delegates to carry out the work. This way—
perhaps a compensation for that desolate and barren
feeling of having nothing to do!—I achieved a sense of
fruitfulness and activity vicariously. . . .*

*I wanted Lawrence to understand things for me. To
take my experience, my material, my Taos, and to formu-
late it all into a magnificent creation. That was what I
wanted him for.*

The feeling of vacuity here expressed is common in the
writings of women. It rarely appears, as it does here, in
conjunction with such insistent self-assertion. There were

few obvious external restrictions on Mabel Dodge Luhan's life; most of the time, after coming to Taos, she depicts herself as doing whatever she wishes. She is not forced to work hard and to feel inadequate at domesticity (she makes a brief attempt at picturesque domestic activity to please Lawrence, but soon abandons it), she is not beset with the cares of a large family, she is aware of no difficulty in establishing and maintaining personal relationships, she makes no effort to suppress her emotions or to conform to a feminine norm. She is eccentric and "free." Yet no external freedoms can solve the problem of one who organizes her sense of identity around other people. Finally she consults the distinguished psychoanalyst A. A. Brill, who tells her she must find work to do. She tries to work, writes pathetic letters to Lawrence, asking how to do it. The work she sees herself doing is *his* work, writing, and her books testify that she never learned to do it well. Her prose insists on her significance until the reader shares her doubt of it. Repetitive, undisciplined, self-indulgent, it conveys the essential confusion of the woman whose sense of reality was always vicarious—unable fully to accept herself as a "finger post," unable fully to exist as a separate self.

Seven

THE WORLD OUTSIDE

As if the two sexes had been in a state of war, the gentlemen ranged themselves on one side of the room, where they talked their own talk, and left us poor ladies to twirl our shuttles and amuse each other by conversing as we could. By what little I could hear, our opposition were discoursing on the old English poets, and this subject did not seem so much beyond a female capacity, but that we might have been indulged with a share in it.

—ELIZABETH CARTER

Women serve as guardians of culture, upholders of society. They go to the symphony on Friday afternoon, they act as volunteer guides in the art museums, they campaign for clean water and against dirty movies.

They talk about the culture men create.

When I was little, my mother joined an organization called Sorosis. In our small southern town, it seemed a very classy group. Its members belonged to the best families; it was gratifying to be among them. They met once a month, discussing a book at each meeting. Someone would discourse on the work she had selected, then the other women contributed their reactions—activity more intellectual than the garden club, and equally conducive to general improvement. It exemplified culture and society as women experience them: "culture" meaning "refinement in manners and taste"; "society" meaning people of social standing collectively, the fashionable class." But these two large nouns have other meanings as well—"male" meanings. "Culture," as the dictionary tells us, designates also—simply and grandly—"civilization." "Society" defines "the system or condition of living together as a group." And the large and limited definitions oppose one another: culture as refinement is antithetical to culture as the creativity of civilization; society as defined by class produces myopia when its victims attempt to examine the broader group in which they participate.

Virginia Woolf's obsession with the absence of a woman Shakespeare reflects her awareness that women have not created our culture. Patted on their heads and told to enjoy their inner lives, they are also assumed—and allowed—to be preoccupied with trivia in the external world. Twirling their shuttles should sufficiently entertain them. My students manifested the results of the implicit pressures thus created. They expected, even assumed, that literature by women would be second-rate. Quite aware that there was no woman Shakespeare, they had trouble summoning the names of any woman poets at all. Emily Dickinson? Sort of crazy, they knew. Sylvia Plath? *Very* crazy. Sara Teasdale? someone inquired. No one else had ever heard of Sara Teasdale. They'd heard of George Eliot and Jane Austen, whom they associated with the dull books one is forced to read in seventh grade. (Is it part of a great antifemale conspiracy that so many generations have had to struggle through *Silas Marner?* My husband remembers weeping over *The Mill on the Floss*—not for the pathos of Maggie's lot, but because it was such an unendurably *long* book to have to read in tenth grade. He has not become a George Eliot enthusiast.) They knew about *Jane Eyre* and *Wuthering Heights,* but not that such novels should be respected: they were escape reading for girls, scorned by males. These well-bred young women understood already, at seventeen or eighteen, that women belong to the periphery. A course in writing by women would skirt serious literary concerns.

One is polite in being "cultured" and "socially adept," impolite being insistently creative. Edith Wharton in her autobiography recalls "once saying that I was a failure in Boston (where we used to go to stay with my husband's family) because they thought I was too fashionable to be intelligent, and a failure in New York because they were afraid I was too intelligent to be fashionable." Her effort to reconcile the opposed values of fashion and intelligence (meaning, in her case, creativity) shaped the drama of her life as she understood it.

It also formed her novels—as similar conflicts have formed those of other women. The intersection of society

and the individual has traditionally supplied novelistic
structure. Society—depending on one's definition of it—may
restrict or enlarge the female imagination, providing internal as well as external measures of possibility. The relation
between outer and inner reality assumes a special complexity in the experience of women, traditionally society's
victims, but sometimes able to use social values to private
purposes. George Eliot, perhaps the most thoughtful and
perceptive woman fiction writer to consider such matters,
reveals the "specialness" of the woman's situation.

Eliot titled her most intensive fictional study of a
woman's psychology—strikingly—with the name of a nearby
community. *Middlemarch*, like all Eliot's work, recognizes
the devious ways the interaction between individual and
society functions. To talk only about culture and society in
Middlemarch, obviously, must leave much unsaid; yet the
divergence between the large and the limited meanings of
those terms defined Dorothea Brooke's insoluble problem
and helps to locate both the moral grandeur and the curious poignance of this novel.

Like *The Mill on the Floss* and *Daniel Deronda*, though
with a sharper focus, *Middlemarch* takes up the problem
of female vocation. More clearly than the other novels, it
presents this as a social issue. The portrayal of Saint
Theresa with which the book opens provides a standard
by which to judge Dorothea and a guide to understanding
her. Evoking Theresa as a heroine whose "passionate, ideal
nature demanded an epic life," Eliot reminds her readers
that women later-born than Theresa have often lacked the
opportunity for epic self-fulfillment specifically because
they "were helped by no coherent social faith and order
which could perform the function of knowledge for the
ardently willing soul." The version of "social faith" that
Dorothea Brooke encounters in fact perform the functions
of ignorance, protecting their participants from the dangers of reflection. In Dorothea's world, "women were expected to have weak opinions; but the great safeguard of

society and of domestic life was, that opinions were not acted on. Sane people did what their neighbours did, so that if any lunatics were at large, one might know and avoid them." A girl with an imagination larger than her opportunities must be particularly careful to control her actions, not to manifest too much, not to seem a lunatic. Vocation, what a person does in the world, represents literal social possibility. The divergence between what Dorothea is able to do and to imagine defines the limits of her society—limits that operate in various ways on every character in the novel.

Dorothea has no difficulty perceiving that her immediate society destroys rather than affirms significant value. She has consistently experienced repression, denial. Nobody "in the neighbourhood of Tipton would have had a sympathetic understanding for the dreams of a girl whose notions about marriage took their colour entirely from an exalted enthusiasm about the ends of life, an enthusiasm which was lit chiefly by its own fire, and included neither the niceties of the *trousseau*, the pattern of plate, nor even the honours and sweet joys of the blooming matron." Like an Edith Wharton heroine, Dorothea in her premarital state demonstrates the opposition of imagination and society. Dreaming of *doing* rather than *having*, she can find no sustenance in a world that values only wealth and birth. Her nature struggles "in the bands of a narrow teaching, hemmed in by a social life which seemed nothing but a labyrinth of petty courses, a walled-in maze of small paths that led no whither." Imagining marriage as a course winning social approval yet allowing larger scope for individual development than the petty labyrinth she has previously inhabited, she finds it a yet more baffling structure of socially enforced restriction. Now she dwells in "the stifling oppression of the gentlewoman's world, where everything was done for her and none asked for her aid—where the sense of connection with a manifold pregnant existence had to be kept up painfully as an inward vision, instead of coming from without in claims that would have shaped her energies."

Dorothea's vision of "a manifold pregnant existence" with which she may find connection implies a different notion of society from any she has experienced directly. She imagines human beings bonded by feelings, a network real and perceptible, founded on need and response to need; she lives among networks of trivia, petty labyrinths, "thought and speech vortices" sucking in hapless individuals—countless threats to personal integrity. She must survive in defiance of her experience—unsupported by any "coherent social faith."

To live in society—Middlemarch society, or the more elevated but equally limited version of the county aristocracy—means finding one's large concerns constantly reduced. Eliot provides many variations on this theme. Lydgate experiences the phenomenon as a result of his marriage to a woman who epitomizes the superficial values of her world. In anticipating marriage he reveals that "society" has already damaged his perceptions. "All his faults ... were those of a man who had a fine baritone, whose clothes hung well upon him, and who even in his ordinary gestures had an air of inbred distinction": a man, in short, preeminently socially acceptable. His "distinction of mind" does not "penetrate his feeling and judgment about furniture, or women, or the desirability of its being known (without his telling) that he was better born than other country surgeons." His snobberies, in fact, resemble Rosamond's, despite his superior mental capacities. Blessed with a true vocation, he mentally isolates it from his social existence. But psychic experience, however diverse for an individual, must be finally single; such separations cannot endure. Lydgate falls victim to a society that first reduces, then incorporates.

Rosamond, as much as her husband victimized, lacks tragic stature, having no larger capacities than her world encourages. Her single fine gesture, of revealing Will's innocence to Dorothea, stems, like her less admirable acts, from concern with what people will think of her. Yet her small soul is not of her own manufacture. Partly a social product ("she was a sylph caught young and educated at Mrs. Lemon's"), that soul derives from an education insistent about the importance of appearances over substance; her inability to respond to her husband's appeals for understanding derives partly from so rigorous a training in behavior that she may be excused for believing that behavior alone matters (by no more than a turn of the neck does she ever evince bad temper).

Of course Rosamond can't altogether be excused. We bear responsibility for ourselves, George Eliot says repeatedly, although society provides many excuses for individual insufficiency. Rosamond inhabits the same universe, almost the same society, as Dorothea, although her social status is lower; she must be judged in relation to her contemporary, and judged wanting: in natural capacity, in education, in moral responsibility. Society makes nobility difficult but does not, from Eliot's point of view, justify failure. Even Casaubon, most unworldly of men, is tricked by generally accepted assumptions which lead him to expect automatic fulfillment in marriage. "He had done nothing exceptional in marrying—nothing but what society sanctions, and considers an occasion for wreaths and bouquets." Our sympathy for him enlarges through the perception that he, like Rosamond at the opposite extreme of self-definition, suffers from mistakes in which his community encourages him. But no matter how fully encouraged he has been, he too remains responsible for those real mistakes, his wrongings of Dorothea as palpable as Rosamond's of Lydgate.

As my references to Casaubon and Lydgate along with Dorothea and Rosamond indicate, Eliot presents men and women who share versions of the same problem. Their possible solutions, however, differ. Men have more "public" resources (Casaubon can publish, or project publishing; Lydgate can achieve, or project achieving, medical discoveries); women, it seems, develop more significant "private" ones. Two extensively developed woman characters in this novel, Dorothea and Mary Garth, accept full responsibility for themselves and their lives, unwilling to claim, as they might, any external excuse for inadequacy. No male character, except the idealized and relatively unconvincing figures of Caleb Garth and Farebrother, both in the background of the action, does the same. Will Ladislaw, Dorothea's eventual consort, drifts from one occupation to another. "It is undeniable that but for the desire to be where Dorothea was, and perhaps the want of knowing what else to do, Will would not at this time have been meditating on the needs of the English people or criticizing English statesmanship: he would probably have been rambling in Italy sketching plans for several dramas, trying prose and finding it too jejune, trying verse and finding it too artificial, ... and observing that, after all, self-culture was the principal point; while in politics he would have been sympathizing warmly with liberty and progress in general." To be sure, this account occurs in the middle of the book; perhaps we are to assume that Will's final commitment to the needs of the English people, the criticism of English statemanship, and the development of his own is motivated by profound devotion to a cause rather than by the desire to be with Dorothea. We learn only that he "became an ardent public man, ... getting at last returned to Parliament by a constituency who paid his expenses." Eliot, having made it difficult to credit his ardency of commitment, evades the issue at last: one does not finally know the relation of his imagination to his achievement. Lydgate, a man also "ardent" in his aspirations for significance accomplishment, compromises in the full knowledge of compromise, attributing his limitation to his wife and what she represents. Casaubon's intellectual endeavors from his point of view excuse his moral and emotional evasiveness. Fred Vincy blames others, blames the world, for the mishaps that befall him; he is partially "educated" by his experience, but almost entirely through the influence of other people.

From all these characters tested by imagination and social possibility a curious paradox emerges. Men, with easier opportunities for doing, possess acknowledged right to varied vocations, the right to function publicly, to compensate for inner misery by outer action directed toward important achievement and recognition. But the men in *Middlemarch* (Caleb Garth the only exception) are in fact dreamers, dissipating their opportunities of education, knowledge, social freedom, creating their own bondage. However gratifying the ultimate consequences she allows (Fred's happy marriage, Will's marriage and final public success), Eliot hints a rather patronizing view of men: given rich social possibility, they lack the individual capacity to use it; only when taken in hand by a good woman can they succeed.

Women, on the other hand, subject to severer social pressure, may in some ways accomplish more. Even petty Rosamond manages to acquire total power in her family. Mary and Dorothea exceed their men not only in moral stature but in significant achievement—though of course one may quibble about what "significant" means: these young women are not Saint Theresas. Their accomplishment, private rather than public, amounts to forming their husbands; in fact, contrary to the anticipated sterotype, they *do* rather than dream.

Mary, at a lower economic level than Dorothea, must labor for her sustenance. Dependent on the will of others, she anticipates pursuing an occupation she hates until her father's prosperity rescues her. Not beautiful, socially distinguished, or wealthy, she has power over the hearts of two men, but no social power whatever. Her commitment to Fred contains an element of sacrifice. She clearheadedly undertakes the task of making him into a man, thus confirming the possibilities of her womanhood. Lodging for no wider sphere of action, she glorifies the sphere she inhabits by her willingness to work without making excuses for herself or for others. If she wanted more, she could not have it: hers is the heroism—real enough—of carefully controlled aspiration.

Dorothea, on the other hand, has trouble controlling and focusing her aspirations. As an unmarried girl, she enjoys drawing plans for ideal cottages, her enthusiasm misleading Sir James Chettham into believing himself a welcome suitor—a result of which Dorothea blames "the intolerable narrowness and the purblind conscience of the society around her." Her embarrassment expresses itself in grandiose questions: "What was life worth—that great faith was possible when the whole effect of one's actions could be withered up into such parched rubbish as that?" The question, which seems at the moment an effluence of youthful pique, echoes ever more seriously through the rest of the novel, as Dorothea suffers the "withering" effect of her sterile husband, her sterile society.

Her relation to "culture" epitomizes her psychological problem. Educated in the polite accomplishments of a young lady, she has been taught nothing of culture as continuity, as an expression of lasting human meaning. Her uncle's travels have stocked his house with miscellaneous "casts and pictures." "Too poor Dorothea these severe classical nudities and smirking Renaissance-Correggiosities were painfully inexplicable, staring into the midst of her Puritanic conceptions: she had never been taught how she could bring them into any sort of relevance with her life." Her wedding trip takes her to Rome, great repository of art and culture, which she finds mainly bewildering. Lacking the "knowledge which breathes a growing soul into all historic shapes, and traces the suppressed transitions which unite all contrasts," she sinks under the "weight of unintelligible Rome," feeling the past as divorced from the present. She appeals to Casaubon for some understanding of history, to Will for some guide to art. Neither man evinces much interest in her spiritual need. She returns to her sense of social responsibility as an escape: "I should like to make life beautiful—I mean everybody's life. And then all this immense expense of art, that seems somehow to lie outside life and make it no better for the world, pains me." Her untrained imagination limited by the realities of a woman's education, she must rest in a notion of social service that, however admirable, derives as much from what she is not allowed to comprehend as from what she really knows. Her "great faith" necessarily derives from personal fantasy, the desire to make everybody's life beautiful epitomizing its vagueness and its impossibility. The connection between faith and culture, the power of art as testimony of faith: these things Dorothea can never know. The true "withering" effect of society expresses itself more profoundly than even so perceptive an observer can understand.

Her imagining of a possible vocation is also limited by her social education. She longs to find meaning where women are supposed to find it: in marriage; but learns with disappointment how little need for her ministrations exists in her husband's prosperous parish. She turns her imaginative energy instead to an even more socially acceptable fantasy of total devotion to her husband's aims. But Casaubon has little room for her in his emotional or intellectual life, and his aims prove neither large nor even real. As enormous social issues become reduced for Middlemarch voters to a question of how a merchant can retain his customers, "the glow-worm lights of country places" dimly illuminating the problems dividing a nation, so Dorothea's dreams of meaningful action diminish in the faint light of her husband's exiguous sensibility. When he dies, her freedom hardly enlarges. She cannot help Will, as she yearns to do, because social pressure, though intangible, seems irresistible. "So heavily did the world weigh on her in spite of her independent energy, that with this idea of Will as in need of such help and at a disadvantage with the world, there came always the vision of that unfittingness of any closer relation between them which lay in the opinion of every one connected with her."

The force of the narrow society that constricts Dorothea's life and frustrates her imagination operates most powerfully through opinion: "public opinion," the sum total of individual private opinions, which assume public force. *Middlemarch* demonstrates this fact through every detail of presented social attitudes, from assumptions about marriage to political views: what people think, and what people think people think, invariably controls possibility. "Who can know how much of his most inward life is made up of the thoughts he believes other men to have about him, until that fabric of opinion is threatened with ruin?" The question, relevant to everyone in the novel, arises in connection with Bulstrode, destroyed by the readily aroused doubts of his community after many years' security in public esteem. Rosamond confirms its implications. From her point of view, her husband's possible distinguished work would possess value only if it enabled him "to attain a high position in some better place than Middlemarch." When scandal touches Lydgate, she feels her trouble no "less than if her husband had been certainly known to have done something criminal. All the shame seemed to be there." Such dependence on what others think can only issue in the total paralysis of individuals by their society. Dorothea, resisting paralysis for others as well as herself, defies "public opinion" in her defense of Lydgate. Unwilling to believe in opposition to her independent, largely intuitive, assessment of the man, she expresses her faith in him before allowing him to justify himself; self-justification thus becomes possible for him, as it has not been before. Dorothea's rarity illuminates itself in this act. Her capacity, not to ignore or defy public opinion so much as to declare it irrelevant, defines a large and significant freedom, which becomes fully meaningful as it allows Dorothea the possibility of evading social pressure in her own case as well as that of another.

The danger of rejecting social sanctions is the danger of total egotism. Rosamond, a supreme egotist, before her husband's catastrophe has no need to separate her own interests from those of her society because she epitomizes so fully—and feels herself to epitomize—what that society values. Even when the world turns on her, she remains conscious of flawless conduct and knows that she can be disapproved of only because of her husband, not for herself. Doomed to an unfortunate alliance by a misguided choice, she resorts to self-pity that such disaster should overwhelm one so deserving of good fortune. Her brother, Fred, displays a similar form of socially supported egotism, achieving partial freedom from it only through his association with the Garths. Casaubon's purer egotism, lacking social support, claims the transcedent importance of his most minute intellectual preoccupations. "We are all of us born in moral stupidity, taking the world as an udder to feed our supreme selves." Dorothea has tried hard to emerge from such stupidity, most importantly through devotion to her husband. But her willingness to subordinate herself to his interests does not automatically enable her to understand that he too has a sense of self, different from hers, which must make all experience look different from his point of view. Each ego creates a different order, and the demands of one upon another are difficult to adjudicate.

Dorothea's effort to comprehend her husband's needs, to be active on his behalf rather than passively accepting of his demands, ends with his death. At this point her bruised ego might assert itself. So much of her difficulty has derived from the pressure of other people—husband, family, society at large—that her most apparent need is independence. She seeks it: in living alone at Lowick, in investigating ways of using her money well, in standing up for Lydgate, in allying herself with Will. Yet all except the first of these activities involves primary acceptance of her obligation to other people. "People glorify all sorts of bravery except the bravery they might show on behalf of their nearest neighbours," she says, with specific reference to her espousal of Lydgate's cause. She seems to understand that her neighbor is he who hath need of her; she will divide herself from "society" as a massive pressure—it's the same distinction as in *The Mill on the Floss*—for

the sake of "other people." So when she declares herself
ready to assure her husband of the absolute devotion he
requests, she recognizes that "neither law nor the world's
opinion compelled her to this—only her husband's nature
and her own compassion, only the ideal and not the real
yoke of marriage." And when she comes to Lydgate's
defense, her friends remind her that "the world" opposes
her. "Would you not like to be that one person who believed in that man's innocence, if the rest of the world
belied him?" she inquires, glimpsing the strength of solitary faith. She looks from her window, in a time of deep
personal distress:

*On the road there was a man with a bundle on his back
and a woman carrying her baby; in the field she could see
figures moving—perhaps the shepherd with his dog. Far
off in the bending sky was the pearly light; and she felt
the largeness of the world and the manifold wakings of
men to labour and endurance. She was a part of that involuntary, palpitating life, and could neither look out on it
from her luxurious shelter as a mere spectator, nor hide
her eyes in selfish complaining.*

This new vision of "manifold pregnant existence," an imaginative grasping of connectedness, suggests that true
commitment to society as human fellowship may involve
rejection of society as clique and class. Taking full responsibility for herself implies recognition of her place in "the
largeness of the world" and her tie to the "involuntary,
palpitating life" of others. She has moved from a sense of
the necessary conflict between the individual imagination
and society's demands to a redefinition of society which allows the imagination to be a guide to social responsibility.

But just as she has decided to adhere to "the ideal and
not the real yoke of marriage," it is an ideal rather than a
real society to which she commits herself. She has had no
opportunity fully to know the real; and the power of the
real endures. Mary and Dorothea are heroines of the

imagination, despite their consistent action. Their imaginative grasp of their own places in relation to others enables them to achieve a steadfastness and stature that few men equal. Yet the limitation of their literal opportunities becomes the final focus of the novel's attention. Dorothea sees herself as part of a universal human fellowship, a society more than national. She acts, however, only in a tiny sphere. The vision of a large society liberates minds; the fact of a small one controls actions. "For there is no creature whose inward being is so strong that it is not greatly determined by what lies outside it. A new Theresa will hardly have the opportunity of reforming a conventual life, any more than a new Antigone will spend her heroic piety in daring all for the sake of a brother's burial: the medium in which their ardent deeds took shape is for ever gone." Dorothea gives "wifely help" to her new husband. She rears two children and lives a life full of "beneficent activity" (unspecified) which other people mark out for her.

Many who knew her, thought it a pity that so substantive and rare a creature should have been absorbed into the life of another, and be only known in a certain circle as a wife and mother. But no one stated exactly what else that was in her power she ought rather to have done—not even Sir James Chettham, who went no further than the negative prescription that she ought not to have married Will Ladislaw.

The problem of power returns. Little is in a woman's power; Dorothea's actual alternatives remain very limited. Her "rareness," her heroic moral stature, may in fact derive from her struggle with social fact; but social fact triumphs in her experience if not in her mind. Her "heroic piety," her impulse toward reform, must express themselves in a clogging medium: the author's last word on her suggests that she is one of " the number who lived faithfully a hidden life, and rest in unvisited tombs." That her faithfulness centers in her belief in ineluctable social ties only intensifies the irony of her severe constriction by the reality of such bonds.

Society as a fact of experience and society as a fact of imagination, then, may play opposite parts in a woman's life. As an imaginative fact, it becomes an enlarging force, drawing the woman to understand grand and hidden possibilities of her traditional activities, making her richly conscious of ways she can affect others. As an experiential fact, it limits women, restricting their possibilities of action. For men, in *Middlemarch*, different patterns shape themselves. "Society," in their experience, limits them relatively little, in comparison with women (even foolish Mr. Brooke can present himself as a political candidate— though his personal limitations eventuate in his harsh rejection by the community), permits them much. But a curious constriction of the imagination seems to result. Men—Fred, Casaubon, Lydgate—imagine personal accomplishment, public recognition, their fantasized contributions to the world important mainly as means to recognition. Encouraged in simple forms of egotism, they do not develop beyond them. Women, required to make heroic efforts to surmount the temptation to indulge in passive compliance with the power it offers (the power of Rosamond and, in more benign form, of Celia), grow more surely than men; but society, finally, cuts them off from full expression of the meaning of their growth.

The complicated pessimism of George Eliot's attitude toward society exemplifies the characteristic tone of women writing on the subject. Edith Wharton, her pessimism simpler but equally profound, refuses to acknowledge even that the female imagination can surmount or transform society's restriction. Her heroines suffer more totally than Dorothea, achieve far less. Her reflections on those vast realities, culture and society, recognize the duality of their meanings and reveal how women, pressed to offer allegiance to both understood in limited ways, may suffer damage from facts hidden within the terms' grander implications as well as from immediate social limitations.

Wharton's last novel, *The Buccaneers*, left incomplete at her death in 1938, seems an intentional comment, from a female point of view, on *Portrait of a Lady*. Like her friend Henry James, Mrs. Wharton made her manifest subject the relation of manners to morals, but her point of view differs from James's specifically in the ways it acknowledges the exigencies of female experience. The heroine of *The Buccaneers*, Nan St. George, is like Isabel Archer an American innocent, a moral orphan. Her parents are living but inadequate to her needs, unaware that experience might have a moral as well as a social or financial dimension. An Italian governess, Laura Testvalley, a benign parody of James's Madame Merle, initiates Nan into the world of literature and morality. Her imagination stimulated, she goes to England, where she marries a wealthy duke, misled into over-valuing him by his association with the artifacts of romantic tradition. The Duke of Tintagel, as it turns out, really cares only about clocks. Less vicious and calculating than Gilbert Osmond in *Portrait of a Lady*, he is equally incapable of treating his wife as more than a possession. She challenges his marital right to her body; the novel breaks off on the verge of her discovery that she loves another young Englishman, Guy Thwarte, widely experienced in the large world (he has married and become a widower in Brazil), who can appreciate her as well as his own inherited traditions and estate.

Mrs. Wharton wrote a plot synopsis that makes clear her intentions for the novel. Nan, encouraged by Laura Testvalley, was to elope with Guy, forced by his choice of her into exile from his homeland and the family house he loves for its history as well as its immediate reality. Laura, meanwhile, embarks (in her middle age) on a happy love affair with Guy's father. Her support for the young lovers requires her to relinquish her own happiness, since Guy's act violates his father's convictions. She ends in solitude,

as Guy and Nan conclude in exile, all three justified by
the moral and imaginative solidity of their choices. A large
supporting cast (elaborately depicted in the 355 pages of
a completed text) dramatizes various alternative possibilities of marriage: emotional deprivation, commercial alliance, social fiction; all corroborate the implication that
Nan has chosen the right course.

Working out this idea might have been difficult: could
Mrs. Wharton have substantiated the view that morality
may consist in violating the laws of society as well as the
sacrament of marriage? The imaginative texture of her fiction is thinner than that of James, no individual paragraph
as persuasive as, say, James's evocation of the final encounter between Isabel and Madame Merle. (Edith
Wharton remarked in her autobiography, "The real marriage of true minds is for any two people to possess a
sense of humour or irony pitched in exactly the same
key. . . . In that sense Henry James was perhaps the most
intimate friend I ever had." Her novels, however, provide
few equivalents of James's subtle, pervasive irony.) Yet
The Buccaneers has in potential a kind of authority that
James would never claim: that of absolute conviction. Although Nan's decision to leave her husband might appear
at least as morally ambiguous as Isabel's choice of returning to hers, Wharton's tone ignores ambiguities. Her characters may recognize them, she refuses to. She supplies a
cumulative weight of social evidence by which to understand individual decisions, insisting by implication (as
James does not) that social facts possess overriding eviden-
tial value.

But individual experience matters too. Marriage—not the
end but often the real beginning of a woman's life—is a social institution (hence, partly, its crushing power), but
above all, an exercise of the imagination. In committing
herself to a mate, the woman tries to make her dreams reality. As a girl, she lives in dreams. Her sex entitles her to
the indulgence of an inner life, its nature determined by
the quality of her mind and spirit. In most instances,

Edith Wharton indicates, the life of daydreams focuses on the imaginary man who will some day come to fulfill all the woman's needs. Lily Bart, in *The House of Mirth*, sees a girl whose face turns "toward her companion's like an empty plate held up to be filled." The image summarizes the psychic state of most unmarried women of her day. Nan St. George, like Isabel Archer, is unusual in her capacity—unfocused though it is—to imagine other sources of personal fulfillment than a man. Yet the social passivity of women, in Wharton's world and James's, blocks them from visualizing fulfillment through personal effort. They see themselves, and others see them, as inevitable recipients; but what will they receive?

Marriage may fill empty plates, but the hard crusts of actuality often contrast bitterly with the banquets of fantasy. Marriage, not just two people living together, involves a social contract full of hidden provisos. Women aware of this fact in advance may find themselves unable to marry at all. In Lily Bart, Wharton studies a girl trained to consider her person and charm essentially commercial resources and to understand marriage as a financial and social transaction in which the *quid pro quo*, perhaps unspecified, can always be understood. "Isn't marriage your vocation? Isn't it what you're all brought up for?" Selden inquires. He is a figure of sanity in the background, a kind of Greek chorus, his luxury of uninvolvement (until his belated and improbable discovery of love) possible only because he is male. Of course he's right in his rhetorical questions, Lily readily agrees with him—but it costs him nothing to be right. It costs Lily everything. She knows well enough that it's literally her "business" to get married and, consequently, to appear at the right parties, wear the right clothes. But she pays for such knowledge by death. Too aware of the meaning of what she might do to do it, she dies in an effort to escape the unendurable pressure of reality, dies from an overdose of chloral, in an escapist fantasy of motherhood, an imaginary infant in her arms.

The House of Mirth has the energy of parable, offering
a fable of woman's social condition and its impingement
on her personal integrity. Edith Wharton's other novels,
less unremittingly bleak, reiterate the same points about
marriage. Wharton's heroines, like Austen's or Eliot's, anticipate marriage as their destiny and their goal. Discovering in it their bondage, they are asphyxiated. "She had
left Anne when Anne was a baby of three; left her with a
dreadful pang, a rending of the inmost fibres, and yet a
sense of unutterable relief, because to do so was to escape
from the oppression of her married life, the thick atmosphere of self-approval and unperceivingness which
emanated from John Clephane like coal-gas from a leaking
furnace" (*The Mother's Recompense*). Even a man can
see that most marriages depend on "a dull association of
material and social interests held together by ignorance on
the one side and hypocrisy on the other" (*The Age of Innocence*), but he can find no alternative. When Nan, in
The Buccaneers, recognizes her own "desperate sense of
being trapped" or sees herself as "a life-prisoner behind
iron bars" or feels a noose tightening round her, she articulates the despair of virtually all Wharton's heroines. Less
sensitive women, like Nan's friend Conchita, may escape
the miseries of marriages in the unreflective indulgence of
love affairs; or fulfill themselves by gratifying social aims;
or rest content with receiving the admiration accorded to
a decorative artifact. Doom pursues the sensitive. Edith
Wharton's memoir, *A Backward Glance,* contains little
reference to her own marriage. "He was thirteen years
older than myself, but the difference in age was lessened
by his natural youthfulness, his good humour and gaiety,
and the fact that he shared my love of animals and out-
door life, and was soon to catch my travel-fever." This superficial characterization contains virtually all we learn of
her unnamed husband, who turns out finally to suffer from
some vague mental ailment. At no point in Edith Wharton's account of herself does her husband appear to have
any connection with her significant experience.

The connection of husbands with real female experience is dim, too, in the novels. Among the questions that marriage focuses for a woman—in James as well—a crucial one centers on the relation between imagination and reality. If marriage, as an effort to make dreams reality, unites the two, its working out usually suggests no such simple identity. At least two kinds of imagination prey on the novels' characters: the individual variety which produces visions of ideal personal fulfillment, and a collective fantasy which embodies the values of "society" in both its large and limited senses. Fortunate women in Edith Wharton's novels—women whose lives display the ease associated with lack of introspection—possess individual imaginations in no way at odds with the imagination of their society. Their dreams of marriage, accepting a social institution, demand no more than such an institution can provide. But Wharton's heroines are never in this sense fortunate women. What they want, what they dream, diverges from what their society wants and dreams.

"In reality they all lived in a kind of hieroglyphic world where the real thing was never said or done or even thought, but only represented by a set of arbitrary signs." Newland Archer, in *The Age of Innocence*, speaks for the author, who demonstrates the same point in all her work. "Society" has little relation to "reality." Oh, that Eglinton girl!" Nan St. George exclaims. "She looked at us all as if we weren't there." Her mother responds ("heroically"), "Well, that's the way for a lady to look at strangers." Triumphant social accomplishment can deny the reality of others. The weight of social imagination rests in denial, repression, concealment. In a particularly brilliant autobiographical passage, Edith Wharton tells of the archery competitions she remembers from her youth, where women competed less in marksmanship than in beauty. Since the chief mark of feminine beauty was "a complexion," young women wore "veils as thick as curtains," often made of wool. "It must have been very uncomfortable for the wearers, who could hardly see or breathe; but even to

312

my childish eyes the effect was dazzling when the curtain was drawn, and young beauty shone forth." The writer adds that "the young gods and goddesses" she watched at archery meetings became the prototypes of her first novelistic characters, the sight of them stimulating her imagination to creativity.

The image of young women whose beauty depends on concealment summarizes an important theme of Wharton's fiction. In *The Age of Innocence* she uses the archery meeting—this time belonging to a later era than the one reported in her memoir: no more literal veils—in a way suggesting the symbolic significance of the veiled maidens. Archer sees his wife emerging in costume (white dress, wreath of ivy) to shoot, her attitude "full of a classic grace." He remembers how she looked the night of her engagement. "In the interval not a thought seemed to have passed behind her eyes or a feeling through her heart; and though her husband knew that she had the capacity for both he marvelled afresh at the way in which experience dropped away from her." Experience drops away because it's supposed to; the ideal woman remains untouched by life as her skin remains untouched by sun. Archer speculates that his wife's supreme "niceness" may be "only a negation, the curtain dropped before an emptiness." The imaginative power of veils derives from their mystery; but concealment may be destructive. The ideal image, the *social* image, of women as beings of untouched serenity and beauty is—like the real veils it recalls—one of potential suffocation.

In Wharton's America as in Fanny Burney's England, the ideal young woman exemplifies perfect innocence—an "innocence that seals the mind against imagination and the heart against experience!" Innocence barricades its possessor "against the alarming business of living." That phrase comes from *The Mother's Recompense,* a tale of innocence sacrificed in a failed search for freedom. Edith Wharton offers no easy answers, hardly any answers at all, to the social problems she poses. Archer sees his fiancée,

May, as a "terrifying product of the social system he belonged to and believed in, the young girl who knew nothing and expected everything": the ideal artifact of the social imagination, a being so bred that she can neither imagine nor claim her freedom. One may be cynical about her, preferring, like Archer, her sophisticated cousin, the Countess Olenska. But Archer marries May, never consummating his real love. Significant relations in Wharton's novels rarely reach consummation, society being so organized—pathetically or tragically—that they should not.

The collective imagination of women as innocent, guarded from experience, receptive and malleable, produces against real feeling; the world tolerates love affairs partly because they are structures of lies—"A lie by day, a lie by night, a lie in every touch and every look; a lie in every caress and every quarrel; a lie in every word and in every silence." Women, assumed to be—in all their "innocence"—natural liars, remain subject creatures, "and versed in the arts of the enslaved." (The phrase exemplifies the bitter energy of Wharton's understanding of the female lot.) Forced into lives of falsehood, they discover that reality has disappeared. Mrs. Clephane, the heroine of *The Mother's Recompense*, recalls the lover for whom she left her husband: "as unreal as somebody in a novel, the highly coloured hero (or villain) on the 'jacket.' From her inmost life he had vanished into a sort of remote pictorial perspective, where a woman of her name figured with him, . . . herself as unreal as a lady on a 'jacket.'" Society teaches us to "call all our generous ideas illusions, and the mean ones truths," creating a structure of lies and limitations, for men as well as women (Selden, in *The House of Mirth*, makes the point about generous versus mean ideas), although men suffer less because of their permitted capacity to do as well as receive.

But that society opposes reality is only half the truth—it being equally true that society *is* reality. Selden perceives Lily as "so evidently the victim of the civilization which had produced her, that the links of her bracelet seemed

like manacles chaining her to her fate." (All the Wharton
novels provide rich imagery of chains, slavery, prison, suffocation.) He sees her thus early in the book whose entire
action simply substantiates his perception. Shortly before
her death, she understands that "if one were not a part of
the season's fixed routine, one swung unsphered in a void
of social non-existence. Lily, for all her dissatisfied dreaming, had never really conceived the possibility of revolving
about a different centre: it was easy enough to despise the
world, but decidedly difficult to find any other habitable
region." The terms have shifted—one feels the gap between the male notion of "civilization" and the female
reference to "the season." Yet trivia may reflect magnitude: "the season," "the world" of high society, emanate
from the fundamental realities of "civilization." Though
the possibility of revolving around a different center theoretically does exist—one can alienate oneself even from civilization—its difficulties make it virtually impossible. Mrs.
Clephane, in *The Mother's Recompense*, demonstrates the
point. The most antisocial of Wharton's heroines (although Nan St. George might have developed farther in
the same direction), she violates social expectation by
abandoning husband and child to flee with a lover.
Eighteen years later, her husband and rigid mother-in-law
dead, she returns to her grown daughter and to the social
world. No one speaks of what has happened, nothing has
changed, nothing (despite the death) has escaped.
"It was all, in short, as natural and unnatural, as horrible,
intolerable and unescapable, as if she had become young
again, with all her desolate and unavoidable life stretching
away ahead of her to—this."

The dual recognition of society as unreality, society as
reality, that emerges in all the novels as well as the autobiography (which justifies itself by claiming to be an
attempt to preserve even the "smallest fragments" of the
social structure the author knew in her youth, but in fact
records her efforts to evade the falsifications of that structure) creates the dilemma that Nan St. George faces in

The Buccaneers. Because the rejections of American society torment her mother, Nan flees to its English equivalent. Its laws are not hers; for a time the invading Americans (the "buccaneers") seem able to create a new freedom. Their attractiveness to the English derives from this illusion. Nan marries the duke because he contains for her the past as well as the present. The ambiguity of such containing emerges only gradually, as she finds herself firmly held in a web of social custom whose strength comes partly from its long continuance. The very letters she writes must be copied from a model. She has lost her self in her social image: "There were moments when the vain hunt for her real self became so perplexing and disheartening that she was glad to escape from it into the mechanical duties of her new life. But in the intervals she continued to grope for herself, and to find no one."

Perhaps *The Buccaneers* is unfinished because it had to be. Mrs. Wharton worked on it for several years, following closely her synopsis, written early in her effort. But she made of her heroine a victim of society so richly imagined that it's difficult to conceive that she can evade the structure that holds her. When she suggests to her mother-in-law that she's made a mistake in marrying the duke, the old dowager affirms (with specific reference to Nan's new English nationality), "Nothing can change that now." *Nothing*, thrice repeated, rings like a knell. Some things, indeed, never change. Mrs. Clephane found no freedom in flight; Nan may find no more. She believes, without understanding, that her private imaginative experience may rescue her, that Guy exists to confirm what her imagination tells her. But Edith Wharton provides abundant testimony that imagination, although it may compensate for external restrictions, breaks no real bonds. Her own imagination, indeed, led her to increasingly vivid perception of the reality of social bondage.

The author's account of her early childhood stresses her lack of interest in the fabulous and legendary, claiming that her imagination needed little sustenance from outside.

"My imagination lay there, coiled and sleeping, a mute hibernating creature, and at the least touch of common things—flowers, animals, words, especially the sound of words, apart from their meaning—it already stirred in its sleep, and then sank back into its own rich dream, which needed so little feeding from the outside that it instinctively rejected whatever another imagination had already adorned and completed." Antagonism between the imagination and "the outside" soon developed, centered on the demands of social life. The child Edith was so eager to be decorous that when an aunt inquired her plans for the future she declared her intention of being the best-dressed woman in New York, feeling this purpose as a dutiful following in her mother's footsteps. But deeper demands emerged from within. "I had to obey the furious Muse; and there are deplorable tales of my abandoning the 'nice' playmates who had been invited to 'spend the day,' and rushing to my mother with the desperate cry: 'Mama, you must go and entertain that little girl for me. *I've got to make-up.*'" There was not one of her playmates, Mrs. Wheaton adds, whom "I would not have renounced forever rather than have my 'making up' interfered with."

"Making up," a solitary activity, involved no intent of communication. It did not occur to the child to reconcile her obligations by telling stories to her playmates, or even to write down the narratives she imagined: the experience was essentially interior. Many years later, visiting England with her husband, Mrs. Wharton discovered with astonishment literary ladies like Alice Meynell and Mrs. Humphry Ward treated with respect, even deference, by their families, writing generating prestige. "Accustomed at home to dissemble" her "literary pursuits (as though, to borrow Dr. Johnson's phrase about portrait painting, they were 'indelicate in a female')," Mrs. Wharton had preserved her childhood's sharp distinctions between outer and inner experience. Her storytelling "takes place in some secret region on the sheer edge of consciousness. . . . What happens there is as real and as tangible as my encounters with my friends and neighbours, often more so, though on an entirely different plane. It produces in me a great emotional excitement, quite unrelated to the joy or sorrow caused by real happenings, but as intense, and with as great an appearance of reality; and my two lives, divided between these equally real yet totally unrelated worlds, have gone on thus, side by side, equally absorbing, but wholly isolated from each other." As in her childhood, she deliberately sustains her isolation. With all her imaginative capacity, Edith Wharton seems never to have imagined that social existence and creative life could interpenetrate: the barriers between them felt absolute. Social existence threatens personal reality and integrity; creative life preserves them.

Many of Edith Wharton's fictional characters are unable or unwilling to use their imaginative capacities: like Mrs. Peniston in *The House of Mirth,* they keep their imagination "shrouded, like the drawing-room furniture." Like the furniture, or like a corpse: the atrophy of imagination kills the spirit. But it protects, paradoxically, against the shock of reality. People unable to grasp their environments through imagination thus armor themselves. Lily Bart, altogether lacking in "moral vision," can understand the lives of others only in terms of her own. She longs for a reductive view of life that might enable her to understand everything "as a perpetual adjustment, a play of party politics, in which every concession had its recognized equivalent," fearing the implications of more expansive imagining. May Welland, in *The Age of Innocence,* impresses her new husband by the coexistence within her of great depths of feeling and total absence of imagination; years later he understands that she has expended all her slender resources of poetry and romance during their courtship, when imagination seemed temporarily a useful tool. Such women as Lily and May know of imagination's torment. Images from her past agonize Kate Clephane, in *The Mother's Recompense;* she can't confess to her daughter Anne that the daughter's fiancé is the mother's ex-lover, largely because she believes that "a hideous indestructible image of her would remain, overshadowing, darkening the daughter's future." Newland Archer lives on his images:

> ... *he had built up within himself a kind of sanctuary in which she throned among his secret thoughts and longings. Little by little it became the scene of his real life, of his only rational activities; thither he brought the books he read, the ideas and feelings which nourished him, his judgments and his visions. Outside it, in the scene of his actual life, he moved with a growing sense of unreality and insufficiency, blundering against familiar prejudices and traditional points of view as an absent-minded man goes on bumping into the furniture of his own room. Absent—that was what he was: so absent from everything most densely real and near to those about him that it sometimes startled him to find they still imagined he was there.*

Imagination functions for Newland analogously to its absence in his wife May: to protect him from the "real," as defined by others. "Real life" and "rational activities" he locates in the irrational inner sphere; prejudice and tradition, belonging to other people, seem unreal and insufficient. May, believing prejudice and tradition real, guards against the feeling that might violate them by refusing to imagine the possibility of feeling outside of social convention. But both fictional characters embody the same point, Edith Wharton's crucial point: what is unimagined is unreal. It does not necessarily follow—indeed, it's dangerous to believe—that the imagined, conversely, must be real. That is, in fact, Newland Archer's tragedy: he substitutes existence in his "sanctuary" for life with a real woman in the real world. Fantasy is easier. But to imagine, even as Kate Clephane imagines, envisioning only horror, is to believe in possibilities, believe that important things can happen—to keep oneself alive, thus, as a being in an unpredictable universe. Little can happen to May, because she will not allow herself to imagine: only to predict the predictable, and find it coming true.

Nan St. George defines herself as a heroine of unusual potential in Edith Wharton's world by her moral growth, which is also imaginative development. She yearns from the beginning to indulge her fancy. "Her own universe was so crammed to bursting with wonderful sights and sounds that, in spite of her sense of Virginia's superiority—her beauty, her ease, her self-confidence—Nan sometimes felt a shamedfaced pity for her. It must be cold and lonely, she thought, in such an empty colourless world as her sister's." Eager to find and make color in her world, she endows the Duke of Tintagel with far more glamour than he possesses and imagines her marriage as enlargement. This effort to reconcile the life of fancy with that of reality fails; by the time she starts to discover her affinity with Guy Thwarte, she can remark, "It's rather lonely sometimes, when the only things that seem real are one's dreams." Forced back on fantasy, she despairs of reconciliation. Yet she continues to believe that the "layers and layers of rich deep background" she finds in England must have solid and discoverable relevance to her personal experience. She and Guy unite in responding to this background; their love creates an alliance of two people equally committed to the effort to combine the life of the imagination with that of reality.

The artist, of course, by definition achieves such a union, translating his inner life into terms communicable and acceptable to the world at large. But the artist plays almost as ambiguous a role in Edith Wharton's work as Gilbert Osmond, the connoisseur of art, in *Portrait of a Lady*. Chris Fenno, the lover of both mother and daughter in *The Mother's Recompense*, during the period of Mrs. Clephane's involvement with him professes to be a painter. He explains that he would be a *famous* painter if his parents hadn't forced him into a stockbroker's office. Kate Clephane rises early every day to make up her face (older than he, she is her own work of art); she sits and meditates while he sketches the scenery. In due time, in the carefree fashion of the artist, Chris leaves her. When he reappears as her daughter's lover, he has become a poet: "All he cares about it his writing," Anne declares. Another commentator reports, approvingly, that Chris is giving up his job as private secretary to a bibliophile: "He says he must have more mental elbow-room; for his writing, I mean. He can't be tied down to hours and places." His creativity attested by assertion rather than accomplishment, he fascinates women through the mysterious glamour of his position. He is the imagined male equivalent of such real figures as Marie Bashkirtseff and Mary MacLane; because he *is* male, assumed therefore to act significantly in the world, he can step into the established romantic role of "poet," declaring his independent masculinity by violating convention and readily winning love by his display of "specialness." All rules are different for men, who get the rewards.

Mrs. Clephane, when Chris belongs to her daughter rather than herself, observes "that slight slackness of the mouth that had once seemed a half-persuasive pout, and was now only a sign of secret uncertainties and indulgences," perceiving at his core "the central failure," "a sight not meant for her." Belatedly, she notes his total narcissism. But her daughter in her full devotion cannot be dissuaded: Anne, wishing to be an artist herself, but as a woman needing to achieve in order to be recognized, needs also vicarious expression through the man who so firmly—regardless of what he may or may not accomplish in the world—defines himself as artist: a being whose imagination justifies his existence, automatically elevating him beyond the obligations of social convention. The artist, thus, in his own fantasy and that of others, becomes the free man. Kate Clephane goes beyond this fantasy to perceive Chris's limitations, but going beyond it offers no reward. She neither has nor can discover her own freedom, asserting herself only through refusal: to stay in America, to accept the love of conventional, devoted Fred

Landers, to continue any significant relation at all. Her daughter, however fantastic her vision of freedom as and with an artist, is a happier woman.

When Isabel Archer begins her final confrontation with her husband, toward the end of *Portrait of a Lady*, she finds him in his study copying the drawing of an antique coin in delicate watercolor on immaculate paper. His art the imitation of an imitation, the exquisite reproduction of surfaces, he is a collector rather than a creator. But his consistent association with beautiful objects serves more than an ironic function in the narrative. His power over Isabel derives partly from the authority of his flawless taste, partly from his capacity to incorporate social forms into a private vision of artistic structure. The notion of that structure, and of the man capable of conceiving it, speaks to her imagination. "She still wished to justify herself; he had the power, in an extraordinary degree, of making her feel this need. There was something in her imagination he could always appeal to against her judgment." Her judgment declares her marriage a monstrous mockery; her imagination suggests another way of seeing it. Osmond articulates her imagination's understanding: "I'm not aware that we're divorced or separated; for me we're indissolubly united. . . . Because I think we should accept the consequences of our actions, and what I value most in life is the honour of a thing!" Isabel sees that his words "represented something transcendent and absolute, like the sign of the cross or the flag of one's country. He spoke in the name of something sacred and precious—the observance of a magnificent form." To this form, this magnificence, Isabel chooses to return, rejecting for it a life of sexual possibility, a committed lover.

Nan St. George, in *The Buccaneers*, marries a man who appeals to her imagination not by what he is but by what he represents. The Duke of Tintagel, far less articulate than Gilbert Osmond, has a mother to defend the observance of forms. "There's only one way for an English Duchess to behave—and the wretched girl has never learnt it. . . . I daresay that's the trouble with Annabel—she's never assumed her responsibilities. Once one does, there's no time left for trifles." The dowager's characteristic tone, testy rather than, like Osmond's magisterial, reaches the miserable young wife's imagination. Nan admires, despite herself, the "control" achieved by absolute commitment to social form. She feels the moral grandeur of submitting to the restrictions at which she chafes; feels "in a confused way that the business of living was perhaps conducted more wisely at Longlands" in spite of her recognition that living thus intensifies her own suffering.

James's imaginative comprehension of Gilbert Osmond is far more subtle and elaborate than Wharton's of the Duke of Tintagel or his mother. Unfortunately, since the final portion of *The Buccaneers* was never written, it's impossible to compare the authors' imagining of their heroines' crucial choices. But the preparation for Nan's decision to leave her husband and the life of social forms for a man who speaks more profoundly to her imagination may arouse speculation about what the shapes of the two novels—fully realized or not—mean.

Both possibilities that confront Isabel are possibilities of flight; she must choose what to flee from and to. She acts decisively, but not out of calculation; once more her imagination rather than her judgment dominates. Imagination tells her that Casper's love is "the hot wind of the desert"; that the "rapture" of momentary psychic submission to him is "a rushing torrent" in which she may "sink and sink." The "magnificent form" to which Osmond is devoted becomes in Casper's description a "ghastly form": Casper turns everything upside down. She chooses to flee the destructive potentialities of his devotion for her, the chaos of his assertions, the hot wind of his sexuality, the "lightning" of his kiss, to flee down "a very straight path" to the moral security of Osmond's sacred, absolute devotion to form. She might instead flee the sterility of her marriage for the deepenings of love, rejecting society's restrictions in favor of personal needs. James does not unequivocally endorse his heroine's choice of flights, but neither does he clearly condemn it. He ends the novel with a moral question mark: What have the major characters learned from their experience, have they grown or only solidified? The reader has seen the emptiness of Isabel's marriage, but also heard the persuasiveness of Gilbert's rhetoric: what Gilbert stands for is not merely contemptible, although the man himself may be exactly that. The author invites one to recognize the heroism of Isabel's fidelity to commitment even while he reveals that it is partly the fidelity of fear: the terror of drowning underlies the choice of aridity.

Edith Wharton allows no such indulgence in the pleasure of paradox. Perhaps it is a male luxury to speculate thus—and the last chapters of *Portrait of a Lady* all dramatize subtle speculation—about the meanings of female choice. At any rate, however divided her characters, the author never equivocates her own point of view. The flight from form to feeling on which Nan will embark follows no straight path, yet leads to salvation. Heroism of Isabel's sort may be seen as a woman's temptation: the temptation of avoidance, to which most of the women in Wharton's novels succumb in one form or another. Gilbert Osmond avoids reality in its more demanding aspects by collecting and copying ancient artifacts, cultivating style rather than substance; Isabel avoids the reality that frightens her by returning to Gilbert, making her life an artifact of flawless style. If true art has saving power (the art constantly alluded to in *The Buccaneers* through the paintings and tapestries of great English homes, the poetry central in Nan's education), false art destroys. The forces of social convention lure women toward corruption of the imagination. One variety of temptation through false art is embodied in Chris Fenno of *The Mother's Recompense*, who substitutes the role of artist for the reality of creation. (Wharton recognizes the falseness as well as the success of such substitution.) The more common temptation for a woman is to convert herself into the work of art, perverting her imagination by limiting its scope, losing her self by intense concentration on how she presents herself. Selden's first impression of Lily Bart, in *The House of Mirth*, is "a confused sense that she must have cost a great deal to make." He sees her as a creation of porcelain, "as though a fine glaze of beauty and fastidiousness had been applied to vulgar clay." Much later, he witnesses a tableau in which Lily has made herself into the image of a Reynolds painting. "It was as though she had stepped, not out of, but into, Reynolds's canvas." She is very beautiful. Selden, moved, feels that he sees "before him the real Lily Bart, divested of the trivialities of her little world."

But the attempt to divest oneself of the trivialities of the world is as dangerous as the effort to live entirely by the trivial. Women are *not* works of art, separated from the commonplace, any more than they are mere social mechanisms. Society encourages them to selfworship and to satisfaction with the trivial. Every woman in *The Buccaneers* except Nan and the governess Laura falls into one course or the other. Laura, of course, has no social pretensions, consequently does not face the problem of living within the conventions she brilliantly teaches: despite the manifold restrictions of the governess's lot, the endless forced silences and discretions, she has more essential freedom than her charges. Nan learns from what she sees as well as what she feels. She chooses life over death, the fertilized rather than the stultified imagination—making the most crucial of human choices. To allow the imagination to die, to restrict it to even the most magnificent of forms, is to reject life. Most women do exactly this, encouraged by the conventions of culture and society, in terms of which a girl earns more esteem for making herself look like a Reynolds painting than for responding richly to one.

Society, in Edith Wharton's vision, offers no support for the female imagination which in her writing too appears to provide the only hope for individual salvation. More immediately, though, imagination creates personal misery. The woman who allows herself to imagine beyond the

325

categories provided for her by social codes generates dissatisfactions which life rarely allows her to dispel. Imagination will lead her to perception of inequity; repression and denial alone can protect her. She can choose the blindness of conformity or the vision of personal discovery; but vision makes a difference only to her inner life. Like George Eliot's heroines, Edith Wharton's have no possible vocations beyond the domestic. Lily Bart's attempt to do something in the world ends in disaster: she can't even trim hats successfully. The impossibility of vocation symbolizes the hopelessness with which these women endure society's pressures: with open-eyed acceptance of misery, like Mrs. Clephane; with willful blindness, like May Welland; with self-destructive floundering, like Lily Bart. The imaginers, in all their misery, seem morally superior to the eye-closers, but happiness belongs to no one, the forces of society are far too powerful for individuals to resist. Nan St. George attempts to make imagination her vocation, seeking happiness with open eyes. Wharton's earlier novels suggest that she will fail.

Trying to circumvent society, women always fail. They also fail, some novelists suggest, if they attempt to embody society's values. Mary McCarthy's fiction belongs to an era in which, one might think, the problem of vocation has been solved. Her heroines hold jobs, can even have careers. Yet, with infinite possibilities of doing and being, they perceive vividly how rigid laws control them within every possibility. In *The Company She Keeps*, the heroine wishes to conform—although what she wants to conform to is never precisely clear; or, rather, it keeps changing, thus blurring. She also wishes the imaginative vision characteristic of Wharton heroines; but the focus and meaning of that vision aren't clear either.

Society in a Wharton novel is "the best people." Mary McCarthy considers the ambiguity of *best*. In her superficially unrestricted world a woman can lead a "free" life without penalty, but her heroines too need the approval of "the best people"—lacking any assurance of who exactly they are. New alignments take place; men and women define themselves in relation to changing standards, shifting assumptions. One may know them by the company they keep; but *The Company She Keeps* reveals the full ambiguity of *that* idea. Political allegiances now become part of social status, the choice of a psychoanalyst creates a label as precise as that determined earlier by receiving or failing to receive an invitation to a ball. Edith Wharton notes a mother's alertness to what name (first or last) a hairdresser uses in referring to the customer's daughter; Mary McCarthy shows a woman worrying over the impression she will make on her fellow passengers in a club car. Attitudes toward international affairs, personal philosophies, jobs, clothes: all function as social counters. Some ideal of social conformity rules as definitively as in Edith Wharton, although reality, utterly different, utterly unpredictable, comprising a moral chaos, shapes individuals in more various ways. Rules are no longer clearly defined: a shabby coat may confer more status than a lavish one. Great tension therefore prevails, rewards and punishments remain obscure. Mary McCarthy examines meticulously the painful ambiguities of personal experience in a setting that implies rigid demands without ever clarifying the nature of those demands.

Margaret Sargent, the central character of the six loosely related episodes of *The Company She Keeps*, young, intellectual, attractive, presents a life history in some respects resembling Mary McCarthy's own. Three episodes concentrate directly on her experience, telling of her first divorce, her seduction by an unattractive man on a train, and her psychoanalysis; the other three centrally concern her male companions: a crooked art dealer for whom she works, a professional host who wishes to help her, a Yale man, temporarily Margaret's colleague, whose political opinions become his means to success. The young woman leads a varied life, surrounded by and interested in diverse people, engaging in various occupations and roles.

Especially roles: far more definitive than occupations. The novel studies woman-as-actress and how society conditions her to this position. Not that society conditions only women—the three sketches focused on men emphasize that men, with similar problems, show similar effects. Margaret, an actress, lives among actors. Mr. Sheer, the crook, seems bizarrely different from others but bizarrely resembles everyone else. "Masquerade was life to Mr. Sheer. He could not bear to succeed in his own personality, any more than an unattractive woman can bear to be loved for herself." To risk the self for judgment would be dangerous; to discover the self, impossible. As Mr. Sheer becomes more successful in legitimate business, he begins to despair. His associates protect him from the consequences of his trickery; his efforts at risk taking (playing the stock market, seducing a client's wife) backfire—the client has been yearning to ditch his wife, the gallery Sheer works for covers his losses. Unable to tolerate the pain of being a commonplace self, Mr. Sheer begins to risk his body. Acting the invalid if he can't act the confidence man, arranging to have portions of his anatomy (appendix, gall bladder, teeth) removed, he dramatizes the self-destructiveness implicit in the steady presentation of false faces to the world.

All the stories, like parables, implicitly claim universal relevance despite their reliance on specific social detail. Pflaumen, the perfect host, inhabits a narrative in the second person singular. The "you" designates Margaret Sargent, but in the strained technique justifies itself by suggesting that the reader too struggles in the same social structure and dilemmas. Pflaumen's genius derives from his capacity to create "the illusion of a microcosm, ... the sense of a little world that was exactly the same as the big world, though it had none of the pain and care. Each of Pflaumen's guests had been selected, as it were, for his allegorical possibilities." The allegories played out around Pflaumen's table involve clashes of value (or displays of clashing values: a rather different thing), the inception of

love affairs, rivalries, enmities, the assigning and acceptance of work to be done; and a steady drama of social
emotion—appreciation (of food, wine, wit, beauty), political passion, literary, musical, and dramatic interest. All
feeling is merely part of the show—a fact accounting for
the manifest uneasiness of participants in the display.

"Portrait of the Intellectual as a Yale Man" enlarges the
arena and shifts the terms, but not the point. Pflaumen
generates suspicion; Jim Barnett, the Yale man, dispels
uneasiness by his very existence. The apparent type of
healthy American conformity, his vigorous wholesomeness,
the earnestness of his conviction, validate his radical opinions. "He made you think of Boy Scouts and starting a fire
without matches ... and the Our Gang comedies and
Huckleberry Finn. ... He might have done very well as
the young man who is worried about his life insurance,
the young man who is worried about dandruff, the young
man whose shirts won't fit him, the young man who looks
up happily from his plate of Crunchies ..." However
imaginable in all the stereotypical roles of American folk-
lore and advertising, Jim in fact plays another part: "he
was worried about Foster and Ford and the Bonus March-
ers and the Scottsboro Boys." He acts a charade of radicalism, making the parade of commitment into another
stereotype; working for *Destiny* (a thinly disguised version
of *Fortune*), he achieves all he wants: money, freedom,
the chance to dramatize himself as a divided man. Seeing
his wife as "the Average Intelligent Woman, the Mate," he
feels gratified that "his domestic life was wholesome and
characterless, like a child's junket.... He had a profound
conviction that this was the way things ought to be, that
this was life." His insistence on finding reassurance everywhere makes him reassuring to others; in all his shifts of
opinion, the world remains to his perception profoundly
logical: endangering no one, he moves to inevitable
success.

In the course of his rise Jim goes to bed once with
Margaret Sargent, whom he judges, with considerable

condescension, as foolhardy, rash, extreme. She defends unfashionable opinions though obviously scared, gets herself fired from a job she needs, lacks the worldly wisdom which comes naturally to him. But his brief liaison with her assumes for him "an allegorical significance" as a turning point in his career. He conducts endless imaginary dialogues with Margaret; sleeping with his wife, he pretends she's Margaret: the thrill of adultery without penalty. Gradually he realizes how much he resents her, because her existence comments on his: she has the power to make his life seem "a failure, not a tragedy exactly, but a comedy with pathos." Despite the persistent unreality of her own experience, she represents for him, ironically, the reality principle. Her presence makes him dimly realize that he only plays roles, limits his psychic expenditure, relies on pretend money while convincing himself that it is real.

As in *Middlemarch*, the novelist suggests that men and women endure similar social pressures, suffer similar problems. Men here seem no more reprehensible than women in the solutions they discover—identical solutions: acting parts in self-created dramas that society applauds or, unhappily, fails to applaud. Margaret's apparent moral superiority to Jim Barnett, in her superior faithfulness to a political position, wins her no applause. Although it makes Jim uneasy, it seems a trifle foolish: no testimony to the virtue of women, evidence rather of one woman's lack of practicality, eventually meaningless even to herself. Jim Barnett, however morally inadequate, achieves "success." Margaret Sargent feels more and more utterly a failure.

Why does Margaret go to bed with Jim Barnett? We never know. In another part of the narrative, though, we learn how she finds herself in bed with an even more unlikely companion, a "porcine" businessman in a Brooks Brothers suit whom she meets on a train. Her sexual career proceeds from one arbitrary event to another. She divorces her husband because she feels compelled to enact the drama of divorce; by the time she leaves for Reno, she realizes that she'll never marry her lover, and she already enjoys and fears her fantasized role as Young Divorcée. Her involvement with the businessman occurs on a trip west to tell her aunt of her approaching second marriage, which never takes place either. In her psychoanalysis she recalls a long sequence of meaningless love affairs, and finally a severely limiting, childless marriage to an architect who tyrannizes over her. Through sexuality she tries to resolve her uncertainty about her femininity: "what she was really asking all along was not that the male should assault her, but that he should believe her a woman." Men "could only respond by leaping at her—which, after all, she supposed, was their readiest method of showing her that her impersonation had been convincing." But the response remains unsatisfactory: conscious of herself as actress (by acting a role too well she ends up with the improbable Mr. Breen), she wants an audience—not fellow performers on the same stage.

The nature of the response to dramatic performance in society comprises the most complicated and compelling issue in *The Company She Keeps*. Men and women, equally driven to "perform" in the social world here depicted—stage metaphors dominate every section of the novel—are alike obsessed with audience response. Yet Margaret, the only woman with more than a walk-on part, suffers more sharply than her male counterparts: not because of her superior sensitivity (though that is a hinted possibility) but because of the social significance of her sex.

Mr. Sheer, Pflaumen, Jim Barnett want, and to varying degrees get, applause. The tragic side of Mr. Sheer's comedy emerges when he's reduced to applauding himself, giggling at the dangers of his surgical operations, because no one else will provide the kind of admiration he craves. Pflaumen offers the artifacts of his apartment, his wines, his menus, his maid, as objects of praise; all represent himself. He gets what he wants, grudgingly given because of his glaring need. Jim Barnett cannot achieve the success of creativity—his great book remains unwritten—but he wins the success of the world: universal admiration and sympathy. Men, in other words, applauded by self or others, achieve, if not happiness, at least a measure of satisfaction specifically from their self-presentation to the world at large.

The comparable satisfactions of women, if Margaret is representative, never compensate at all for their private miseries. Society, in encouraging a sense of infinite possibility for women (Margaret's available roles seem more abundant than Jim's), only intensifies the individual's awareness of inadequacy. Jim Barnett and Pflaumen may wish to do and be more than they can do and be, but their community asks of them no more than they offer. Margaret, on the other hand, can never escape the feeling that something more is wanted: her audience's reaction never satisfies her. If they seem thrilled by the high drama of her divorce, they probably won't be thrilled tomorrow. If someone takes her to bed in a Pullman berth, he vulgarizes her; if he admires her high style he makes her feel ridiculous; if he sends her a telegram of sympathy, she throws it out—standing in, as it were, for her audience, of which she remains always vividly conscious. Her social milieu, intricate and ill-defined, but very precise in her imagination, both creates and reflects her. She may appear to move outside it, as in the brief encounter with Mr. Breen, but she soon manages to incorporate such happenings within her understanding of her social definition. Driven by the obligation to be "interesting"—to herself first of all, that self epitomizing her society—she finds the possibilities always diminishing. Never can she predict fully the consequences of an act: this she discovers with her divorce. A psychoanalytic hour miniaturizes her total experience, as she says what seems interesting, what seems to insist on her "specialness," only to discover unforseen uncertainties as the result of such self-assertion.

The Company She Keeps studies female *hubris*—not the arrogance of overweening self-assertion beyond the laws of God and man, but the apparently more modest assertion of insistent self-display as the perfect representative of society. What Margaret is seems fully defined by where she is, in time and space: this fact generates her pain. She articulates the complicated and often contradictory values of her world, demands of herself that she articulate them flawlessly. If these values have little solidity, she too will be utterly fluid. Her highest achievement is insight, for which she prays: "If the flesh must be blind, let the spirit see. Preserve me in disunity." But what she can see remains severely limited. Like her creator, she has an acute eye for social detail: her malicious portrait of her analyst and her self-castigating description of her own middle-class life display the same sharp perception of the relation between minutiae and meaning. She sees her own posing and the poses of others, but no possibility for authenticity; she feels doomed to be "the equivocal personality who was not truly protean but only appeared so," taking pride only in the fact that "she could still detect her own frauds."

What Margaret can perceive is limited, as she and her world are also limited. Her irony belongs to the society described: smart, witty, self-deprecating, destructive. Yet clear seeing represents a genuine value. McCarthy as author demonstrates how imaginative vision, even operating in a context of severe moral disorder, can assert at least limited meaning. The multiple points of view, the varied fictional techniques of the novel provide stylistic equivalents for the multiple roles available to the heroine. Her inability to make any final commitment reflects her society's lack of clarity and testifies her willingness and capacity to survive, to endure the suffering of her many selves despite her open-eyed perception that her environment provides only temporary illusions of meaning. Interior insight confirms exterior disunity, the imagination promises nothing: except the heroine's faith, her only available faith, in her perceiving self.

"... That extraordinary gift, that woman's gift, for making a world of her own wherever she happened to be":

Virginia Woolf's phrase, from *Mrs. Dalloway*, like the other Woolf novels a book deeply imbued with awareness of how the world outside impinges on the woman's meaningful possibilities for creating her own. A man perceives this "woman's gift" in the novel, unaware of the cost and of the severe limitations on the exercise of the gift. Edith Wharton and Mary McCarthy by no means exhaust the ways women render in fiction the relation between the individual female self and the enveloping social context. Instead of reiterating, like Wharton, the conflict between society's demands and those of the imagination, or depicting like McCarthy, imaginations painfully subordinated to shifting social pressure, some writers have suggested that the solitary imagination can turn what society offers to its own purposes, making a world of its own less an alternative to than a transformation of the "real" world. Yet those who offer such optimistic assertions also, if only faintly, question them. *Mrs. Dalloway* shares some fundamental assumptions with two otherwise dissimilar novels: Mrs. Gaskell's *North and South*, from the late ninteenth century, and Eudora Welty's *The Optimist's Daughter*, published in 1972. The three books, from different eras and societies, all exemplify a qualified faith in the possibility of an individual female self-assertion which need not conflict with values asserted from without.

Society and culture, in their large and smaller meanings, reside in values and in objects. Both values and objects supply opportunities for the imagination. The most crucial transformation that women effect, as novels by authors in all obvious respects very different testify, converts forms to feeling. *Mrs. Dalloway*, for example, recording with exactitude the patterns of social existence in a confined sphere of upper middle class society, glorifies its heroine by demonstrating how through the conventions of that society she expresses and enlarges interpersonal emotion.

Looking in the mirror, Mrs. Dalloway almost automatically alters the face she sees. She purses her lips to give her countenance "point." "That was her self—pointed;

dartlike; definite. That was her self when some effort, some call on her to be her self, drew the parts together, she alone knew how different, how incompatible and composed so for the world only into one centre, one diamond, one woman who sat in her drawing-room and made a meeting-point, a radiancy no doubt in some dull lives, a refuge for the lonely to come to, perhaps." This summary (a trifle disturbing in the disjunctiveness of its metaphors) sketches both Mrs. Dalloway's achievement and its cost: artifice: making incompatibilities disappear, the living woman become all "one diamond." The "self" thus created, existing only in response to "some call on her," seems less than an independent entity. The cost contradicts the achievement: to create community, generate light, offer refuge—functions associated with the very "nature" of women. Peter, admiring Mrs. Dalloway in her drawing room, sees that she makes it "a sort of meeting-place; she had a genius for it." He sees also that this accomplishment depends on adherence to minute social forms: "that network of visiting, leaving cards, being kind to people; running about with bunches of flowers, little presents; ... all that interminable traffic that women of her sort keep up." Yet he concludes that "she did it genuinely, from a natural instinct."

Is it "natural" to be artificial in Clarissa Dalloway's fashion? Despite her consciousness of cost, she understands social effectiveness as her "gift," her special form of genius. Responding intensely to people, she wants to "bring them together." She does so; *must* do so because of her feeling. ("And she felt quite continuously a sense of their existence; and she felt what a waste; and she felt what a pity; and she felt it only they could be brought together; so she did it.") She understands that this effort, this achievement composes her "offering; to combine, to create; but to whom?" The mystery of motivation and of meaning lies at the heart of her accomplishment. The meaning of Mrs. Dalloway's actions derives from their effects on others— but also, and more complicatedly, from their effects on herself: the novel studies the ambiguity of those effects.

At any rate, Woolf suggests that the power of giving such parties as Mrs. Dalloway gives is more than trivial; to describe it as a "social" gift is inadequate, given the limited meaning of *social*, and imprecise in relation to the large meaning. Her gift, "social" because it concerns the union of people, depends on the transforming force of an underlying personal perception of union's significance, restoring consciousness of "society" as the meeting of individuals, grasped and valued in their individual natures. To bring people together is not merely Clarissa Dalloway's gift, it is the woman's gift—more novelists than Virginia Woolf suggest this point. And its ambiguities dereive not merely from its personal cost.

In *North and South*, the "gift" must display itself in the context of serious clashes of value: between representatives of the manufacturing north and the agricultural south; also, somewhat less consistently, between men and women. Both sexes, in the novel, belong to both sides, to the "north" and to the "south." Mr. Thornton's formidable mother embodies as completely as he the values and assumptions of the manufacturing world; Margaret's father, as gentle as she, commits himself even more fully to the desirability of humane studies. Thornton is unquestionably the main spokesman for trade, standing for the future rather than the past. "We do not look upon life as a time for enjoyment, but as a time for action and exertion. Our glory and our beauty arise out of our inward strength, which makes us victorious over material resistance, and over greater difficulties still." Margaret knows herself his antagonist. She perceives him immediately as "sagacious and strong, as becomes a great tradesman," but feels total contempt for tradesmen—defined as "all who have something tangible to sell." At first Margaret seems merely a snob, but we soon learn that she, like Mrs. Dalloway, exemplifies and proclaims the importance of feeling as moral guide, declaring the life of selling corrupt because it attaches emotion to tangible rather than intangible gain. Her own social class—her father is a clergyman, although religious doubts precipitate his premature retirement; her mother has social pretensions, even in reduced circumstances they can afford two servants—defines for her the realm of moral possibility. Her life involves scrupulous self-examination, reading and meditation, service to others. In the South, with which at first she identifies herself, she tended to the material, intellectual, and moral welfare of her father's parishioners. In contrast to Thornton, whose relationship with his devoted mother is spectacularly undemonstrative (in a mutual agony of worry the two of them stay up all night in adjoining rooms, to communicate with one another, decorously, only in the morning—Thornton remaining unaware till then of the very fact of his mother's wakefulness), Margaret devotes herself to the expression and eliciting of feeling with her mother. Encountering in the street a consumptive working-class girl, she assumes the responsibility of visiting and comforting her. She "brings people together" not in Mrs. Dalloway's fashion, not through parties nor from possession of a "gift," but out of a moral responsibility that becomes social. Through her influence Higgins, the working-class union organizer, and the manufacturer Thornton come together, to arrive at mutual respect and an understanding of their common interests.

Four social classes emerge distinctly in Mrs. Gaskell's novel: the workers (represented by Higgins, his sick daughter, and their neighbors), the manufacturers (Thornton and his mother), the educated nontrading middle class (Margaret, her family, her father's good friend Mr. Bell, an Oxford don), and the idle rich, precursors of Mrs. Dalloway's society. The rich, although they of course include men, comprise an essentially feminine world, Margaret's Aunt Shaw and her beautiful cousin Edith at its center. Margaret disapproves of their society (despite her affection for her relatives) but it parodies her own. Edith is all surface, Margaret all depth; yet Edith too concerns herself obsessively with her own psychic life, superficial though it may be, and enjoys and values an existence far from contaminating contact with trade. Her dinner parties exploit feeling. "Every talent, every feeling, every acquirement; nay, even every tendency towards virtue, was used up as materials for fireworks; the hidden, sacred fire, exhausted itself in sparkle and crackle." Margaret's repugnance at such grotesque distortions of feeling and community helps drive her toward a life of action. When she inherits money, she embarks on a vaguely evoked course of social enterprise, more highly organized, more a matter of public commitment, than anything she has done before. Although she has always had aspirations toward a "brave and noble life," they have belonged more to the realm of fantasy than to that of action. "She remembered promising to herself to live as brave and noble a life as any heroine she ever read or heard of in romance, a life sans peur and sans reproche; it had seemed to her then that she had only to will, and such a life would be accomplished." Trying for nobility, she has uttered a lie for the sake of her brother—a lie that poisons her relation with Thornton (for whom she has discovered her love) and her sense of self. Tempted to retreat from action into feeling, to dwell in the consciousness of her sin rather than risk further sin, she has learned other possibilities from her contact with the manufacturing world she scorned. When her would-be lover Henry Lennox praises Milton's inhabitants for "their energy, their power, their indomitable courage in struggling and fighting," he always wins Margaret's attention—though she feels obliged to remark that the manufacturers work for ignoble ends, dominated by the profit motive. Her own commitment to feeling and fellowship has been modified by contemplating both Edith's self-indulgent idleness and Thornton's purposeful activity.

In a novel that never mentions "class," *The Optimist's Daughter*, Eudora Welty dramatizes through the American South the same clash of values that preoccupied Mrs. Gaskell. Two women oppose one another: Fay McKelva, a lower-class Texan, superficially absorbed into aristocratic

society by her marriage to a Mississippi judge, and her
stepdaughter Laurel Hand, a southern aristocrat by birth,
although now living and working in Chicago. Fay stands
for fighting; Laurel, for feeling. The action of the novel
(Judge McKelva dies, mourned in curious ways by many
survivors) solidly endorses Laurel. Yet here as in the two
earlier novels some faint ambiguity of value survives.
What does commitment to feeling, that upper-class luxury,
really cost?

For Laurel, who "belongs" community exists without
effort. She returns from New Orleans with her father's
body (and her stepmother) to meet her six ex-bridesmaids,
eager to support her. Neighbors bring food, townsfolk
reminisce about her father, she finds herself effortlessly re-
absorbed into a society rich in forms that express feeling.
"We're grieving *with* you," one of the bridesmaids assures
her; the powerful atmosphere of *with-ness* controls possibility. Laurel doesn't know "how to stand and face the
person whose own life had not taught her how to feel."
Fay, a great believer in standing and facing, but ignorant
of how to feel, longs to find someone who speaks her language, feeling alone among aliens, yet unable to accept
full community even with her own family: a fighter, therefore solitary. "*I* haven't got one soul," she reiterates; while
Laurel, as the mayor of Mount Salus points out, is "surrounded by her oldest friends!" Fay's mother promptly but
wrongly challenges the stability of friends (as opposed to
"kin"); Fay and her kind are always wrong. The novel's
compassion for them rests on the perception that their social origin—the *meaning* of their social origin—has deprived
them of the capacity for outward-directed emotion.
Forced to concentrate on themselves, on what they can
get, they have been emotionally deprived. They possess
the active virtues that Mrs. Gaskell associates with the
manufacturers and Virginia Woolf with the socially-con-
scious Lady Bruton: energy, power, courage in conflict.
Mrs. Gaskell imagines that the active virtues of relatively
unexalted social classes may combine with the emotional

richness of the upper class, their union symbolized by the marriage of Margaret and Thornton, but also by Thornton's new concern (enlightened self-interest) for the welfare of his workers, Margaret's new respect for and partial commitment to a life of focused action (she offers her money for Thornton's manufacturing needs). Eudora Welty sees no such possibility, nor any real need for it. The virtues of Mississippi society, the commitment to feeling and to a set of forms designed for its expression, are self-sufficient. Fay, the fighter, will survive; but with more dignity, wisdom, scope—qualities embodied in the social stratum from which she emerges—so will Laurel.

"You don't know the way to fight," Fay challenges Laurel. "I had a whole family to teach *me*." But the lower class cannot be allowed such a simple advantage.

> *But of course, Laurel saw, it was Fay who did not know how to fight. For Fay was without any powers of passion or imagination in herself and had no way to see it or reach it in the other person. Other people, inside their lives, might as well be invisible to her. . . . She could no more fight a feeling person than she could love him.*

> "*I believe you underestimate everybody on earth,*" *Laurel said.*

The terminology of this passage reflects on all these novels. By "passion" and "imagination," capacities closely linked, or even identical, human beings make one another visible. Only through them can one "estimate" properly another person's quality. The gift of feeling—Mrs. Dalloway's gift, Margaret Hale's, Laurel's—may derive from right use of social convention. Mrs. Dalloway as "perfect hostess" is subject to male mockery for a role that seems merely a matter of social conformity but is in fact an act of transcendence. Convention becomes a means to the supremely human end of making passion and imagination socially operative. Thornton misperceives Margaret as arrogant, in his early encounters with her, instead of dignified. "She

340

felt no awkwardness; she had too much the habits of society for that." Her "straight, fearless, dignified presence," the result of social training, in fact expresses her sense of personal integrity and allows room for the straightforward expression of interpersonal feeling. In a crucial conversation between Margaret and Thornton, they differ over the relative value of the terms *man* and *gentleman*. Thornton prefers the former, for its "full simplicity" and its reference to the individual's "relation to himself,—to life—to time—to eternity." *Gentleman*, in contrast, he says, "only describes a person in his relation to others." Margaret loses the chance to "speak her slow conviction," but we are left in no doubt that she values the social term (she has precipitated the discussion by using it herself as the language of definition), presumably *because* it refers to the individual's relation to others. To be a gentleman, or a lady, creates the freedom in which one can relate.

Social conventions, then, Elizabeth Gaskell and Virginia Woolf and Eudora Welty suggest, train the capacities for passion and imagination by providing assured channels for their expression. More than that, social forms almost generate these crucial capacities. Fay's passion and imagination are not merely unchanneled; they seem simply not to exist, or to exist only in destructive forms. Fay lies—a perverse activity of the imagination: she claims that her family (who arrive en masse for the funeral) are all dead. She has temper tantrums: perverse passion. Laurel finally realizes that "very likely, making a scene was, for Fay, like home." The coherent society to which Laurel belongs creates order, meaning, energy. Some social energy goes to repression: Margaret, like other Victorian Heroines, frequently must try to master her tears; Laurel's friends must be polite even to boors; Mrs. Dalloway must go through social motions regardless of her feelings. But the best social forms depend on the assumption that to estimate people rightly is not merely a convenience for polite intercourse but a means of maintaining personal integrity; that convention, in other words, may supply the medium for growth. So Mrs. Dalloway has grown; Laurel, returning to her roots, reasserts the possibility of such development; Margaret triumphantly incorporates the vitality of the North without abandoning the *politesse* of the South, which also contains abiding value.

Margaret's ideal solution claims the possibility of having everything. Yet questions remain. The insistence with which Laurel asserts her total superiority to Fay, as fighter and feeler; the extent to which Mrs. Dalloway is criticized not only by observers but by external action taking place around her; the very fact that Margaret, finally, must have Thornton to give her life meaning (mother, father, and father-surrogate having successively died)—such elements in these books convey ambiguity.

In *Mrs. Dalloway* the subordinate character of mad Septimus Smith comments obliquely on social conformity as a way of life. Seeing visions, hearing voices, despairing because he believes he has perceived to the hidden heart of social reality, Septimus cannot conform. The expensive doctor he consults preaches and exemplifies "proportion": moderation—one child, one wife, salmon-catching vacations—opposed alike to excessive childbirth, excessive despair. The sister of "proportion" is "conversion," who "offers help, but desires power; smites out of her way roughly the dissentient, or dissatisfied"; who "loves blood better than brick, and feasts most subtly on the human will. For example, Lady Bradshaw [the doctor's wife]. Fifteen years ago she had gone under." She has "gone under" into a life "smooth and urbane," a life, like Mrs. Dalloway's, of dinner parties and polite social contact. An image of horror, she troubles Septimus' desperate wife, Virginia Woolf, the reader.

Mrs. Dalloway *uses* the forms that Lady Bradshaw merely submits to; but they are the same forms, the women inhabit the same society. So does Lady Bruton, another peripheral character, who has "perhaps lost her sense of proportion" in her devotion to the cause of emigration. For her the cause's vitality derives from its liberation

of the pent egotism, which a strong martial woman, well nourished, well descended, of direct impulses, downright feelings, and little introspective power . . . , feels rise within her, once youth is past, and must eject upon some object—it may be Emigration, it may be Emancipation; but whatever it be, this object round which the essence of her soul is daily searched becomes inevitably prismatic, lustrous, half looking-glass, half precious stone; now carefully hidden in case people should sneer at it; now proudly displayed. Emigration had become, in short, largely Lady Bruton.

The imagery recalls Mrs. Dalloway's earlier contemplation of herself as "diamond," perceived in a literal looking glass. Lady Bruton does not much resemble Mrs. Dalloway (although they feel a deep kinship with one another), but she enlarges and complicates the problem of evaluation. Mere conformity—the hidden meaning of Sir William Bradshaw's "proportion"—is deadening. We are glad when Septimus evades the doctor who would deprive him of his despair; but appalled that he seems able to escape the death of the spirit only by the death of the body. Lady Bradshaw is actively oppressive in her relations with others, the agent of her husband's lust for power, but her own curious vaguenesses and confusions betray something dead in her. Lady Bruton, all vitality, reveals something wrong too, in her conversion of a powerful egotism to total identification with an arbitrary cause. Lady Bradshaw and Septimus Smith become victims of Sir William's egotism, Lady Bruton, the victim of her own.

And Clarissa Dalloway? Her otism as powerful as Lady Bruton's, she has found a means of expressing it through the same social conformity that vitiates Lady Bradshaw. Although she uses social forms so fully as to transcend them, she cannot entirely escape the negative consequences of utter commitment to a system. Peter, remembering an episode in which Clarissa, still a girl, responds with social prudery to a neighbor's sexual indiscretion, remembers also understanding it as "the death of her soul." Sally Seton, Clarissa's unconventional girlhood friend, begs Peter to rescue Clarissa from such men as Richard Dalloway, who would " 'stifle her soul' . . . , make a mere hostess of her, encourage her worldliness." A hostess she becomes.

And yet for her own part, it was too much of an effort. She was not enjoying it. It was too much like being—just anybody, standing there; anybody could do it; yet this anybody she did a little admire, couldn't help feeling that she had, anyhow, made this happen, that it marked a stage, this post that she felt herself to have become, for oddly enough she had quite forgotten what she looked like, but felt herself a stake driven in at the top of her stairs. Every time she gave a party she had this feeling of being something not herself, and that every one was unreal in one way; much more real in another.

This union of reality and unreality, equally inherent in hostess and guest, reflects the anomalies of the social system as a means for utilizing emotion. To achieve the state of hostess in some ways liberates rather than stifles or deadens the soul. Yet Sally and Peter accurately perceive the danger involved. To become a post, a stake, something not oneself, an "anybody," is to deny the self. Clarissa's most triumphant self-assertion—the assertion of her "gift"—comes through such denial. But her affinities with Lady Bradshaw and Lady Bruton, the extent to which Septimus Smith's more enveloping denial comments on her—these elements in the novel challenge any ready assumption that Mrs. Dalloway's achievement means *only* triumph. It is a woman's triumph: ambiguous.

So, too, with Laurel and Margaret, although in *The Optimist's Daughter*, and *North and South* one can be less sure of the *author's* perception of ambiguity. Laurel, unquestionably the moral and emotional superior of Fay, rightly asserts that her wisdom of imagination and feeling gives her an advantage even in Fay's chosen area of combat. Yet her life, widowed, feeding on memories, implies withdrawal and rejection as well as rich commitment to tradition; her vitality, though real has something attenuated about it. The phalanx of Mount Salus society, to which Laurel effortlessly belongs, drives Fay away; but, like Faulkner's Snopese, she will return; from her point of view, she will win. Other points of view are grander, more satisfying; the reader identifies with Laurel's. But we have been reminded of a perspective in which the sustenance of feeling by forms is simply irrelevant to concerns that matter. Similarly, in *North and South*, the severe assurance with which Mrs. Thornton rejects the value of studying the classics leaves reverberations in the air. We know she's wrong, yet her very existence challenges what Margaret stands for. Perhaps only from a twentieth-century viewpoint does Margaret's agonizing over her innocent lie seem wire-drawn and potentially sterile—certainly Victorian novels abound in such crises of conscience, assumed to be matters of moment. But Mrs. Gaskell, providing images of more outward-turning lives, thus questions her heroine's greatest achievement, making the reader conscious that Margaret's reliance on propriety as the ultimate defense for the life of feeling, though admirable, implies the possibility of diminishing vitality, diminishing involvement with vast external realities. Margaret's largest imagination of social action leads her to visit the poor; her lover envisions changing the fundamental relation between classes. His vision implies the possibility of losing touch with real people; hers risks contentment with narrowed purpose. Thornton needs Margaret to remind him of certain realities; she needs him to rescue her from her own version of an attenuation comparable to Clarissa Dalloway's and Laurel Hand's.

Artifacts help to convey complexities of value in all

three of these novels. Laurel finds in objects assurances of the continuities by which she lives. Her father's desk may be marred by drippings of Fay's nail polish, but nail polish can be scraped away. Her mother's desk survives, manufactured from "the cherry trees on the McKelva place a long time ago," an emblem of continuance; and she still has her mother's letters, snapshots, two-inch-long boat of river stone, left from her courtship days. Most important of all, her mother's breadboard, made by Laurel's long-dead husband, scarred and grimed by Fay's nutcracking and carelessness, but still enduring. "She supported it, above her head, but for a moment it seemed to be what supported her, a raft in the waters, to keep her from slipping down deep, where the others had gone before her."

Objects of a different sort define and support Fay: clothes and jewelry, mostly; possessions important to her merely as things owned; particularly, the coffin in which her husband is buried. "I was proud of you today," her mother tells her. "And proud for you. That coffin made me wish I could have taken it right away from him and given it to Roscoe." "Thank you," Fay replies. "It was no bargain, and I think that showed." Miss Adele, one of Laurel's bridesmaids, understands that Fay's preoccupation with "the most expensive casket, the most choice cemetery plot"—even though that most choice plot seems in some respects the least desirable—expresses her limited kind of feeling: "By her lights!" Objects *do* express feelings, and reveal values. Fay's "objects" are vulgar, Laurel's speak of tradition, but both alike epitomize cultural as well as personal convictions.

Laurel's success, finally, is to relinquish ties to objects, leaving the breadboard behind. "The past isn't a thing to me," Fay asserts. "I belong to the future, didn't you know that?" The past is everything to Laurel, who knows that the future rests on it; but she comes to understand that memory must be independent of possession. "Memory lived not in initial possession but in the freed hands, pardoned and freed, and in the heart that can empty but fill again, in the patterns restored by dreams." Memory, the ultimate support, affirms feeling's value and persistence, recalls the continuities of social and cultural tradition and of individual experience, preserves the past as vital principle but frees the possessor from its bondage. The evocative rhetoric of freedom, heart, dreams, insists that memory solves all problems. Yet that rhetoric's total reference to an inner world may leave the reader with some question about exactly what range of problems such a solution confronts. If society encourages women finally to retreat within, guarding precious private heritages, it thus fosters a straitened maturity, involving the giving up of external claims. The optimist's daughter seems from this point of view an emblem of despair. Similar despair, that a woman may claim at last only her privacy, underlies the positive-sounding assertions of *Mrs. Dalloway* and *North and South*.

In *North and South*, with houses the most important artifacts, architecture and decor suggest the nature of the dwelling's inhabitants. No available house in the manufacturing town meets the demands of the Hales' "taste." Even gentle Mr. Hale remarks with dismay "the overloading such a house with colour and such heavy cornices!" this with reference to the place they actually rent. Margaret assures him that he can hide the gaudy paper with bookcases, symbolizing the Hales' commitment to the life of large culture. But her apparent confidence conceals misgiving and bafflement: "She had never come fairly in contact with the taste that loves ornament, however bad, more than the plainness and simplicity which are of themselves the framework of elegance."

The summary's tone suggests Mrs. Gaskell's full endorsement of her heroine's assessments, and much of the narrative supports this endorsement by revealing the link between taste, that largely cultural and social phenomenon, and personal feeling. The Thorntons, who have suppressed feeling, express that suppression in their house.

*There was no one in the drawing-room. It seemed as
though no one had been in it since the day when the furniture was bagged up with as much care as if the house
was to be overwhelmed with lava, and discovered a thousand years hence. The walls were pink and gold; the pattern on the carpet represented bunches of flowers on a
light ground, but it was carefully covered up in the centre
by a linen drugget, glazed and colourless. The window-
curtains were lace; each chair and sofa had its own
particular veil of netting, or knitting. Great alabaster
groups occupied every flat surface, safe from dust under
glass shades.*

This only begins the long description of a room summed
up as creating an "effect of icy, snowy discomfort." Mrs.
Gaskell writes of such details with a peculiar intensity of
feeling which declares her conviction that objects *matter*,
both revealing and controlling the lives played out in their
context. When the Thorntons entertain, they remove all
the veils: "the apartment blazed forth in yellow silk
damask and a brilliantly-flowered carpet." But brilliance
means the same as concealment. "Every corner seemed
filled up with ornament, until it became a weariness to the
eye." The Thornton dinner, in its "sumptuousness,"
"pride," "magnificence," reveals the assumption that the
"exchange of superb meals" rather than the interchange of
feeling defines social intercourse. Margaret, who finds it all
"oppressive," once more clearly speaks for her creator.

After her parents' death, Margaret returns to the "luxurious house" of her aunt and cousin. Here the prevailing
taste, self-indulgent rather than vulgar, substitutes objects
for intangible foci of meaning. Edith, recovering from
childbirth, feels "impatient to get well, in order to fill Margaret's bed-room with all the soft comforts, and pretty
knick-knacks, with which her own abounded." Soft comforts and pretty knick-knacks epitomize polite London life;
Margaret, without criticizing the objects themselves, suf-

348

fers from the attribution of exaggerated importance to them: still entirely "right" in her judgment.

Yet what a house should properly look like cannot entirely be determined by reference to Margaret's taste. When her guardian takes her for a visit to her father's old parsonage at Helstone, she doesn't like what she sees, though not only for reasons of taste: she suffers from the change in actuality of artifacts preserved intact in her memory. (The challenge of actuality to memory is not faced by Laurel—or, in *The Optimist's Daughter*, by Eudora Welty.) But taste figures in her judgment:

The garden, the grass-plot, formerly so daintily trim that even a stray rose-leaf seemed like a fleck on its exquisite arrangement and propriety, was strewed with children's things; a bag of marbles here, a hoop there; a straw-hat forced down upon a rose-tree as on a peg, to the destruction of a long beautiful tender branche laden with flowers, which in former days would have been trained up tenderly, as if beloved.

The new owner explains that they are converting Margaret's room to a nursery and "throwing out a window to the road" in what was once Mr. Hale's study, a spot formerly marked by its "green gloom and delicious quiet." Mr. Bell, Margaret's guardian, who shares her aesthetic values, mocks Mrs. Hepworth by the ironic "admiration he thought fit to express for everything that especially grated on his taste." Although Margaret's taste is equally exacerbated, her concern with the feelings of others causes her to rebuke Bell for his rudeness. He justifies himself: "If she had not shown you every change with such evident exultation in their superior sense, in perceiving what an improvement this and that would be, I could have behaved well." The manifest logic of this argument silences Margaret.

Mrs. Gaskell's position no longer seems perfectly clear. But it *is* clear that Margaret and her guardian, in their concern for good taste, prove singularly insensitive to another realm of value. The continuing life of children, of a family, appears to them to make no claim compared with that of the rose branch which should be "trained up tenderly." The crucial issue, once more, concerns vitality. Is the tending of rose branches, the life of seclusion in green gloom and delicious quiet, altogether preferable to the tumult and comparative vulgarity of family life? Can taste, after all, adequately determine value? Surely one feels through this episode the reality of the need which Thornton, in the prospective marriage, will supply. Without him, Margaret risks sterility, both literal and metaphoric. Her real commitment to feeling, often intensified by her commitment to social forms, can also, paradoxically, be vitiated by her adherence to forms.

Peter Walsh, in *Mrs. Dalloway*, reflects on what he sees: "A splendid achievement in its own way, after all, London; the season; civilisation." The precise degree and focus of irony in that final word are difficult to assess. What Peter Walsh sees as "civilisation" depends largely on clothes—probably this novel's most significant artifacts. Men and women alike declare their social status by what they wear; and Virginia Woolf's frequent references to what they wear epitomize her delicate perception of the value and the ambiguities of taste.

The upper-class ladies and gentlemen of the book really do represent, in one sense, a civilization. A "girl, silk-stockinged, feathered, evanescent"; "laughing girls in their transparent muslins"; shop windows full of "lovely old sea-green brooches in eighteenth-century settings"; young people in "pink stockings; pretty shoes"; "a high stepping old dame, in buckled shoes, with three purple ostrich feathers in her hair"; a room full of "lovely clothes" (so Ellie Henderson sees Mrs. Dalloway's party), Clarissa wearing "ear-rings, and a silver-green mermaid's dress"; Lady Bruton as "a spectral grenadier, draped in black"; Elizabeth Dalloway, unrecognizable to her father because "she looked so lovely in her pink frock": these references (each from a different part of the novel) sum up a society. At the opposite extreme cowers Miss Kilman, who "dressed in a green mackintosh coat. Year in year out she wore that coat; she perspired." Miss Kilman herself knows clothing important. "She could not help being ugly; she could not afford to buy pretty clothes." She claims that people don't ask her to parties because she's "plain"; bad dressing accompanies plainness, and both put one outside the social pale. Elizabeth, whom Miss Kilman adores, stands at a bus stop "in her very well-cut clothes," and people start comparing her "to poplar trees, early dawn, hyacinths, fawns, running water, and garden lilies." The conjunction of the artificial and the natural points ironically to the fact that well-cut clothes may engineer deception, but unironically to their real creation, or revelation, of beauty: an unambiguous value.

Yet how precarious a "civilization" predicates itself on appearances! Clarissa Dalloway, having just heard of Septimus Smith's death, goes alone into a little room. "There was nobody. The party's splendour fell to the floor, so strange was it to come in alone in her finery." Finery belongs to society, other people, by dress a woman expresses herself to others. "Death," Mrs. Dalloway feels, "was an attempt to communicate." The seriousness of the attempt—however unsuccessful—mocks the superficiality of efforts to communicate through clothing, and suggests how fatally the inhabitants of this society are cut off from one another. "Absorbing, mysterious, of infinite richness, this life," Peter Walsh reflects. Clothing emblemizes the richness, the mystery, of life; but also the surface quality of life as experienced in polite society. Miss Kilman neither morally nor aesthetically equals Mrs. Dalloway. Yet it is dangerous to assume—as Laurel Hand and Margaret Hale might also—that her aesthetic inferiority necessitates moral inadequacy.

If all three of these novels at least faintly question the notion that the values of a small society can sustain the moral life of individuals within it, they none the less share a view of "society" and "culture" more optimistic than that implied by George Eliot, Edith Wharton, or Mary McCarthy. The values of society provide a screen behind which women can conduct their inner lives; they may, at best, actually supply a means for expressing the dimensions of inner reality. And inner reality is a woman's most valuable possession—whether, like Dorothea Brooke's, it constantly challenges the assumptions of the world outside or, like Clarissa Dalloway's, it uses such assumptions for its own purposes.

Eight

FREE WOMEN

---

*Having a vocation is always something of a
miracle, like falling in love. . . . I can understand why Luther said that a man is justified
by his vocation, for it is already a proof of
God's favor.*

—PAUL GOODMAN

A man is justified by his vocation. But a woman?

Beatrice Webb was next to the last of ten children of the prosperous Victorian Potter family. She had eight sisters and a single brother, who died at the age of three. Her mother, who according to Beatrice "disliked women," absorbed herself totally in her single son, born when Beatrice was four years old. After his death, she virtually ignored her daughters. She herself "had started life heavily handicapped by the unqualified indulgence and adoration of a wealthy widowed father, who insisted on her brothers' regarding her as a paragon of virtue, beauty and learning. . . . Fortunately for her happiness, and I think also for her character, she found the same unqualified adoration in marriage. . . . In all other aspects her life had been one long series of disappointments." The mother had imagined for herself a life of intellectual accomplishment which she never achieved; after her son's death she retreated to her room, where she entertained herself by learning languages in devious ways—studying German, for example, from a grammar written in Bulgarian.

Beatrice's first memory was of being flung naked into the hallway, her clothes thrown after her, by her infant brother's nurse. Her mother had little interest in her. "Beatrice is the only one of my children who is below the average in intelligence," she wrote in her diary. The child grew up among servants. As she recalled, no one paid any special attention to her education; she taught herself, reading in a well-stocked library. Often ill, bored, and depressed, early in her life she secreted a vial of chloroform with a vague intention of suicide. Intensely self-critical, she wrote harshly in a diary at the age of ten about her reprehensible habit of "building castles in the air." In such fantasies, she confesses, she plays "always the charming heroine without a fault." Her mother intervened only to criticize; her stern authority intensified the child's sense of hopeless inadequacy.

For a girl born into a wealthy English family in 1858, the demands of society were clear. Beatrice Webb formulates them lucidly:

Marriage to a man of their own or a higher social grade was the only recognized vocation for women not compelled to earn their own livelihood. It was this society life which absorbed early half the time and more than half the vital energy of the daughters of the upper and upper middle class; it fixed their standards of personal expenditure; it formed their manners and, either by attraction or repulsion, it determined their social ideals.

Her own course was that of "repulsion." Before she reached adolescence, she had decided not to follow the "recognized vocation." Her solitary childhood ("I was neither ill-treated nor oppressed: I was merely ignored") encouraged her sense of difference from other girls; the impossibility of pleasing her mother must have made her feel she could not be successful in a woman's traditional roles. But more positive influences also controlled her development. One was the frequent presence in the household of the philosopher Herbert Spencer, a close friend of both her parents. "To the children of the household the philosopher always appeared in the guise of a liberator." He opposed the restrictions of governesses, encouraged the development of individual talents, took an interest in Beatrice's "lonely studies," allowed her to help him in his work. Passionately desiring his approbation, she learned from him "the relevance of facts; a gift said to be rare in a woman." A more complicated element in her life was her father, whom she describes as "notwithstanding frequent absence, ... the central figure of the family life—the light and warmth of the home." The terminology suggests the expected place of a woman, but to a considerable extent the positions of men and women were reversed the Potter household. Although Beatrice insists that her father "controlled the family destinies," she also describes him as self-sacrificing, emotional, devoted to others. In a diary entry written when she was twenty-five she summarizes, "With him the instinctive feelings are paramount. He would sacrifice all, to some extent even his self-respect, if he thought the happiness of some loved one were at stake." It is not a description of orthodox masculinity. Moreover, he "worshipped his wife, he admired and loved his daughters; he was the only man I ever knew who genuinely believed that women were superior to men." At a luncheon of suffragists around 1889, Beatrice herself declared, "I have never met a man, however inferior, whom I do not consider to be my superior!" She was being deliberately provocative (she had not been given a cigarette when she wanted one), but in fact for some time she felt herself a serious antifeminist. Her father's effect had not been unambiguous.

With this Miss Julie-esque background, Beatrice seems to have taken Herbert Spencer as her role model. (She remained his devoted friend until his death, for more than thirty years.) At any rate, her process of sublimation involved a conscious effort to extirpate some "feminine" aspects of her nature. From early adolescence, her self-criticism in her diary concentrate on her besetting sin of "vanity." Here is a poignant entry written when she was fourteen:

But one thing I have learnt is, that I am exceedingly vain, to say the truth I am very digusted with myself; whenever I am in the company of any gentleman, I cannot help

*wishing and doing all I possibly can to attract his atten-
tion and admiration; the whole time I am thinking how I
look, which attitude becomes me, and contriving everything to make myself more liked and admired than my sisters. The question is, how can I conquer it, for it forwards
every bad passion and suppresses every good one in my
heart; the only thing I can think of, is to avoid gentlemen's society altogether.*

Three years later, at seventeen:

*I must work harder, try and become more truthful both in
my acts and in my conversation, less vain and admiration-
seeking, and never let my thoughts rest with complacency
on any little distinction I may have of body or mind.*

Her struggle to achieve intellectual distinction for its
own sake caused her agonies of doubt: Was she really
pure of heart? How could she eliminate the pernicious
desire to be "liked and admired"? Deep conviction told her
that no one *would* like and admire her for the qualities
she so desperately cultivated in herself. Incorporating en-
tries from her youthful diary in the first volume of her autobiography, published when she was in her sixties, she
comments retrospectively, "However useful intellectual
curiosity and concentrated purpose may be to the scientific
worker, they are not attractive gifts in a child or in a mar-
riageable young woman." Despite her own happy marriage, she never lost her conviction that the attractive and
the intellectually useful oppose one another in a woman.
Making the choice of intellect, she quite consciously abandoned hope of traditional feminine fulfillment.

The difficulties Wellesley students perceive so vividly in
the possible feminine choice of nonconformity, particularly
nonconformity through commitment to the mind, are precisely those that Beatrice Webb battled. She made her
choice early. The most youthful excerpts from her diary,
written when she was nine or ten, display a measured

prose full of concealments. Morality defends against emotion from the beginning. The pattern set by the young child, scolding herself for her failings, discoursing of the dangers of novels as reading for the immature, constructing sentences that declare in form as well as content her balance and control—the same pattern dominates the old woman she became. Writing a preface to the first volume of her autobiography, Mrs. Webb suggests that all life stories reveal a struggle between "an Ego that affirms— and an Ego that denies." But when she explains these suggestive terms in relation to herself, she abstracts and generalizes the issues beyond all recognition: the struggle is "really," she maintains, between science and religious faith, the central concern of her autobiography. In fact her original formulation is much more precise: the real drama of her life centers on the conflict between self-abnegation through total absorption in noble work and self-affirmation of the sort that makes love possible.

The remarkable childhood journals of the French psychoanalyst and writer Marie Bonaparte, dissimilar as they are to Mrs. Webb's writing, may illuminate the drama of Beatrice Webb's life. Writing in English between the ages of seven and ten, the Princess Bonaparte filled her copybooks with bizarre and often incomprehensible stories. Late in her life she published them, with a painstaking commentary based on her own psychoanalysis with Freud. Freud, she explains, deduced many of the facts these prepubescent journals conceal before he saw the books themselves. When she read them to him, he found in them confirmation of the discoveries of her analysis.

Marie Bonaparte's adult commentary on her childhood self concentrates on the sexual issues raised by the collection of fantasies. Her early history, like Beatrice Webb's, was unusual. Her father, a nephew of the Emperor Napoleon, married a young heiress, daughter of the man who founded (and made a fortune from) the casino at Monte Carlo. His bride, tubercular, died a month after giving birth to Marie, less than two years after her marriage.

Newspapers created a minor scandel from this event, suggesting that the heiress had been poisoned by her husband and his tyrannical mother, who lived with the young couple. That mother, Marie's grandmother, continued to preside over the household as the child grew up. In retrospect the author repeatedly describes her as "masculine" or "virile." A series of nurses and a governess supervised Marie's development; her father was a remote, adored intellectual—frequently absent on mountain-climbing trips to Switzerland—with whom the child was allowed to have lunch and dinner once a week. Despite the loving attention of nurses and governess, restrictions emanating from the grandmother governed the girl's life: she could not roll hoops, play in tall grass, swim, run fast, go out in cold weather; she had to drink red wine, which she loathed, endure frequent enemas, and take large doses of a morphine-based medicine at the first sign of illness. Her childhood, too, was in many ways solitary, and crucially influenced by the fact that for many months of her infancy, her nurse engaged in repeated sexual activity with the head coachman in the baby's room. Marie saw and heard what was happening; although she repressed her guilty knowledge, it remained.

Beatrice Webb, on the other hand, offers no specific sexual information about herself. We can only guess what she saw or knew. At any rate, the problem she faced, of dealing with the implications of a mother essentially absent, bears some relation to Marie Bonaparte's; and so does her solution. For the French child, the dilemma presented itself in more clearly sexual terms (although of course the stories she tells disguise their sexual meaning). She feared her womanhood. To be a woman was to be penetrated by the male, impregnated, killed. One might avoid such a fate by identifying entirely with the masculine. In her case, "the masculine" was her intellectual father. Her journals display a persistent identification of ink with seminal fluid, declaring ink the masculine instrument, writing the way to salvation. The keeping of a journal becomes life's most crucial activity, even for the small child.

A single example may suffice to suggest the kind of importance journal writing had for Marie Bonaparte, and the kind of emotion it involved.

my sad moments

1. my most sad moment is: it is that when the peapel scold me and when I muss work after and study my lesson: in this sad moment I would go to loose myself in the streat.

· · · · · ·

4 when I am riting in this book and that they will not not. I would go and lose my self

5 when they—tell my to wort at an aur and that at the aur I muss let this book. I would go and loose my self

(The anomalies of spelling and syntax, of course, derive from the fact that English was for the seven-year-old Marie a second—hence a "secret"—language.) The author in her commentary points out that imposed lessons, in this case suggested to be the consequence of a scolding, did not appeal to her. She also explains that the desire to "go to loose" herself in the street, equivalent to a suicide wish for the sheltered child, represented her strongest expression of despair and protest. Such despair is reserved for the loss of love (when "the peapel" scold her) and for interference with her activity of writing in her notebooks. "In writing them I found unspeakable relief, a supreme catharsis. I fled into an imaginary world, far from this world with its torments, its conflicts and its disappointments. . . . This reflex of taking refuge in writing whenever I have been hurt by life has remained with me. Disappointment or grief, so far from preventing me from working, always drives me irresistibly to seek solace in literary or scientific creation." The only consolation for lack of love, the child believes—as does the adult—is "free intellectual work"; deprived of that, she feels suicidal.

Free intellectual work also consoles Beatrice Webb, and the first adjective is particularly significant. The intellectual can be a sphere of freedom. The woman who finds her vocation in it may seem to escape the social limitations of femininity. Functioning as mind rather than body, she avoids the problems that often determine female destiny. She solves the conflict of thought and feeling which my students found so central a concern by associating her strongest feeling with thought: a unification of sensibility in which intellect precedes and dominates emotion. One may think of Gertrude Stein, author, as Phyllis Greenacre points out, of four different autobiographies, none of which admit in their titles their actual subject of discussion. For her the choice between life of the body and of the mind seems to have been definitive, and to have brought her in abundance that independence which women often claim to want. "If the anxiety of the individual, of the biological ego, in the face of its own sexuality, which threatens its narcissim, is universal," Marie Bonaparte observes, "woman's anxiety, founded on the fear, inherent in all protoplasm, of being broken into seems deeper and still more intense." Gertrude Stein, one may surmise, dealt with that anxiety, supported her narcissim, by declaring her vocation or métier the most important element of her life. As she puts it through the persona of Alice B. Toklas, speaking of Miss Stein, "She is passionately addicted to what the french call métier and she contends that one can only have one métier as one can only have one language. Her métier is writing and her language is english."

The notion of an exclusive métier obviously precludes the possibility of combining marriage, that orthodox feminine vocation, with other spheres of activity. And Gertrude Stein's concept of what she wishes to achieve in her writing attempts to eliminate emotion as a component of métier. Unlike Marie Bonaparte, who understands her writing as a way of channeling and finally transcending emotion; unlike Beatrice Webb, who writes most passionately about her intellectual preoccupations, Gertrude Stein tries not to write passionately at all, her passion reserved for the *idea* of métier.

She knows that beauty, music, decoration, the result of emotion should never be the cause, even events should not be the cause of emotion nor should they be the material of poetry and prose. Nor should emotion itself be the cause of poetry or prose. They should consist of an exact reproduction of either an outer or an inner reality.

Robinson Crusoe, with its accumulation of precise detail, is the model for *The Autobiography of Alice B. Toklas* and for this ideal of nonemotional exactitude. By such exactitude one controls experience, recording it with precision, fixing it forever. Writing as métier is thus more than usual a declaration of independence. "It was like life was happening to her, she wasn't living it," a student remarked of Anna in *The Golden Notebook.* Gertrude Stein represents an opposite extreme. She refuses to allow anything merely to happen to her; instead she dominates the world by reproducing it, and by denying the primacy of emotion. Her life, full of people, lacks real attachments; she preserves her freedom by severing herself from most aspects of "normal" feminine experience. Alice B. Toklas must associate with the artists' wives because Gertrude Stein will not. Or cannot, having denied in herself whatever is special to women.

Beatrice Webb assumed from the start her primary obligation to be good. Her problem—one version of her problem—was how to be good without just settling back in herself. For many years she seems to have assumed that, having chosen for her "goodness" an arena larger than that of most women, she must therefore be doomed to unhappiness. "You really mustn't grow up into a blue-stocking," Marie Bonaparte's nurse told her. "Men don't like it, darling! . . . If a woman wants to keep a man she must be coquettish, very coquettish, and take an interest in her appearance, and she must be good at housekeeping and keep her eye on the servants and the cooking, in short, first, last, and all the time, she must look after her home!" Hers is the voice of late-nineteenth-century society (the copybooks were filled in the early 1890's). In Beatrice Webb's experience, the injunction that a woman "must look after her home" did not imply merely keeping a man: it was the message of morality. Her mother died; her seven married sisters united in declaring it her responsibility, as the eldest unmarried daughter, to devote herself to her father and her home. Marriage would have been the only legitimate mode of freeing herself from the burden. Beatrice, with "aspirations and plans for self-culture and self-expression," had to choose between self-affirmation and self-denial. Believing herself to have made the positive choice by concentrating on her determination to do ultimate good in the world, she then discovered the intolerable difficulty of implementing her decision. The only acceptable mode of higher education for a woman was through social intercourse. Beatrice, no Gertrude Stein, had not cut herself off from the usual life of her generation. For two years she served as her father's hostess, relegating her intellectual life (her attempt at systematic reading) to the hours between five and eight in the morning. A kind of schizophrenia resulted: "Now my life is divided sharply into the thoughtful part and the active part, completely unconnected one with the other," she writes in an 1883 diary. As for the "thoughtful part": "In my heart of hearts I'm ashamed of it, and yet it *is* actually the dominant internal power." Because she never talks of what really concerns her, she suffers from predictable neurotic symptoms: loss of energy, a sense of unreality. By the next year, she despairs:

The whole of my life from the age of nine, when I wrote a priggish little note on the right books for a child to read, has been one continuous struggle to learn and to think, sacrificing all to this, even physical comfort.... Why should a mortal be born with so much aspiration, so much courage and patience in the pursuit of an ideal, and with such a beggarly allowance of power wherewith to do it? And even now, now that I have fully realized my powerlessness to achieve, have perhaps ceased to value any achievement which I in my dearest dreams thought open to me, even now, my only peaceful and satisfactory life lies in continuous enquiry.

At approximately this point in her autobiography, when her dilemma seems tragically hopeless—twenty-six years old, still the slave of her family—she abandons the personal almost entirely and for close to a hundred pages discourses on the state of philanthropy and social investigation in late-nineteenth-century England. Such lengthy digressions are by no means uncommon in her writing. More and more, her autobiography begins to record her work rather than her life; or her work and her life become identical. The very title of the first volume, *My Apprenticeship*, emphasizes the degree to which she interprets all her experience, and assumes its interest for others, only in relation to her demonstrable accomplishment. The negative emotion she allows herself to express almost always relates to her desire to do useful work: its most common avatars are depression about the apparent impossibility of freeing herself for meaningful work, and over her sense of moral (and sometimes intellectual) inadequacy for what she wants to do.

The writing of a diary releases feeling. Despite the characteristic formality of their prose, the Webb diaries often reveal a great deal. Looking back over her life, Beatrice Webb quotes extensively (though obviously very selectively) from her early journals, which contain the most vivid prose in her account of herself. By comparison, the judgments and summaries she offers from the vantage point of maturity are judicious to the point of deadness; and her apparently growing conviction of the irrelevance of the personal makes her version of herself increasingly generalized. She seems to think of herself, finally, as an institution rather than a person. But at the age of twenty-six, she wonders about herself and her needs quite directly:

It would be curious to discover who it is, to whom one writes in a diary? Possibly to some mysterious personification of one's own identity, to the Unknown, which lies below the constant change in matter and ideas, constituting the individual at any given moment. This unknown was once my only friend; the being to whom I went for advice and consolation in all the small troubles of a child's life. Well do I remember, as a small thing, sitting under the damp bushes, and brooding over the want of love around me (possibly I could not discern it), and turning in upon myself, and saying, "Thou and I will live alone and if life be unbearable we will die."

Her sense of the mystery of personality contrasts sharply with Marie Bonaparte's penetration into her own nature and with Gertrude Stein's arrogant disregard of mystery, but her awareness of the drama of division parallels theirs. Once more she seems to see the split in her personality as between the public and the private self. She, like Marie Bonaparte, suffers from lack of love (although her self-critical orientation makes her speculate at least perfunctorily that the problem may have been her own failure of perception), she too reacts by withdrawal and suicidal fantasy. But she values the self she does not really know, and her determination to preserve the integrity of that inner being saves her from the Victorian trap of selflessness.

In other moods, she formulated the split as one between thought and feeling. "I saw myself as one suffering from a divided personality; the normal woman seeking personal happiness in love given and taken within the framework of a successful marriage; whilst the other self claimed, in season and out of season, the right to the free activity of 'a

clear and analytic mind.' . . . It would not have been prac-
ticable to unite the life of love and the life of reason." In
action, she chose the life of reason, abandoning the dreadful burden of being a society hostess to pursue sociological
investigations in the East End of London. She could
bolster her self-esteem by reminding herself that she was
doing what women had never done, but the attempt to
isolate the life of reason from that of love produced increasing despair. At the age of twenty-eight she describes
repetition of the breaking waves of feeling." She speaks of
herself as "living without hope! . . . No future but a vain
repetition of the breaking waves of feeling." She speakes of
her "hopeless independence of thought that makes my
mind so distasteful to many people; and rightly so, for a
woman should be more or less dependent and receptive.
However, I must . . . be true to myself." And then, thirty-
four years old, she met Sidney Webb, her life was transformed—and the second volume of her autobiography
could be called *Our Partnership*.

The famous partnership was both intellectual and emotional: but intellectual first. Beatrice reports some comic
scenes of courtship: "We talked economics, politics, the
possibility of inspiring socialism with faith leading to
works. He read me poetry, as we lay in the forest, Keats
and Rosetti, and we parted." (Early she confessed, recalling Darwin, that "the whole realm of poetry was closed to
me: I was poetry blind, as some persons are color blind.")
She accepted Sidney as "the predominant partner in the
firm of Webb" because she admired his grasp of socialism,
because he enlarged her mind, because he accepted her as
a co-worker. If physical passion aroused them, she never
mentions it, although she makes it clear that they had sexual relations before their marriage. But in a curious passage of *Our Partnership* she considers sexual union as a
possible mode of education:

*Friendship between particular men and women has an
enormous educational value to both (especially to the*

*woman). Such a friendship is practically impossible (or, at
any rate, impossible between persons who are attractive to
each other—and therefore, most remunerative as friends)
without physical intimacy; you do not, as a matter of fact,
get to know any man thoroughly except as his beloved
and his lover—if you could have been the beloved of the
dozen ablest men you have known it would have greatly
extended your knowledge of human nature and human affairs. . . . But there remains the question whether, with all
the perturbation caused by such intimacies, you would
have any brain left to think with? I know that I should
not—and I fancy that other women would be even worse
off in that particular. Moreover, it would mean a great increase in sexual emotion for its own sake, and not for the
sake of bearing children. And that way madness lies.*

Beatrice Webb was forty-eight years old when she
wrote this extraordinary paragraph. It sums up many of
the complexities of her personality and suggests the important implications of her paradigmatic case history. The
crucial terms of her life are "love" and "work," particular-
ized versions of "emotion" and "reason." Only through her
work does love become possible: she can accept her female nature only after she has developed the intellectual
capacities that her society saw as opposed to it. In her
earlier discussions of her own nature, those words "free"
and "independent" occur with striking frequency in relation to intellectual activity. Her "independence of
thought," her doom, also defines her personality. She must
have scope for "free activity" of her mind. Her work *is* her
freedom, as she understands it. And it gives her the
freedom to love. Work establishes the context for her
worshipful devotion to her husband; their long and happy
life together was one of shared work. Work even creates
the possibility for sexual fantasy: she can speculate
about promiscuity for its "enormous educational value."
"Knowledge of human nature and human affairs" is what
she most needs for her vocation as social investigator; the

"you" she apostrophizes is the one she has earlier identified as the object of her writing in her diary—her secret self.

But the work of the mind which creates her vocation and her freedom creates also her limitation. She cannot allow herself sexual indulgence, even with "the dozen ablest men" she has known, because it might weaken her brain. And because it is morally unthinkable, involving as it does "a great increase in sexual emotion for its own sake." Morality and work are closely linked; morality and passion, opposed. So the love derived from or associated with work is permissible, but emotion cannot be self-justifying. Love is conditional on its justification, in this scheme of things; and work, the source of the woman's freedom, is finally her tyrant.

The issue of freedom came up often in my class. As we moved from one depressing vision of feminine experience to another, freedom started to seem the central issue. The restrictions on women made their lives intolerable. If we could just find someone who declared herself independent, who explored the full possibilities of feminine freedom . . .

Kate Brown, the middle-aged heroine of Doris Lessing's *The Summer Before the Dark*, spends a good deal of time thinking about hair. Her own, at the novel's opening, is tinted auburn and gently waved about her face in approved suburban style. When she transforms herself from housewife to executive her hair becomes, at the hands of an expensive hairdresser, dark red, the color of her youth, cut to swing heavily as she moves, releasing an almost frightening influx of physical self-love. As Kate travels through Spain with her ailing young American lover, a band of gray gradually appears at her parting. Back in London, the gray has spread, the red turned brassy, the heavy silkiness become unmanageable bush. Kate ties her hair back with an unsuitable ribbon or knots her head in a scarf. Ill, she cannot bear to sit under a dryer. She accepts her bushy gray hair, like her aging face, as given. That was the summer, we are told, that Kate Brown grew old.

Other people in the novel also have conspicuous hair. Maureen, the young woman with whom Kate briefly shares a flat, is blonde. Her gleaming mane lends itself to various arrangements, always emblematic of her youthful, thoughtless power. When she chops it short, in a gesture of vague protest, it remains seductive: the attractiveness of youth is ineluctable. At the theater Kate sees hair of all colors and reacts with disgust. "Their hair was the worst: mats and caps and manes and wigs of hair, crimped and curled and flattened and lengthened and shortened and manipulated, hair dyed all colours, and scented and greased and lacquered. It was a room full of animals, dogs and cats and wolves and foxes that had got on their hind legs and put ribbons on themselves and brushed their fir." This grotesque perception of human effort at beautification epitomizes the point of view the heroine finally achieves. "We are what we learn," Kate believes. One thing she learns is the loathsomeness of self-adornment.

Maureen learns nothing of the sort. Her fascist lover accuses her of spending all her time decorating herself; she tells him he's wrong. And in fact her self-display, though elaborate, seems effortless. No need to dye her hair; her cosmetic manipulations focus, rather, on such bizarre effects as eyes painted around her nipples. She appears in various roles—Dutch girl, twenties vamp, hippie—all created by dress and makeup. Of course she isn't happy (the only happy person in the novel is a woman who has mysteriously arrived at adulthood with no sense of morality or guilt), but she seems entitled to far more than Kate Brown is.

Entitled to more partly because she understands less. We are what we learn, and what we learn is our limitation. Most hair, sooner or later, turns gray; the question is what to do about it. Animals on their hind legs, human beings attempt to disguise their animality and their aging; or perhaps they simply fail to recognize such facts. Kate

Brown learns that she is aging, that aging is not a process which awaits a fixed future date to begin. Accepting what she has learned, she cannot continue coloring her hair. Her willingness to violate accepted standards of "attractiveness" is a triumph. Or maybe a defeat. To rage against the dying of the light is the traditional heroic way to confront old age; Kate's female heroism limits itself to acceptance. The implication of her series of allegorical dreams seems to be that she has discovered, or recovered, or rescued, her very being by such acceptance.

Maureen, on the other hand, seeks secondhand knowledge to protect herself. She wants to learn from and through Kate, although she also knows that such learning is impossible. Kate would like her dreams to enlighten Maureen as well: "Do you think dreams are just for the person who dreams them? Perhaps they aren't?" But Maureen's answer, although characteristically couched as another question, is definitive: " '*I* didn't dream it,' said Maureen. 'Did I?' " The implication is particular as well as general: not only is it true that dream insights are not transferable, it is more especially true that what a middle-aged woman discovers has no conceivable meaning for a young woman.

But what exactly is it that Kate has learned, in that summer of her growing old? The tone is the message, in this as in other Doris Lessing novels, and the tone is singularly ambiguous. At the beginning of the action Kate leaves her suburban family life, at the end she takes it up again. In between, she has dreamed about a long journey during which she returns a dying seal to life-saving water. She has embarked upon a literal journey with a young American, their sexual contact confined to a single night because he immediately becomes ill; when she follows him into illness, she's forced to leave him. She has endured a period of physical suffering, a subsequent bout of mental confusion, a time of living among young people. She has realized that a woman's sexual attractiveness depends upon her interior state and upon ways of walking, looking, being that reflect this state; that her insistence on helping her family has often supplied tyranny rather than support; that her husband's sexual peccadilloes arouse her contempt . . . and that she must not dye her hair.

That again: How are we to feel about it? And about her other insights? The novel's tone makes it difficult to answer such questions, to know whether the "dark" that follows the summer is necessarily destructive, whether Kate's return to domesticity must mean her resignation to the intolerable.

Now that it was important to her, a matter of self-preservation, that she should be able to make a statement, that she should be understood, then she would, and would not, do certain things to her hair: substance squeezed slowly out through holes in her scalp like spaghetti out of a machine, the only part of her that felt nothing if it was stroked, pinched, or handled. . . . Now she was saying no: no, no, no, NO: a statement which would be concentrated into her hair.

This concentrated form of statement, Kate believes, is less ambiguous than the verbal communication she has been bred to. It is also—this she doesn't say—much simpler: the great refusal implicit in nonconformity to fashion and expectation is clear enough, but the extent of it and the reasons for it are not. One wonders, finally, how clear those reasons are to Kate; for that matter, to Doris Lessing, whose tonal ambiguity seems to derive from sets of contradictions not fully realized or confronted. The definition of hair offered in those sentences about the denial implicit in not taking conventional care of it makes the substance, squeezed out like spaghetti from holes in the scalp, thoroughly repellent. Early in the novel, the hairdresser sends Kate out "with very dark red hair cut so that it felt like a weight of heavy silk swinging against her cheeks as she turned her head. As she remembered very well it had once done always. It was disturbing, this evocation of her young self." The vision of the hair as spaghetti rather than heavy silk is a response to the disturbance. It represents an attempt to deny not only the burden of social expectation but the burden of sexuality. Kate has it in her power to remain a sexual being; she chooses, consciously and deliberately, not to. And she chooses hair, the part of her that cannot feel, as her symbol of rejection. One suspects that the "rejection" is of feeling also, sexual feeling and the other, often painful, emotions.

The capacity to choose develops from her experience. At the summer's beginning, she reflects, "Choose? When do I ever choose? Have I ever chosen?" At its end, she uses a newly discovered capacity in the service of denial. Her rhetoric of decision ("no, no, no, NO") conceals her uncertainties. The insistence of her rejection suggests that she herself takes a heroic assessment of her decision to allow herself unattractiveness; but her stress on the mechanical and unfeeling in her description of hair hints the cost of such decisiveness. What else is given up along with hair dye? The pleasure as well as the anxiety of seductiveness, the pride of sexual identity. Such pleasure, such pride perhaps should properly be relinquished—but Doris Lessing's language consistently points to the strain of the relinquishment. The dream-fable about the seal has a happy ending, focused on the "large, light, brilliant, buoyant, tumultuous sun that seemed to sing"—to sing that rescue is possible though arduous. Kate comes to believe that the only proper object of rescue is the self. But the book's characteristic rhetorical device is the question: "Her reactions of the last few months had been nothing more than that? She had not been loved enough, noticed enough, licked and stroked enough? Was that all it was?" And the novel's statement about a woman's middle age amounts to an enormous self-punishing question? Can one win only by giving up? If an affirmative answer seems implied, it only generates further questions; and the novel's power derives partly from its willingness to rest there, to rest in questions.

In fact questions loom large everywhere in female perceptions of middle age. "The faces and movements of most middle-aged women are those of prisoners or slaves," Kate realizes. How does one avoid the slavery?

Oh it was all so wearying, so humiliating . . . had she really spent so many years of her life—it would almost certainly add up to years!—in front of a looking glass? Just like all women. Years spent asleep, or tranced. . . . For the yhole of her life, or since she was sixteen . . . she had looked into mirrors and seen what other people would judge her by. And now the image had rolled itself up and thrown itself into a corner, leaving behind the face of a sick monkey.

          —THE SUMMER BEFORE THE DARK

I believe Mr. Anderson talks partially of me, as to my looks; I know nothing of the Matter. It is eleven Year since I have seen my Figure in a Glass. The last Reflection I saw there was so disagreeable, I resolv'd to spare my selfe such mortifications for the Future, and shall continue that resolution to my Live's end. To indulge all pleasing Amusements and avoid all Images that give Disgust is in my opinion the best method to confirm Health.

          —THE LETTERS OF LADY MARY WORTLEY MONTAGU

Lady Mary was in her fifties, if her testimony is to be believed, when she gave up looking in mirrors. This real eighteenth-century woman's denial is not the same as that of fictional Kate Brown—or not the same as the one Kate Brown admits. Lady Mary assumes that looking in mirrors is a proper occupation for those who find something pleasant to look at. She has no desire to give up attractiveness, but she believes that it has given her up; still, one hears the undertone of gratified vanity in her remark about Mr. Anderson. Treating her mirror image as merely one among the many images available as sources of pleasure or pain, she commits herself firmly to the side of pleasure. Her rejection is pragmatic: if she doesn't enjoy looking at herself, she will find something else to look at. When Kate Brown sees the face of a sick monkey in her mirror, she feels that thirty years of mirror watching have been a waste of time; Lady Mary does not regret the vanity of the past merely because it is not justifiable in the present.

Yet the gaps between eighteenth and twentieth centuries, between real woman and fictional creation, between vanity passionately rejected and vanity reluctantly relinquished, are in some respects less important than the fundamental unity of perception across those gaps. Both women, in their denials and in their affirmations, reveal the crucial importance of physical attractiveness in feminine psychology. Both suggest the necessity for finding defenses against the loss of attractiveness which means a loss of woman's most obvious power. If the defenses are different, the fear that calls them forth is the same: a fear of finding one's limited freedom altogether destroyed.

Before Kate Brown gives up mirrors, in that final summer of her sexuality, she tries another way to assert her freedom and power: a liaison with a younger man. Its lack of satisfaction for her depends upon circumstances that she suspects to be precipitated by the laws of psychology rather than of fate. At any rate, she finds herself feeling more like mother than mistress; her lover has nothing to give her; solutions must lie within. Lady Mary, in a less analytic era, left no record of speculations about the forces driving her in a similar direction, but much evidence from which readers can draw their own conclusions. She was forty-seven years old when she met Francesco Algarotti, almost precisely half her age. Four months later, she was passionately in love with him. "My feelings are too ardent," she writes. ". . . What has become of that philosophical indifference that made the Glory and the tranquility of my former days? I have lost it never to find it again, and if that passion is healed I foresee nothing except mortal ennui." A significant bit of foreseeing:

375

without passion, in a woman's imagining, there can be only boredom—which one may choose to glory as "philosophical Indifference," but which offers no hope of satisfaction or fulfillment: the psychic darkness which must follow the summer. A few weeks later, Lady Mary writes yet more clearly about her situation.

One must have a Heart filled with a strong passion, to be touched by trifles which seem of such little importance to others. My reason makes me see all its absurdity, and my Heart makes me feel all its importance. Feeble Reason! which battles with my passion and does not destroy it, and which vainly makes me see all the folly of loving to the degree that I love without hope of return.

. . . You must believe that you possess in me the most perfect friend and the most passionate lover. I should have been delighted if nature permitted me to limit myself to the first title; I am enraged at having been formed to wear skirts.

Part of Lady Mary's rage perhaps derives from some suspicion that Algarotti was in fact homosexual. Her love was to achieve no happy ending: Algarotti played her off against Lord Hervey, ignored some of her most passionate advances, and finally evaded her although she pursued him to Italy. But she had learned from the experience, as the passage above suggests—learned to be angry at her woman's fate of feeling, but learned also how the heart can be a source of insight. If her reason leads her to understand the folly of loving, the lesson of the heart—which makes her feel all love's importance—yet remains potent; she appears to regret that reason cannot be simply paramount, but also to take pride in her emotional complexity, which makes her world, she believes, more intricate than the one her lover inhabits, and more interesting. (It is beside my point at the moment that Algarotti's bisexuality probably generated complexities in his experience beyond the scope of Lady Mary's imagining.) Of course she is posing, as she boasts of her love without hope of return; but not only posing: expressing also a female sense of superiority. As Anne Elliot puts it in her debate with Captain Harville toward the end of *Persuasion*, "All the privilege I claim for my own sex (it is not a very enviable one, you need not covet it), is that of loving longest, when existence or when hope is gone."

Lacking the fulfillment of her passion, despite her declared willingness to go anywhere, do anything for Algarotti, Lady Mary had to find new outlets for the feelings of her heart. She suspected that she was not beautiful enough—fifty years old, still pursing him—for the young Italian. "I am horribly silly . . . to let myself be swept away by that Demon ["Inclination"], while you forget me before the eyes of some Idol of a Parisienne, painted and gilded, who receives (perhaps without appreciation) the homage that would make all my happiness." She doesn't say "a *young* Parisienne," but that's what she means, haunted by a vision of younger women, adept at physical self-adornment, as devoted as she to the dashing Algarotti. Yielding to her "Inclination," she makes herself vulnerable: that is the point her letters reiterate. Vulnerability is a woman's natural condition: Mary McCarthy—among many others—was to perceive the same truth.

But attractiveness is entitlement: that, after all, is the ultimate source of Maureen's power in *The Summer Before the Dark*. Her physical charm makes insight relatively unnecessary for her, a luxury. She can lay demands upon the world because the world admires her. Kate's discovery is that demands imply counterdemands. If red hair forces men to notice you, it also forces you to respond. Freedom comes, Kate eventually believes, from giving up entitlement, rejecting its ambiguities as representing too high a cost. To yield to age is, paradoxically and surprisingly, to declare independence. That independence exists only in a small circle of confinement, but better to know the bounds of your circle. Kate's future life, as she goes toward it at the novel's end, is unimaginable; one cannot feel satisfied by the ending. Of course that's part of the point. The ending is not satisfactory for Kate either, but it represents the best of bad alternatives. The rejection she has achieved is the great necessity, implying a belief that to accept limited possibility is at least to recognize the existence of possibility as well as of limitation.

Lady Mary plays her story through. Following Algarotti to Italy, she discovers what she might have known already: he doesn't want her. She wants him, wants expression for her feelings, a focus for her ardent heart. Deprived of such expression, such focus, where women traditionally find them—in a man—she must redirect her energies. She stays in Italy, almost to the end of her life, creating for herself a new and original form of existence, gardening, building, raising silk-worms, writing thoughtfully and at length to her married daughter about how girls should be educated, what it means to be a woman. She neither seeks nor finds immediate intimacies, although the long-distance relationship with her daughter becomes increasingly important. Nominally married still, Lady Mary, after she has given up on Algarotti, indulges in no more flirtations. She too has yielded the privileges and the burden of attractiveness. Less programmatic than Kate Brown, she appears to arrive at a similar understanding of woman's condition and its possibilities. Less is more, to give up is to gain. George Orwell has made up associate such generalizations with tyranny; they represent the desperate and necessary conclusion of many tyrannized women, forced as they lose physical attractiveness to understand how much it has defined their power, forced to comprehend the ambiguities of such power, to understand how little they've really ever had, to embrace diminished lives and convert accepted limitation to qualified triumph. Lady Mary, in her letters, seems far more appealing in age than in youth. No longer obsessed with making an impression, free, like Kate, to discover who she is, she reveals a new sweetness. She expresses, directly and indirectly, some wistfulness about her life, but it does not obscure her pleasure in simple pursuits late discovered.

Kate, seeing middle-aged women as prisoners and slaves, comes to believe that only the young and unattached can preserve a convincing illusion of spacious freedom. Lady Mary is explicit in making a similar point:

To say Truth, there is no part of the World where our Sex is treated with so much contempt as in England. . . . We are educated in the grossest ignorance, and no art omitted to stifle our natural reason; if some few get above their Nurses' instructions, our knowledge must rest conceal'd and be as useless to World as Gold in the Mine.

* * *

I am never in pain for any of that Sex [men]. If they have any Merit there are so many roads for them to meet good Fortune, they can no way fail of it but by not deserving it. We have but one of establishing Ours, and that surrounded with precipices, and perhaps, after all, better miss'd than found.

. . . that tyrannical sex, who with absurd cruelty first put the invaluable deposite of their precious honor in our hands, and then oblige us to prove a negative for the preservation of it. I hate Mankind with all the fury of an old maid (indeed most women of my age do), and have no real esteem but for those heroines who give them as good as they bring.

If social conditions are no longer such that a heroine might plausibly complain that she can receive no education or that only one road leads to a woman's fortune, still all these eighteenth-century grievances echo in twentieth-century writing by women. The necessity for a clever woman to conceal her cleverness in order to relate happily to men, the degree to which it is still assumed that a woman's fortune will depend on her marriage, the prevalence of complex sexual double binds created by men for women—these remain issues for modern feminists, causes for suffering in modern women, subjects of modern novelists and poets. The more things change . . .

But as significant as the problems are the solutions. Fictional Kate Brown and real Lady Mary both declare that a woman must deal with her condition by manipulating her psyche. Aware though they are of social forces restricting female possibility, they conclude that their own significant resources derive from their ways of perceiving themselves and the world. Yielding reliance on physical attractiveness, recognizing the kind of freedom and power that attractiveness has provided, they come to believe that true freedom depends on the willingness not to rely on such power: not, in fact, to need power at all. They do not, like Beatrice Webb, understand sexual vanity as sin but, finally, as weakness. Their "freedom" unnervingly resembles resignation.

Women's struggles for larger sorts of freedom may produce grander resolutions, but many resemble Kate's and Lady Mary's in being essentially products of the imagination.

Ella says drily: "My dear Julia, we've chosen to be free women, and this is the price we pay, that's all."

"Free," says Julia. "Free! What's the use of us being free if they aren't? I swear to God, that every one of them, even the best of them, have the old idea of good women and bad women."

"And what about us? Free, we say, yet the truth is they get erections when they're with a woman they don't give a damn about, but we don't have an orgasm unless we love him. What's free about that?"

—DORIS LESSING, *The Golden Notebook*

There are those who can rise above life, transform it, free themselves, and for these the revolution is not necessary. I can see how necessary it is for those who cannot escape into creation, create an illusory world, those who cannot dream or create an individually perfect world.
—THE DIARY OF ANAÏS NIN, *1936–1939*

The distinguished "emancipated" women who have written about themselves in our century often reveal the extraordinary difficulties of feminine freedom. As women approach freedom, they find it receding; as they accept limitation, it comes to look strangely like its opposite. Colette is first liberated to write when locked into her room and ordered to produce by a domineering husband who publishes her work under his name; Beatrice Webb yields to Sidney's intellectual control, even while consistently referring to him as "my dear boy." Simone de Beauvoir struggles against her sense of Sartre's superiority, hence dominance, and confesses that her lover is the center of her world. All these facts disturb students.

But even Lillian Hellman, whom students eagerly admire, working in a more "liberated" era and in a Hemingwayesque style which makes no apologies, exemplifies in her memoir, *An Unfinished Woman*, the degree to which feminine freedom may depend on ignorance, derive from fantasy, and produce paradoxical limitation. Miss Hellman dreams of living successfully by masculine standards: honor, courage, aggression. Her stories of triumph, considered as testimonies to the possibility of feminine freedom, thus have an ironic edge, of which she seems unaware. She relates Hemmingway's praise of her: "So you have *cojones,* after all. I didn't think so upstairs. But you have *cojones* after all." Although she tells him to go to hell, she treasures the episode: Such praise, defining her difference from the rest of her sex, testifies to her distinction. She can spit in Dashiell Hammett's eye, literally; the capacity makes her worthy of the companion. And she can endure bombardments, travel with the Russian Army, defy

Hollywood moguls, the equal of any man. She sees the relation between men and women as a battle, and believes reflection on the difficulties of a woman's lot to be reprehensible weakness, "stuff proper for the head of a young girl."

However ugly her battles, she fights them. Often she wins, although her account of Hammett records his abundant victories. He asserts his power by creating a conflict and making her back away from it. By the time they reach the corner, he declares, she must decide never to discuss a certain subject again: otherwise, they will take permanently different directions. She must stop "juggling," maneuvering relationships, or he will leave her. He will not dine with a house guest who bores him; he will ignore her good friend Dorothy Parker, however embarrassing his refusals. When she rebukes him for his injustices, his insistence on his own way, he grinds a burning cigarette into his cheek to keep himself from doing it to her. "We never again spoke of that night because, I think, he was ashamed of the angry gesture that made him once again the winner in the game that men and women play against each other, and I was ashamed that I caused myself to lose so often."

Miss Hellman's shame at causing herself to lose—as women so often do—reflects the "masculine" orientation of her pride: Hemingway's praise of her for having "balls" is to the point. But it reflects also her selective blindness, a curious quality of her memoir. Although its author's interest for the public at large must depend on her reputation as a playwright, the narrative dwells hardly at all on her experience as a writer. Her accounts of her loves and of her work are oblique, as if neither aspect of experience were vital to her (although the real meaning of the fact may be that both are too vital to be shared). Her summary comment on Hammett, with whom she spent thirty years, sounds deliberately but disturbingly flat: "He was the most interesting man I've ever met." Her most analyti-

cal comments about herself observe that she was "difficult"
or "headstrong"—adjectives which classify her as her
parents might, from without, but which provide little insight into her inner workings. The cumulative effect of her
lack of self-penetration, her apparent uneasiness in love
relationships, her reluctance to contemplate her own writing, her acceptance of a travelogue version of her experience, is to suggest that her central effort has been to
create, for her own benefit as well as for others, a character to meet masculine standards. This is not a mere
image": her life substantiates it. The life of constant
action (in this case "masculine" rather than "feminine"
accomplishment) rests on a foundation of intense self-
concentration. Lillian Hellman's work has been to make a
self, rejecting in the process many traditional concomitants
of femininity.

She made my class nervous, despite their admiration:
she didn't fit the established categories. If she exemplifies
the possibilities of independence (and without working
hard in school! as one student pointed out), she also suggests unexpected dangers and qualifications. For one
thing, she makes more distinct the possibility that
"bitchiness" goes with "doing something in the world."
"None of the women we've encountered sit home and bake
cookies," a student observed. True. But before Lillian
Hellman, no one we read raised serious questions about
the value of "niceness." Self-absorption is the foundation of
Miss Hellman's freedom: the freedom to manufacture a
more satisfactory self from the headstrong, difficult, unruly
girl—always her father's "rumpled daughter"—so inadequate by standards of ladylike behavior. Her acquired
strength appears to make bearable for her her occasional
discovered weakness which, like most people, she can
sometimes enjoy: another paradox troubling to the young.
This truth she reveals without seeming ever to understand
it. "There may be a need in many of us," she writes, "for
the large, strong woman who takes us back to what most

of us always wanted and few of us ever had." Strong women and strong men have clearly been important to Miss Hellman. She devotes three chapters of her memoir to describing four central figures in her life, all dominating personalities. Her yearning for dependence, her delight in discovering others, men and women, at least sometimes more forceful than she, suggest that the freedom to be weak may be as vital to a woman as the freedom to be strong. But vulnerability is dangerous—that she knows with full awareness. Only the strength of self-obsession and determination allow the memoirist space to construct a self, to make her yearning for masculine accomplishment into fact.

Isak Dinesen defined for herself a curious vocation: to live in Africa. Impermanent though it proved—yielding, in a logical process, to the more orthodox vocation of writing—this life commitment created for her a freedom larger, more demanding, yet richer in possibility than she had previously conceived. Africa offered specifically a freedom of the imagination, providing an atmosphere analogous to that of dreams, which Dinesen values for their aura "of unlimited freedom," the opposite of nightmare's constriction. Africans, she tells us, seek imagination as the crucial quality "in a master or a doctor or in God." "When the Africans speak of the personality of God they speak like the Arabian Nights or like the last chapters of the book of Job; it is the same quality, the infinite power of imagination, with which they are impressed." Africa released this "infinite power" in the Danish woman by providing a meaningful focus for energy outside the self, and outside the woman's traditional commitment to caring for others. Unlike Lillian Hellman, Isak Dinesen finds freedom by transcending self-absorption, creating a self-image congruent with, evolved from, the continent. The image, product of an imagination engaged with the outer world, amounts to an idealized version of the self, responsive to pressures from without and within. Although its existence influences the activities and the yearnings of the real person it reflects, image and person never become identical. The capacity to generate such an image defines the person's power. And the image itself, artificial though it may be, provides a means to self-knowledge.

To accept living in Africa as a vocation rather than an accident of fate demanded energy, intelligence, honesty, courage. A woman wishing to retain her integrity, to assert her own sense of self, had to resist, first of all, the natives' tendency to mythologize her beyond recognition.

Because of their gift for myths, the Natives can also do things to you against which you cannot guard yourself and from which you cannot escape. They can turn you into a symbol. I was well aware of the process, and for my own use I had a word for it,—in my mind I called it that they were brass-serpenting me. . . . I believe that in spite of all our activities in the land, of the scientific and mechanical progress there, and of Pax Britannica itself, this is the only practical use that the Natives have ever had out of us.

Practical is an odd word here. The brass serpent in the Bible actually protected the Israelites against the poison of "fiery serpents," thus possessing literal practical value; Isak Dinesen provided for the Africans only imaginary protection, asserted meanings that meaning of symbol. To be converted to a symbol is an ambiguous fate for a human being.

I thought it a painful, a very painful process to be hung upon the pole, I wished that I could have escaped it. Still, many years after, there will be occasions when you find yourself thinking: "Am I to be treated in such a way?—I, who have been a brass-serpent!"

Pain and pride: the pain of becoming an instrument for other's purposes, the pride of feeling one's individual value enlarged. But what if, instead of contenting oneself with being mythologized, one mythologizes the self? Such was Isak Dinesen's course: learning the lessons the country could teach, she did not simply resist Africa's pressures but converted them to her own use, appropriating and redirecting the habits of mythologizing imagination.

Her myth of herself developed with great complexity. Perceiving Africa—land, people, animals, plants—as a world with close affinities to that of art, she developed responses to it analogous to her responses to paintings or statues. Her metaphors insistently establish connections between life and art. The forest appears to her a phenomenon from a tapestry, her dogs belong to another wall-hanging, scenes present themselves as an illustration to Heine or a picture from a fairy tale or a Chinese pattern or an event on a stage, a man seems an actor of comedy or tragedy, or a picture, or a piece of sculpture. As she lovingly contemplates all that surrounds her, the same meticulous attentiveness focusing on fawn or chieftain, charging lion and dancing natives, the landscape and its inhabitants acquire the grandeur and profundity of a fairy-tale environment. Isak Dinesen as a figure of her own imagination has the same quality.

The values by which she survives bear striking similarities to Lillian Hellman's. Indeed, this woman with a male pseudonym (as a writer) lived in many respects the active life of a man. Free and independent in an external sense, she controlled an estate like a feudal barony, some two thousand natives its other inhabitants, all acknowledging her authority, many willing to accord her semi-divine status. During the First World War, she led a vast expedition across the plains, carrying supplies for the government. She hunted big game, celebrated the epic virtues, valued herself for endurance, leadership, bravery. Her womanhood seems largely irrelevant to her actual experience. No one ever suggests that her sex may be an obstacle in anything she wishes to do. Her life might belong to Lillian

Hellman's fantasy, so free and powerful does she seem, so devoid of social or personal sense of limitation.

Yet her mythical self-image is intensely that of a woman, her implicit definition of womanhood suggesting her special imaginative way of confronting the African experience. Before she establishes the vision of herself as "good woman," she evokes a counterimage of "bad woman," in connection with the vividly evoked figure of Old Knudsen, the Dane who inhabits a cottage on her farm, a constant spinner of fantasies about himself and the world. In Old Knudsen's imagination, he is a hero inhabiting a world of infinite possibilities which he possesses the power to exploit. In actuality, he shows himself altogether impotent, unable to realize any of his grandiose schemes or to reconcile his vast imaginings to his literal shrunken status and capacity. Isak Dinesen, whose interest in him depends on the high value she places on imaginative activity, who shares his delight in fantasies of heroism, conjures up for him an altogether imaginary antagonist, a woman, whom she christens "Madam Knudsen." Madam Knudsen represents a harsh version of reality. "She was the woman who ruins the pleasure of man, and therein is always right. She was the wife of the curtain-lectures, and the housewife of the big cleaning-days, she stopped all enterprises, she washed the faces of boys, and snatched away the man's glass of gin from the table before him, she was law and order embodied. . . . Madam Knudsen did not dream of enslaving by love, she ruled by reasoning and righteousness." An embodiment of absolute power, "always right" in her rigid adherence to established principle, she is, from the author's point of view as from Knudsen's, an image of horror. Such power, control without love, is possible for any woman. It destroys imagination, its source of authority a notion of reality altogether opposed to pleasure, fantasy, possibility. The woman who resorts to it reduces herself, even in asserting her claim of enormous force.

But the commitment to reality is as necessary, Isak

Dinesen believes, as the commitment to imagination. Her ideal image of woman, of herself, combines the two. She evokes it most distinctly in a moving scene near the end of *Out of Africa*, where she and a woman friend join in saying farewell to the farm. Economic necessity is driving her way, out of Africa, back to Europe. Her friend understands, as only a woman could, what the loss of the farm means to her. She helps the dispossessed woman to combat her loss by acknowledging it in the fullest possible detail. Together the two traverse the estate, mourning every animal, every plant, counting, naming, *recognizing* everything. Their recognitions include awareness and acceptance of the friend's better fortune in being able to stay; finally, they acknowledge together the meaning of their roles. "In spite of our old khaki coats and trousers, we were in reality a pair of mythical women, shrouded respectively in white and black, a unity, the Genii of the farmer's life in Africa."

In reality. The phrase emphasizes the difference between Isak Dinesen's notion of the real and Madam Knudsen's. For the potential writer (already entertaining herself in the evening by composing "fairy tales and romances"), only mythic perception can grasp reality. Seeing herself as the presiding genius of the farmer's life in Africa, she recognizes herself also as archetypal woman—an archetype at the opposite extreme from Madam Knudsen. She stands for love, love of the object world, full attention and response to the outside. Her "work," the work of fully being where she is, uses her every capacity for love, to which *Out of Africa* testifies. The book does not call itself an autobiography or memoir, does not even claim to be about the self. It reveals the self in its attention to the other. The author declares relationship in every act of her existence—with her workers, her friends, her animals, her chance acquaintances; and with the vast world of Africa, animate and inanimate. Through relationship she discovers and defines herself as mythical woman, affirming her woman-

hood through imagination while demonstrating in action
her capacity to surmount all womanly limitations.

The tale of the stork epitomizes the artistic faith that
underlies *Out of Africa*. The author remembers it from her
childhood, recalls how the narrator would trace on paper
as he told the story the devious routes taken by a man
plagued by endless mishaps—stumbling over stones, falling
in successive ditches, forced to plug leaks in a dam, and so
on. He wakes in the morning, looks out the window, and
sees—as the delighted child listener also sees—that his
stumblings have created the figure of a stork. "He must
have wondered what was the idea of all his trials, he
could not know that it was a stork. But through them all
he kept his purpose in view, nothing made him turn round
and go home." Dinesen makes the application to her own
life, seeing the possibility of transformation through art:
"The tight place, the dark pit in which I am now lying, of
what bird is it the talon? When the design of my life is
completed, shall I, shall other people see a stork?"

Such storks must be both created and discovered. The
imagination, instrument of creation and discovery, generates patterns that link people and continents, the art of
Europe and Asia illuminating the actuality of Africa, to
make sense of experience. And to enable its possessor to
love, insisting not simply on the value of the self but on
the self's capacity to embrace the created world. Through
suffering and pleasure alike, the writer's imagination affirms her freedom while testifying her kinships. It
preserves the female vocation of loving as part of the artist's vocation: to see, to recognize, to shape. Living in Africa, as Isak Dinesen describes it, involves—demands—all
these activities.

Like Lillian Hellman, Anaïs Nin writes of herself in
ways that have the power to challenge standard assumptions; unlike Miss Hellman, she appears to take great pride
in "losing." The published volumes of her diary emphasize
her unfailing self-sacrifice, her willingness to live without

so much as a pen while supplying her writer friends with typewriters, her eager yielding to others' demands. It is true that this pattern was directly responsible, Miss Nin declares, for a psychic breakdown, but her commitment to the values of orthodox "femininity" remained unchanging. Yet she is also committed to an ideal of personal freedom, which she—like Marie Bonaparte—explicitly associates with the life of imagination—with "escape," the "illusory," "dream." Unlike Isak Dinesen, she demonstrates few connections between imagination and actuality.

The counterpart to the story about Lillian Hellman's "*cojones*" is an episode centered on Anaïs Nin's breasts. She complains to her analyst, Dr. René Allendy, that her breasts are too small, asking for appropriate medicine. "Are they absolutely undeveloped?" the doctor inquires. She replies no, then: "As I flounder in my descriptions, I say: 'To you, a doctor, the simplest thing is to show them to you.' And I do." The doctor begins, she reports, to rhapsodize: "Perfectly feminine, small but well shaped, well outlined in proportion to the rest of your figure, such a lovely figure, all you need is a few more pounds of it. You are really lovely, so much grace of movement, charm, so much breeding and finesse of line." Shortly thereafter, we discover that he has "lost his objectivity"; he can no longer help her. She reflects, "I asked Dr. Allendy to help me as a doctor of medicine. Was this quite a sincere action? Did I have to show him my breasts? Did I want to test my charm on him? Wasn't I pleased that he reacted so admiringly?"

Instead of Lillian Hellman's vocabulary of battle and endurance, Isak Dinesen's mythologizing, Anaïs Nin uses the language of self-deprecation and self-doubt. She avoids talk of "winning" as she modestly records her victories over the succession of people who fell in love with her: Henry Miller, Henry Miller's wife, her father (he reappears after having deserted his family years before, and soon begins to fantasize that everyone will think her his mistress, then loudly to regret that she is in fact his daughter), Dr. Allendy, Dr. Otto Rank, who succeeded Allendy as her analyst, an Indian revolutionary, a French astrologer. Yet the need to triumph as well as the intermittent compulsion to "lose" resembles Hellman's, although the arena is different.

Unlike Hellman, who claims realism as one of her virtues and berates herself even for introspection, Nin commits herself explicitly to the value of imaginative reconstruction of reality and to the centrality of writing in her life. Suffering from the twentieth-century problem of fragmentation, she solves it as a diarist, and defines her freedom as the product of her writing: "Because writing, for me, is an expanded world, a limitless world, containing all." But her real "work" appears to be self-contemplation and self-display, of which writing is only one mode. The source of her artistic energy, she believes, is her femininity. Love, service to others, those traditional forms of feminine expression, are other aspects of her self-presentation. "Yes, I see myself always softening blows, dissolving acids, neutralizing poisons, every moment of the day. I try to fulfill the wishes of others, to perform miracles." Despite her obsessive introspection, she conveys a view of herself in some ways as external as Lillian Hellman's self-portrait, because her concern centers so completely on the creation of effects. Her sense of freedom depends on her ability to manipulate those effects, to control her environment (different rooms painted different colors to encourage different moods), her clothing ("original"), and her companions, in order to show herself to advantage. When she gives birth, in agony, to a six-month fetus, dead at birth, she reports, "Towards eight o'clock I had several spasms of pain. . . . I combed my hair, I powdered and perfumed myself, painted my eyelashes. At eight o'clock I was taken to the operating room." Using all the paraphernalia of feminine attractiveness, she insists on loving and being loved, on working and having her work valued, on her symbolic position, as Woman, at the center of the uni-

verse. Demanding freedom, she declares herself to have
achieved it.

Much more openly than Hellman, Anaïs Nin admits the
great importance in her life of writing, publication, and
relation with others. She seems willing, in fact, to admit
just about anything. One does not feel that she tries to
form herself in any particular mold; she quite simply loves
and displays whatever she happens to be at any given moment. Yet the sense of limitation is as strong in her lengthy
account of a "free" life as in Lillian Hellman's. The Hellman memoir suggests that the cost of freedom from relationship is emotional impoverishment and restriction, but
the cost of relationship, for such a woman as the author, is
likely to be submission, emotional limitation. Nin's diaries
emphasize her resort to frequent bouts of psychoanalysis
to rescue her from the desperate restrictions of an untrammeled life. Absorbed in narcissism, she flounders among
the multitude of selves she perceives. Committed to fantasies of feminine power, she involves herself therefore in
endless responsibilities to others. Her self-display requires
an audience, her audience makes demands, her freedom
eludes her. Her relationships lead her back only to herself.
It seems a strangely symbolic fact that her husband has
disappeared, apparently by his request, from her published diaries. The stillborn fetus might, for all we are
told, be a virgin birth: the figure of Anaïs Nin, surrounded by others, exists nonetheless in a terrifying isolation of
self-concern.

All autobiography must rest on a foundation of self-absorption; men as well as women indulge in self-manufac-
ture and self-display. What is perhaps peculiarly feminine
about the autobiographical writing of Lillian Hellman and
Anaïs Nin, dissimilar though the two authors are, is the
obsessiveness of its implicit or explicit concern with the
question of freedom, psychic and social, and the nature of
its revelations about freedom's limitations for women. But
one may also speculate about the essential femininity of
what may be called "defensive narcissism." For Ernest

Hemingway or Norman Mailer, writing about themselves, narcissism is a mode of aggression, a way of forcing the world to attend. In woman writers, even writers so assertive as Lillian Hellman, so exhibitionistic as Anaïs Nin, the characteristic note suggests something close to desperation: it is as though they were writing to convince themselves. The ordering of experience in memoir or diary, the implicit assertion that this life makes sense, seems in these cases a way for the author to remind herself of the value of her own experience, to hold on to the meaning of her life.

The note is particularly clear in the capsule autobiographies of two young women committed to Women's Liberation as social program and as personal style: Ellen Willis ("Up from Radicalism: A Feminist Journal," *US* Magazine, 1969) and Sally Kempton ("Cutting Loose," *Esquire*, July 1970). Both are concerned with political and personal freedom for women. Both reveal the close connection between freedom and fantasy, with similar images: Miss Kempton describes herself lying in bed beside her husband, wishing she had the courage to bash in his head with a frying pan; Miss Willis half-seriously suggests a future in which women will express their political rage by killing men. Yet such aggressive fantasies coexist with the crucial feminine fear of desertion: both women confess, paradoxically, to identical limitations of their sense of possibility—they share the fundamental terror of losing their men. And both share also a repetitive, emphatic tone which suggests that, however public their announced concerns, they are finally talking to themselves, trying in print to resolve dilemmas that women have never resolved.

"Man, my friend," Colette observes, "you willingly make fun of women's writings because they can't help being autobiographical." The issue of freedom looms large in women's fiction as well as more direct forms of autobiography. No more securely than diaries or memoirs do novels reveal how to do it—how a woman is to find freedom for work and for love and to use it effectively—but they multiply the clues.

In novels written by women in the nineteenth century, when social liberation was hardly a real possibility for women, the connection between imaginative vitality and psychic freedom was clear and striking. Charlotte Brontë's passionate heroines, existing in conditions of artificial social isolation—orphaned heiress, poor governess, English teacher in a foreign land—asserted their imaginations as alternative to the deadening conventionality that surrounded them. One remembers Jane Eyre: "My sole relief was to walk along the corridor of the third storey, . . . and allow my mind's eye to dwell on whatever bright visions rose before it—and, certainly, they were many and glowing; to let my heart be heaved by the exultant movement, which, while it swelled it in trouble, expanded it with life; and best of all, to open my inward ear to a tale that was never ended—a tale my imagination created, and narrated continuously; quickened with all of incident, life, fire, feeling, that I desired and had not in my actual existence." Elizabeth Gaskell, less dramatic in her evocations of the imagination's yearnings, allows Margaret, in *North and South,* to look out the window at night, see a poacher, and find herself—despite her irreproachable credentials as minister's daughter—sympathizing and identifying with him. But Charlotte Brontë's tempestuous spirits invariably find fulfillment in marriage to a dominant man, and Mrs. Gaskell's Margaret, after enduring the full experience of desertion, as her parents and guardian die, after experimenting briefly with independence in the doing of good works, subsides contentedly into marriage. And indeed, given the detailed exposition of the lot of old maids in Miss Brontë's *Shirley,* it is difficult to conceive other viable alternatives for these young women: they can sustain their freedom only in their imaginings.

In the twentieth century, social possibilities are greater, and the image of the "free woman"—often promiscuous, often intellectual, priding herself on being emotionally undemanding but often seen nonetheless as "castrating"—has been established in fiction by men and women authors alike. The most self-conscious and elaborate study, in imaginative terms, of the "free" woman's problems is *The Golden Notebook*, first published in 1962, now read with passionate involvement by college girls who have difficulty believing that women of their mothers' generation confronted the dilemmas Doris Lessing describes, which seem to the young uniquely their own. It was the last book we read in the course, a fact that gave it in advance a curious special position. Because it was the last—and because I had hinted all semester that this was the book that *really* described the condition of the contemporary woman—unique expectations developed around it. This was the novel, my students hoped, that would answer their questions.

At any rate, it *asks* their questions. Five sections of the book bear the title "Free Women," a phrase surrounded by invisible inverted commas of steadily increasing emphasis. From without, from the point of view of society at large, Anna, the novel's heroine, and her friend Molly seem to lead "free lives, that is, lives like men." Anna is, in every accepted social sense, free: from financial pressures and domestic ones, from the blindly accepted restrictions of conventional morality, from traditional class-definitions, from inarticulateness, ignorance, stupidity. She is, for exactly these reasons, to men an appropriate object for casual lust: when their wives go to the hospital to have babies, they expect to be welcomed to Anna's bed. Her "freedom" thus becomes a means for her victimization.

In her own self-perception, she is bound by her physical nature as woman; every month her period makes her "feel helpless and out of control." Her emotions limit her possibilities: particularly the diffuse and irrational sense of guilt which she shares with women in general; and, even more emphatically, her felt need for love and protection. And the nature of society and of her responses to it severely restrict even her imagination of freedom. The novel's central symbol is her "writer's block," her inability to create in communicable terms, caused partly by her sense of how inadequate is any individual response to social horror. Imaginary Vietnamese peasants look over her shoulder; the challenge of reality invalidates every rendition of the real.

Anna is in fact far from free. Her personal political situation thus reflects the international one rendered in the final section of her red notebook, the one devoted to the Communist Party:

The red notebook, like the black notebook, had been taken over by newspaper cuttings, for the years 1956 and 1957. These referred to events in Europe, the Soviet Union, China, the United States. Like the cutting of Africa in the same period [recorded in the black notebook], they were about, for the most part, violence. Anna had underlined the word "freedom" whenever it occurred, in red pencil. When the cuttings ceased, she had added up the red lines, making a total of 679 references to the word freedom.

Freedom is only a word, its implications always contradicted by reality, and the idea of a free woman is illusory as that of a free society. To make freedom a fact is the central effort of all political struggle.

In Anna's personal feminine politics, one responds to felt limitation by fragmentation. Women have long been accustomed to divide their lives into compartments; Anna's mode of keeping things separate, isolating parts of her experience in individual notebooks, although more complicated, literary, and self-aware than that of most women, has the same meaning. She replies to the threat of chaos, which makes freedom meaningless, by creating limited orders, necessary, but necessarily false; recognizing their falsity, she sees herself therefore as an enemy of possibility.

But the notebooks contain also the seed of possibility, for they record not only fact but its imaginative reshaping.

The black notebook—about Africa, about her writing, about her finances—offers the truth of feeling, dominated by what Anna comes to consider her "lying nostalgia" for the past. The truth of social perspective shapes the red notebook, about Anna's relation to the Communist Party; the yellow one, for fiction, offers the truth of imagination; the blue, a conventional journal, provides the truth of detail. Truth is multiple and fragmentary, and so is fiction. Only the yellow notebook is intended for fiction, but all four notebooks contain it, since precise linguistic rendition of simple actuality is unachievable. Language necessarily mediates between fact and imagining, transforming experience into meaning. Language is for Anna the only conceivable means to freedom. Her experience produces dead ends, defeats teaching nothing but hopelessness; yet writing about experience can redeem it. The lessons Anna must learn are taught her in dreams: salvation comes through the release of the subconscious. *The Golden Notebook* ends in a chaos of recorded and imagined experience, with the reader unable to tell for certain which is which. It ends also with considerable emphasis on the fact that a novel, this novel, has been written—the single clearly redemptive fact, a fact of freedom. Freedom is only a word, but the word has power.

Writing is Anna's work, for a long time her emblem of the impossible. It does not provide the freedom of escape, as Anaïs Nin claims her writing does, but of integration: the containing and ordering of experience. Partly an alternative to experience, it points up the difficulties of a woman's finding freedom directly in her life. The problem of relationship, for the fictional character, Anna, as for living women, Lillian Hellman, Anaïs Nin, Isak Dinesen, focuses the perplexities of femininity. Anna's consciousness that she needs the love of a single man dominates her understanding of all that happens to her. Recognizing that it makes her out of tune with her life and her time, she yet has no control over the need.

A complaint frequently made about *The Golden Note-*

book is that its failure to depict any emotionally adequate men amounts to a serious falsification of actuality. But the paucity of good men helps to focus the problems of good women—"good" in quite a new sense. "For wommen like me," reflects Ella (Anna's "fictional" version of herself), "integrity isn't chastity, it isn't fidelity, it isn't any of the old words. Integrity is the orgasm." Ella, like Anna, experiences orgasm only with men she loves. And love is, for a woman, part of *wholeness*—integrity in the root sense.

To be a whole human being is the heroine's central struggle. Wholeness is, finally, the necessary condition for freedom: and it is, for Anna, unattainable. The ambiguous ending of *The Golden Notebook* records two conspicuous defeats—Molly's marriage of convenience, Anna's job at "matrimonial welfare work"—along with the partial victory of Anna's freedom-through-imagination in her writing of the metaphorical golden notebook, the novel. Molly and Anna have recognized the impossibility of wholeness, which depends for a woman, the novel suggests, on connection with another. Acknowledging the severe limitations on their freedom, they resign themselves to working within them: defeat and victory are the same. The condition that makes ultimate freedom impossible is the human condition, the same for men and women. But—so Molly's and Anna's positions imply—because women must have love, not only for orgasm but for integrity, their struggle is perhaps more intense, their triumph less conceivable, their partial freedom more entirely dependent on imagination, than those of men.

Such, at any rate, is the assumption on which much of *The Golden Notebook* rests. Molly and Anna imagine that the emotional needs of men and women are different; although they declare that this difference defines masculine freedom, their tone reveals their contempt for the emotional superficiality and exploitativeness they associate with the male. The amplitude of sexual possibility for men is, from their feminine point of view, an index of moral inferiority. The novel depicts limited men, associates such limitation with masculinity, declares it to be "freedom." The difficulty of a woman's achieving comparable freedom becomes a subtle emblem of her virtue. To differentiate between the sexes in such terms may be seen as yet another operation of defensive narissism: self-love disguises itself as humble acceptance of things-as-they-are, betrays itself by the nature of its evaluation of the Other (i.e., the masculine), but provides protection by embracing limitation while seeming to regret it, and by defining feminine limitation in flattering terms.

"Anna's notion of freedom isn't real because real freedom depends on a relation between two people in which responses don't have to be guarded."

My students, many of them, clung to a hope that freedom was not incompatible with love.

In *The Four-Gated City*, Doris Lessing grants that the masculine need for love is as fundamental as its feminine counterpart, but she also explicitly declares narcissism the means of salvation. What in *The Golden Notebook* seemed a link between fantasy and freedom here becomes in fact an identity. The novel's significant definition of freedom is provided—without any relieving irony—by psychotic Linda. "I keep quiet about what I know," she says. "I have to, you see. . . . That's freedom, isn't it? Everyone has a bit of freedom, a little space. . . . That is freedom. . . . That's mine. It's all they let me have. They wouldn't let me keep that if they knew how to take it away. But if I say to them: I don't hear voices, you've cured me, the voices have gone . . . . they can't prove anything. That's my freedom." Her freedom is her madness, and her privacy in it. Martha Quest, the novel's heroine, comes to believe that madness is, or derives from, true insight; her own "work," she decides, must be to achieve equivalent insight herself.

This work becomes part of the battle of being a woman. As consistently as Lillian Hellman, Mrs. Lessing in this novel employs military metaphors to describe feminine activity, here understood as largely defensive. Martha has to defend others from the petty and major ills of the world, and, more important, has to defend herself from encroachment: has to create and preserve her own freedom. Her effort involves rejection of love and marriage, finally a gladly accepted sexlessness. She expresses gratitude at the fact that young girls "borrow" her clothes, the paraphernalia of feminine attractiveness. "The rejuvenation a young girl gives her mother or an older woman is a setting-free into impersonality, a setting-free, also, from her personal past." The point foretells the ideology of *The Summer Before the Dark*.

The solution to the problem outlined in *The Golden Notebook*, then, of the limitation to freedom implied by one woman's declared inability to have orgasms without love, is to eliminate sex as well as love from one's life. The solution to the restrictions implicit in all personal relations is "a setting-free into impersonality." Critics have complained about the "science fiction" final section of *The Four-Gated City*, in which dedicated "seers" and "hearers," who have developed to a high degree capacities formerly identified with madness, help to save the world, or pieces of it, from total annihilation. But the disturbing quality of this section, its sense of remoteness, its theoretical tone, in fact dominates a large part of the novel's second half. As Martha concentrates more and more on her inner life, the outer world becomes (not only to her: to the reader) increasingly attenuated. Relationships multiply, but their complexities are stated rather than felt. Sexual possibilities continue, but they are not important. The world moves toward its destruction, the political and social scene reflecting the unsureness of individuals: in a sense this is the novel's subject. But it does not feel important either, except as a weighty demonstration of the urgency of Martha's efforts toward self-discovery. Only this exploration of her own inner life matters.

Martha's external conduct is that of the "good" woman: she devotes her life to others. Her inner life, on the other hand, a life of obsessive self-concentration, denies the real significance of others and makes it clear that, in her case at least, the good woman's actions, however socially useful, do not reflect her essence. The asserted paradox central to *The Four-Gated City* is that self-obsession of Martha's kind can produce a social salvation; analogically, the horrifying physical mutations caused by radiation and other forms of contamination may involve psychic alterations which will likewise contribute to the world's redemption. But the problem of individual female salvation dominates the novel, which seems to assert a solution to that problem. Martha Quest, living a life almost entirely formed by the needs of others, lacks the external concomitants of freedom but achieves the inner dependence that comes from intense self-commitment, accepting the dangers of self-immersion. Her creator appears to claim that such solipsism, multiplied, may save the world; but the novel suggests rather that this kind of freedom, like others; may become itself a trap.

Indeed, the suspicion that here too is a trap is a subterranean theme of contemporary fiction by women. Mrs. Lessing's *Briefing for a Descent into Hell* has a masculine protagonist whose problem recapitulates Martha's, and Linda's, in more intense form. Imprisoned in his own madness, he sees in its fantasies sources of redemption for the world, but his insight is incommunicable. He can only return to sanity and meaningless community. *Play It as It Lays*, in which insanity means total isolation; *Up the Sandbox!*, with fantasies supporting the mundane while appearing to challenge it—such books reveal that in our era of widespread fascination with madness and romantic speculation about its power to lay hold on truth, woman novelists, sharing the fascination, also convey doubts—often apparently inadvertent, often shared with men—about its viability.

The idea that women may find their most significant freedom through fantasy or imagination need not imply any commitment to madness. Saner visions of the imagination as salvation, which underlie many pre-twentieth-century novels about and by women and at least a few autobiographies, substantiate the possibility that the liberated inner life may create new freedoms of actual experience.

The difficulties of feminine freedom, as suggested by Hellman, Nin, and Lessing, inhere in the actualities of feminine experience. To arrive at freedom, these women indicate, through direct self-presentation or fictional creation, is to triumph over actuality. The qualified triumphs they adumbrate depend at least partly on denial or avoidance: Hellman denying significant difference between the sexes, Nin avoiding self-confrontation by self-display, Lessing's heroines retreating from intolerable experience into the wider expanses of conscious or subconscious reshaping of it. But the imagination can also lead toward acceptance, as Dinesen's loving but unsentimental attention to details of the natural world suggests, providing such intense imaginative concentration on actuality that its possibilities expand. To be sure, Isak Dinesen's experience bears little relation to the "normal" lives of women—but Hellman's experience, Nin's, the careers of Lessing's heroines, are not "normal" either. Welcoming what happens to her, valuing and using her richest capacities, Isak Dinesen accepts her womanhood but insists on her freedom within it. Her capacity for acceptance repudiates the despair of such books as *Briefing for a Descent into Hell*—a despair that declares immutable the gap between the real and the imagined.

Afterword

When I write I think I live in a golden castle that shines in the sunlight.
—CAROLINE MARÍA DE JESÚS

What does it mean to a woman to write? For the real person Anaïs Nin and the fictional character Anna Wulf, writing represented the only viable possibility for freedom. Most woman writers, in fact and in fiction, neglect to specify the significance of their literary activity, whether vocation or avocation. One may guess, though, that the equation between writing and freedom holds for more than those who have articulated it. The cliché that women, more consistently than men, turn inward for sustenance seems to mean, in practice, that women have richly defined the ways in which imagination creates possibility: possibility that society denies.

"We must not suppose," Amelie Rorty, a recent woman commentator on the social plight of women, announces, "that our most brilliant solutions will enable us to lead lives of glory, joy, and total freedom. If we do suppose that, we will create new myths by which to condemn ourselves." As a substitute for social action, myths prove dangerous; and the myth of infinite possibility—of the joyous life awaiting us if only we make the right choice—is especially dangerous, with its inevitable concomitant of despair. But myths have multiple meanings: from the point of view of Medea's children, what does the story signify? To read books by women answers few questions, raises many. The books do not destroy or even seriously challenge the old, man-created myths about women, but they shift the point of view.

For example: the Freudian description of women as

405

masochistic, passive, narcissistic. Autobiographies and fiction by women supply abundant evidence of these traits. Everywhere women gaze into mirrors, embrace suffering, welcome roles of helpless submissiveness. Maggie Tulliver, deliberately excluding from her life the possibility of joy; Esther Greenwood, bleeding as a result of her sexual yielding to a man she doesn't know; Kate Clephane, in *The Mother's Recompense*, choosing the misery of alienation: such women are willful sufferers. If the term *masochistic* were only descriptive, it would describe them. But it is interpretive as well, as all myths are interpretive, and to experience many books by women means to recognize the relativity of interpretation. To prefer suffering to pleasure may seem perverse from one point of view, profoundly wise from another. Even Esther in her psychosis seeks misery not as an end in itself, not even only as a testimony of uniqueness, but as a necessary means to self-assertion. Maggie and Kate Clephane would prefer to be happy. Their capacity to accept, even welcome, unhappiness derives from their refusal to compromise, their unwillingness to conform to social definitions of what should constitute happiness, their determination to preserve the integrity of the self.

Similarly, the vivid narcissism that seems disagreeable in Isadora Duncan, awe-inspiring in Mary MacLane, terrifying in Catherine Linton, fascinating for its disguises in Charlotte Perkins Gilman—one could go on and on—that narcissism also provides a means to self-preservation in settings intensely antagonistic to the full preservation of the self. And the passivity of the perfect wife often conceals the assertiveness of a woman willing to cover but not to abandon her drive for power. Of course orthodox psychoanalytic theory would acknowledge that masochism, narcissism, and passivity may constitute stratagems for maintaining the personality; women's writing supplies awareness of the necessity for such stratagems, given conditions of life that make direct tactics of survival impossible.

Women, like men, their writing tells us, yearn for the
often incompatible fulfillments of power and love. They
are permitted, or encouraged, to seek and to express
love—although even this aspect of their role is not altogether straightforward: the adolescent woman's agonies
over whether she is sufficiently lovable frequently extend
into adult life. Allowed the vocation of loving, women
nonetheless receive no guarantees that their love will win
return. They can cultivate the apparent stoicism of Jane in
Pride and Prejudice; or go into a decline like Caroline, in
Shirley; or control themselves against the very appearance
of being in love, like Camilla; or declare the irrelevance of
love outside the realm of fantasy, like Mary MacLane.
They can say, 'Tis better to have loved and lost.... But
they cannot finally protect themselves against the ravages
of feeling, more dangerous to them than to men, often, because they often have lacked other occupation.

As for power—well, the seventeenth-century Duchess of
Marlborough observed, in her old age, "Women signify
nothing, unless they are the mistress of a prince or first
minister." Women have traditionally operated through
men, finding vicarious satisfaction for their need to control; or they have ruled within the narrow sphere of the
home, achieving absolute dominion of a few other lives.
The classic disposition of women's energies is domestic,
marriage the traditional arena of power; the orthodox female vocation of caring for others, the orthodox female
posture of dependency, contain, as we have seen, hidden
possibilities for exercising control. Women in their self-
presentations rarely suggest that such possibilities seem finally satisfactory: only the semi-comic tradition of writers
like Betty MacDonald supports in autobiography the notion that women achieve through domesticity adequate
gratification of their need to control. Fiction more often
supports this comforting view. Eighteenth- and nineteenth-century novels apparently rest on the assumption
that marriage will provide sufficient outlet for a woman's
energies. Strikingly, though, when women write these nov-

els they allow at least subterranean challenges to the
vision they appear to accept. Feminists have long since
claimed Charlotte Brontë for their own; but Jane Austen,
George Eliot, Elizabeth Gaskell, even Fanny Burney—all
raise questions about women's lot which they do not answer. Do not because, clearly, they can not. Fanny Burney, able to recognize that male regard for female beauty
effectively transforms women into objects, simply denies
the problem she has revealed, forming the plot of *Camilla*
as if she believes that marriage resolves all difficulties, although each of her novels contains hints that she knows
the contrary. Jane Austen, in her meticulous delineations
of what can go wrong between people, suggests that her
insistence on self-responsibility and self-development
derives partly from desperation: this version of cultivating
the inner life at least produces growth, it may possibly improve the quality of human relationships. Austen, Eliot,
Gaskell all depict unhappy marriages with a care pro-
claiming their consciousness that the odds favor frustration
and psychic diminution as the consequences, for a woman,
of final commitment to a man.

By the twentieth century, of course, women might contemplate public accomplishment as a potential means of
control. Many still preferred to content themselves with
fantasies of accomplishment—Marie Bashkirtseff a vivid
real-life example, Martha Quest her fictional equivalent.
But others besides Mary McCarthy learned the power implicit in art. The best alternative to being *good* is being
gifted. If women less readily than men are forgiven their
sins for their talents, if women suffer greater conflicts in
making the initial commitment to self-expression rather
than self-abnegation, it yet remains true that the woman
artist, like her male counterpart (although usually at
greater cost), can insist on her right to be "special." Even
Jo in *Little Women*, though she subordinates herself finally
to a dominant man, earns by her writing a more interesting life than her sisters; and Lily Briscoe, apparently
limited in talent as in accomplishment, achieves clearer,

fuller perceptions than those around her, gains a sense of her own dignity independent of the value others place on her—unlike Mrs. Ramsay, she doesn't need to be needed. Anna Wulf, in *The Golden Notebook*, suffers more than most housewives (even the desperate housewives of contemporary fiction); but she rescues herself at least partially by the act of artistic creation. Real women artists reveal the same patterns of suffering and compensation: Anaïs Nin, glorying in her awareness of female and artistic specialness; Isadora Duncan, with a similar personal drama; Mary McCarthy, using her artistry to understand her experience; Lillian Hellman, defining a heroism of endeavor; Isak Dinesen, transcending limitation through perception.

But women learning the power of art inevitably wonder about love. Is the cost of achievement the loss of relationship? One may, like Isadora Duncan, develop romantic dreams of triumphing in both areas; or, like Dora Carrington, destroy oneself in despair of reconciliation. Accomplishment in other fields of endeavor raises the same question. Beatrice Webb asks it repeatedly; Charlotte Perkins Gilman sees her public achievement as compensation for private failure. Moreover, women have not created important fictional heroines who find gratification through doing something in the world. Doris Lessing's Kate Brown finds it easy to be successful at a "career," but success remains irrelevant to her real problems. Lily Briscoe, one of relatively few female artists in fiction, doesn't paint very well. Gwendolen Harleth only dreams of a stage career which she could never bring about; Maggie Tulliver and Dorothea Brooke can't even find a mode of accomplishment to dream about. Margaret Sargent, in *The Company She Keeps*, gets fired from the only job that matters to her, and it doesn't matter much. It seems the idea of success has failed to engage the female imagination.

The idea of virtue, on the other hand, appears to have considerable imaginative appeal. Sometimes—in fiction and in fact—mere misery can constitute an emblem of goodness. Edna Pontellier, in *The Awakening*, demonstrates the possibilities of unhappiness as a vocation testifying in itself to a high order of psychic virtue. Mrs. Thrale, announcing her submissiveness to a life that in many ways she detests, like the pioneer wife reporting her illness, proclaims the equation between suffering accepted and female virtue. But the female consciousness of domestic virtue need not associate itself with helpless suffering. Mrs. Ramsay feels virtuous (and should) for her preservation of order; Ada (*Vein of Iron*) and Beth (*Little Women*) for their capacity to endure; Shirley values herself for her ingenuity in manipulating a man; Jane Eyre is conscious of accomplishment in caring for Rochester; Betty MacDonald's "virtue" is not only her suffering but her gaiety in the face of suffering. Virtue is power in a particularly advantageous form: it seems also a way to win love. Yet women forced toward goodness may feel it as burden rather than opportunity, and female anger often rings most clearly in accounts of lives given up to others.

This summary, like any summary of the implications of women's writing, sounds dismal. It is not surprising that anger so often supplies undertones or overtones, if rarely explicit subject matter, in books by women. Virginia Woolf was right in seeing it everywhere. Anger generates the energy in twentieth-century fictional presentations of the careers of female adolescents, whose experience of frustration seems likely to continue into their adulthood. It shapes serious considerations of the relation between woman and society, however judicious and accepting their superficial tone. We encounter it in a mad wife's laughter and mutterings, in Charlotte Perkins Gilman's "nervous breakdown," in the Duchess of Newcastle's anxiety to be remembered, vicariously in Heathcliff's hanging of little dogs, in Eugenia's outburst about beauty, in Lady Mary Wortley Montagu's comments on female education. Over and over, it sounds the most authentic woman's response: a response to bafflement, to dead ends bumped into, to society's failure to speak to women's needs.

For society's failure is the large fact that emerges from contemplation of women's writing. Women's needs, one feels after reading many of their books, are identical with men's. Perhaps the balance may be different, but the substance is the same: for work and love, for independence and dependency, solitude and relationship, to enjoy community and value one's specialness. All too often, though, these polarities present themselves to women as insoluble contradictions rather than paradoxes; because general assumption condones one set of goals for women to the exclusion of the other. Love, dependency, relationship, community: proper feminine goals. Their opposites are assumed to be of questionable value for a woman, and the woman who presumes to seek them—real woman or fictional projection—pays a price. Lily Bart, yearning for more reality than marriage offers, wishing to maintain independence, must die. Dorothea Brooke can't even build cottages, she can only rear children. Martha Quest, who wants to discover herself and to do great things, denies herself and does nothing at all. Mabel Dodge Luhan cringes before the injunction to work, although only through work can she hope to resolve her psychic difficulties. Charlotte Perkins Gilman never surmounts her sense of guilt at demanding public opportunities for self-assertion. Even Lillian Hellman reveals the strain of insisting on the value of doing and enduring, suggesting that its penalty is the failure of relationship.

The dreariness of social frustration, then, permeates much writing by women. Yet the effect of reading such writing is by no means dreary. If women say again and again that society denies them clear paths to fulfillment (acknowledging often, at least by implication, that such paths are difficult for men, too, to find: but men face no such systematic pattern of obstacles), they also affirm in far-reaching ways the significance of their inner freedom. That escape through writing declared possible by Anaïs Nin and Anna Wulf emblemizes an even larger kind of escape, through imagination: the recourse not only of artists

411

but of fictional heroines with no pretensions to artistic accomplishment. In much of the most interesting fiction by women, romantic fantasies about the self sustain a character, to be criticized and finally modified (but not entirely rejected) by the action of the novel. Jane Eyre daydreams, and incorporates Rochester into her dream; but she learns that she does not really want so enlarged a sphere of action as she thinks she longs for. Gwendolen Harleth sees herself as a glamorous heroine, but is educated through suffering to the difference between fantasy and reality. Maggie Tulliver struggles from romanticism to realism; Edna Pontellier, unwilling to face the full implications of that struggle, drowns in her own romanticism. Anna, in *The Golden Notebook,* has up-to-date versions of romantic fantasy, yearning to be a political savior or a perfectly free (i.e., happily promiscuous) lover; her drama, too, involves the confrontation of limitation. Like Emma Woodhouse, these heroines must learn to be sensible, to reconcile themselves to the facts of external experience, which deny the freedom and power they feel in their inner lives, to "grow up," become mature. But although they must reject exalted visions of themselves and of their possibilities, imagination remains for them a significant dimension of reality.

Isak Dinesen, after her return to Denmark from Africa, reports some confusion in the first months. "I had great trouble," she writes, "in seeing anything at all as reality. . . . The landscapes, the beasts and the human beings of that [African] existence could not possibly to my surroundings in Denmark mean more than did the landscapes, beasts, and human beings of my dreams at night. Their names were just words." Africa meant no more than her dreams: but no less. The fruitful interchange of dream and reality, the awareness of the strangeness of fact, the authenticity of fancy: these often constitute the special strength of women as writers, the positive result of the social alienation they suffer. The "negative" result is their anger: a response to impotence, a source of energy. Neither fancy nor anger in itself solves social problems. Both may lead to personal resolutions of dubious value—to indulgent selfpity, to passivity, masochism, narcissism as postures of defense so rigid that they prevent growth. But both can also provide means for growth.

"I'm still, I think, male-oriented more than self-oriented," a student wrote, in a summary comment on my course. She added, in parentheses, "I get cold chills as I write that." Her cold chills register her consciousness of a perplexing paradox, shared in the awareness of more than college women. Isak Dinesen seems relevant once more, in her account of the Somali women who "cannot own themselves but must needs belong to some male, to a father, a brother or a husband, but they are still the one supreme prize of life. . . . The young girls, who had no men to squeeze . . . were making the most of their pretty hair and looking forward to the time when they should be conquering the conqueror, and extortionating the extortioner." The passivity implicit in a social condition of "belonging to" the other sex, the powerlessness of existence as a "prize" merge strangely into the activity and power of "conquering" and "extortionating"—alternative definitions of the identical social condition. From the women's world of "walls and fortifications" the battle of the sexes is waged; behind those walls one feels "the presence of a great ideal, without which the garrison would not have carried on so gallantly; the idea of a Millennium when women were to reign supreme in the world. The old mother at such times would take on a new shape, and sit enthroned as a massive dark symbol of that mighty female deity who had existed in old ages, before the time of the Prophet's God."

The situation of the Somali women, extreme though it is, provides a paradigm of the female condition as seen by women of Western cultures in the past three centuries. The vision of female dominance in the background has not, of course, existed in the same form in the Western world. But women dominate their own experience by imagining it, giving it form, writing about it. Their imag-

413

inative versions of themselves as supporters of the social structure, guardians of the species, possessors of wisdom unavailable to men—versions derived partly from the arrogance of anger—in effect re-create the "mighty female deity." In their exact recording of inner and outer experience they establish women's claim for attention as individuals. They define, for themselves and for their readers, woman as she is and as she dreams.

Works Cited

Alcott, Louisa May, *Little Women*, Boston, 1871.

Anderson, Margaret, *The Fiery Fountains*, New York, Hermitage House, 1951.

_____, *My Thirty Years' War*, New York, Covici, Friede, 1930.

Austen, Jane, *Emma*, *The Novels of Jane Austen*, ed. R. W. Chapman, 6 vols., Oxford, Oxford University Press, 1922–1954, vol. 4.

_____, *Persuasion*, *Novels*, vol. 5.

_____, *Pride and Prejudice*, *Novels*, vol. 2.

Bashkirtseff, Marie, *Journal*, tr. A. D. Hall, New York, 1890.

Beauvoir, Simone de, *The Second Sex*, tr. H. M. Parshley, New York, Knopf, 1953.

Benedek, Therese, *Psychosexual Functions in Women*, New York, Ronald Press, 1952.

Bonaparte, Marie, *Five Copy-Books*, tr. Eric Mosbacher, 4 vols., London, Imago Publishing Co., 1953.

Brontë, Charlotte, *Jane Eyre*, London, Oxford University Press, 1969.

_____, *Shirley*, London, Dent, 1944.

_____, *Villette*, London, Dent, 1922.

Brontë, Emily, *Wuthering Heights*, New York, Oxford University Press, 1907.

Burney, Frances, *Camilla: Or, A Picture of Youth*, 5 vols., London, 1796.

_____, *Cecilia, or Memoirs of an Heiress*, 2 vols., London, 1901.

_____, *Diary and Letters*, ed. Austin Dobson, vol. 6, London, 1905.

————, *Evelina*, ed. Edward A. Bloom, London, Oxford University Press, 1970.

————, *Journals and Letters*, vol. 3, ed. Joyce Hemlow with Patricia Boutilier and Althea Douglas, Oxford, The Clarendon Press, 1973.

Carrington, [Dora,] *Letters and Extracts from her Diaries*, ed. David Garnett, New York Holt, Rinehart and Winston, 1971.

Cavendish, Margaret, Duchess of Newcastle, *The Life of William Cavendish, Duke of Newcastle, to which is added The True Relation of My Birth, Breeding and Life*, London, 1886.

Chesler, Phyllis, *Women and Madness*, Garden City, N.Y., Doubleday, 1972.

Chopin, Kate, *The Awakening*, New York, Capricorn Books, 1964.

[Churchill,] Sarah, Duchess of Marlborough, *Memoirs*, ed. William King, London, Routledge, 1930.

Colette, [Sidonie,] *Break of Day and The Blue Lantern*, tr. Enid McLeod and Glenway Wescott, New York, Noonday Press, 1966.

Cooper, Arvazine Angeline, "Journey Across the Plains," *Growing Up Female in America*, ed. Eve Merriam, Garden City, N.Y., Doubleday, 1971, pp. 121–40.

Dinesen, Isak, *Out of Africa*, New York, Random House, 1952.

————, *Shadows on the Grass*, New York, Random House, 1960.

Duncan, Isadora, *My Life*, New York, Boni & Liveright, 1927.

Edgeworth, Maria, *Belinda*, London, 1896.

Eliot, George, *Daniel Deronda, The Writings of George Eliot*, Boston, 1908, vols. 15–17.

————, *Middlemarch, Writings*, vols. 12–14.

————, *The Mill on the Floss, Writings*, vols. 5–6.

————, *The George Eliot Letters*, ed. Gordon S. Haight, 7 vols., New Haven, Yale University Press, 1954–55.

Ellmann, Mary, *Thinking About Women*, New York, Harcourt, Brace & World, 1968.

Works Cited

Freud, Sigmund, "The 'Uncanny,'" *On Creativity and the Unconscious*, ed. Benjamin Nelson, New York, Harper Torchbooks, 1958, pp. 122–61.

Gaskell, Elizabeth, *North and South*, London, 1920.

_____, *Wives and Daughters*, London, 1911.

Gilman, Charlotte Perkins, *The Living of Charlotte Perkins Gilman*, New York, D. Appleton-Century Co., 1935.

_____, "The Yellow Wallpaper," *The Oven Birds*, ed. Gail Parker, Garden City, N.Y., Doubleday, 1972.

Glasgow, Ellen, *Vein of Iron*, New York, Harcourt, Brace, 1935.

_____, *The Woman Within*, New York, Harcourt, Brace, 1954.

Greenacre, Phyllis, "Woman As Artist," *Emotional Growth*, 2 vols., New York, International Universities Press, 1971, vol. 2, pp. 575–91.

Hellman, Lillian, *An Unfinished Woman*, Boston, Little, Brown, 1969.

James, Henry, *Portrait of a Lady*, *Novels and Tales*, 26 vols., New York, Scribner's, 1961, vols. 3–4.

Janeway, Elizabeth, *Man's World, Woman's Place: A Study in Social Mythology*, New York, Morrow, 1971.

Josipovici, Gabriel, *The World and the Book: A Study of Modern Fiction*, Stanford, Calif., Stanford University Press, 1971.

Kempton, Sally, "Cutting Loose," *Esquire*, 74 (July 1970), pp. 53–57.

Kris, Ernst, *Psychoanalytic Explorations in Art*, New York, International Universities Press, 1952.

Lessing, Doris, *Briefing for a Descent into Hell*, New York, Knopf, 1971.

_____, *The Four-Gated City*, New York, Knopf, 1969.

_____, *The Golden Notebook*, New York, Simon & Schuster, 1962.

_____, *Martha Quest, Children of Violence*, vol. 1, New York, Simon & Schuster, 1964.

_____, *The Summer Before the Dark*, New York, Knopf, 1973.

Luhan, Mabel Dodge, *Intimate Memories: Background,* New York, Harcourt, Brace, 1933.

————, *Intimate Memories: Edge of the Taos Desert,* New York, Harcourt, Brace, 1937.

————, *Lorenzo in Taos,* New York, Knopf, 1932.

MacDonald, Betty, *The Egg and I,* Philadelphia, Lippincott, 1945.

MacLane, Mary, *I, Mary MacLane: A Diary of Human Days,* New York, 1917.

————, *The Story of Mary MacLane,* Chicago, 1902.

————, *The Story of Mary MacLane* ("a new edition with a chapter on the present"), New York, 1911.

Mailer, Norman, *The Prisoner of Sex,* Boston, Little, Brown, 1971.

McCarthy, Mary, *The Company She Keeps,* New York, Harcourt, Brace, 1942.

————, *Memories of a Catholic Girlhood,* New York, Harcourt, Brace, 1957.

Millett, Kate, *Sexual Politics,* Garden City, N.Y., Doubleday, 1970.

Milner, Marion, *On Not Being Able to Paint,* New York, International Universities Press, 1967.

Montagu, Lady Mary Wortley, *Complete Letters,* ed. Robert Halsband, 3 vols., Oxford, The Clarendon Press, 1966–67.

Nin, Anaïs, *The Diary of Anaïs Nin, 1931–1934,* New York, Harcourt, Brace, Jovanovich, 1966.

————, *The Diary of Anaïs Nin, 1934–1939,* New York, Harcourt, Brace, Jovanovich, 1967.

————, *The Diary of Anaïs Nin, 1939–1944,* New York, Harcourt, Brace, Jovanovich, 1969.

————, *The Diary of Anaïs Nin, 1944–1947,* New York, Harcourt, Brace, Jovanovich, 1971.

Piozzi, Hester Lynch Thrale, *Thraliana,* ed. Katherine C. Balderston, Oxford, The Clarendon Press, 1951.

————, Unpublished journals (5 vols.) in the Houghton Library of Harvard University.

Plath, Sylvia, *The Bell Jar,* New York, Harper & Row, 1971.

Rorty, Amélie Oksenberg, "Dependents: The Trials of Success," *The Yale Review*, 63 (1973), pp. 43–59.

Schneir, Miriam, ed., *Feminism: The Essential Historical Writings*, New York, Random House, 1972.

Stein, Gertrude, *The Autobiography of Alice B. Toklas*, New York, Harcourt, Brace, 1933.

Swift, Jonathan, *The Battle of the Books*, ed. A. Guthkelch, London, 1908.

Trilling, Lionel, *Beyond Culture*, New York, Viking, 1955.

Vicinus, Martha, ed., *Suffer and Be Still: Women in the Victorian Age*, Bloomington, Indiana University Press, 1972.

Webb, Beatrice, *My Apprenticeship*, New York, Longmans, Green, 1926.

———, *Our Partnership*, New York, Longmans, Green, 1948.

Welty, Eudora, *The Optimist's Daughter*, New York, Random House, 1972.

Wharton, Edith, *The Age of Innocence*, New York, Appleton, 1920.

———, *A Backward Glance*, New York, Appleton-Century, 1934.

———, *The Buccaneers*, New York, Appleton-Century, 1938.

———, *The House of Mirth*, New York, Scribner's, 1914.

———, *The Mother's Recompense*, New York, Appleton, 1925.

Willis, Ellen, "Up from Radicalism: A Feminist Journal," *US* Magazine (1969).

Woolf, Virginia, *Mrs. Dalloway*, London, Hogarth Press, 1925.

———, *A Room of One's Own*, London, Hogarth Press, 1929.

———, *To the Lighthouse*, New York, Harcourt, Brace, 1927.

———, *A Writer's Diary*, ed. Leonard Woolf, London, Hogarth Press, 1953.

Index

NOTE: Fictional characters are listed by their full names (where these are provided) rather than by their surnames. Elizabeth Bennet of *Pride and Prejudice*, for example, will be found under E rather than B.